THE ANALYSIS OF
SOCIAL SYSTEMS

THE ANALYSIS OF
SOCIAL SYSTEMS

Harry C. Bredemeier
and
Richard M. Stephenson

RUTGERS · THE STATE UNIVERSITY

HOLT, RINEHART and WINSTON, INC.
New York · Chicago · San Francisco
Toronto · London

90123 22 98

PREFACE

We are aware that to add another to the mountain of introductory textbooks already in the field smacks of presumptuousness. We do so anyway, because over a period of twelve years of teaching together and trying many different texts, we have evolved what we believe is a very fruitful synthesis of some of the most promising recent developments in sociology. The approach of this text is one that has worked very well with our own students, on whom, in fact, we have tested the present text in mimeographed form for three years, making revisions from time to time as our students taught us.

What recent developments do we presume to have "synthesized"? Perhaps foremost we have found the structural categories of Talcott Parsons to be powerful organizing concepts. We have also found some of his more dynamic concepts to be richly illuminating, especially in connection with socialization and deviance, and also as he has developed them with Neil Smelser in *Economy and Society*. But the recent work of George Homans, employing the conceptual tools of economics and of learning theory, has also influenced us heavily. We have, in addition, been impressed by the convergences between economic analysis and sociological analysis that are at least implicit and usually explicit in the recent work of Howard S. Becker, William J. Goode, Alvin Gouldner, and Thomas Schelling. Finally, for emphasis, Robert K. Merton's influence on us, as teacher, clarifier of concepts, and subtle and supple analyst will be apparent to everyone who knows his work, even without the many references to his contributions to be found throughout this book.

We believe that we have applied in an illuminative way the gifts of those sociologists, and of the many others we cite throughout, to most of the central concerns of sociology: culture, socialization, deviance, social control, marriage and the family, magic, science, religion, ideology, stratification, industrialism, and politics. We also believe that we have done this on a level and in a language understandable to beginning students, without talking down to them or supplanting the instructor.

Several things that, admittedly, might be done in an introductory text, we have *not* done. In the first place, there are several substantive foci of current sociological attention that we have not dealt with intensively. There are no chapters on demography, urbanism, racial and ethnic relations, small-group analysis, or bureaucracy. So far as they are concerned, we have chosen, instead, to weave our analysis of them into other substantive chapters where, we feel, their theoretical and *systematic* relevance becomes more apparent to an introductory student. We do not have a chapter on methods of sociological research. So far as "methodology" is concerned, we chose the horn of leaving it out instead of the horn of adding another two hundred pages, because we were aiming toward a book that would stimulate undergraduates' interests rather than overwhelm them with complexities. (When we get them as majors, we feel, is the time for some of those things.)

Another thing we have not done, deliberately, is to include extensive and detailed descriptions of an illustrative kind. We have included *enough,* we believe, to make each analytical or theoretical point clear and even interesting, but certainly not so much as many other texts do. We have chosen this course for several reasons. In the first place, there are now so many excellent books of readings available that we thought it would be redundant to duplicate them. Furthermore, since as instructors we prefer to select our own outside readings as supplementary assignments, we believe that other instructors will prefer to do likewise. In the second place, we wanted, above all, to keep the material in this book on as systematic and general a level as possible, in order to emphasize to the student the omniapplicability of this mode of analysis of social systems. We did *not* want to risk losing the thread of the analytical argument in detailed preoccupation with concrete phenomena. It has been our own pedagogical experience, which we can only hope is not completely atypical, that this notion of omniapplicability best comes across to students when they first read the analysis, then read elsewhere some descriptive account or the report of a research activity, and *then* tie the two together in class discussion or in term papers.

The illustrative and elaborative reports that can be used for this purpose are suggested in two ways. In the first place, at the end of the text we offer a chart showing, for each of the twelve chapters, the pages in each of eleven different collections of readings that we believe would make excellent additional assignments. (We might have incorporated those readings, or summaries of them, in our own text easily enough, but our conviction is that to have done so would have made a cumbersome book and, in addition, would have been pedagogically less sound. We prefer to have students read the original reports and make their own connections.) In the second place, the reader will find that the text is studded with references to illustrative studies and reports, which, depending on the library facilities of the user, can also be used as additional assignments.

We wish to repeat our belief, however, that the text alone provides enough illustrative material to make the general points clear. For that reason we believe that it can be used either for a one-semester course or for a two-semester course, the difference, naturally, being in the amount of supplementary readings assigned from our suggested list or from the instructor's own bibliography. We have used it in both ways.

Two final notes should be made, and their conventionality should not obscure their importance. The first is that this book and our own thinking in general would have been far inferior if it had not been for the patient but trenchant criticisms of our colleagues who have taught with us over a period of several years: Alisa Lourie, Gillian Lindt, Nechama Tec, Emily Alman, Jay Schulman. The second is that neither those persons nor the sociologists mentioned above can be responsible for any of the ways we have fallen short of their standards.

H. C. B.
R. M. S.

New Brunswick, N.J.
February 1962

CONTENTS

THE ANALYSIS OF
SOCIAL SYSTEMS

1

CULTURE AND DEFINITIONS
OF SITUATIONS

S ociology is one among many approaches to understanding human behavior. Each approach consists of taking a few aspects of human action and studying them in detail.

What sociology selects to emphasize are two aspects that, taken together, are among the unique characteristics of human beings: the fact that men have culture, and the fact that they live in groups.

Sociologists, of course, are not the only ones to fasten their attention on those aspects. Playwrights, novelists, and poets also seize on the cultural and group characteristics of human life and illuminate important facets of human action that may be passed over by sociologists. So do many philosophers. What distinguishes sociology from other interesting approaches is the combination of a focus on culture and "groupness" *plus* an effort to use a scientific method to analyze them.

Needless to say, much is left out of the sociological account, just as much is left out of a psychological account, a chemical account, or a poetic account. Neither sociology nor any other conceivable discipline can possibly deal with *all* of reality. *Aspects* of reality must be abstracted for purposes of analysis, if only because of the limits of the human mind, which can take in only so much at a time.

On the basis of these brief considerations, we can state fairly simply what sociology is about. It is an effort to illuminate as much of human behavior as can be illuminated within two kinds of limits: the limits imposed by a scientific frame of reference and the limits imposed by focusing attention only on two aspects—culture and "groupness." It is important to bear in mind the limits, just as it is important to appreciate the illumination this approach is able to shed.

We shall begin with a preliminary analysis of culture.

1

THE NATURE AND SIGNIFICANCE OF CULTURE

It may be needless to say, but for the sake of complete certainty, it should be said anyhow, that we do not use the term "culture" in the sense of "going to college to become cultured," or in the sense of "highbrow, middlebrow, or lowbrow culture." What we mean by culture is a set of *shared symbols*[1] *and their definitions.* The shared definitions are manifested in collective patterns of behavior and in artifacts, the objects that man fabricates from nature. The definition of the chair you are sitting on as something to be sat on is part of your culture. The definition of a sociology course as something that might reward you in some way is part of your culture. The definition of a professor as someone who does not, in the middle of a lecture, decide to take a bath is part of your culture.

"Things," such as chairs, courses listed in catalogues, or people standing in the front of the room with their jaws moving *are never seen by you in their total concreteness.* You see only some aspect of them: that aspect that you have learned to abstract by learning your cultural symbols and the meaning of those symbols. This is the phenomenon Walter Lippmann was summarizing in his famous aphorism, "First we look, then we name, and only then do we see." You have to name the thing a chair before you "see" (that is, respond to) it as something to be sat upon. You have to name the person a lecturer before you "see" him as someone to be listened to. Suppose, for example, you were to name the thing you are sitting on a "priceless antique." Then you would probably "see" it as something *not* to be sat on. Or we could name it a variety of different things, and each time we named it something else, you would "see" something else. For example, we could name it a "weapon," and you would see it being broken over someone's head, or we could name it "a piece of primitive wood carving," and you would picture a different thing altogether.

A good illustration of Lippmann's point is provided in a pastime that

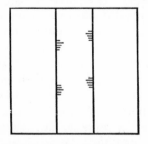
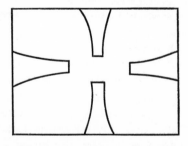

[1] By "symbol" is meant any verbal form, bodily gesture, act, or other means of communication that arbitrarily stands for some perceived characteristic or set of characteristics of the sensory environment or a posited environment beyond direct sensory perception.

was popular during the early 1950's, "Droodles." Drawings, such as those on the preceding page, were shown to people, who were asked what they were. What the drawings "really are" is indicated in the footnotes.[2] Notice how you first "look" at the drawings without much comprehension, and then "see" them after you know their "names."

Apart from parlor games, the same principle has vast significance in "real life." Coal, petroleum, and iron, for example, were in the ground of North America when the Indians owned it; but the presence of such natural resources could not result in an industrial civilization until *culture* had evolved to the point at which there were appropriate symbolic definitions of such things. Coal without a definition of coal is irrelevant to human beings.

The compelling nature of language as it affects perceptions should not, of course, be exaggerated. Men are capable of learning from experience, at least in the long run; so that even though it is possible for someone to define what we call "coal" as mashed potatoes and to act on that definition, such a definition is not likely to endure as part of any group's culture. We are not saying, in other words, that the laws of physics and biology are suspended by culture. In the long run there has to be *some* correspondence between what people define as real and what is really real. What we are saying, rather, is that there are many, many "real" aspects of the world, but only some of them are recognized as such by a culture and therefore only some of them are paid attention to.

D. V. McGranahan has put this well: "The effect of language on perception appears to be to make those features of the objective world that are represented by linguistic forms stand out in greater articulation, to give greater individuality to the object or event so represented, and in general to influence perception in the direction of the speech form."[3]

The fact remains, however, that people must define things before they can respond to them. This is the fundamentally important fact summarized in Lippmann's aphorism: human beings don't respond to stimuli; they respond to their *definitions* of stimuli. This is the fact that makes the unique element of culture so critically important in understanding human behavior, for culture is something that *intervenes* between the human organism and its environment to produce action. As someone has said, culture is an envelope that seals men off from direct contact with their environment, including other men.

What you have to understand in order to understand a man's behavior are the symbols and their definitions that intervene between him and any

---

[2] *Bear climbing a tree. Four elephants at a drinking tank.*

[3] D. V. McGranahan, "The Psychology of Language," *Psychological Bulletin*, 33: 202 (1936).

stimulus to which he is exposed. You have to know what the stimulus *means* to him. It is just this necessity, in fact, that makes the behavior of some insane persons so puzzling—we can't imagine how they are defining the situation. If, on the other hand, we are told that this patient is defining himself as Napoleon, part of our bewilderment disappears. We may not understand how in the world he got to such a definition, but at least we are then able to make some sense out of his behavior: we can imagine how such and such a stimulus *could* produce such and such a reaction, *if* it were defined from Napoleon's point of view.

It would be very hard to find any human action *not* influenced by cultural definitions. Even basic biological drives—the closest things human beings have to instincts—are controlled and modified, sometimes beyond recognition, by cultural definitions. Hunger, above the level of starvation, for example, doesn't drive people to eat. First, something has to be defined as food; and caterpillars, no matter how nutritious they might be, are not *defined* as food by Americans. Sex doesn't drive people to intercourse. First an object must be defined, not only as suitable, but even as interesting. A great variety of different objects *can* be defined as sexually interesting and suitable; but objects that are biologically suitable, such as parents or brothers or sisters, are often rejected as a result of their cultural *meanings*. Even internal physiological processes, such as digestion or the secretion of glandular fluids or the beating of the heart, come to be regulated symbolically—as any person recognizes who has ever been in love.

Again, we do not, in using these examples, mean to say that straightforward biological impulses *cannot* determine men's actions. Some people, when driven by hunger, have eaten caterpillars; some shipwrecked sailors have resorted to cannibalism; some parents and their offspring do have sexual relations. What we do mean to call attention to is that these are exceptions which result from a failure to "acculturate" the individuals adequately or from unusual situations where cultural definitions may not operate. Our point is that culture very often can lead people to violate their biological tendencies. People fast unto death; they deliberately commit suicide for such an abstraction as "saving face"; there are women who would choose "death rather than dishonor"; and many persons are celibate.

THE BENEFITS AND COSTS OF CULTURE

The very process of thinking is dependent on culture. As Benjamin Whorf has put it:

We dissect nature along lines laid down by our native languages. The categories and types that we isolate from the world of phenomena we do not find there because they stare every observer in the face; on the contrary, the world is presented in a kaleidoscopic flux of impressions which has to be organized by our minds—and this means largely by the linguistic systems in our minds. We cut nature up, organize it into concepts, and ascribe significances as we do, largely because we are parties to an agreement to organize it in this way. . . .[4]

The linguistic symbols men use structure their perception and tell them what to "pay attention to" or ignore by placing dissimilar objects, events, and experiences in the same symbolic category or by making fine symbolic distinctions that differentiate them in great detail. The Eskimo has three different words for types of snow, whereas we have only one. The Navaho use three words for our one word "rough," to describe the surface of a file, rock, and road. A tribe in the Philippines had twenty words to describe rice in its various stages of growth and harvesting. The Arabs are said to have had a thousand words for "sword," and our medieval ancestors had an elaborate repertoire of symbols to describe different ways of dressing fowl. But then, imagine the utter dismay of these peoples when confronted by our symbolic distinctions concerned with cars, with all the elaborations entailed in "year," "make," and "model."

The fact that human beings respond to their *definitions* of things, hardly ever to the things themselves is, then, obviously critical for the understanding of human behavior. It means that the *range* of things to which human beings can respond—that is, the range of different things that can be stimuli—is enormously greater than it is for other animals. Other animals can respond only to something that can impinge directly on their senses. They have to be able to smell it or see it or feel it or hear it before it can be a stimulus. But man can learn and "think" about his world without direct physical contact with it. It also means that man's conception of his world need not represent its objective nature. The legend that tomatoes were once called "love apples" and were appreciated for their esthetic value, but not eaten because they were "poisonous," illustrates the point. In the same way, the northern Ojibwa Indians refrained from eating berries from a number of different nonpoisonous plants because they were collectively referred to as "snake berries," a symbol which denoted poison.[5]

In addition, the dependence of human beings on their definitions of

[4] Benjamin Lee Whorf, "Science and Linguistics," in Theodore M. Newcomb and Eugene L. Hartley, *et al.* (eds.), *Readings in Social Psychology* (New York: Holt, Rinehart and Winston, Inc., 1947), p. 214.

[5] A. I. Hollowell, "Cultural Factors in the Structuralization of Perception," in J. H. Rohrer and M. Sherif (eds.), *Social Psychology at the Crossroads* (New York: Harper & Brothers, 1951).

things means that symbols must be *shared,* so that perceptions of reality and appropriate responses to it are held collectively. Human beings who share a common language have a standardized set of concepts denoting *similar* generalizations about classes of things to *each* individual. Although it is true that something has to impinge on man's sensory mechanisms in order for a response to be given, the range of things that can be stimuli is vastly increased by his capacity to respond to symbols in the same way that he and other animals respond to "things." As symbols come to stand for things, man is able to respond to things when they are not present in his immediate environment; that is, he responds to the sound of other symbols that stand for the thing, just as he would respond to the thing itself. Furthermore, he may transfer his response to this sound to other sounds, which may, then, evoke the same response. In this way, the response he gives to a thing may be transferred to a sound that has no relationship to the thing, or indeed, to anything that exists or ever existed as a thing.

Thus, the response we feel in one situation may be transferred to a sound or to another situation by means of a sound. Our physiological and chemical responses to sickness, injury, loud noise—in other words, our biological response to substantive things that impinge on our senses—may be transferred to sounds, such as Democrat, George Washington, traitor, hero, devil, witch, good, bad, female, and all the other sounds we make. The same is true of substantive things, when sounds are attached to them, such as a cathedral, a grave, the White House, a rabbit's foot, a painting, or another person. As these sounds and things impinge on our senses, we may respond with feelings of awe, pain, glee, fear, hate, love, nausea, or any other "emotional" response of which human beings are capable. But note that the sound or the thing does not, of itself, necessarily evoke the response. Clearly, different people will respond in different ways to the same sound (Democrat, for example) and the same thing (modern art, for example). The history of man confirms his capacity to respond to things and sounds in an infinite variety of ways. Psychiatric and clinical techniques reveal the same capacity in those whom we call mentally ill.

Even with their limitations, nonhuman animals can acquire a very great repertoire of complex skills, to be sure. Dogs can be conditioned to "speak" for food, to "stay," to walk tightropes, to salivate at the sound of bells or buzzers, and so on. Psychologists have done amazing things with pigeons and mice, such as teaching them to cooperate in pressing a complex sequence of levers to get food. But two limitations sharply set these phenomena apart from man's use of symbols.

One is the fact that *one pigeon doesn't train another pigeon. A psychologist* trains them; not a more advanced pigeon. The second is the fact that even the psychologist can't teach a pigeon to press a lever *in the absence of the lever.* One human being can give another human being a description of a lever and can "train" him to press it *next week*, without either person stirring from his armchair. In performing their tricks, pigeons and dogs are doing one thing that human beings do, but not another. In salivating at the sound of a buzzer the dog is *abstracting* from the total situation only one aspect and responding to it. So far, this is just what human beings do when they stop work and open their lunch boxes at the sound of the noon whistle (and, as a matter of fact, both learn their "tricks" in very much the same ways, as we shall see when we take up the process of "socialization").

But human beings not only abstract from complex situations; they *generalize* their abstractions. They can store up in their minds, as it were, the experience of hearing a whistle and the experience of eating lunch; and they can form connections between those two experiences without ever having experienced them simultaneously. That is, someone can say to them (once the "storing" process has occurred) "You know what a whistle sounds like? You know how to open a lunch box? Well, *next time* you hear a whistle, that means it's time to open your lunch box." No dog can do this for another dog, and no psychologist can do it for a dog.

This ability to *symbolize* a whistle and a lunch box, and to generalize about them on a *symbolic* (not experiential) level, has given *Homo sapiens* an extraordinary advantage over other animals. It has unquestionably made man the "king of the beasts," for it enables him to profit from other people's experiences and to accumulate from one generation to the next the most effective ways of acting. It means that each generation does not have to discover the wheel or fire for itself; each successive generation can start where the previous generation left off. One physicist can tell another physicist about his ideas and experiments, and the second can *symbolically* connect those reports with other reports he has stored up in the fantastic "electronic calculator" that is his mind. A scientist like Newton can abstract from the situation of a falling apple such aspects as velocity, mass, and distance and connect them with similar aspects of the situation of planets orbiting.

These advantages are not entirely unmixed with disadvantages, however. The very ability to abstract from situations certain properties and symbolize them may *prevent* solutions to problems as well as aid in solving them—and for the same reason: Symbols canalize perception and response. They act as "blinders" that focus attention on some aspects of things and not others. This means, of course, that we may not pay attention to some things that we ought to if we want to find a solution to some kind of problem. The notion, for example, that germs cause disease may blind us to other possible causes, just as the notion that devils cause disease blinds some primitive peoples to the possibility that germs may cause disease. For another example, it is often the case that if a man is named a "Negro," other people (and possibly even he himself) are automatically blinded to all the *other* things he is also, other things that actually might be much more important, such as the fact that he is an able physician or carpenter, a good soldier, a man with wife and children, and so on.[6] Another disadvantage of symbolic communication that parallels its advantage is the fact that each generation may learn the "errors" of the previous generation, rather than profit from its experience. "Enlightened" men required a long time to accept the fact that lack of sanitation in medical care, which they thought did not matter, or blood letting, which they thought did, were practices that defeated the very results they were aiming at in medicine. This was true even when evidence of the error was made known. Perhaps the most obvious case is found in the history of witchcraft in Western civilization.

Another disadvantage of symbolic capacity is that one can have the *feeling* of certainty and comprehension where they are entirely inappropriate. By applying a symbol that stands for something we do know (or think we know) to something we do not know, we may get the feeling of comprehension. But the feeling of comprehension comes from the feeling evoked by the symbol, not the "something" that is unknown. Thus, thunder and lightning are understood with absolute certainty as a huge man pounding on an anvil, or mental illness is understood as possession by the devil, who, in turn is "seen" in semihuman form as a red man with horns and a long, pointed tail.[7] Achieving a sense of comprehension by a feeling evoked by a symbol rather than the process or thing to be understood, has been called "verbal forgery"; for example, people can forge a "genuine" understanding of hard times by blaming "Wall Street," or "the Communists." Furthermore, as man transfers his feeling of comprehension from one thing to another, symbolically, he also transfers his other feelings. If mental illness is caused by the devil, and the devil is fearful and hateful, then one fears and hates the mentally ill.

One final example of the problems posed by symbols should be mentioned. Sometimes because we create a sound, we assume that a thing exists; but the sound may stand for a relationship of things rather than *a* thing. A nation, a group, a social system, an "economy" are not substantive things. They are shorthand symbols that point to a whole complex of processes and relationships among things. If we are not careful, however, we shall forget this and begin to think of them as things that act as things. This is particularly true in social science, and the reader should be cautious, if the writers are not, in approaching such symbols.

From the foregoing discussion, it can be seen that man's use of symbols

---

[6] For an excellent discussion of such phenomena, see S. I. Hayakawa, "Meaning, Symbols, and Levels of Abstraction," in Newcomb and Hartley, *op. cit.*, pp. 190–203.

[7] These samples illustrate anthropomorphism, the ascription of human characteristics to nonhuman things.

presents a certain dilemma. On the one hand, they are the only tools he has for ordering social existence. Commonly shared definitions, right or wrong, are necessary for human group life. In order for the individual to act, he must have some definition of the situation; and in order for him to act in a division of labor with other people, he must *share* a *common* definition with them. Even very invalid conceptions may facilitate human existence by giving the individual necessary relief from the strain of complete uncertainty and by providing groups of individuals with the ability to understand and predict one another's responses. On the other hand, of course, are all of the difficulties associated with symbolic communication that we have just discussed.

As a result of his capacity to use symbols, man places a cultural screen between his self[8] on the one hand and his biological processes, his environment, and other men, on the other hand. In consequence, the limits and the mechanisms of the development of mankind are radically different from those of other animals. This can be seen by considering the role of organic evolution in human affairs. The basic processes of organic evolution are three: first, random variations or mutations in genetic structure; second, selection by the environment of some of these genetically produced innovations as being adapted to the environment; and third, reproduction.

It took this process to *produce* human beings, with their upright posture, stereoscopic vision, tool-using hands, large, complex brains, and symbol-using *capacity*. Once human beings as we know them were produced, however—once culture arose to intervene between the organism and the environment—strictly organic evolution ended for human beings.

That might sound like a controversial statement. Nearly everyone has heard about or read accounts of the probable disappearance of the appendix in human beings, or the disappearance of hair or of the twisted cartilage of the outer ear because they are not longer advantageous or— in the case of the appendix—are even liabilities. Such ideas arise from a failure to distinguish between two separate steps in the evolutionary process. First is the step of genetic variation or mutation. This, to be sure, has as yet not been directly affected by culture (although man may not be far from controlling even this step). The second step is selection—and this is radically affected by culture. In organic evolution, the genetic variation that gives one individual a slight competitive advantage over another in the struggle for survival means that the one with the advantage is more likely to live to reproduce. Given a *cultural* mode of adaptation, however, we do not allow that to happen. The individual with a genetic

---

[8] We understand, of course, that grammarians frown on the phrase "his self," but, as we shall see, it is a valid and important concept, different from "himself."

immunity to smallpox has no advantage over the person with a genetic susceptibility to it; the latter merely gets a vaccination—a *cultural* adaptation. In the same way, man can control many other aspects of his physical environment so as to overcome their selective capacity. Variations in temperature, fluctuations in food supply, natural disasters of flood and fire, and the like, can be controlled or neutralized so that their potential power to select one human type rather than another is inhibited. As these examples suggest, man does not have to change biologically in order to adapt to changes in his physical environment. Biologically, man is essentially the same the world over, and has been historically since his origin, despite the radical difference in his physical environment in both space and time. Furthermore, reproduction among human beings is not a matter of biological attraction; it is a matter of cultural definition. Still further, the genetically determined physical qualities that are "selected" are not selected by a physical environment; if there is any selection at all, it is a result of cultural *meanings* attached to the physical qualities.

What this means is that, as a result of genetic variation or mutation, if some persons do get born without appendices, without hair, or without external ears, they are no more likely to reproduce than anyone else. (Or, if they are more likely to reproduce, that will not be because hairlessness or earlessness is a biologically superior adaptation; it will be because hairlessness or earlessness is *culturally* defined as desirable; hairlessness, in other words, becomes more fashionable.)

Human beings, then, cannot rely—as termites can—on genetic variations to adapt them to the world they live in. They must rely on cultural variations. This, of course, is usually put the other way around: termites "have to" rely on genetic variations; human beings "get to" use culture (or that special species of culture, "science").

The matter is not so one-sided, however. We culturally produce DDT; the termites counter with a genetic immunity to DDT. We come up with penicillin; viruses evolve an immunity to penicillin. The contest is by no means ended. Moreover, as we implied above, it is scarcely certain that man's culture will *always* be able to serve him in lieu of genetic changes; and it may even be that his culture will so modify the physical environment that genetic changes will be produced in spite of himself. The potentialities of atomic radiation are a vivid case in point.

Whatever the ultimate outcome, the fact remains that if we are to understand human action, human history, human adaptation, human life chances, it is cultural *meanings*—symbols and their definitions—that we must understand. A step toward that understanding can be taken by attempting to dissect this thing called culture into its different parts—by considering how the different elements of culture can be classified.

Analysis of Culture

The first, and in a sense the most elementary, classification is one that distinguishes between cultural definitions telling people *what to perceive* and those that tell them *how to respond* to what they perceive. The first kind we call "cognitive" meanings. They tell people what *is* (or was, or will be, or might be). They include ideas of cause and effect relationships. For example, all the following are cognitive ideas:

> The earth is flat.
> The earth is round.
> God created the world.
> There is no God.
> All men are mortal; Socrates is a man; therefore, Socrates is mortal.
> If I go through a red light, the chances are 65 out of 100 that I'll get a ticket.

Notice that in these examples there is no necessary implication that cognitive ideas are "correct," or even that it is possible to ascertain whether or not they are correct. Obviously, the earth is not both round and flat, and obviously there is no scientific way of knowing whether there is or is not a God. All the ideas, nonetheless, are cognitive ideas because they tell people what *is* or "what the chances are" that something will happen. They might, to be sure, tell them incorrectly, but we are not at the moment concerned with correctness or incorrectness. Our point is that if people's cognitive ideas tell them that something is so, they will *act* as if it were so. This is only a special case of our basic proposition that human beings respond to their *definitions* of situations.

Not only do people depend upon symbols to tell them "what is" (that is, to channelize their perceptions); they also depend on symbols to channelize their *responses* to these perceptions. We can distinguish between two kinds of these response-channeling definitions. One we call, "cathectic" ideas; the other we call "moral" or "evaluative" or "normative" ideas.[9]

Cathectic ideas consist of cultural definitions that define what is pleasurable and what is painful. At first glance, it may seem to be stretching things a bit to say that human beings need symbolic definitions to tell

[9] Normative definitions are frequently referred to as "social norms." The term "norm" is also used in a statistical sense to indicate the average or most frequent attribute of a group. Neither usage is more "correct" than the other, but the distinction should be kept in mind. Throughout this book we shall use "norm" to mean a shared moral evaluation.

them what is pleasurable and what is painful. But, in fact, the human dependence on cultural meanings does extend even to this point. It is one thing, for example, to *cognize* caterpillars as possibly nutritious and a very different thing to define them as tasty. A moment's thought will tell you that we could find hundreds of illustrations of this point in the realm of food alone. It is enough merely to mention such expressions as cannibalism, dog steaks, fried cat liver, and rat soup to make the point.

We could also find hundreds of illustrations in the realm of sex, beauty, music, fashion, or housing. For example, the difference between even white teeth and filed pointed teeth, between the attractive feminine figure of the 1920's and that of Brigitte Bardot, between the music of Brahms and rock 'n roll—these will do to illustrate the point. So thoroughly do cathectic ideas intervene between men and the environment that they can determine such basic physiological responses as glandular secretions, sexual appetites, the pulse rate, the directions of peristalsis, and so on.

The second kind of definition helping to determine responses consists of "moral" or "normative" ideas. These are different from cognitive and cathectic ideas in that they add a dimension to human responses that, so far as we know, is completely absent from other animals. All animals, after all, perceive some aspects of reality and have tastes—although their perceptions and tastes are, to be sure, largely *biologically* dictated. But human beings also respond to the "goodness" or "badness" of things, the "virtuousness" or "wickedness," the "properness" or "impropriety" of things.

Evaluative ideas often take precedence over both cognitions and cathexes in determining action. Some things that are positively cathected may be morally tabooed, as in the case of many sexual pleasures; and some things that are *negatively* cathected may be *morally required*, as in the case of firemen entering burning buildings or men allowing women and children to leave a sinking ship first. Furthermore, actions that are *cognized* as being very efficient ways to achieve some gratification may be *morally prohibited*, such as cheating on an examination or poisoning one's rival in a love affair. All Americans cognize the horse and buggy as a means of transportation, but only Mennonites feel *morally* obliged to use it.

With these concepts in mind, it is possible to gain a better understanding of the way in which culture guides human behavior. The "barbarian invaders," as Ralph Linton has termed the infants of each generation, learn from their parents, teachers, and older children how to cognize, cathect, and evaluate the situations in which they are called upon to act. (The process by which they are taught their culture is aptly called by sociologists the "socialization" process. It is the process by which they are changed from nonsocial to social beings. We shall consider it in detail in Chapters 3 and 4.)

The compelling nature of social "definitions of situations" has been dramatically demonstrated in laboratory experiments. Sherif has shown how group definitions affect individual perception in unstructured situations, while at the same time suggesting how such definitions become a property of the group.[10] In his experiment, he made use of the "autokinetic effect," in which a *stationary* point of light in a completely dark room *appears* to move. First, he had his subjects individually indicate over a period how far they thought the light moved. He found that each individual tended to establish a range of movement peculiar to himself. Next he put the individuals into two groups to see how the group would affect the individual's perception. One group was composed of individuals who had previously made judgments as individuals; the other, of individuals who had not previously participated in the experiment. In the group situation, he found that each of those who had previously established his own range of movement tended to converge judgment so that a group standard was established. Those who faced the experiment for the first time also developed a group judgment, but their convergence was closer than the initiated group. Furthermore, when an individual faced the experiment *alone*, after his group experience, he carried over in his individual perception the standard of his group.

Solomon Asch demonstrated that the effect of group definitions on individual judgment operates even in situations where objective differences could be readily perceived. His experiment involved judging the length of lines by matching a given line with one of three others, only one of which was of equal length to the line to be matched. Asch instructed a group of assistants (who pretended to be subjects along with one "naïve" subject) to insist that line A matched line B, when in fact line A did not. He found that the naïve subject in such a case nearly always changed his own objective judgments in favor of the group distortion.[11] Such experiments as these, repeated with variation by many researchers, have amply demonstrated that an individual's "definition of a situation" is affected by that held by the group. Projecting these findings into "real-life" situations, we can begin to understand how the cognitive, cathetic, and normative definitions held by groups of people are taken over by individuals, particularly when they are introduced in infancy and reinforced by the group for an extended period.

As the Sherif experiment suggests, the more vague and unstructured a

[10] M. Sherif, *The Psychology of Social Norms* (New York: Harper & Brothers, 1936).

[11] S. E. Asch, "Effects of Group Pressures upon Modification and Distortion of Judgments," in G. E. Swanson, T. M. Newcomb, and E. L. Hartley *et al.* (eds.), *Readings in Social Psychology* (2d ed.; New York: Holt, Rinehart and Winston, Inc., 1952).

stimulus, the greater the effect of factors not inherent in the stimulus itself. Where no objective standard exists, as in the autokinetic situation, the individual is particularly vulnerable to standards of judgment set by the group. In the case of *moral* judgments, which have no ultimate objective standards, it would appear that people are especially subject to group values, particularly in childhood, when such values are first established in the individual. Asch's research suggests that where objective standards do exist, the amount of concerted group consensus and pressure required to affect the judgment of individuals is greater, but that nonetheless such group pressure is extraordinarily difficult to withstand.

When fully socialized as members of a group, people have learned to single out certain aspects of situations as "the" significant aspects. They cognitively abstract from the total situation certain key characteristics, which have moral or cathectic *meanings* to them. Those aspects also have further cognitive meanings.

For example, when you enter a classroom or a lecture hall as a sociology student, there are literally thousands of aspects of the total situation which you do *not* cognize (if you have been socialized properly). The age of the chair you sit in, the kind of wood from which it is made, the architectural style of the building, the fact of your blood circulation, the chemistry of your digestion, the physics of the acoustics, and so on and on. You perceive only selected aspects—the professor glancing at his watch, for example, and that aspect has a meaning for you. You instantly deduce from it certain further cognitions ("He's going to start lecturing in a minute"); certain evaluative convictions ("He shouldn't start before everyone has a chance to get settled"); and perhaps certain cathexes ("I wish it were summer again!").

VARIATIONS IN CULTURAL DEFINITIONS

The cognitive, cathectic, and evaluative expectations comprising the structure of situations may vary in several ways, in addition to the obvious variation in content. In the first place, they vary with respect to their precision. Some situations are precisely and minutely defined; the expectations are prescribed in minute detail and no deviation is permitted. Soldiers on parade, certain religious ceremonies and rituals, and formal Japanese tea ceremonies are examples. In most situations, however, the definition of the situation is less rigid. Students, for example, are supposed to be "attentive"; women are supposed to dress "attractively"; men are supposed to be "considerate" of their dates. But there is a wide range of behavior which would still be called "attentive," "attractive," or "considerate."

In the second and related place, different expectations fall at different points along a positive-negative continuum. Behavior might be required, preferred, permitted, tolerated, disapproved, or tabooed (prohibited). In the third place, expectations differ with respect to the person, situation, and time. Some apply to everyone in a group or a society (for example, the Ten Commandments); others are applicable only to subgroups within a culture (for example, women may and sometimes must wear hats in Catholic churches, men must not; haberdashers may advertise, physicians must not; in some parts of the South whites must be called "Miss" or "Mrs." but Negroes must not be). Some apply in nearly all situations, such as concepts of virtue or integrity; others apply only in specific situations, such as the exercise of competition in business relations but not in friendship. Some are perceived as relatively transitory, such as fads and styles, whereas others are held to be valid for all times, such as religious and ethical beliefs.

PATTERN VARIABLES

A fourth kind of variation emphasized by some analysts is concerned with the kind of "action problem" the definitions help individuals to solve. Talcott Parsons has suggested that five such problems are inherent in every situation, and that the structures of different situations vary with respect to how they are solved. The five problems or "dilemmas" distinguished by Parsons are as follows:

1. Is Person A supposed to pay attention to what Person B *is* (a Negro, a woman, an American, a professor) or what he can *do* (cook, run, advise, teach)?
2. Is A supposed to be chiefly concerned with B's relationship to *himself* (*my* mother, *my* wife, *my* teammate), or with B's relationship to general principles (laws, standards of competence, rules of the game)?
3. Do evaluative standards take precedence over cathectic ones ("Die for your country!"), or is the reverse true ("Run for your life!")?
4. Is this a narrow, specific relationship (such as giving a waitress your dinner order), or a broad, diffuse one (such as asking your mother to fix your favorite food *and* iron your clothes *and* nurse you when you're sick *and* give you money, etc.)?
5. Is Individual A supposed to watch out only for his own interests ("What's in this for me?"), or is he supposed to give priority to B's interests ("What's best for him?")?

The different answers to these five questions give different definitions of situations.[12] We shall discuss each of these five problems in the order given above.

QUALITIES VS. PERFORMANCES

A distinction of far-reaching significance in social affairs is the distinction between two institutionalized ways of defining people: on the basis of their abilities or on the basis of certain of their qualities.

In one sense, this is a familiar distinction to Americans, who learn almost from kindergarten that "what a man *is* doesn't matter; it's what he can *do* that should determine his fate." These two opposing definitions are, of course, at the root of the national crisis over the treatment of Negroes. One tradition says that the *performances* of Negroes should determine their relationship to whites; another says that the sheer quality of "being Negro" should be the determining factor.

Since it is in the context of racial, ethnic, and religious conflict that most Americans think about the difference between emphasizing performances and emphasizing qualities, it is understandable that most people think of the "quality" orientation as "discrimination." This is misleading, however, for what we have been noting all along in this chapter is that people *must* discriminate one object from another before they can act. What is critical is the question of the *basis on which* their cultural definitions lead them to discriminate.

All cultures, in some contexts, define certain qualities as "the" important things; in other contexts, certain performances are defined as important. In the American culture, when Individual A is a man looking for a wife he is *supposed* to discriminate on the basis of a quality: B's sex. Most people would be horrified and indignant if in such a situation he insisted on giving priority to what people can *do,* and chose to marry a homosexual male on the grounds that the latter could clean house and cook better than any of the available females. But there is nothing "automatic" about this; it is a matter of cultural definitions, as the following report by an anthropologist, Ralph Linton, indicates:

> Men whose personalities were completely uncongenial to the warrior role assumed a special status, that of *berdache.* They wore women's costumes and carried on women's activities. . . . They continued to hunt and a little of the general pattern of male superiority still attached to them. Thus they were expected to be somewhat better than women even at women's tasks. The highest compliment which could be paid to

[12] They are *variable* ways of *patterning* relationships and probably for that reason the sociologist who originated this mode of analysis, Talcott Parsons, called it the "pattern variable" schema. See Talcott Parsons, *The Social System* (New York: The Free Press of Glencoe, Inc., 1951), pp. 58–67.

a woman was to tell her that her beadwork was as fine or her lodge as well kept as that of a *berdache*. Some of the *berdache* were homosexual, but the majority apparently were not. In either case, the society's attitude toward them was entirely neutral. Even when they married other men there was only mild disapproval, and this fell upon the "husband," not the *berdache*. He was condemned for trying to get a partner who would not only keep his house but also hunt for him.[13]

In many other respects also, the American culture defines situations by assigning rights and obligations to people on the basis of their qualities. The difference between "women's work" and "men's work"; the different expectations of boys' and girls' behavior on dates, the privilege of voting simply by virtue of being twenty-one years old; the obligation of enlisted men in the armed forces to initiate the salute between commissioned officers and themselves—all these are examples of structured expectations based on qualities.

UNIVERSALISM VS. PARTICULARISM

A second way in which social structures differ is in terms of the kind of morality institutionalized—what we might call the "morality of principle," on the one hand, or the "morality of loyalty," on the other. The "morality of principle" consists of the expectation that one should treat everyone according to the same abstract, general, *universal* principles. The "morality of loyalty" is the expectation that one should treat people differently, depending on their *particular* relationship to one. Principle morality or universalism, for example, says that if you see your best friend cheating, you should report him to the professor. Loyalty morality or particularism says that you should lie to the professor to protect your friend. Particularism says, "My country—may she ever be right; but right or wrong, my country!" Universalism says, "May she ever be right—if she wants my support."

When a professor gives grades to students "impartially," based only on the students' relation to *third* things, such as the exam questions, he is behaving universalistically. When he favors his son or daughter who happens to be in the class, thus emphasizing the student's relationship to *himself*, he is behaving particularistically.

These two contrasting expectations are often deeply rooted in people and invested with strong emotions. Such epithets as "traitor," "squealer," and "disloyal" attest to the indignation aroused by people who violate particularistic institutions. But the same people who indignantly cry "traitor" at someone who behaves universalistically in one situation will

[13] Ralph Linton, *The Study of Man* (New York: Appleton-Century-Crofts, Inc., 1936), p. 480.

just as indignantly cry "corruption" at, let us say, a judge who *fails* to apply the law impersonally in another situation. This is a good illustration of our basic point that what arouses indignation is the violation of social definitions—which, however, vary from situation to situation. Thus, to illustrate the principle in another context, the woman who behaves particularistically as a jury member is dishonest, but if she does *not* behave particularistically as a wife, she is unfaithful. The situations in which loyalty is institutionalized are sharply different from those in which universalism is called for; and, as we shall see later, the two kinds of definitions have very different consequences.

AFFECTIVITY[14] vs. NEUTRALITY

A third basic difference in the definition of different situations concerns the question of which has priority—cathectic definitions or evaluative ones? Every situation contains opportunities for people to get immediate gratifications—that is, it provides ways in which people can maximize their immediate pleasure. In some situations it is proper for them to do so, and in others, it is not. When it is proper, they are expected to be "affective"; when it is not, they are expected to be "neutral."

We briefly cited some examples of this above. Firemen, for example, could maximize their immediate gratifications by refusing to enter a burning building. Soldiers under fire could get great pleasure from deserting. There are opportunities for sexual pleasure in every situation involving males and females. Almost everyone could increase his immediate gratification by turning off the alarm in the morning and going back to sleep.

All such pleasures—avoiding pain or death, sex, sleep—are expected in some situations but not in others. When the definition of the situation calls for gratification and pleasure-oriented behavior, then people who insist upon giving priority to evaluative ideas are treated with indignation and scorn, or perhaps even as psychologically sick. The frigid woman or the impotent man, for example, who are too obsessed with the "immorality of sex" to be able to play adult sexual roles are familiar examples. The date who must leave the party at eleven o'clock in order to "get a good night's sleep" is a not unfamiliar bore.

It is significant, however, that the indignation felt toward people who

[14] The term "affectivity" in this context comes from the word "affect," which, regrettably, has several different legitimate meanings and, to make matters worse, is widely used incorrectly as a synonym for "effect." Funk and Wagnalls' dictionary gives two meanings when the word is used as a verb: (1) To act upon or have an effect upon; (2) *to touch or move emotionally.* It is the second of these meanings that is the root of "affectivity" as used here. An attitude of "affectivity" is one that allows the person to be touched or moved emotionally.

are *neutral* when the situation calls for *affectivity* is considerably less than that felt toward people who are *affective* when the structure demands *neutrality*. The impotent man is more likely to be an object of ridicule than of hostility; but the reverse is true of the cowardly man. The reason for this, we may speculate, is that neutrality is rather harder to learn than affectivity, which "comes naturally," as it were. The infant is born with the ability to attempt to maximize pleasure and does not hesitate to complain about pain or discomfort. It takes a long time and considerable effort and frustration to acquire the ability to inhibit the desire for immediate gratification of every impulse and whim. It is on the side of neutrality, then, that the weight of a society's tradition tends to be thrown; and the greatest wrath is reserved for those who threaten to upset the hard-won victory over impulse.

Furthermore, the need for reliability and predictability of behavior is so great in the delicately balanced human division of labor that impulsive behavior is a serious threat. Compulsive behavior, on the other hand, which might prevent someone from being affective, is merely irritating. It has nowhere near the same possibilities of disruptive consequences. It is as if society prefers the risk of going too far in inhibiting some people to that of not going far enough in controlling the impulses of others.

For these reasons uncontrolled impulsiveness is likely to be more seriously punished in all societies than uncalled for restraint or inhibition. The American culture, moreover, has had a special dose of neutrality injected into it by Puritanism, which probably went as far toward devaluing affectivity as it is possible to go.

DIFFUSENESS VS. SPECIFICITY

A fourth way in which definitions of situations differ is with respect to the range of different activities the participants engage in with one another or the range of different experiences they share. In some situations, the expectations that A may legitimately (that is, according to the common definitions) have of B are sharply limited, involving only a fraction of A's and B's total personalities. The expectations are *specified* narrowly, as in a contract in which A promises to deliver ten tons of coal to B next Friday in exchange for $100, *and that's all*. Any other expectation these two might have of one another is illegitimate. For example, B must find someone else to mow his lawn, another person to teach him sociology, still another to cook his meals, and so on. Indeed, if B even so much as asks A to put the coal in the coalbin instead of dumping it on the sidewalk, it might be institutionally appropriate for A to retort, "That's not in our contract!" (or to communicate the same idea by inviting B to go where coal is highly redundant).

Specific relationships, in other words, are specialized ones. Situations that are defined *diffusely,* on the other hand, are situations in which the limits to the expectations one person might have of another are not specified. They perform not one but many functions for one another—or at least, it is legitimate for them to expect one another to do so if need should arise. Friends, for example, are traditionally supposed to "know no limits" to the sacrifices they will make for one another. In small rural communities or in preliterate, simple societies, neighbors and clan members may do virtually everything for one another—they hunt, fish, plant, harvest, nurse, worship, live, eat, and sleep together.

In modern, specialized, complex societies most situations are specific. Even the marriage relationship, as many sociologists have pointed out, no longer involves many of the functions that husbands and wives used to perform for one another. It is scarcely an exaggeration to say that there is virtually nothing the modern husband receives from his wife that he could not *legitimately* get elsewhere—and better, provided he could pay for it—save sex, love or companionship, and "blood children." Canning, cooking, washing, sewing, house cleaning, even child care are available from specialized experts; and many wives, in fact, simply act as liaison agents between the family and those specialists.

A simple test of whether a relationship is defined *specifically* or *diffusely* is to ask, "Who has the burden of proof—the person who wants to *in*clude something in the relationship, or the person who wants to *ex*clude something?" In a *specific* relationship, such as the coal seller–coal purchaser relationship, the person who wants to *in*clude something must prove that he has a right to do so—that it is legitimately a "part of the contract." In a *diffuse* relationship, such as a husband-wife relationship, the person who wants to *ex*clude something has the burden of proof. It is entirely possible, of course, that in a specific relationship the person who wants to include some new element in the relationship—or even many new elements—may be able to carry the burden of proof.

For example, a professor-student relationship is specific; it is supposed to be confined strictly to the interchange of knowledge about a certain subject. If a professor says to one of his students, "Where were you last Saturday night, whom were you with, what were you doing, and what time did you get home?" the student might very well reply, "That's none of your business." The student, properly, is denying the professor's right to include such subjects in their specific relationship. Still, the professor may be able to prove that he *does* have a right to include them *in terms of the specific relationship.* If he is a sociology or a psychology professor, for example, he may explain that he needs to know those things in order to be able to carry out his *specific* task of explaining some point to the student.

In the same way, the members of a *diffuse* relationship may be able to "prove" that a certain element which the other member wants to include in the relationship, in fact, should not be included. If a husband asks his wife to steal something, for example, the wife may legitimately refuse *if* the culture places her obligations to the larger society on a higher level than it places her obligation to her husband.

SELF-ORIENTATION VS. COLLECTIVITY ORIENTATION

The fifth and final way in which Talcott Parsons has suggested that social definitions might differ significantly is with respect to the kind of motivation institutionalized. On the one hand, individuals may be expected to attempt to further their own interests in the situation; on the other hand, they may be expected to subordinate their own interests to the interests of some larger collectivity. For example, when you buy a car you expect the salesman to give you a "sales talk," and you know that the sales talk will be designed not to meet *your* needs but the salesman's. By contrast, when you consult your physician about your health, you know fairly confidently that he will tell you what is best for *you*, even if he could use the extra money from an expensive operation.

It is easy to become confused about this distinction by arguing that the physician as well as the salesman is trying to further his own interests, only the physician is in a position in which he would get in trouble if it were discovered that he was prescribing operations on the basis of his own monetary needs rather than his patients' health needs. The difference in their "positions" is exactly the point we are making. The salesman is *expected* to ignore the customer's needs—they are up to the customer to protect in this situation. The "customer" as *patient*, however, is *not* supposed to protect or meet his own needs; the physician is.

This distinction has nothing whatever to do with the question of which is "more selfish" or "more altruistic"—the physician or the salesman. "Selfishness" and "altruism" are evaluative terms referring (not very informatively[15]) to individual character traits. We are dealing with only cognitive terms, in the first place; and in the second place, we are not talking about character traits. We are talking about *shared expectations*. Physicians, teachers, lawyers, engineers—all professional persons (at least) —are institutionally required to put their clients' interests ahead of their own, in the sense that all the clients have to do is to make their problems known in order to *obligate* the professional person to try to solve them to

---

[15] Like all evaluative terms, they describe nothing about the person to whom they are applied, but simply report the attitudes of the person applying them. The evaluative sentence "He is selfish" is translatable into the cognitive sentence, "I think he ought to behave differently."

the best of his ability. In a sense, the client is the employer of the professional person (even though indirectly, as in the case of the student
client); and he has an institutional right to expect his "employee" to give
him his best effort and not to "rob the till," so to speak. The salesman,
however, is not remotely the employee of the customer. They are inde-·
pendent bargainers.

The professional people may be extremely selfish, greedy, antisocial
persons, so far as their personal characters are concerned; and the salesmen may be paragons of charity, sweetness, and altruism. None of that is
relevant. The selfish physician must still pursue his ends by doing his best
to meet his *patients'* problems; the kindly car salesman must meet his by
making sales. (If he attempts to further his customer's interests, as one of
the authors once did in a part-time job as a department store salesman,
by telling the customer to go to another store where he could get a better
bargain, the salesman simply won't be a salesman long!)

These five respects in which the structure of situations vary will appear
again and again in our analysis of integration, adaptation, and decision
making in later chapters. The terminology is not the important thing, so
the reader need not fret about such unfamilar language as "specificity
and diffuseness, affectivity and neutrality," and so on. When it is convenient to use the terms later on, they will be explained again. What is
important is to understand what the terms are labels *for;* that is, to understand the difference between the structure of a situation calling for
"affectivity," for example, and that of a situation calling for "neutrality."

FOLKWAYS AND MORES

So far we have discussed four different ways in which sociologists find
it convenient to distinguish among the cognitive, cathectic, and evaluative
definitions that comprise "culture." We called attention to differences in
the minuteness with which they regulate behavior; we noted that some
are phrased positively, some permissively, and some negatively (thou
shalt, thou may, thou shalt not); we observed that some apply to all the
members of a group or a society whereas others apply only to special subgroups; and we described alternative ways in which five basic issues of
social definition might be culturally resolved. Now, and finally, we must
point out another way in which it is sometimes useful to analyze the prescriptions and prohibitions of culture into separate categories.

This is a classification that has become by now a part of everyday
speech, in such familiar terms as "folkways," "mores," "customs," "enacted
law," and "common law." These categories of social definition result from
focusing attention on three characteristics of the *normative* or evaluative
aspects of culture: their origin; the degree of importance attached to

them by the members of a society or group; and the manner in which they are enforced.[16]

Two kinds of origin may be distinguished—tradition and organized enactment. That is, norms are simply divided into two categories—those whose origins are "lost in the mists of antiquity," such as the taboo on sexual relations between parents and children; and those that were enacted by a legislature of some kind, such as traffic laws or the national prohibition amendment. Second, norms are grouped into those about which people feel strongly and those about which they feel mildly. Third, they are divided into those which are enforced by some formal machinery, such as police and courts; and those which are enforced informally, through such means as spontaneous group ridicule or lynchings.

When these three distinctions are put together, the classification shown in Table 1-1 emerges.

TABLE 1-1

Classification of Norms

	INFORMAL ENFORCEMENT		FORMAL ENFORCEMENT	
	Strong group feeling	Mild group feeling	Strong group feeling	Mild group feeling
Traditional	MORES	FOLKWAYS	COMMON LAW	
	(CUSTOMS)			
Enacted	XXX	XXXX	ENACTED LAW	

Mores, as Table 1-1 indicates, are norms that are traditional, informally enforced, and invested with strong group feelings. Folkways are like mores in that they are informally enforced and traditional; but the members of the group do not attach so much importance to them. Both mores and folkways together are "customs."

The common law is traditional law, but unlike folkways and mores, the legal norms are formally enforced, simply by definition. No distinction is made between common-law norms about which the group feels strongly and those about which it feels mildly—that distinction would appear in the severity of the sanctions meted out by the enforcement agency. Enacted law, similarly, is formally enforced, with no distinction between "important" and "unimportant" statutes, except in terms of their sanctions.

As the two sets of X's in Table 1-1 indicate, there are no terms for

---

[16] We are here following the analysis presented by Allen Barton, "The Concept of Property Space in Social Research," in Paul F. Lazarsfeld and Morris Rosenberg (eds.), *The Language of Social Research* (New York: The Free Press of Glencoe, Inc., 1955), pp. 51–52.

norms that are enacted but for which no enforcement machinery exists. As Allen Barton suggests,[17] examples of these might be found in statutes prohibiting racial or religious discrimination, but with no "teeth" in them. They are not likely, then, to be very effective.

STRUCTURE AND INSTITUTIONALIZATION

When people know how to act in a situation—when they know what to expect of others and what is expected of them—we say that the situation is "structured" for them. This is to say that they have a common *definition* of the situation. When these expectations are not only cognized but are positively evaluated as well, the structure is said to be *institutionalized* in this group of people. That is, when expectations are institutionalized, people not only can predict how they and other members of the group will behave, but believe that they *should* behave that way. Moreover, they usually *want* to behave in the expected manner. If someone behaves contrary to an institutionalized expectation, other people are startled, indignant, scornful, or hostile. Punishment of one sort or another is visited on the violator, who himself ordinarily feels guilt or shame and embarrassment.

Situations, however, may be structured for individuals without the structure being institutionalized in the group. This is the case, for example, when two friends know they can count on one another to cheat but also know that cheating is "wrong"—at least in the eyes of most members of the group and probably in their own eyes as well. This distinction between structured and institutionalized interaction is made in order to emphasize the fact that people may interact in predictable, patterned ways that deviate from the normatively expected ways of the group.

The conditions under which people violate institutionalized definitions will be taken up later in Chapter 5. Here we shall continue in another direction by noting that sometimes people encounter situations that are "unstructured" in either an institutional or a noninstitutional sense. Sometimes people may be brought together in situations where there are no institutionalized or structured expectations. Sometimes people may enter groups where there are highly institutionalized expectations, but they have not yet learned what these are. Sometimes, too, different persons may have incompatible expectations; they bring different definitions to the same situation. It is in such situations that the human dependence on shared cultural definitions is made vivid, for the feeling of not knowing what to expect—or even worse, what is expected—can be completely paralyzing; and the experience of discovering that one's expectations have

---

[17] *Ibid.*, p. 52.

been widely at variance with someone else's can be either infuriating or embarrassing, depending on the circumstances.

For example, when a boy sees himself as playing Romeo to a girl's Juliet, while all the time she sees him as playing Laertes to her Ophelia— both persons are in for a shock. At some point she is going to discover that the way he is holding her hand is not exactly brotherly; and at that point someone's definition of the situation is going to have to change. The situation will be restructured.

Such a situation illustrates the necessity not only of *clear* expectations but also of shared and complementary expectations. Individual A must know confidently what Individual B is like, how she will interpret his actions, what her responses will be, what response he is then supposed to make to her response, and so on, before he can act. But, in addition, she must know exactly the same things before they can *interact* in any stable way. Everyone, in other words, is dependent on symbolic definitions to tell him what things are and how to respond to them; but if the symbolic definitions are to be part of a *culture*, they must be widely shared by the members of a social system. Put another way, people can act on the basis of private, idiosyncratic, symbolic definitions; but if they are to *inter*act in a structured situation, there must be a *culture*—that is, *shared* definitions.

In the example we have chosen, of course—courtship, or the "dating game"—an element of uncertainty about the other person's response is itself institutionalized (in the American system) as part of the expectations. A slight amount of uncertainty, especially when institutionalized, adds a certain zest or thrill to the situation, as in any game. But the importance of even the uncertainty's being institutionalized becomes readily apparent if one considers introducing the same amount of uncertainty into the situation after a man and woman are married. Marriage, by definition, is an institution in which the expectations are supposed to be certain—which, for some people, is precisely what makes marriage dull and boring. But it is also precisely what makes it possible for the marriage partners to eat and sleep and to think about something besides the limpid pools of liquid twilight that are the beloved's eyes.

It should be emphasized, however, that not only is the "uncertainty" *institutionalized* in the dating game, as in a baseball game or a bridge game, but also the rules and signals governing the "players'" behavior must be institutionalized before any interaction, except warfare, can take place. Just how far the boy is supposed to go, just what degree of resistance he is supposed to recognize as real rather than as part of the game, just which responses on the part of the girl mean encouragement— all these symbols, which might be very subtle, must be institutionalized if the situation is not to degenerate into open conflict. The tragicomedies of dating and courtship often result from boys and girls moving from a group in which one set of rules and signals were institutionalized into a different group with a different set.

The extreme of lack of structure occurs when the individual simply does not know what is expected. No doubt many readers can illustrate from their own experiences the anguish and near paralysis felt when they found themselves in a strange situation with no clear understanding of how to act. If the situation is one which in fact has a structure, although the individual in question does not know it, the remedy is the fairly simple one (however painful it might be) of learning it. In some cases, however, the situation is in fact unstructured; and then before interaction can go on, a structure must be found or created on the basis of past experience with similar situations. Something like this happens not infrequently perhaps in boy-girl relationships in the United States. One of the persons make a very vague, general, essentially meaningless remark. (The ability even to take this first step, of course, requires a vast amount of past experience with symbols and their definitions.) In order to respond, the other person must pick out some range of meanings the remarks *might* have and give some response to that imputed meaning. If the response is in the direction desired by the first speaker, he or she responds to it in a manner corroborating the second speaker's guess, and the situation becomes gradually structured. The art of ambiguity in this kind of dialogue can be developed to a very fine point, indeed.

James D. Thompson and William J. McEwen have called this the "sounding out" process, and have described it as follows in the context of an effort to *shift* the structure of a situation from one kind to another.

> The sounding out process can be illustrated by the problem of the boss with amorous designs on his secretary in an organization that taboos such relations. He must find some means of determining her willingness to alter the relationship, but he must do so without risking rebuff, for a showdown might come at the cost of his dignity or his office reputation, at the cost of losing her secretarial services, or in the extreme case at the cost of losing his own position. The "sophisticated" procedure is to create an ambiguous situation in which the secretary is forced to respond in one of two ways: (1) to ignore or tactfully counter, thereby clearly channeling the relationship back into an already existing pattern, or (2) to respond in a similarly ambiguous vein (if not in a positive one) indicating a receptiveness to further advances. It is important in the sounding out process that the situation be ambiguous for two reasons: (1) the secretary must not be able to "pin down" the boss with evidence if she rejects the idea, and (2) the situation must be far enough removed from normal to be noticeable to the secretary. The ambiguity of sounding out has the further advantage to the participants that neither party alone is clearly responsible for initiating the change.[18]

[18] James D. Thompson and William J. McEwen, "Organizational Goals and Environment," *American Sociological Review*, 23:23–31 (1958), p. 30.

With such very special exceptions as this, however, and this one in only a limited sense, human beings find most unstructured situations intolerable. Indeed, in a basic sense, they *are* intolerable, since human beings are as dependent on cultural definitions as insects are on "instincts." It has been reported, for example, that among certain primitive Australian tribes, where only a limited number of structures are recognized and those mostly kinship relations, the following action takes place whenever two strangers meet. They immediately begin to trace their lineage back through the generations, in the hope of finding at some point a common ancestor. If they succeed, they know the relation in which they stand to one another, and they then know how to act. If they fail, they have only one recourse—to attempt to kill each other.

SUMMARY

Human responses to physical and biological stimuli depend upon the meaning assigned to those stimuli by cultural definitions. Cognitive ideas tell people what to "see" in the environment; cathectic definitions tell them what is pleasant and unpleasant about what they see; and evaluative ideas tell them what is morally good and bad about what they see.

Cultural definitions not only permit people to abstract different aspects of concrete reality; they also permit people to generalize about them. Both abilities—to abstract and to generalize—permit human beings to understand and respond to many aspects and relationships that are beyond the purview of nonhuman animals. Human beings also, however, may be as much the prisoners of their definitions as other animals are of their instincts.

In order for people to interact with one another, it is necessary for them to share common definitions. Five "dilemmas of actions" must be resolved by a common culture—the dilemmas indicated by these concepts: (1) qualities vs. performances; (2) universalism vs. particularism; (3) affectivity vs. neutrality; (4) diffuseness vs. specificity; (5) self-orientation vs. collectivity orientation. The cultural solutions of these as well as other cognitive, cathectic, and evaluative definitions may vary with respect to their origin, the importance attached to them, their mode of enforcement, their minuteness, and their universality.

2

GROUP LIFE

Ralph Linton once wrote that men are anthropoid apes trying to live like termites.[1] This wryly put thought sums up a good deal of perceptiveness.

Several kinds of insects and human beings have evolved a mode of life that sharply distinguishes them from other insects and animals. Instead of meeting the survival problems of nourishment and protection individually, as, for example, bears and turtles do, termites and people meet them cooperatively, through a division of labor.

The cooperative method has certain advantages, in that if some members of the species can specialize in certain tasks, while others specialize in other tasks, over-all efficiency can be increased. But the cooperative method also raises certain new problems. How is the labor to be divided, and which members are to do what in the division of labor? Since specialization means that individuals are dependent on one another (by definition no specialist meets all his own needs), how are the fruits of specialization to be made available to other specialists? How can it be assured that the various specialists will all do their part, so that the whole thing "hangs together"?

Once the evolutionary step is taken away from individual methods toward cooperative methods of survival, these *internal* problems become just as urgent as the *external* problems of adapting to the environment. Insects that have adopted the social mode of adaptation solve the internal problems of integration and "motivation" in the same way that they (and all other forms of nonhuman life) solve the external problems—biologically. Through biological differentiation within the species, specialists are

[1] Ralph Linton, *The Tree of Culture* (New York: Alfred A. Knopf, Inc., 1955), p. 11.

28

created to perform the various activities that make up the division of labor within the social group.

Thus, in an ant society, the ant with the role of laying eggs is *genetically* prepared to lay eggs. She can no more avoid laying eggs than a fish can avoid swimming or an infant can avoid breathing. Similarly, the "neuter" ants (neither male nor female), which care for the queen ant, can no more avoid caring for her and giving her what she needs than she can avoid laying eggs. And the soldier ants, with their genetically determined powerful jaws, are likewise bound to do what they have to do in the division of labor and take what they receive as "reward," because that is the way they are *genetically* built.

With man it is different. The same problems must be met, but there are few genetic mechanisms for meeting them. This is what Linton meant. Man's genetic equipment is much more like that of an individualistic ape than it is like that of a cooperative termite. Yet, through evolution, man has moved away from the ape's mode of survival and has become committed to that of the termites. No human being *has* to bear offspring, as a queen ant has to lay eggs; no human being *has* to be a soldier; no one is genetically forced to be a worker; and so on. Moreover, there is no biological compulsion for a human mother to play her role well; nor is there any biological necessity for a human soldier to be a "good" soldier or a "poor" one.

What substitutes (more or less effectively) for the genetic solutions to integrative and "motivational" problems in human societies is the same thing that substitutes for genetic solutions to adaptive problems: culture. The human mother's activities, like those of the human soldier or the human worker, are determined by learned *definitions of situations.* How this is brought about and what "more or less effectively" means we shall consider later. Here we must first introduce a number of concepts that will help in understanding how culture operates in human social life.

Social Structure

STATUS

As we have pointed out, culture consists of symbolic definitions in terms of which people act. Clearly, no one person knows all the culture that exists, even in his own immediate environment—not to mention what has existed in the past. Just as clearly, no one person acts at any given time or place in terms of all the culture he *does* know. Some is acted upon at one time and place and with one person or group; some, at other times and places and with other persons or groups. In other words, which symbolic definitions are used depend on the specifics of time, place, and person or group.

The term we use to designate these specifications is *status*. A status is a position within a division of labor. It should be understood, of course, that a status is not a physical position. It is, rather, a set of cultural definitions that specify how a person is supposed to perceive and respond to objects and people when he is in a particular relationship with them. The status "father," for example, consists of the ways a man is supposed to cognize, cathect, and evaluate certain other people and things. A father in American society is one who is supposed to love his children, get respect and love from them, be a good provider, have pride in his home, and so on. As this example shows, a status is a relational concept; it cannot be defined except in terms of how its occupant is supposed to think and feel and act toward occupants of *other* statuses.

One way of describing this relational aspect of the concept "status" is to point out that the social definitions comprising a status consist of a set of rights and obligations directing interaction with other people. *Status rights* consist of what a person can legitimately expect from others when he is occupying a particular status. *Status obligations* consist of what others can legitimately expect from him in that status. It is the mutual cognition of status rights and obligations that gives "structure" to social interaction. It is the institutionalization of those expectations that permits orderly, consistent, and relatively enduring relationships among people. It is in this sense that statuses are analogous to biological differentiation within a species such as ants or termites. Status differentiation does the same thing for human beings that biological differentiation does for social insects.

ROLE

The concept "role" has been used by different sociologists in slightly different ways. We shall return to the concept below, when we take up the concept of "role-set;" but for the immediate present we can do no better than quote the lucid statement of Robert K. Merton:

> For some time now, at least since the influential writings of Ralph Linton on the subject, it has been recognized that two concepts—social status and social role—are fundamental to the description, and the analysis, of a social structure.
>
> By status Linton meant a position in a social system occupied by designated individuals; by role, the behavioral enacting of the patterned expectations attributed to that position. . . . Linton went on to observe that each person in society inevitably occupies multiple statuses and that, for

each of these statuses, there is *an* associated role. This proved to be a useful first approximation, as later research amply testifies. In this first approximation, however, Linton assumed that each status has *its distinctive role.*

Without engaging in heavier deliberation than the subject deserves, we must note that a particular social status involves, not a single associated role, but an array of associated roles.[2]

A "role," then, is not *all* the "behavioral enacting" of the status; it is only the behavioral enacting of a *part* of the status—the part which prescribes how the status-occupant should act toward *one* of the persons with whom his status rights and obligations put him in contact.

SOCIAL SYSTEM

To say that a status is a position (one of the "divisions") in a division of labor is to imply interdependence such that the action of a person in one status is contingent upon the action of a person in another status. In other words, there is a relationship of social *inter*action that is guided by the statuses involved. Such interrelated statuses we call a *social system.* To take our previous example, a man, when he is in the status of "father," interacts in specified ways with his children and their mother. The statuses "father," "mother," "son," and "daughter" (assuming these to be the ones involved in a particular family—say, the Joneses) taken together constitute a social system, which we call a "family" in our society. Statuses, then, are the building blocks or the constituent parts of a social system. They are the symbolic definitions, shared by members of the system, which differentiate behavior of people acting in the system.

One of the things you will notice about the Jones family is that any member of this system calls upon only part of his total repertory of symbolic definitions when he is acting in the family system. Mr. Jones does not interact with his ten-year-old son as he would with a forty-year-old friend, some other person's son, a female acquaintance, his boss at the office, or his medical doctor. Although all the complex aspects of Mr. Jones as a person are physically present when he is interacting in the family, only those which are appropriate to his status in the family are ordinarily acted upon. The same is true, of course, of the other family members. This is why the basic unit of a social system is not a person; it is only one of the *statuses* of that person.

[2] Robert K. Merton, *Social Theory and Social Structure* (rev. and enl. ed.; New York: The Free Press of Glencoe, Inc., 1957), pp. 368–369. The work by Linton to which Merton refers is *The Study of Man* (New York: Appleton-Century-Crofts, Inc., 1936), Chap. 8.

SOCIAL GROUP

A plurality of people such as the Jones family is called a *social group*. (This is not the same as a social *system;* we shall get to the contrast below.) What sets the Jones family apart, as a "group," from other people? Among other criteria, three seem central. First, they are in a relationship in which the action of one is taken into account in the actions of the others; that is, they interact within a shared culture. Second, they consider themselves members of the family group and are so considered by the other members. Third, the rights and obligations binding upon them, within *their* group, are not binding upon nonmembers. Thus, we distinguish the Jones family from the Smith family, and both from the groups of people that compose the local Baptist church, the neighborhood, the downtown department store, Troop 9 of the Boy Scouts, and so on.

A group such as the family is often referred to as a *primary* group.[3] Primary group members usually interact directly (face to face), with a relatively high degree of frequency and personal involvement, in a relatively stable and enduring group. A friendship, a neighborhood, a boy's gang are also examples of a primary group. Such groups are relatively small. People are also members of larger groups—groups the size of a business organization or even a whole society or nation. These groups have been called *secondary* groups. Sometimes they are referred to as "collectivities," and primary groups are simply called "groups."[4] We prefer the primary-secondary distinction because the difference appears to be one of degree rather than of kind. Relationships in a secondary group, in contrast to those in a primary, are more indirect, less frequent, or more transitory, or demand less personal involvement—or are all of these. However, the term used is of little importance so long as the differences are kept in mind. The student of social science will soon learn that the vagaries of terminology are such that the same term may be defined differently by different analysts and different terms may be used to communicate the same concept. The student should not be dismayed by this fact, but acknowledge it as a mark of a developing and searching discipline.

[3] The term "primary group" was introduced by Charles H. Cooley and is discussed in detail in *Social Organization* (New York: Charles Scribner's Sons, 1909), Chap. 3. He did not specifically use the term "secondary group," and the origins of this term are obscure.

[4] Robert K. Merton, the Columbia sociologist, has discussed his preference for this terminology in the essay "Continuities in the Theory of Reference Groups and Social Structure," in Merton, *op. cit.*, p. 299. We have drawn from this seminal article for many of the terms used in this chapter.

FORMAL AND INFORMAL GROUPS

The terms "formal" and "informal," when applied to groups, refer to the way in which the institutionalized structure of a group has developed and is organized. *Formal groups* are those whose structure is rationally conceived and organized. As used in this context, "rational" means that the social structure is deliberately and consciously created and organized to realize some specific end or goal. In other words, formal groups are formed with a specific purpose in mind and their structure is instrumentally organized to attain the purpose. Examples of formal groups are governmental bureaucracies, military establishments, large business and industrial enterprises, universities, and the like. Although the distinction between formal and informal groups is relative rather than absolute, it can be said in a general sense that *informal groups* are those whose structure has not been consciously or deliberately created and whose organization, while bearing on the attainment of goals, is not deliberately formed for specific ends. Examples of informal groups are the family, friendships, cliques, and the like. As these examples suggest, formal groups are usually secondary groups; and informal groups, primary.

Probably the more sociologically significant difference between formal and informal groups is found in the difference in organization of structure rather than in differences in the origin of structure. Formal organization is distinguished by a number of characteristics.[5] Without going into the details of all these characteristics, we may say that formal organization usually involves a unity of purpose to which each status is specialized to contribute; the status rights and obligations ordinarily are written in a formal code or status specification; these rights and obligations are enforceable, activity is coordinated, and decisions are made by specified authority in an organized chain of command; group members are recruited on the basis of specialized training; and the continuity of the social system over time is independent of particular status-occupants.

When informal groups increase in size but maintain their group identity, they tend to assume the characteristics of formal groups. As communication among group members decreases, as the coordination of their activities becomes more difficult, and as their statuses become more specialized with increased size, some type of formal organization tends to develop. Similarly, formal groups or "organizations" tend to foster the

[5] The source of much of the discussion of formal organization is to be found in Max Weber's analysis of bureaucracy. See, for example, *From Max Weber: Essays in Sociology* (trans. H. H. Gerth and C. Wright Mills; New York: Oxford University Press, 1946). For more recent discussions see C. I. Barnard, *The Functions of the Executive* (Cambridge, Mass.: Harvard University Press, 1938) and Herbert A. Simon, *Administrative Behavior* (New York: The MacMillan Company, 1947).

development of informal groups. There are probably a number of reasons for this, but we shall mention two. First, members of a formal group hold statuses in a wide variety of other groups. Only one status (or a limited number) is oriented toward the formal group. Their other statuses provide a basis for a wide variety of informal group interactions within the formal group. Cliques are likely to develop on the basis of similarities of marital status, race, religion, education, community of origin, and the like. Second, no formal organization ordinarily provides for all the needs of its members while they are acting in the system. The rational calculations upon which the organization of the structure is based rarely, if ever, take into account all the factors that are involved in all the statuses and the personal make-up of the members of the formal group. Furthermore, frequently the requirements of the organization of the formal group may be such that needs which arise from these sources are deliberately denied or controlled.[6] Informal groups are likely to develop to satisfy these needs or support those attitudes and values not met or supported by the organization of the formal group. It can be readily appreciated that the existence of informal groups within a formal group may give rise to many problems. Analysis of the relationships between formal and informal groups has been a central focus of industrial sociology and the sociology of formal organization.

SOCIAL GROUP AND SOCIAL SYSTEM

Why use two terms ("group" and "system"), when one would do? The answer is that one will not suffice; these concepts point to different "things." When we speak of a social group, we refer to particular people who are physically present and interacting in terms of their statuses. When Mr. and Mrs. Jones and their children are together and interacting in terms of their family statuses, one speaks of them concretely as a social group. When these people are apart from one another, acting in other groups, they do not form a group in any concrete sense. We may, however, speak of their familial interactions, apart from their presence together, in terms of their family as a social system.

A more important distinction can be made, moreover. The members of a family are not replaceable. Except in the case where a wife or a husband is replaced as a result of death or divorce, or a child is replaced by

---

[6] In the analysis of formal organization, Cris Argyris sets forth the thesis that there is an inevitable conflict between formal organizational needs and "personality" or individual needs, and that informal organization develops as a necessary means for meeting the personal needs denied by the formal organization. See Cris Argyris, *Personality and Organization* (New York: Harper & Brothers, 1957).

adoption, the same family members remain in the system throughout its existence. Even in these exceptions, a new status is likely to be brought into play—such as the "stepmother"—rather than the replacement of a status holder by new personnel. In other words, the social system is bound to particular members. This is not true of most other social systems. In a college, a corporation, a government bureaucracy, a banking institution, or a lodge, the system may remain the same irrespective of who is occupying its statuses. Although a college, for example, graduates its senior class, takes in a new crop of freshmen, and promotes and replaces some of its faculty and administrators, it does not necessarily change its status structure in any way. The system remains the same, even though the group of people acting in it (or a goodly portion of them) has changed. Thus the social system is one consideration; the social group acting in terms of the system, another. Another way to put the distinction is to say that the *units of a group* are "people acting in terms of a social system," whereas the units of a social system are "statuses in terms of which groups of people act." Thus, a social system is an abstract concept, considered apart from particular people who give it concrete existence in a social group. And, by the same token, a social group is a concrete reality that acts in terms of an abstract social system, by virtue of people "holding in their heads," collectively, the status structure of the system.

There is a third sense in which the distinction between "group" and "system" is a useful one to make. People may interact in a system without forming a group, as we have defined that term. In a large urbanized and industrialized society such as our own, we interact frequently with many people with whom we do not share group membership, except in the sense that we are members of the same society. In the course of a day, a person may interact with a bus driver, a policeman, a cashier at the bank, a lunch counter attendant, a clerk in a grocery store, and a ticket seller at the movies. None of these relationships constitutes a group as we have defined it. Nonetheless, all of them have a clearly defined structure, usually institutionalized, that permits orderly and predictable interaction. Mutually shared definitions of the situation contained in the statuses involved present a "system" within which the interaction takes place.

STATUS-SET

In our discussion of the Jones family, we pointed out that Mr. Jones's "father" status is only one among several which he occupies. This points to the fact that any concrete person occupies many different statuses; that is, he has a position in several different systems. Mr. Jones is a father in one system, an accountant in another, a friend in another, and when interacting with his doctor, a patient in still another system. This, of course, only begins to unfold the statuses he occupies at various times as he interacts in different systems. He also has a sex status, an age status, a political or religious status, a citizenship status, and so on. All of his statuses taken together, at a given time, are called his *status-set*. One of the interesting sociological questions we shall examine later concerns the degree of congruence or conflict within an individual's status-set. For example, to what extent are the expectations governing Mr. Jones's work status compatible with his status as father and husband or his religious or friendship statuses? The degree of conflict or compatibility within a status-set can have important consequences for both Mr. Jones and the members of the various groups in which he has membership.

STATUS-SEQUENCE

The phrase "at a given time" has been introduced into our definition of "status-set" because a person may occupy different statuses at different times in his life, as he drops some at one time and assumes others at another. Most obviously, a person's age status changes over time. In our society, for example, we have the relatively clear status distinctions of infancy, childhood, adolescence, adulthood, and old age. Although these statuses are linked to chronological age, the expectations governing the biological fact of age may be only loosely based upon it. "Infancy" as a status may be extended in one culture, contracted in another. "Adolescence" is quite highly structured as a status in our society, but this same age range may not be sharply distinguished as a separate status in a primitive society. Certainly the rights and obligations of "old age" vary greatly from society to society.

As this example of age suggests, some statuses are arranged in a progression so that in order to occupy one, a person must have occupied another that preceded it. Such an arrangement of statuses is termed a *status-sequence*. Other examples are found in the freshman, sophomore, junior, and senior sequence in a college, the movement "up the ladder" in a business organization, or the hierarchy of "degrees" in the Masonic Lodge. As in the case of a status-set, a status-sequence may be inconsistent and conflict, so that what has been learned in one status has to be unlearned in another that follows it. Such conflict presents a "discontinuity" and gives rise to adjustment problems similar to those found in an inconsistent status-set. Such problems and ways of handling them will be discussed in detail later. At this time, we should simply be aware of the possibility of discontinuity in a status-sequence.

The limits to the different statuses that may be included in a status-set and the regularities in status-sequences may, like all cultural definitions, be prescribed, preferred, or permitted. Some limits to the content of a status-set may stem from the exclusive nature of certain statuses. For example, one may not be able to be a Jew and a Catholic at the same time, although one *may* be able to be a German and a Catholic simultaneously. In other cases, the limits are formally stated and enforced with an explicit rationale. For example, the President of the United States cannot be a citizen of another country. Status-sequences, similarly, may be formally recognized, as in the sequence of high school graduate–college student; or, while being factually demonstrable, they may be verbally denied by the system members. It may, for example, be a prerequisite to employment in certain large law firms to have attended an Ivy League law school, although this may be formally denied by everyone concerned.

RANK

Among the various statuses we have mentioned thus far, the reader will note that some are evaluated more highly than others. Mr. Jones's occupational status, "accountant," for example, is ranked higher than, say, Mr. Smith's position as a janitor. Similarly, a third-degree Mason ranks above those of lower degree, a senior above a freshman, and so on. When statuses in a system are evaluated in a graded series by system members we refer to *rank*. Not all statuses, of course, are ranked in a graded series. Mr. Jones's status as "father" is not evaluated over Mrs. Jones's status as "mother." Differences in rights and obligations are involved, as well as some similarities, but they are not compared invidiously with one another. This is true in our society because the marital relationship is structured on an equalitarian basis. Somewhat the same is true normatively (if not in actual practice) of the male and female statuses. In some other societies, these statuses are differentially evaluated so that the husband ranks above the wife and the male above the female. In the case of such ranked statuses, we say that one has more "prestige" than another.

A common confusion has arisen in the use of the term "status" because the early Greek and Latin usages have developed historically so that it has come to mean roughly both status and rank, as we have defined these terms. Thus, "status" is frequently used to mean not only the institutionalized expectations of how system members should behave, but also the "rank" an individual has by virtue of occupying a certain status. This misleading usage is found in such expressions as "He has a lot of status" or "He has lost status." Such confusion can be avoided by saying, "His status has high rank," "His status has lost prestige," or "He has moved from a status with high prestige to one with low prestige."

ROLE-SET

Any given status in a particular system involves the person in inter-action with a *number* of persons in other statuses. The actual acting out of a status in interaction with another status-occupant we call a *role*.[7] For example, within the family, the status "father" involves our hypothetical Mr. Jones in interaction with his son, his daughter, and their mother. They constitute his *role-partners*. Note that the status rights and obligations vary with each of the persons mentioned. Thus, the particular behavior patterns laid down by any given status are specified in accordance with the status of the persons with whom one interacts. In the status "father," Mr. Jones also interacts with people outside the family system. As a father, he may have social relations, for example, with his children's teacher or with members of the P.T.A. All the role-relationships that a person in a particular status has with people in other statuses we call a *role-set*. A role, then, is the prescribed interaction of a status-occupant in *one* of the relationships in which a given status involves him. A role-set is all the prescribed interactions in which a given person is involved by virtue of the fact that he occupies a given status.

REFERENCE GROUP

The term "reference group" is used to indicate the source of the insti-tutionalized definitions that guide behavior or form the attitudes of par-ticular people in particular situations.[8] Although a person's attitudes and behavior may be influenced by his status-set, his membership in groups is not the sole source of the standards that guide his action or influence his attitudes and values. Any group may be a reference group if it is a source of a person's self-conception or his conception of the groups to which he belongs. In other words, a person does not have to be a member

[7] We are drawing again on the development and clarification of these concepts made by Professor Merton, *op. cit.*, pp. 368–370.

[8] The term "reference group" was coined and used by Herbert H. Hyman in "The Psychology of Status," *Archives of Psychology*, No. 269 (1942). Robert K. Merton presents a systematic analysis of reference group theory and related concepts in *Social Theory and Social Structure*, Chaps. 8 and 9. Further analysis based on a wide range of empirical research may be found in Muzafer Sherif and Carolyn W. Sherif, *An Outline of Social Psychology* (rev. ed.; New York: Harper & Brothers, 1956).

of a group in order for him to accept that group's definition of the situation and act in terms of it. Similarly, a person may occupy a status in a group (his *membership group*) without that group's being the source of his cathexes and evaluations.

The use of the word "group" in the term "reference group" may be confusing because the point of reference may not be a "group," as we have defined that term. It may be a social category rather than a group. A *social category* consists of persons who possess similar social characteristics, such as age, sex, income, race, or religion, but do not act in terms of those characteristics as a group. Another term used to signify such categories is "peers," although in common usage this term is usually associated with equality of rank and, as used by some writers, has come to refer primarily to equal age. Such status-categories, as well as groups, may serve as "reference groups." For example, people of low income may aspire to high income or strive to emulate the behavior of people who have high income, or age peers may be the "reference group" for the adolescent rather than his family group.

Reference groups may be positive or negative. *Positive reference groups* are those whose norms are favorably perceived and adopted by individuals. *Negative reference groups* are those whose norms are rejected. Both serve as frames of reference for the individual's definitions of situations. For example, parents may serve as a positive reference group for their children, with respect to the value of education. The attitudes of the Brown family, who live "on the wrong side of the tracks" and view education differently, may serve as a negative reference group. A youth's parents may be a negative reference group with respect to dating or use of leisure time. The positive reference group with respect to evaluation of these activities may be the children's school or neighborhood friends or some other group or social category which they strive to be like or to join. Any group or social category, then, may serve as a reference "group" with respect to any social definition if a person strives to be like the others or to join them, strives to be unlike them or seeks to avoid them, or uses the group or category as a standard of comparison for his behavior and attitudes or for those of his group.

Functional Analysis of Social Systems

In the preceding discussion we have tried to describe briefly, by means of a series of concepts, how human behavior is culturally structured so as to permit the division of labor and the relatively orderly, consistent, and

enduring interactions that make human social existence possible. In introducing the term "status," we pointed to the fact that culture differentiates
human behavior to form a division of labor among people. The cultural
prescriptions of a status link the action of one person to others in other
statuses who share a common culture to form a social system. The people
acting in terms of the social system constitute a social group when they
not only act within a common culture but consider themselves and are
considered by others to be members of a plurality and when the rights
and obligations within this plurality are binding on them but not on nonmembers. Any member of the group ordinarily is linked to other groups
by virtue of his status-set. As he moves from group to group his action is
differentiated by the appropriate status he holds in the system that distinguishes the group interactions. Over time, he may drop a status in one
system and assume a new status in another. When movement to one
status is contingent on a preceding status, he is acting in a status-
sequence. Some statuses in a system are evaluated more highly than
others so that they are ranked in a graded series, providing differential
access to rights and obligations and further differentiating action in the
system. Within any single status, the person interacts with several other
status-occupants in a specified role-relationship, both within and outside
the system of which the status is a part. Thus, in any given status, a
person's behavior is differentiated by his role-set. Statuses, status-sets,
sequences, rank, roles and role-sets thus provide the structure of human
action and the basis of human social life.

We have only touched upon some of the major facets of the structure
of group life; much more remains for discussion, but it cannot all be done
at once.[9] For the present, we want to turn our attention to how these
concepts may be used in the analysis of social systems.

FUNCTIONAL ANALYSIS

To learn how any system (an automobile engine, a biological organism,
or a human society) operates is to learn what the objective consequences

[9] Nor can all of the more subtle distinctions involved in these concepts and the
vexing problems that frequently arise in their usage be dealt with here. We leave this
for the more advanced student or the student who wishes to explore in detail the
many different discussions of these and related concepts to be found in the field. We
can only hope that conceptual problems ultimately will be solved and trust that the
present exposition will serve as provisional and working concepts for purposes of this
introductory text.

of any one part are for another part or parts or for the system as a whole. This approach has been called a *functional* mode of analysis.[10]

The label "functional analysis" may, as we shall see, be a little misleading. To guard against misunderstanding at the outset, let us begin with a clear distinction between "functions" and "consequences." By "consequences," we mean all the results of a given act or a given rule or structure that would not have occurred except for that act, rule, or structure. But *all* the results are numberless. (For example, the results of your taking a single breath include a slight decrease in the oxygen supply in the environment; a slight increase of the oxygen in your body, activities of your heart, your blood, your liver; a slight increase of carbon dioxide when you exhale; all the implications of carbon dioxide for plants; all the implications of plants for food; and so on.)

Obviously, to take account of *all* the consequences would be an unending task. A systematic distinction among consequences must be made. The first distinction made in "functional analysis" is between those consequences, on the one hand, *that are directly relevant to the system being analyzed;* and those consequences, on the other hand, that are not so directly relevant (however relevant they may be for some *other* system). The second distinction made is between those *relevant consequences,* on the one hand, that are "helpful" or "useful" to the system in some way, and those relevant consequences, on the other hand, that are "harmful" to the system in some way. The *helpfully relevant* consequences are called "functions"; the *harmfully relevant* consequences are called "disfunctions."

A functional approach is probably most familiar to the reader in connection with biological systems. We say, for example, "A function of blood is to provide a circulating medium to carry nutritive elements to the cells of the body." The statement points to a useful objective consequence of the presence of blood for other parts of the biological system.

Sociologists, and other social scientists as well, use this mode of analysis in much the same way, except that the system they are interested in is a social system rather than a biological or mechanical system. Nor are the

[10] A review and critique of a wide range of the literature on functional analysis may be found in Professor Merton's important article, "Manifest and Latent Functions," in *Social Theory and Social Structure,* pp. 19–84. A complex elaboration of the functional analysis of social systems is contained in the writings of Professor Talcott Parsons and associates. See, for example, Parsons, *The Social System* (New York: The Free Press of Glencoe, Inc., 1951). We are particularly indebted to Merton's incisive comments on functional analysis in our discussion. For a convincing argument holding that "functional analysis" *is* "sociological analysis" see Kingsley Davis, "The Myth of Functional Analysis as a Special Method in Anthropology and Sociology," *American Sociological Review,* 24:557–572 (1959).

parts of a social system biological or mechanical. They are social structures—cognitive, cathectic, and normative definitions, statuses, roles,
status-sequences, and so on. These are the items or parts to which the
social analyst imputes functions, just as the biologist imputes functions to
biological structures (the brain, the kidneys, the blood, and so on).[11]

FUNCTIONAL REQUIREMENTS

When the biologist imputes a function to a particular biological structure, he implies that it has a useful consequence for a condition of another
structure or perhaps ultimately of the total biological system. The biologist usually deduces some *necessary* condition or requirement of the
organic system and then proceeds to analyze how the parts contribute to
these requirements. The term "functional requirement" has been used to
indicate such necessary conditions. For example, if the blood is to perform the function of providing nutriment to the cells, then some structure
must be provided to circulate or pump the blood to the other parts of
the body. This is a function of the heart. If the total system (the human
body) is to exist at all, its various parts must perform certain functions
necessary to sustain life.

Again, this is very much the way one proceeds in applying functional
analysis to social systems. If a social group is to exist at all, some division
of labor (some social system) must be developed such that each member
of the group is able to get from some other member or members what he
needs to perform his roles in the group, and such that the group as a
whole can adapt in some degree to its environment (both the physical
environment and other groups). In other words, the group must be provided by the social system with some degree of integration and adaptation. The *integration* of a group refers to the extent to which the group
members get from one another the attitudes, services, and goods they
have learned to need. The *adaptation* of a group refers to the extent to
which the group as a whole gets from other groups the attitudes, services,
and goods its members have learned to need, and the extent to which it
gets from its physical environment the things it needs. As far as we can
deduce, integration and adaptation would be two basic and essential requirements for the operation of any social system. Others may be involved, but they are likely to be encompassed by these two, and we wish,
at this point, to keep our analysis as simple as possible.

[11] It should be clear to the reader that we are here discussing similarities in modes
of analysis, *not* in what is being analyzed. We do not wish to engage in confusing or
fruitless analogies between biological and social systems.

FUNCTIONAL AND DISFUNCTIONAL CONSEQUENCES

Let us apply a functional analysis to a structure in a social system. Anthropologists have observed that the incest taboo (the prohibition of sexual intercourse between certain members of the family) is universal in the nuclear family (mother, father, and children), with the exception of certain specific cases and under certain specific conditions. Here we have a structure—in this instance, a normative definition binding upon the status-occupants acting in terms of the social system. What is its function for the system? It should be noted at once that several different functions have been imputed by observers, which calls attention to the fact that any structure may perform more than one function; that is, it may have *several different* useful consequences for the system or for *other* systems. *One* consequence for the system is that the incest taboo contributes to family integration by preventing rivalry for sexual favors. Thus, it is said that a function of the incest taboo for the family is to foster integration by inhibiting sexual rivalry among family members.

Without our going into details at this point, the reader should be made aware of the fact that to indicate the function of a structure is not to indicate why it "exists." To determine why a particular pattern exists is to entail a search for its historical origins, not its present functions. How something came into being cannot be determined by what its consequences are. The great French sociologist, Émile Durkheim, among others, warned of this error some time ago: "To show how a fact is useful is not to explain how it originated or why it is what it is. The uses which it serves presuppose the specific properties characterizing it but do not create them. The need we have of things cannot give them existence, nor can it confer their specific nature upon them."[12]

Similarly, the great German social scientist, Max Weber, was certainly aware of this limitation in functional analysis and another, as well. Commenting on differentiation in insect societies, Weber wrote:

> It is relatively easy to grasp the significance of the functions of these various differentiated types for survival. . . . But this is not enough. We would like especially to know first what factors account for the original differentiation of specialized types from the still neutral undifferentiated species-type. Secondly, it would be important to know what led the differentiated individual in the typical case to behave in a way which actually serves the survival value of the organized group.[13]

[12] Émile Durkheim, *The Rules of Sociological Method* (trans. Sarah H. Solovay and John H. Mueller; ed. George Catlin; Chicago: The University of Chicago Press, 1938), p. 90.

[13] Max Weber, *The Theory of Social and Economic Organization* (trans. A. M. Henderson and Talcott Parsons; New York: Oxford University Press, 1947), p. 105.

Putting this in terms of a human group, we would like to know the origins of a particular structure, and we would like to know what motivates people to act in terms of that structure. Weber somewhat wistfully notes, particularly in terms of the first inadequacy, that "the limitations of analysis to the functional level is only a necessity imposed by our present ignorance which it is hoped will only be temporary."

To return to our discussion of the incest taboo, note that this particular structure functions to foster integration, and thus contributes to the operation of the system. When a structure contributes to the integration or adaptation of a system, it is said to be *functional* for the system. Structures, of course, may impede or hinder integration or adaptation. When they do, they are said to be *disfunctional* for the system.[14] Let us examine a structure that is disfunctional for a particular system and at the same time illustrate how a structure in one system may have consequences for another system, as we indicated above that it might. If the reader will bear with us, we shall return again to Mr. Jones and his family for our example.

Let us assume that if Mr. Jones is to retain his position in the firm for which he works, he must devote a great deal of time and energy to his occupational status. This is part of the institutionalized obligation of his status as accountant in the occupation system in which he acts. Because his time and energies are limited, he must withhold part of them from his interaction in the family system. This, in turn, may mean that he is unable to observe fully the obligations that are institutionalized in his statuses of husband and father in the family system. Now, the obligations of his work role may be functional for the adaptation and integration of the firm because, for example, they give the firm competitive advantage over other firms and because Mr. Jones completes the necessary accounting procedures needed by executives to make certain decisions. However, these same status obligations may be disfunctional for the integration and adaptation of the family because, for example, they deprive Mr. Jones's wife and children of the attention, response, or counsel that is their status-right and expectation or they impede the Jones family from meeting its social obligations to the Smith family. It should be noted in passing that here we have an example of a conflict in a status-set, to which we called attention earlier in our discussion.

---

[14] There is, of course, a third logical possibility. Some structures may have no consequence for the integration or adaptation of the system. It is important to bear in mind that this category exists, so as not to make the mistake of thinking that every structure must be functional or disfunctional for a system. We are primarily interested in functions and disfunctions and, therefore, shall drop this third category from further discussion at this time.

MANIFEST AND LATENT CONSEQUENCES

We have said that a functional analysis of a social system involves determining the *objective* consequences of some structure for some system, especially for the integration and adaptation of that system. But let us be careful to distinguish between an objective analysis of how certain structures or actions contribute to (are functional for) or impede (are disfunctional for) adaptation or integration, on the one hand, and the subjective motives and ideas of the actors on the other. To say something about the functions of the incest taboo is to say nothing, necessarily, about the ideas and attitudes of people. Most people, obviously, think as little about integrating the family by preventing rivalry through the incest taboo as a heart thinks about helping to nourish cells.

The consequences of an act *may* be understood by people, but they may not be. If they are, the functionality or disfunctionality of those consequences *may* be understood, or they may not be. Finally, *even if* they are understood, they may or may not have been the "reasons" or the "motives" of the actors in acting that way. In other words, it is necessary to distinguish not only between consequences that are functional and those that are disfunctional, but also between those that are recognized and those that are not recognized by the actors. And still further, it is important to distinguish between the consequences that people *want* to produce and those that they actually do produce. It may be that what they want to accomplish—their goal—is to be virtuous and go to heaven and that is "why" (from their point of view) they obey the incest taboo. If so, that is very important for the sociologist to understand; but *another* important job still remains—namely, to consider what the objective *consequences* of their obedience are. (Whether or not their obedience actually succeeds in achieving their goal of salvation, or getting to heaven in this case, is, of course, outside the ability of the sociologist or any other scientist to know.)

In short, we should be fully aware that objective consequences (what can be determined empirically to be a consequence) are not always those intended or anticipated by the persons acting in the system. To take an example previously discussed, when the job specifications of "accountant" were formulated in the firm, it is unlikely that it was intended or even considered that these status-obligations would have consequences for the status-occupant's family. Nevertheless, objectively they do, and they may be vital considerations in analyzing the operation of the family system. When a structure has positive (that is, contributory) consequences for a system that are unintended or unanticipated, they are referred to as *latent functions.* On the other hand, the structure of the job in the firm very likely was formulated with anticipation of certain positive consequences for the business system. In this case, we speak of the *manifest functions* of the structure—those avowed or intended or recognized as the contributory consequences of the structure. In the same way, we may speak of *manifest* and *latent disfunctions.*

This is an important distinction to keep in mind, because a wide range of structures operate latently in human affairs. The fact that they do may be easily overlooked unless we are sensitized to observe carefully. We cannot rely upon the avowed anticipations of the system members concerning a structure if we are to make accurate analysis of its functions or disfunctions. They may not be aware of or recognize its latent functions, and the *anticipated* consequences may not be the ones that, in fact, take place.

This can be seen in the analysis of certain magical practices among primitive people. For example, a tribe may have institutionalized a rain dance, the function of which, tribal members anticipate, is to bring rain. In fact, however, the consequence of a rain dance has nothing to do with rain.[15] Yet the dance may have latent functions for the tribal system. It may, for example, bring together periodically the scattered groups that make up the tribe and provide the reinforcement and interaction necessary for the integration of these dispersed groups into a tribal system. Without it, they might lose contact with one another, and the common culture that binds them together might gradually erode away. To destroy the structure might result in the destruction of the tribal system, a fact of which anyone who anticipates "enlightening" the tribal members concerning their rain dance should be fully aware.

The concepts of manifest and latent functions and disfunctions are summarized in the table below.

TABLE 2-1

Classification of Consequence of Structures

	CONSEQUENCES THAT FOSTER INTEGRATION AND ADAPTATION	CONSEQUENCES THAT IMPEDE INTEGRATION AND ADAPTATION
Intended or recognized consequences	Manifest function	Manifest disfunctions
Unintended or unrecognized consequences	Latent functions	Latent disfunctions

[15] Without involving ourselves in the metaphysics of this, on top of all the complexities of our present discussion, at least we can say that modern man's empirical knowledge leads *him* to this conclusion.

STRUCTURAL ALTERNATIVES

This consideration leads us to another. Is the rain dance the only structure that can perform this integrative function? The answer is no. Any structure that would bring the people together periodically in common interaction where shared cognitive, cathectic, and normative definitions are reinforced might do as well. For example, they might meet periodically to recount ancient tribal lore or participate in traditional tribal games. The point to be observed here is that many different structures may perform the same function. Alternative structures may act as substitutes for the rain dance by producing its latent function. It is the function that is necessary for tribal integration, not a particular structure. Such substitutes or equivalents may be referred to as *structural alternatives*.

Again it is important to point out such a fact, since we may be led to the easy conclusion that since a particular structure performs a necessary function that structure must necessarily be practiced. As a matter of fact, a functional alternative might better serve the needs of the group. Dancing for rain may prevent the discovery of the natural laws governing rain and prevent man from controlling rain altogether, in accordance with his needs. In this sense, the rain dance is "disfunctional" for making rain. Man's history contains numerous similar examples. The transformation of the witch doctor to the medical doctor is notable (but do not overlook the fact that the medical doctor may perform some of the latent functions of the witch doctor!).

Adaptation and Integration

THE NECESSITY OF EXCHANGE

We have said that the structure of a human group involves a division of labor among its members. The essence of division of labor is specialization; and specialization demands exchange among the group members, since each is unable to get all his needs met independently. Although human needs could be catalogued endlessly, three basic *kinds* of needs seem to be essential in group life. First, people need certain *attitudes* from others and the expression of those attitudes in certain responses. For example, if people are to act in a group, there must be some attitude of inviolability of the person. Without such a definition of the person, accepted and practiced by group members, each is against the other and group life is impossible. The same is true of property. There must be some institutionalized definition as to the rights that group members have in the material things of cultural significance to the group's way of life. Beyond this, in different interactions in various groups, people need the favorable response of others based on attitudes of love, respect, esteem, and the like.

A second need of people interacting in group life is the need for *services*. People need certain kinds and amounts of labor, protection, entertainment, information, advice, leadership, and so on, from others. Finally, as a third need, they must be provided with certain *goods*. They may need tools, food, clothing, shelter, medicine, and a host of other such things, which they do not themselves produce.

THE MECHANISMS OF EXCHANGE

Any given member of a group gets what he needs by giving to someone else what the latter needs and the former possesses. Interaction within the group consists of exchange among its members. If one needs love, he must love in return. If he needs inviolability, he must not violate others. If he needs goods and services, he must provide them for others. These exchanges are part of the rights and obligations of his status in the group. Each group member is specialized to produce something for the others that they wish to procure, and they are specialized to produce something that he wishes to procure. In other words, each has something he needs to procure and something he needs to dispose of. Indeed, one way of distinguishing statuses is on the basis of what their "procurement" and "disposal" needs are.

But *how* do these exchanges occur? There appear to be three major kinds of exchange that may be institutionalized. First, people may exchange with others because of mutual *cathexis*. In American society, the father, for example, is supposed to provide for his children because he loves them and finds pleasure in caring for them. In turn, he is supposed to receive from them their love, respect, and esteem. And in our society, a husband and wife are supposed to provide each other with certain attitudes, services, and goods because they are "in love." Similarly, friends are supposed to help one another and exchange their feelings for each other because of their mutual regard. As these examples suggest, this basis of exchange appears to be confined largely to primary group relations. There are many reasons for this, but without going into them all, it can be seen that the primary group forms a basis for the development of mutual cathexis that secondary groups ordinarily do not. At the same time, primary group relations would be difficult to sustain without the presence of some degree of mutual cathexis.

A second kind of institutionalized exchange is *duty* or *obligation*. In this case, a group member provides for certain needs of others, when they are made known to him, as part of his status-obligation, without regard to his cathexis for the person. The person whose need is to be satisfied has a right to get that need met by the status-occupant who is supposed to satisfy it. What he gives in exchange is the acting out of certain corresponding obligations. In an army unit, for example, a supply sergeant is supposed to give over equipment to any member of his unit who can produce the necessary requisition or has the necessary authority. In a community, the principal of a school is supposed to provide educational opportunities to any child who meets the appropriate obligations: for example, appearing at the school, living in the school district, and showing the "proper respect." How the sergeant or the principal feel about a particular person seeking to satisfy a need is supposed to be of no concern in his meeting it.

This basis of exchange is found typically in a formal organization. A somewhat special case is found in a feudal society where, by tradition, the rights and obligations of members of an "estate" bind each to the other in the mutual production and exchange of certain attitudes, goods, and services. The nature of the exchange is implied in the phrase "noblesse oblige," which signifies the obligation of those of high rank to be honorable and generous in their relations with those of low rank.

A third kind of institutionalized exchange is *bargaining*. In bargaining each status-occupant is supposed to get his needs met by making it worth some other status-occupant's while to meet them. The person meeting another's needs does not do so out of love or friendship, nor does he do so out of duty. He does so, if he does so at all, because the first person has something *he* needs and is willing to give it as an inducement. Whereas in the first kind of exchange (cathexis), need satisfaction depends on membership in a primary group, and in the second kind (rights and obligations) it depends on membership in a bureaucracy, in the bargaining case need satisfaction depends on having an inducement to offer.

POWER

In the absence or avoidance of an institutionalized mechanism of exchange, power is the alternative to acquiring what is needed or disposing of what is produced. *Power* is the capacity to carry out, by whatever means, a desired course of action despite the resistance of others and without having to take into consideration their needs. When power is institutionalized in a system, it is referred to as *authority*. The essential features of institutionalized power appear to center around group consensus as to who shall exercise it, how it shall be used, and to what purpose. The ultimate source of power lies in a monopoly of physical force, but power may be exercised effectively whenever one party can grant or withhold what another needs and cannot get elsewhere.

Because of the very nature of power, some controls on its use must be institutionalized in order for group life to take place. Thus, power is never the sole basis of exchange or adaptation *within* a group, although it may be between groups. Power may operate in any of the mechanisms of exchange we have mentioned. The love of a woman for a man who does not reciprocate it may allow him to make inordinate demands on her. The differential distribution of rights and obligations in a bureaucratic structure may permit the abuse of rights and the neglect of obligations. One side in a bargaining relationship may have so many alternatives and the other side so few that bargaining power is totally lopsided. Fraud, manipulation, and other forms of deviance may be used in order to circumvent the institutionalized basis of exchange. In the absence of authority or of effective means for inhibiting or controlling the exercise of naked power, conflict ensues. Since human needs potentially are limitless and always varied and the institutional structures for their satisfaction are by no means perfect, conflict is always potential in group life. A major need for any group, then, is the development of effective mechanisms for handling conflict and the maintenance of a consensus within which conflicts may be resolved.

SUBGROUPS AND SUBSYSTEMS

Thus far in our discussion we have been focusing attention largely on a division of labor composed only of individual specialists who together make up a single group. It is obvious, however, that just as individuals are specialized parts of a group, groups may be specialized parts of larger groups. Groups that are parts of larger groups are called *subgroups;* their systems, *subsystems*. For example, the organization of a business system is broken down into subsystems in the form of sections, which may be further differentiated into departments. Similarly, the marital system is part of the family system, which is part of the neighborhood, which is part of the community, and so on. Whether a particular set of interacting persons one is examining is designated as a group or a subgroup depends upon the purpose of analysis. We may want to analyze how a given status-occupant adapts to other status-occupants, or we may want to analyze how a given group adapts to other groups. The mechanisms of adaptation that we have examined apply in either case. Groups, like individuals, may procure what they need from other groups as a matter of right (for example, the Jones family receives fire protection from the local fire department as a matter of right); it may procure what it needs through bargaining; or it may procure what it needs through appealing to the cathexis of others (for example, the Jones family may appeal to public charity or to its neighbors or relatives). When any of these institutionalized arrangements break down or are nonexistent, a group may have to exploit other groups or submit to them.

We shall from now on speak more generally, then, of the adaptive problems of "units" of a group or system, and what we say will apply both to status-occupants and to groups. When it is necessary to make distinctions between the two kinds of units, we shall make clear which one we are talking about.

OPTIMUM ADAPTATION

Any social unit (a role-player, a subgroup, or a group) is said to be adapted to other units when it is able to meet its procurement and disposal needs. This is simply to say that it is able to procure from its environment the attitudes, goods, and services it wants, and to dispose of those it produces. This does not mean, however, that a unit is able to maximize *all* its satisfactions or realize all its *potential* wants. Needs are potentially limitless, but resources are always limited. Limited resources must somehow be allocated by an adapting unit among its different procurement and disposal needs. Some wants must be sacrificed in order to satisfy others. In short, procurement and disposal always involve some *cost*. The cost to the mother of procuring the affection and response of her children may be that she can procure less attention from her husband. The cost to an artist of producing a masterpiece is all the things he could produce if he were not producing art. The cost of a college education is all the things you could have been spending your time, energy, and resources on if you were not in college. In the same way, the cost of your taking one course is all the courses you thereby are prevented from taking; the cost of getting married is whatever advantages there are in remaining single (and vice versa); the cost of a house is all the things you must give up in order to pay for it; and so on. (We are accustomed to thinking of "cost" in terms of dollars and cents, but it is very important to understand that this is simply a shorthand way of talking about the *real* cost of something. Where money is involved, the real cost of something is all the other things that could have been procured or produced with the money.)

In order for a social unit to be willing to pay a procurement or disposal cost, it must have some notion of what it wants most. In other words, there must be some *hierarchy* of needs such that some satisfactions will be sacrificed in order to get others. Individual and group resources are allocated on the basis of a hierarchy of values in which certain needs or wants take precedence over others. A modest home may be valued more than an expensive car; art, more than easy living; patriotism, more than personal gain; love, more than obedience—or the other way around.

Ordinarily the dilemma of choice is resolved by the normative structure of the system in which people act. Moral evaluations are attached to alternatives and shared by members of the group. Each individual does not have to start from the beginning of man's existence and map out his choices and allocate means for securing them. Although the question of which hierarchy of values or goals is the "right" one (or whether there is such a thing) remains, group structure provides some answer for specific men at specific times as a necessary condition for group life. The fact that social structure always guides human behavior to some degree means that adaptation is not necessarily a conscious or calculated process. It may even be quite accidental and unplanned. A great deal of the action in which people engage is of this nature. The social scientist, however, believes that the consequences of action, either intended or not, can be determined. He cannot determine scientifically what goals *should* be sought or which one *ought* to take precedence over the other. His judgments in such matters are ethical or moral judgments and therefore are not necessarily better or worse than any other person's. Given the hierarchy of values in a system, he may conclude that one goal should be sacrificed or deferred for another. But this is to say that if system members wish to achieve one goal that is more valued than another, then resources must be allocated in certain ways—which is just another way of determining consequences.

Men have long dreamed of a world in which the sacrifice or deferment of one need was not necessary to achieve another—the legend of the Garden of Eden, for example. But the world men have known, ever since their "expulsion from paradise," is one in which everything has a price. This means that, outside the Garden of Eden, adaptation can never be "perfect." It is always possible to conceive of a "better" adaptation—if only there were a "little more time," "a little more energy," "a little more skill," if only the environment were "a little different," and so on and on. At most, we can speak only of an *optimum adaptation;* one that is the "best possible in the circumstances." What is meant by "best possible"?

Optimum adaptation is one in which any increase in the expenditure of resources for one procurement or disposal need would require the sacrifice of another procurement or disposal need that a social unit is not willing to make. It is an adaptation in which any increase in the allocation of resources to one goal would cost too much, understanding "cost" to mean the sacrifice of another valued goal. In other words, we say that if resources were to be transferred away from efforts to get one thing and put to work to get another, and if such a transfer would increase the unit's total satisfaction, then it has *not* achieved optimum adaptation, but it would be better off, by definition, if it made the transfer. In fact, it would be better off if it kept on making such transfers until any further transfer would decrease total satisfaction. At that point, its adaptation is optimum. It cannot be improved.

Let us consider a simple example. Suppose you have the goal of learning French, the goal of learning sociology, and the goal of dating. Unquestionably, you could learn more French if you spent more time at it. But every hour you spend on French, you must subtract from sociology and dating. At some point, increasing your "French time" by one additional hour would so interfere with the achievement of your sociology or your dating goal that you, as a total person, would feel unsatisfied. When you have reached a point at which any further subtraction from sociology or dating for the sake of French would be more frustrating than gratifying, you have achieved an optimum adaptation. You are not necessarily perfectly adapted. You probably still feel "if there were only more time" or "if good grades were only easier to achieve." Furthermore, it may be that there is no allocation of resources that would satisfy you. That is, it may be that any possible allocation interferes with at least one of your goals so that you cannot pursue any of them with satisfaction. In this case, you have failed to set goals that may be achieved with your resources or to establish a hierarchy among your goals so that resources can be allocated to achieve them. Also, you may be unable to adapt to your environment at all because of *its* nature. The educational standards set by the college may inhibit your dating or demand more than your resources permit. In this case, you had better seek another educational system in which to meet your needs or give up the goals of dating or learning French and sociology—unless, in the unlikely circumstance, you can change the college standards.

It is clear that the optimum adaptation of individuals to their environments and the optimum adaptation of *groups* to their environments pose rather different problems—or, rather, the same problems exist, but different mechanism must be used to solve them. The problem in both cases is the fact that resources are limited and must be allocated among many different ends. So far as the individual is concerned, a hierarchy of goals that permits an optimum allocation is a subjective phenomenon and is often the focus of study by psychologists. So far as a group is concerned, the decisions about how to allocate the *group's* resources among alternative ends cannot, obviously, be a psychological phenomenon—a group has no psyche. It is a *political* phenomenon, and one we shall consider in detail in Chapter 12.

Optimum adaptation of an individual requires that the individual's needs and wants in the different roles of his role-set and in the different statuses of his status-set be somehow *integrated* with one another. Although, as we have said, this is in part a psychological problem, there are certain sociological factors and mechanisms that facilitate or impede such integration. We shall consider them in Chapters 5 and 6.

Similarly, optimum adaptation of a *group* requires integration of the parts of the group—its subgroups and its status-occupants. It is this problem of *group* or system integration that we will consider now.

OPTIMUM INTEGRATION: EQUILIBRIUM

When we focus upon a particular individual as a unit of a group, other group members are part of the environment, and therefore, we speak of the *adaptation* of the individual on whom we are focusing to that environment—that is, to other individuals in the group. When we focus upon the mutual adaptations of the members to one another, we speak of the *integration* of the parts of the system (statuses) or of the parts of the group (individuals). The same is true of the analysis of subgroups and subsystems as parts of larger groups and systems that encompass them. Thus what, from one point of view, is the adaptive problem of a unit of analysis is, from another point of view, part of the integrative problem of the larger unit of which it is a part. Integration and adaptation, then, are really two different ways of looking at the same thing. More precisely put, whether we speak of integration or of adaptation depends entirely on which unit we focus our attention on. If, for example, we are analyzing the Jones family as a group, we must define the Smith family as part of its environment and speak of the Jones-Smith relationship as an adaptive problem for the Joneses. If, on the other hand, the group being analyzed is the neighborhood in which both families act, then the Jones family and the Smith family are parts of that group; and then the Jones-Smith relationship is part of the integrative problem of the neighborhood.

In general, then, it should be clear that what is an integrative problem for one social system is an adaptive problem for the subsystems of which that system is comprised. For the sake of emphasis, let us repeat this in reverse: what is an adaptive problem for one system is an integrative problem for the inclusive system of which the first is a part. The adaptive problem of the administrative staff vis-à-vis the faculty of a university is an integrative problem of the university; the adaptive problem of General Motors Corporation vis-à-vis the United Automobile Workers is an integrative problem of the United States, and so on.

Social units (individuals acting in a group or in subgroups that are part of a more inclusive group) are said to be in a state of equilibrium when each is satisfied with the exchange made. "Satisfaction" is dependent on the degree to which the units are able to procure the attitudes, goods, and services they want and dispose of those they produce. In other words, *each* unit has achieved optimum adaptation. Consider some unit (A) that wants something (x) from another unit (B), and has something (y) to offer in exchange. This set of relationships is represented as follows:

A	B
Seeks to dispose of	Seeks to procure
y	y
seeks to procure	seeks to dispose of
x	x

A and B are in equilibrium when four things are true:

1. A gets as much x as it wants.
2. A finds acceptance of as much y as it wants to produce.
3. B gets as much y as it wants.
4. B finds acceptance of as much x as it wants to produce.

To give a simple example, let us assume that in a community a worker (A) offers his services (y) as a shoe salesman and wants wages (x), while a proprietor (B) wants shoe salesmen (y) and offers wages (x). The relation of the shoe salesman and the proprietor are in equilibrium when each gets from the other what he wants and disposes to the other what he has to dispose of.

The notion of equilibrium is probably easiest to understand when the mechanism of exchange is bargaining, and especially when money is involved as a medium of exchange. Thus, it is fairly obvious (because familiar) that the shoe salesman and the employer are in equilibrium when the salesman gets the money he wants and works no harder than he thinks reasonable, and the employer gets the work he wants and pays the wage he thinks reasonable. The same situation applies, however, when cathexis or obligation is institutionalized as the exchange mechanism, although the phenomena may be slightly more subtle.

For example, when a husband gives his wife love, he must receive something in return—if not love, then at least gratitude, respect, appreciation, loyalty, or some equivalent. And if he fails to receive what he considers a "reasonable" return, or if she spurns his love or demands still more love or signs of love, their relationship will be as sharply in disequilibrium as if the shoe salesman were parading in front of his employer's store with a sign proclaiming "Unfair."

In the same way, in a classroom where "obligation" rules as the mechanism of exchange between instructor and students, equilibrium requires that the instructor receive all the attention and respect he believes himself entitled to; it requires that he give no more (and no less) time and help than he thinks he should; it requires that students receive all the clarification and aid they think they are entitled to; and it requires that they be made to concentrate and work no more (and no less) than they think they should. If any of those conditions fails to exist, there is strain and tension—disequilibrium—in the classroom, as both the instructor and the student readers of this book can undoubtedly attest from their own experience.

Moreover, there is clearly a sense in which "bargaining" may be present in both the "cathectic" and the "obligatory" exchanges. *How much* gratitude or respect or attention one person should give in exchange for *how much* love, help, or clarification may be open to question. (That is, there may not be any precise institutionalized definitions.) Indeed, as these examples should indicate, the distinctions among cathexis, obligation, and bargaining are not distinctions with respect to *what* is exhanged; they are, rather, distinctions with respect to how the *terms* of exchange are determined.

What distinguishes the kind of exchange we have called "cathectic" is the cultural norm that there should be no limit to what one person owes another. If A asks B for something, the only question in B's mind should, ideally, be, "Can I do it and will it be good for A?" In the obligation case, on the other hand, there are sharply specified limits. Here, when A asks B for something, the appropriate question in B's mind is, "Is it my duty?" In the bargaining case, the situation is still different. Here, the appropriate question for B to raise is, "What's in it for me?"

To put this in other words, the terms of exchange are settled in the cathectic case by the degree of each person's involvement or identification with the other; in the obligation case, by bureaucratic or legal rules; in the bargaining case, by each person's relative bargaining power—which is determined by the number of alternative sources of supply each person has for the thing he wants from the other person. (For example, if I want x from you and you want y from me, your bargaining power is greater than mine to the degree that there are *many* people from whom you can get y but no one else from whom I can get x.)

As we have noted, when we discuss the adaptation of one unit to another, we are at the same time saying something about the integration of the larger group that includes those units. To point to the conditions under which two units are adapted to one another, then, is to point to the conditions of integration of their inclusive system. A social system has achieved optimum integration when its units are in equilibrium with one another—that is, each unit finds acceptance from other units of what it wants to produce and procures what it wants from other units.

It should be emphasized that this is *not* the same thing as saying that when a role-player or a subgroup is well adapted (has achieved optimum adaptation), the group of which it is a part is well integrated. A unit might be well adapted, for example, by the exercise of power through exploitation or manipulation of others, which may mean that the exploited unit is not well adapted and, therefore, the system that includes them both is not well integrated. This is one of the reasons that it is nonsense to say that "what is good for General Motors is good for the United States." It *may* be, but it also may *not* be. A social system can be said to have achieved optimum integration only to the degree that *all* its sub-systems have achieved optimum adaptation to one another.

GROUP INTEGRATION AND GROUP ADAPTATION

We have up to now been discussing the relation between *unit* adaptation and *group* integration. What about the relation between *group* adaptation and group integration? Are the two independent in the sense that a group can be well adapted to its environment and at the same time be malintegrated, or well integrated and at the same time maladapted? Or are integration and adaptation related in such a way that one implies the other?

The answer to those questions must distinguish between the short run and the long run. In the long run, maladaptation will lead to malintegration. If the group as a whole does not succeed in procuring from and disposing to its environment in accordance with its structural needs, then sooner or later some unit in the group will not have its needs met, and to that degree the group itself is malintegrated. For example, if the purchasing department of General Motors Corporation does not procure steel from United States Steel Corporation or some other environing group, the GM units that depend on steel in order to carry out their roles will be frustrated. In the same way, if the State Department does not procure respect from the Soviet Union, then the Defense Department may increase its needs for manpower, which may frustrate the needs of other units for manpower. On a smaller scale, if Mr. Smith does not succeed in borrowing a lawn mower from his neighbor, Mr. Jones, Mrs. Smith may not have her need for a well-kept lawn met. And if Mr. Smith does borrow the lawn mower, he may thereby incur the obligation to "return the favor" by helping Mr. Jones to paint his house, which may deprive Mrs. Smith of her husband's company for a while; and so on.

Thus, clearly, the needs of units are highly interdependent with the group's adaptation. To point to one important implication of this: in the long run it is foolish to attempt to treat "domestic national policy" independently from "foreign policy."

In the short run, however, there may be a discrepancy between integration and adaptation. That is to say, it may be that a given social structure satisfactorily meets the needs of members and subgroups better than any alternative structure; *but if continued will lead to maladaptation of the group* and hence, in the long run, to malintegration. For an obvious example, it may be that a given way of exploiting natural resources—say, timber—satisfactorily meets the needs of everyone in the nation, but sooner or later is going to exhaust the timber supply, thus frustrating the needs of many units and hence, by definition, producing malintegration. For another example, it may be that American methods of adapting to Cuba or Africa or China or Egypt, satisfactorily meet Americans' needs for raw materials and markets, but gradually leads to a resentful nationalism in those areas that seriously threatens Americans' needs in the long run.

In the short run, in other words, it may be necessary to malintegrate a group—in the sense of frustrating some units' existing needs—in order to prevent a later maladaptation and hence a possibly even greater malintegration. This fact poses one of the most severe problems of political decision making; we shall return to it later in that context.

SUMMARY

The basis of social life consists of a division of labor among participants such that each contributes in some measure to the needs of the other through some degree of specialization. Differentiation within a human group is accomplished by means of a social system composed of statuses. Each status specifies the rights and obligations of the person occupying it in relation to other status-occupants in the system. Any given person ordinarily has membership in many different groups and therefore occupies several different statuses, which collectively are called his status-set. Each status links him to different systems, and any particular status may differentiate his behavior in each system as well as in the system of which the status is a constituent part. When the occupancy of one status is contingent upon having occupied a preceding status, we speak of a status-sequence. When statuses are evaluated in a graded series, we speak of rank. In any one status, a person interacts with people in other statuses. These people, acting in terms of their reciprocal statuses, are the person's role-partners. The interaction taking place in conformity to the statuses involved is a role. All the interactions prescribed by a status is a role-set.

Human groups may be studied by means of analysis of the functions of the structure of the social system governing their activities. Any system must be so organized as to maintain some degree of integration among its units and some degree of adaptation to its environment. Structures that foster integration and adaptation are said to be functional for the system. Those that inhibit integration or adaptation are said to be dysfunctional for the system. Consequences that are intended or recognized or anticipated by system members are called manifest consequences. Those that are unintended, unrecognized, or unanticipated are called latent consequences.

Adaptation may be pursued noninstitutionally by force or fraud; institutionally, by primary group cathexes, by legal-bureaucratic rights and obligations, and by bargaining. The mutual adaptation of units to one another determines the integration of the system; in the long run, the system's integration depends on its adaptation.

3

THE PROCESS
OF SOCIALIZATION

Given a social system made up of statuses, one obvious requirement, if the system is to endure, is that its members learn their status rights and obligations and carry them out. Here is where termites *may* have an advantage: the members of termite societies are biologically compelled to perform their adaptive and integrative functions. For termites, physical and biological existence in the system is itself a relatively automatic guarantee of reliable role performance.

With human beings, however, physical or biological membership in a system merely *poses* the problem of reliability; it is not the answer to it. Man's biology is not sufficient for social life. It only provides a potential which must be developed (and in some ways can only be developed) in accordance with a pattern of social life that exists, at first, externally to the human being. Nor is that pattern itself an inevitable or direct expression of human "biological nature." Except in the very broadest of outline, even if we knew all there was to know about man biologically, we could never predict or even imagine the rich and varied patterns that have culturally evolved as man's ways of perceiving his world, feeling his pleasures and pains, or conceiving his moral rights and obligations.

The integration and adaptation of human social systems, then, cannot depend on the biological equipment the human being brings with him from the womb. It depends on his acquisition of and conformity to the cognitive, cathectic, and normative definitions of his group. In other words, human conformity depends on the individual's coming to *define* conformity (1) as intrinsically pleasurable, (2) as an efficient means to some end that is intrinsically enjoyable, (3) as a moral duty, or (4) as a necessary condition for other people's respect and acceptance. That is to

say, you and I and other human beings *willingly* do what we are supposed to do only if

1. we think it is gratifying.
2. we think it is a useful or necessary way of getting something that *is*
   gratifying or avoiding something painful.
3. we would feel ashamed or embarrassed if we did not.
4. we would feel guilty if we did not.

The "trouble"[1] is, of course, that those are also among the very reasons
that you and I and all other human beings do what we are *not* supposed
to do. We may *deviate* from the folkways and mores defining our statuses
or status-sequences because the tabooed behavior is rewarding, because
it seems more efficient than the prescribed way, because we have the idea
that the behavior expected of us is "wrong," or because we feel that *other*
people would disapprove if we conformed to "these" people's expectations.

The trick, then, if we are to conform to a given set of normative commands and prohibitions and appropriate cognitions and cathexes, is either
for things to be so arranged that we *cannot* deviate (even if we think it
would be fun, useful, right, or applause getting to do so); or else for
things to be so arranged that *the only actions we define as fun, right,
useful, or applause getting are the ones culturally prescribed.* Both
"tricks" are what have been termed "mechanisms of pattern-maintenance."
The first—arranging things so that deviance cannot be engaged in even if
motivated—are *social control* mechanisms, which we shall discuss in
Chapter 6. The second—arranging things so that people *define* fun, morality, utility, and going-along-with-the-crowd only in prescribed ways—are
socialization mechanisms, which we will discuss in this chapter.

The socialization process, in other words, is the process by which
people are developed into *social system members*, who carry in their
heads as cathexes, cognitions, and evaluations the culture of the system.
It is the process by which the "barbarian invaders of each new generation," as Ralph Linton called newborn infants, are turned from uncivil-
ized, ignorant animals into human members of a social system. It is also,
of course, the process by which "barbarian" high school graduates are
turned into college men and women, the process by which "barbarian"
civilians are turned into soldiers, immigrants are turned into citizens,
neophytes into masters. The socialization process, in short, is the process
by which people, who at one time do not define situations in accordance
with institutional prescriptions, are brought, at a later time, to do so.

---

[1] "Trouble" only from the point of view of *conformity*. As we shall see, there are
certain conditions under which *non*conformity is better for adaptation and integration
(let alone ethically) than conformity.

As this implies, the socialization process always involves interaction between two persons or two *kinds* of persons: a "socializee" (infant, raw recruit, immigrant, freshman, and so forth) and a "socializing agent" (parents, sergeants, natives, upperclassmen and faculty, and so forth). To understand this special kind of interaction, the question we must seek to answer is this: How do socializing agents get socializees to define situations as the agents want them to?

Initial Socialization

For two reasons, it is useful to start our analysis with the newborn infant. For one thing, obviously the social fabrication process begins there. Human beings at birth are one of the least functionally organized of all animals. Their responses are confined to a few rudimentary reflex actions occasioned by a very limited range of internal and external stimuli. For example, the infant will suck when an object is placed in his mouth or will eliminate wastes when sufficient pressure is experienced by relevant organs. These responses lack the highly patterned characteristics of the socialized members of society, and they mean that the infant requires an extended period of care by persons already socialized.

For another thing, at least two of the "reasons" for conforming (or deviating) that we listed above are conspicuously absent in the infant, and we must understand how they come into existence. The infant has no sense of guilt or shame. Those motives—or their more "positive" expressions in a sense of morality and a sensitivity to others' opinions—are themselves products (*if* they appear) of the first socialization experiences. In this respect, the infant is different from all other socializees, which, as we will see, is one reason why it is easier to socialize infants than other people.

The infant has only one motive for doing anything: pleasure. What the infant wants (that is, what seems to soothe him when it is present and panic or infuriate him when it is absent) is warmth, dryness, physical support, a full, but not-too-full stomach, a minimum of pressure on his bowels and bladder, a certain kind of tactile stimulation, and, apparently, some exercise and distractions. So far as anyone knows, he would stay infantile all his life if such pleasures were always unconditionally provided for him. "Growing up," which means growing out of this initial Garden of Eden, is other people's idea, not his.

SOCIAL CONDITIONING OF BIOLOGICAL NEEDS

But up and out he must grow—because the people on whom he is dependent for his simple pleasures insist on it. Much as they may love him (*"because* they love him," they say, but that too is their idea, not his!), they refuse to give him what he needs without getting something in return. The price of their support is his conformity to their expectations, and the bargaining power between them is usually so lopsided that he literally has no choice but to pay the price. So, trapped by his own pleasures, and even before he knows what happened, he is gently evicted from his paradise.

"Gently," and "before he knows what happened," in the ordinary case, because the eviction is a masterpiece of subtlety. His mother is the primary agent. She is ordinarily the single source of *all* his specific pleasures: warmth, dryness, tactile stimulation, milk, food, coddling, caressing, support—all of it. It is the satisfaction of such basic biological needs that seems to provide the *initial* basis for the transformation of the biological being into a social being. Dependent as the infant is upon the satisfaction of his biological needs by socialized others, he cannot help be sensitized to the particular objects and events that are culturally significant to his associates. The infant's biological needs form the bridge for the introduction of the mother's cultural definitions, and they provide the motive for the infant's acceptance of those definitions. Being fed, warm, and comfortable are the "rewards" for "accepting" the breast or the bottle, the blanket or the swaddling cloth, the cradle or the crib. As these basic needs are being met, the infant begins to learn to differentiate and respond to those objects that satisfy his biological needs. But which objects will be brought into his awareness and by what manner are determined by his mother, not by him or his biology (except, of course, that biological considerations set the broad limits of what can be responded to and what needs must be met). In the process, the child's discriminatory and selective capacities are conditioned and canalized so that he comes to focus his attention on what is culturally defined as reality, and to base his selections on what is culturally defined as pleasurable and moral. The fact that his sensory and motor equipment are not fully developed at birth facilitates as well as makes possible the very molding of his cognitions. It is in this sense that one might quite literally accept Ruth Benedict's dictum that "no man ever looks at the world with pristine eyes."[2]

[2] Ruth Benedict, *Patterns of Culture* (New York: Mentor Books, New American Library of World Literature, Inc., 1950), p. 2.

Of the many instructive studies of infancy and early childhood that provide inferential evidence of this cultural influence on cognition and its initial dependence upon biological needs, only a few can be mentioned here. Sherif, the American social psychologist, cites a number of such studies. For example, children under eighteen months, when presented with cards having different figures and pictures on them, make no discrimination among the cards. Children of eighteen months or older, however, begin to make discriminations in terms of the pictures that have value to them, but even they fail to discriminate detail in geometric figures or ink blots or drawings that require distinction of length, color, or shape. Now the point is that failure to make such distinctions does not appear to be a consequence of the child's biological *inability* to do so. On the contrary, when properly *motivated* (by having a piece of candy placed behind the design to be discriminated, for example), the child quite readily learns to choose the "correct" design and distinguish it from others. This conditioning of perception also seems to be reflected in the child's first verbal generalizations. The early words generally apply to objects and persons that have significance to the child in meeting his biological needs. Sherif concludes that such evidence indicates that "insight into children's discriminatory reactions must be gained through analysis of their developing capacities and experiences (learning) with objects and their characteristics as these relate to their motives. Herein lies the key to understanding how social influences come to regulate the child's biogenic motives and to affect discrimination of objects perceived as goals."[3]

By linking satisfaction of biological needs to a cultural context, the initial socializing group begins the process of making the satisfaction of intrinsic gratifications conditional on conforming to the structural requirements of the social system. Both cognitive and cathectic orientations are established in the child that are congruent with the structure and functions of the family and other contingent social systems. Within the wide and diffuse range of means for satisfying biological needs, socializers specify and limit the child's sources of gratification to conform to the cultural pattern. In this way, the child is socialized to established patterns for satisfying biological needs, and behavior that is intrinsically gratifying is linked to existing structure.

NEED FOR THE APPROVAL OF OTHERS

Although the biogenic needs provide a means for initial transmission of cultural cognitions and the early canalization of cathexes, they cannot be

---

[3] Muzafer Sherif and Carolyn W. Sherif, *An Outline of Social Psychology* (rev. ed.; New York: Harper & Brothers, 1956), pp. 396–398.

the sole motivation for conformity to the cultural pattern. Even very young children soon learn that they can satisfy their biological needs in a variety of ways, and their physical maturation permits exploratory sampling of an ever-widening range of environment. At the same time, physical growth eventually equalizes "bargaining power" so that the socializers no longer have all the advantage. Furthermore, many social needs transcend biological needs and urges entirely and demand that they be controlled or denied. How are these *social* needs to be transplanted so that they take root as part of the motivational equipment of socialized beings?

Again we return to the initial model of mother-child relationship. When the mother ministers to her child favorably, she is likely to do so with words and tone of voice that the infant comes to associate with pleasure. When she is displeased with him, her words, tone of voice, stance, and facial expression are likely to be significantly different. The infant needs only a modicum of biological normality to come to associate one tone or expression with gratification and another with no-gratification or with deprivation. He learns by this association that her *attitude* toward him is a critical determinant of whether he will be gratified or deprived.

He comes, thus, to value her favorable attitude, which itself is then a new kind of reward. It is a crucial kind of reward for the young child, in two somewhat paradoxical senses. In the first place, once he is dependent on it as a source of gratification, he is "hooked" as a human being. From now on (with a qualification to be introduced below), he must evaluate his actions not only in terms of the pleasure they bring him *but also in terms of what someone else will think of them.* The second sense in which the mother's favorable attitude is a crucial kind of reward is that the child (when socialization is effective) learns that he can control it to some extent. That is, *by controlling his own actions he can control her attitudes. All he has to do is to figure out what she wants him to do and then do it.*

This is "all he has to do," but it means the revolutionary step of coming to care about norms. From then on things are never the same again. The child at this point discovers the strictly human world of "shoulds" and "should nots," which can dominate the biological world of pleasure and pain and even physical and biological reality.

Now he has one of the reasons for conformity that we noted above was missing at birth: the negative reason of avoiding "shame"; the positive reason of securing someone's favorable opinion. That is, he is sensitive to what his mother, at least, thinks; and by extension he comes to be sensitive to what other people think (especially those like his mother and those she approves of—such as his father and people like him). Put positively, the mother can now reward the child for conformity by granting him not only physical gratification but psychological gratification as well. Put negatively, she can punish him not only physically but also by withholding the psychological gratification of her approval. Whiting and Child have described the negative aspect of this source of conformity in the following way.

> A child who breaks a cultural rule, if his transgression is known to his elders, is punished in some way. As a result of such experience he learns to anticipate similar punishment whenever he breaks a cultural rule. The transgression of a rule thus brings to a child one or both of two unpleasant consequences: punishment by his elders, and fearful antici-pation of such punishment. Finally, by further consequences of the learning process, the fear comes earlier. Now the thought of possible transgression, or presence in the situation in which he committed a transgression, is sufficient to arouse the uncomfortable anticipation of being punished or of giving himself grounds to fear imminent punish-ment. This anticipatory state of fear, like other emotional states, serves as a drive to motivate behavior which may lead to elimination of the drive. The behavior that is most effective from this point of view is avoidance of the transgression. If the child moves away from tempta-tion, gets out of the situation, or decisively makes a response in accord-ance with the cultural rule, he no longer has occasion to fear punish-ment. Thus conformity with cultural rules is rewarded by the reduction of fear of punishment.[4]

Once the child is sensitized to the approval of others, he has been socialized to conform beyond the motives of intrinsic biological gratifica-tion and instrumental attainment of it. He is now in the world of social motivation, which is the third source of conformity we have mentioned as part of the socialization process.

As the child begins to distinguish and respond to the verbal cues to which he is exposed, his mother and other family members begin to open up to him the social world that intervenes between his biological needs and the physical objects that may satisfy them. Once the child gains com-mand of the language of his culture (the verbal and other symbols and their meanings), the socialization process is rapidly accelerated. With the discovery that things have names, the child takes a major step away from dependence upon immediate biological needs and immediate situations and objects—a step that other animals never take. As we indicated in Chapter 1, language telescopes the learning process so that the child learns about things without direct experience with them. Language or-ganizes the environment into categories and relates the child to them in specific ways. The critical point here is that in the process of learning

---

[4] John W. M. Whiting and Irvin L. Child, *Child Training and Personality: A Cross-Cultural Study* (New Haven, Conn.: Yale University Press, 1953), pp. 224–225. See also J. Dollard and N. E. Miller, *Personality and Psychotherapy* (New York: McGraw-Hill Book Company, Inc., 1950), Chap. 10.

language, the child takes on the attitude (the cathexes and evaluations) toward his environment held by those round about him. In addition, the acquisition of language provides one basis for the next stage in motivation to conformity.

THE NEED FOR SELF-APPROVAL

Once the child has been sensitized to the attitude of others toward him, he is in a position to add to his reasons for conformity the fourth and final motive mentioned above: the desire to be "moral" or, put negatively, to avoid guilt-feelings. This further step is important in the socialization process for the obvious reason that if conformity were motivated solely by the desire to avoid *other* people's censure or to get other people's praise, there would be no reason to conform when the others were not likely to find out.[5] Conformity is much more certain if the socializing agent's criteria of evaluation can be put inside the socializee, *so that they become the standards by which he assesses himself. Then* he is *really* hooked: He carries the censor of his actions around with him, even when he is by himself.

What determines whether or not this step is taken is not very precisely understood. When it is taken, the norms of the socializing agent are said to have been "internalized" by the socializee, who is said to have "identified" with the socializing agent.[6] But "internalization" and "identification," though suggestive metaphors, are mainly labels attached to the process as names; they are not very illuminating explanations. About the most we can suggest is that, just as the socializee has the biological capacity to imitate the physical motions and vocal sounds of the socializing agent, so he has the capacity to imitate the agent's approval and disapproval.

[5] Whiting and Child's cross-cultural study of socialization suggests that although fear of external punishment theoretically might be the sole source of conformity and even guilt (since such fear may operate even when there is no objective basis for it), it does not seem to be a sufficient or satisfactory explanation in the empirical situation. *Op. cit.*, Chap. 11. Sigmund Freud was among the first to make a detailed distinction between what he called "objective anxiety" (fear of external punishment) and "moral anxiety" (fear of internal punishment or guilt) as sources of conformity.

[6] The role of identification in socialization has been emphasized in psychoanalytic theory, initiated by the writings of Sigmund Freud. See his *New Lectures on Psychoanalysis* (3d ed.; New York: W. W. Norton & Company, 1933). One of the few attempts to ground these speculative theories in empirical research directed at cross-cultural analysis (some seventy-five societies) is found in the Whiting and Child study already cited. They conclude that their study presents "tentative evidence in support of the process of socialization through identification, with origins akin to those ascribed to it in psychoanalytic theory" (p. 260).

Two processes seem to be involved here. In the first place, in learning the language of his socializing agents, the socializee learns cognitions and evaluations simultaneously and as part of the same process. He learns not only that he is a boy, but simultaneously that "boys must not wear dresses." His parents, especially (and later on all his other socializing agents), talk and act as though the world *is*, in fact, divided into "bads" and "goods," "rights" and "wrongs." "Negroes are inferior"; "Foreigners are evil"; "Nice people don't think such thoughts." In learning the lan-guage, he learns to evaluate the world; and in the process, since he is part of the world, he learns in this indirect way to evaluate himself also. If *people* are bad who "think such thoughts," then *he* is bad if he thinks them; if Negroes are inferior, then he is inferior if he fails to act as if Negroes are inferior.

In the second place, he develops evaluations of himself in a more direct way. He can imitate his agents' approval or disapproval of *himself*, directly. He does so just to the degree that the agent's approval and dis-approval are important to him. That is, he imitates the agent's approval of one act and disapproval of another to the degree that he attaches great importance to the agent's attitudes.

He does attach importance to those attitudes, in turn, to the degree that they are the things that seem to control the gratification or deprivation of his *other* needs. If the agent has, or seems to have, a monopoly of the means of satisfying the socializee's needs, *and if* the agent consistently refuses to satisfy them if he disapproves of the socializee's actions, then his approval becomes extremely important. In such a case, the socializee is under great pressure to cognize correctly what the principles are on which this all-powerful monopolist seems to base his blessings, and to attempt to practice them diligently. He is aided in this enterprise by imi-tating his best guess of the attitudes of the agent toward various actions. It is in this sense that he "identifies" with the agent, as an aid in making sure, so to speak, that he behaves in accordance with the agent's prin-ciples. To put it succinctly, since he can't beat 'em, he joins 'em.

DEVIANT SOCIALIZATION

However, we must pause here to emphasize that there is nothing in-evitable about this development. In the first place, the socializee may or may not acquire a need for others' approval. In the second place, even if he does, he may or may not *internalize* their standards of approval. It all depends.

Recall what was said about the child's ability to control his mother's attitudes. "All he has to do," we said, "is to figure out what she wants him to do and then do it." But this is "all he has to do" *when the socialization process operates functionally for pattern maintenance.* It might not. A breakdown in the process might occur at this point, in either of two disfunctional directions. On the one hand, the socializee may be able to control his mother's and other socializers' attitudes *without* conforming to their expectations. They are dependent on him for his conformity, and it sometimes happens that the bargaining power is lopsided in the *child's* favor. In such a case, he may learn that he can make *them* conform to *his* expectations. If he screams loud enough or kicks his heels long enough (and in a public enough place), it may be *they* who surrender first. Popular speech then speaks of a "spoiled" child.

On the other hand, it may be that the parents' attitudes toward the child are in fact *outside his control.* Whether his parents approve or disapprove of him, speak in soothing gentle voices with smiles or in harsh voices with frowns, may depend not nearly so much on what he does as on how they are feeling as a result of some other event in their lives. It may even be impossible for him to please them; they may resent his very existence. In such a case, the child will learn well enough, but *what* he learns may not be the lesson that *conformity* pays off. It is more likely to be either the lesson that one must live in dread of others' unpredictable attitudes and only hope for the best, or else the lesson that there is no way at all of being approved of: one is simply objectionable.

In all these cases, the child can be counted upon to learn excellently. He cannot be counted upon to be socialized excellently, however; that depends on the structure of his learning situation and on what is communicated to him. Moreover, even if he does succeed in taking the first step of learning that he can elicit his parents' favorable opinions and that the way to do it is to conform to their standards, he may or may not move on to *internalize* those standards as his *own.* If there are other people in his environment, for example, who can satisfy his needs and whose standards are different—or if his mother and father differ in their standards—then what he learns is likely to be that it *is* important to be sensitive to other people's values, but *which values all depend on which people.* He is not under pressure to judge himself by their values, except in the sense of being embarrassed if he makes a mistake.

AUTONOMY AND HETERONOMY

Further still, even if he does proceed to the second step of developing a conscience (as everyday speech refers to the values he has internalized) or a superego (as Freudian speech refers to the same thing), his socialization is still not necessarily at an end. (It *may* cease there, of course, and often does, just as it may cease even earlier.) Conformity is now more fully guaranteed than before, but still not as fully as it might be. "Conscience," by definition, implies that the individual has *some* tendency to act in a manner proscribed by the norms he has internalized, but "checks himself." He must exert an effort to *make* himself conform; and so long as this is the case it is always possible for circumstances to arise in which the internalized socializing agent or the "generalized other" may be evaded, circumvented, outwitted, put to sleep, or rebelled against. (Some of the ways in which this may be done will be taken up later; for now let it be sufficient to illustrate by noting the possibility of narcotizing inhibitions with alcohol—which is, indeed, one of the prime functions of alcohol.)

The further and third step in the socialization process is a slightly complex and in one sense a paradoxical one. To put the paradox: The further step, if taken, returns the individual to a situation in which there are once again only *two* reasons for conforming, not four. The two reasons are enjoyment and utility.

To explain this step, we shall draw, with considerable modification, on the classic studies of a Swiss psychologist, Jean Piaget.[7]

Consider two rules—two normative prescriptions—with which little boys are confronted by various socializing agents: The rule that boys should play with marbles, not dolls; and the rule that in playing marbles the base line should be drawn (let us say) four feet away from the circle.

Now at first these rules are like any of the thousands of other rules with which children are confronted: utterly incomprehensible. After a while, however, with socializing agents standing ready to heap ridicule and scorn on the little boy who plays with dolls or "cheats" on the base-line rule, and to reward with approval and respect the boy who spurns dolls and follows the four-foot rule, boys learn that other people's approval depends on conformity. Most boys go on to internalize those rules, and wouldn't be caught dead (even if alone) playing with dolls or cheating.

At this stage, Piaget asked the boys such questions as this: "Well, suppose everybody agreed on having a different rule—say, drawing the base line three feet or five feet away. Would that be all right?"

"Absolutely not," the boys were likely to reply. "The rule is four feet; it's absolute; it can't be tampered with; it always was the rule ever since the ancient days of God and grandfather; and that's that."

Piaget did not ask the boys similar questions about the rule, "Boys should play marbles" (in fact, Piaget does not explicitly deal with this as

---

[7] Jean Piaget, *The Moral Judgment of the Child* (New York: Harcourt, Brace & World, Inc., 1932).

a rule); but we suggest he would have received very similar, if not more emphatic, answers.

When the boys were older, however, and Piaget, asked them the same question, he received a very different answer. "Certainly," they say, "three feet, five feet, two feet—anything at all, *so long as it gets a good game of marbles going and everyone agrees to play by the rule!*"

Now here is a radical change. From being an absolute rule, conformity to which was a measure of one's own respectability, the four-foot rule now has become a mere instrument, to be conformed to or not depending entirely on its usefulness at the moment. It is no longer the case that the boys judge *themselves* by the rule; they now judge the *rule* by its usefulness to them.

How about the rule that *"boys* should play marbles"? Piaget doesn't report on this, but we suggest that attitudes toward it have also changed, though in a different way. At the later stage, it also ceases to be seen as a God-given command; it comes to be seen simply as a statement of what is pleasurable. "Naturally, boys should play marbles; it's more fun than dolls." Here, too, boys no longer judge themselves by the rule; there isn't any rule, there's only "doing what comes naturally."

So pervasive is socialization of this sort that alternatives to the institutionalized pattern are seldom if ever conceived, and the pattern itself may never be questioned. Nowhere is this better illustrated than our conception of the "naturalness" of masculine and feminine traits. To accuse a male in our society of being feminine is to question his natural, biological state and constitutes one of the most ego-threatening epithets. However, cross-cultural analysis of conceptions of masculinity and femininity suggests that many sex traits are largely culturally conditioned and have little direct basis in the biological nature of the sexes. Margaret Mead has described such traits in three primitive cultures, each with a varying conception of what the sexes "really are."

> We have now considered in detail the approved personalities of each sex among three primitive peoples. We found the Arapesh—both men and women—displaying a personality that, out of our historically limited preoccupations, we would call maternal in its parental aspects, and feminine in its sexual aspects. We found men, as well as women, trained to be co-operative, unaggressive, responsive to the needs and demands of others. We found no idea that sex was a powerful driving force either for men or for women. In marked contrast to these attitudes, we found among the Mundugumor that both men and women developed as ruthless, aggressive, positively sexed individuals, with the maternal cherishing aspects of personality at a minimum. Both men and women approximated to a personality type that we in our culture would find only in an undisciplined and very violent male. Neither the Arapesh nor the Mundugumor profit by a contrast between the sexes; the Arapesh ideal

is the mild, responsive man married to the mild, responsive woman; the Mundugumor ideal is the violent aggressive man married to the violent aggressive woman. In the third tribe, the Tchambuli, we found a genuine reversal of the sex-attitudes of our own culture, with the woman the dominant, impersonal, managing partner, the man the less responsible and the emotionally dependent person. These three situations suggest, then, a very definite conclusion. If those temperamental attitudes which we have traditionally regarded as feminine—such as passivity, responsiveness, and a willingness to cherish children—can so easily be set up as the masculine pattern in one tribe, and in another be outlawed for the majority of women as well as for the majority of men, we no longer have any basis for regarding such aspects of behavior as sex-linked. And this conclusion becomes even stronger when we consider the actual reversal by Tchambuli of the position of dominance of the two sexes. . . .[8]

Piaget uses the terms "heteronomy" and "autonomy" to distinguish between the earlier and later orientations of people toward norms. At the early, heteronomous, stage, the norms are conceived as being outside one's self—as having an existence of their own, independent of one's self or of people. At the later, autonomous, stage, they are felt to be simply part of one's self or subject to one's own will. For our present purposes, we can define a *heteronomous* relation to norms as one in which the individual conforms either in order to secure someone else's approval or in order to secure self-approval. An *autonomous* relation is one in which he conforms either because conformity is instrumentally useful or because it is pleasurable.

At the autonomous stage, then, as noted above, the individual is back to the point of being susceptible to only two kinds of rewards: pleasure and usefulness. But, obviously enough, there is an extraordinary difference. The autonomous individual's conceptions of pleasure and efficiency are *cultural* conceptions, extremely complex, subtle, and at least not necessarily egocentric. (His pleasure, for example, may be in his family's success, in discovering penicillin, and so on.) The infant's are biological, simple, and necessarily egocentric.

At the autonomous stage, conformity to norms is fully guaranteed in the case of those norms that have become cathectic definitions. Individuals can be counted upon to do what they are supposed to do because that is just what they want to do. With respect to other norms, however—those that have changed from yardsticks to tools—conformity is guaranteed only if conformity seems to be the most effective *means* of achieving the *goals* specified by the other norms. In other words, at this stage,

[8] Margaret Mead, *From the South Seas* (New York: William Morrow & Company, Inc., 1939), "Sex and Temperament in Three Primitive Societies," pp. 279–280.

norms are divided into two categories: cathected goals and rationally considered means.

No society, so far as we know, has ever succeeded in socializing all its members to all its norms all the way to the stage of autonomy. (There are several reasons for this, which we shall take up at various points in this book.) Moreover, in any society, our guess would be that some people never reach the autonomous stage with respect to any norms, and that very few people in any society reach it with respect to all norms.[9]

CONDITIONS OF AUTONOMY

Let us consider first the conditions that seem to be necessary if the norm is to shift from the heteronomous category of a yardstick against which people measure themselves to the autonomous category of a tool that gets measured in terms of its usefulness. We shall draw again on Piaget's work, with modification.

First of all, what seems to be necessary is *exposure to contradictory norms*, especially when in association with equals. Similarities of status and rank permit children (and adults as well) to interact on equal terms, without the differences of power and prestige implicit in authority. In equalitarian relationships, there is greater possibility of deliberation, experimentation, and mutual influence. When boys who believe faithfully in the absoluteness of the four-foot rule get old enough to play two blocks away and there meet boys who believe just as faithfully in a five-foot rule, something has to give. What may give, of course, is the relationship between the boys. Our marble players would not be the first human beings, nor the last, to respond to diversity with the conviction that the different must be evil. If this is not to happen, with a consequent reinforcement of the heteronomous commitment, a second set of conditions seems necessary—first, that conformity to the new and conflicting norm be rewarding (it gets a good game of marbles going, for example); second, that there be no other way to get the reward; third, that the

[9] A large amount of philosophical, ethical, and religious debate is concerned with precisely the issue of whether the autonomous or the heteronomous orientation is "better." We eschew the debate in this book, but refer the reader to several works in which the subject is dealt with dramatically and absorbingly. See Henrik Ibsen's plays, *Peer Gynt*, *A Doll's House*, and *Ghosts*. (In the latter play, the Reverend Manders speaks for the heteronomous view; in several speeches Mrs. Alving champions the autonomous side.) See also several books by Erich Fromm: *Escape from Freedom*, *Man for Himself*, and *Psychoanalysis and Religion*. Jean Paul Sartre tackles the issue in a brilliant play, *The Flies*.

reward (playing marbles) is greatly valued; and fourth, that there be no external punishment for violating the old norm (for example, the other boys are not around, or if they are, they all support one another in the new experiment).

If these conditions obtain—contact with diversity, greatly valued reward for changing, absence of alternatives, and absence of punishment—the odds are that socializees will redefine the norm in question from an absolute yardstick to a relative tool.

But how about the other shift—from normative yardstick to cathectic definition? This is the change most Americans experience with respect to such norms as "Boys should wear trousers, girls should wear dresses" or "Americans should speak English." Many people experience it with respect to such norms as not cheating on examinations, doing scientific research painstakingly, playing the piano correctly, and so on.

The basic condition that seems to be necessary for this shift to occur is that conformity to the norm not permanently, or even for very long periods, frustrate some need. It is for this reason that normative *proscriptions* are much harder to relate to autonomously than *prescriptions*, *unless some equally gratifying alternative is provided.* If boys, for example, were merely punished for wearing dresses instead of being rewarded for wearing trousers, they would not be so likely to cathect trousers nor so likely to give up completely the desire to wear dresses. In general, the principle seems to be that *punishment* can lead people to *inhibit* some tendency, at least when the punishment is swift and certain; but it cannot lead them to *extinguish* the tendency.[10] The difference between inhibition and extinction, of course, is the difference between refraining from an act because of conscience-demands and refraining from it because one has no desire to engage in it.

In order to extinguish a tendency, what seems to be necessary is to give a greater reward for some action *incompatible* with the tendency than the person could get from expressing the tendency. That is, if Tendency A is to be extinguished, some action, B, must be found such that B is both incompatible with A *and* brings a greater reward. Obviously, this is sometimes impossible to do. Sexual gratification, for example, is for most people a reward so gratifying that not much can compete with it, in the first place; and in the second place, it is hard to think of any activity which is *permanently* incompatible with sexual activity. For these reasons, most sexual proscriptions—for example, the proscription in American society of premarital sexual relations—are conformed to, if they are, either as a result of heteronomous conscience-demands or instrumentally out of

---

[10] See B. F. Skinner, *Science and Human Behavior* (New York: The Macmillan Company, 1953).

fear of pregnancy or venereal disease. Some norms, then, by their very nature cannot be related to autonomously. If such patterns are to be maintained,[11] they must be maintained by one of the other devices.

The Development of the Self

In our discussion so far, we have focused on how people are socialized so as to act in conformity with the social system of the groups in which they have membership. In the process of socialization, people not only develop a conception of their social world; they also develop a *self-conception*. An analysis of this aspect of socialization is sociologically significant because it helps us to understand the interplay between the socialized person and his social environment. Therefore, we now turn to a brief discussion of the development of the social self.

THE SELF-CONCEPTION

Once the child is sensitized to the response of others, he is in a position to formulate a self-conception. He begins to see himself as others see him; or, more precisely, as he thinks others see him. Charles Cooley, one of the first American sociologists to explore this source of the "self-image," referred to it as the "reflected or looking-glass self." "A self-idea of this sort," he writes, "seems to have three principal elements: the imagination of our appearance to the other person; the imagination of his judgment of that appearance, and some sort of self-feeling, such as pride or mortification."[12] In other words, the child begins to see himself as an object and to distinguish it from other selves. He takes on an identity and a distinction in much the same way that he has learned to distinguish and identify other objects in his environment. Just as his conception of the physical world is affected by the image held by his socializers, so is his conception of his self.

By imaginatively taking the viewpoint of others ("If I do this, what

[11] Whether or not such patterns "should be maintained" may be debated on a level of "ethics" or "absolute morality," or on a level of their *functionality* for social system processes. On the first level, of course, sociologists have nothing to contribute. On the second level, they have much. Throughout the text, we shall refer frequently to the functionality and disfunctionality of system norms.

[12] Charles Horton Cooley, *Human Nature and the Social Order* (rev. ed.; New York: Charles Scribner's Sons, 1922), p. 184.

will Mother do?" or "How would my big brother act in this situation?"),
he can anticipate their response to *his* behavior as well as *their* behavior
in a given situation. This can all be done "in his head," before he acts,
and *then* become the basis for his overt behavior. Moreover, the standards of conduct held by the father, mother, or older brother are used as a
basis for self-evaluation. By means of an internal dialogue, the individual
can become an object to himself. Figuratively speaking, he can stand outside himself and take a look at himself, making judgments and evaluations that are used as a basis for action—independent of reference to the
standards of *particular, identifiable* others. It is in this sense that we say
that he has "internalized" the norms of others. Using the standards of
others that he has internalized as his own, he is able to judge himself in
much the same way that others have judged him. As others have rewarded him with their approval for compliance to social standards, he
is able to reward himself with approval. Thus, the social enters into the
individual as, by means of symbolic self-communication, his self becomes
an object that can be appraised and evaluated in terms of the relevant
definitions of the systems in which he functions.

George H. Mead has expressed this development of the self in the following way:

> . . . there are two general stages in the full development of the self. At
> the first of these stages, the individual's self is constituted simply by an
> organization of the particular attitudes of other individuals toward him-
> self and toward one another in the specific social acts in which he par-
> ticipates with them. But at the second stage in the full development of
> the individual's self that self is constituted not only by an organization
> of these particular individual attitudes, but also by an organization of
> the social attitudes of the generalized other or the social group as a
> whole to which he belongs. These *social* or *group* attitudes are brought
> within the individual's field of direct experience, and are included as
> elements in the structure or constitution of his self, in the same way that
> the attitudes of *particular* other individuals are. . . .[13]

To put Mead's point in other words, first the child acquires a self by
learning to say, in effect, "I am he whom Father expects to eat his
spinach." He does this by learning to *predict* Father's reaction to eating
spinach and not eating it. Second, he *generalizes* his conception of
"father" and says, in effect, "I am supposed to eat my spinach" (and not
hit my sister or run outdoors naked, and so on and on). He moves, in
other words, from the idea that he had better learn to anticipate Father's
reactions, to the idea that certain things "just aren't done" or that certain
things "just should be done."

[13] George Herbert Mead, *Mind, Self and Society* (Chicago: The University of
Chicago Press, 1934), p. 158. Copyright 1934 by the University of Chicago. Emphasis
supplied.

In this way people are able to enter into appropriate social interaction with others, *whatever* may be the specific relationship of the others to them. In other words, an individual is able to respond appropriately to an almost indefinite number of statuses, irrespective of what concrete person occupies them, provided only that the status definitions have been incorporated into his self. Thus, people are socialized to interact within a social system in predictable and systematic fashion and to carry out their respective functions in an orderly division of labor. The behavior of each is controlled by the pattern of the whole. Mead's classical statement of this is as follows:

> It is in the form of the generalized other that the social process influ-
> ences the behavior of the individuals involved in it and carrying it on,
> i.e., that the community exercises control over the conduct of its indi-
> vidual members; for it is in this form that the social process or commu-
> nity enters as a determining factor into the individual's thinking. In
> abstract thought the individual takes the attitude of the generalized
> other towards himself, without reference to its expression in any par-
> ticular other individuals; and in concrete thought he takes that attitude
> in so far as it is expressed in the attitudes toward his behavior of those
> other individuals with whom he is involved in the given social situation
> or act.[14]

CONSISTENCY OF SELF-CONCEPTION

Two statements may be made concerning system definitions already internalized. First, social systems usually are structured and people related to them so as to assure some consistency in the expectations to which people are exposed. Therefore, there is likely to be some consistency in definitions internalized. Second, ordinarily, internalized definitions will be ordered in a hierarchy; that is, certain of them will be more positively valued than others. This hierarchy is normatively determined by the systems in which people are socialized. In the family, for example, the child may learn that obedience to his father takes precedence over obedience to playmates, that occupational skills are to be valued more than social dancing skills, that it is more reprehensible to strike than to berate, or that classical music is to be preferred to popular music. In this way, people learn not only what courses of action they may legitimately pursue, but which are to take precedence when they are faced with several alternative, normatively sanctioned choices. It is this consistency and hierarchy of internalized definitions that people seek to maintain.

Within the limits set by striving for stability and consistency of in-

14 *Ibid.*, pp. 155–156.

ternalized definitions, a person tends to act so as to increase his favorable self-conception. As we have pointed out earlier, a person's favorable self-conception is contingent upon his conformity to his internalized definitions. Such definitions become standards for self-appraisal or criteria of self-assessment; people tend to judge themselves in terms of them.

Why do people strive for some consistency of internalized definitions? Since behavior must be predictable, it seems clear from the system point of view why some consistency is functional for system processes. From the point of view of the people in the system, it seems equally plausible that some consistency is necessary in order to act; for if they internalize conflicting definitions of equal saliency, they cannot pursue one desired course of action without violating another that is equally desired. In addition, if new demands conflict with standards already internalized, favorable self-conceptions are threatened. If people conform to these conflicting demands, they may experience feelings of shame, guilt, remorse, embarrassment, and the like. The general tendency is to avoid or reject such demands, where possible, so as to maintain a favorable self-conception. It should be noted that the consistency need not be ordered in a logical sense, as long as people believe that their values are relatively consistent or are unaware of inconsistencies.[15] Also, attention should be called to the fact that people may use certain psychological mechanisms of defense that permit them to repress one side of a conflict while acting in terms of the other. For example, they may avoid the self-criticism likely to result from violation of an internalized norm by rationalizing their behavior in a way that convinces them they are really not doing anything "wrong." We shall have more to say about these mechanisms in Chapter 5.

THE SELF AS A SOCIAL PRODUCT

The extensive and careful observations of child development carried on by Gesell and his associates give instructive, inferential evidence of the sequence of the growth of the self as a social product.[16] The newborn infant has no sense of self and apparently does not clearly distinguish even his physical self from other objects. During his first month of life he is relatively impassive to other social beings; by his second month, he is likely to smile spontaneously when he sees another person's face; in about

[15] See William A. Scott, "Cognitive Consistency, Response Reinforcement, and Attitude Change," *Sociometry*, 22:219–229 (1959).

[16] A. Gesell and F. L. Ilg, *Infant and Child in the Culture of Today* (New York: Harper & Brothers, 1943), pp. 334–340.

four months the smile is self-induced; and at six months he begins to react differently to different individuals, especially to strangers. During this same period and extending through his first year of life, he is making significant discovery of his physical self. During his second year he begins to discover the world of other people in more detail, to be less passive and self-involved, and increasingly to respond to the cues of other persons. In the second year, he begins to respond to his name and develops a sense of self-other identity in terms of such pronouns as "you," "me," and "I." During the fourth year he cites older family members as authority for behavior, and in his fifth and sixth years is quite adapted to the dictates of his immediate culture. At this time he also begins to set up standards for himself and make value judgments about his own behavior in terms of this authority.

This self-development is in stark contrast to those cases of children who have suffered from a minimum of social interaction. Kingsley Davis has reported on two such cases.[17] In both instances, the children were isolated because of illegitimate birth. One of these cases was discovered when the child was six and a half years old. Social interaction apparently had been restricted to her mother, who was a deaf-mute, and took place in a dark room where the child had been hidden from the outside world. She had never learned to speak, and her vocal response was limited to strange croaking sounds. In the presence of strangers, her behavior resembled that of a wild animal and was charged with fear and hostility. Her response to objects that were normally familiar to her age peers was one of indifference or bewilderment. In some respects her behavior was comparable to a child of six months, and according to one observer, she was "apparently utterly unaware of relationships of any kind." Because of the unusual nature of many of her reactions, it was thought at first that she was deaf. Although at one time experts pronounced her feeble-minded, after seven months of careful training she developed a substantial vocabulary, and within two years she reached a normal level of mental and social development. Eventually she entered school to take her place among other children.

From such contrasting studies of socialized and nonsocialized humans it becomes evident that the social self is not something that exists first and then enters into social interaction, but, rather, that it is a product

---

[17] Kingsley Davis, "Extreme Social Isolation of a Child," *American Journal of Sociology*, 45:554–564 (1940), and "Final Note on a Case of Extreme Isolation," *American Journal of Sociology*, 50:423–437 (1947). These cases are discussed in the context of socialization in his book, *Human Society* (New York: The Macmillan Company, 1949). Other cases of socially isolated children are discussed by J. A. L. Singh and Robert M. Zingg, *Wolf Children and Feral Man* (New York: Harper & Brothers, 1942).

that develops out of social interaction. In this sense, the social self reflects and expresses the status-sequence and status-set of the individual. What he "pays attention to" (cognition), what he "feels" (cathexis), and what he thinks is "right" (evaluation) *reflect* the cultural context to which he has been exposed. At the same time, once socialized, he has all four potential reasons that we mentioned earlier for *expressing* (conforming to) those cultural definitions: pleasure, utility, approval of others, and self-approval. Or to put it another—and very strategic—way, there are now four kinds of rewards that can reinforce his conformity to the institutional prescriptions that he has learned.

Diversity and Modality in Socialization

Since, as we have seen, the development of sensitivity to others' opinions, the development of a "conscience," and the development from heteronomy to autonomy all depend so much on the individual's exposure to diversity or consistency, and on the nature of his rewards and punishments, we must now turn our attention to some of the major social structures that affect those variables. That is to say, what are the *structural* arrangements that determine *which* others the socializee will learn to try to please? What are the structures that determine whether he will learn that he can control other's attitudes or learn that he is powerless? What structures determine the amount and kinds of diversity he will be exposed to? What structures influence the rewards and punishments he will experience?

THE FAMILY

It is in the family, particularly, that certain basic normative evaluations are established. These are composed of rather broad and dominant value orientations reflective of the society in which the individual is born and funneled through to him from the societal system by the older family members. To the extent that values in the family system and the societal system coincide and are reinforced by socialization in systems outside the family, the internalized values of each individual in the societal system are likely to be relatively similar. This would be most probable in small societies with little division of labor. In such societies, characterized by cultural homogeneity and the absence of rapid social change, where the child may be socialized to most roles within the family, and where other socializing agents reinforce the family socialization, there is greater opportunity to develop people who express homogeneity in their behavior and possess relatively similar characteristics and traits. Ruth Benedict, the cultural anthropologist, recognized this in her analysis of the patterned nature of human culture and its impact on human personality.

> It is one of the philosophical justifications for the study of primitive peoples that the facts of simpler cultures may make clear social facts that are otherwise baffling and not open to demonstration. This is nowhere more true than in the matter of the fundamental and distinctive cultural configurations that pattern existence and condition the thoughts and emotions of the individuals who participate in those cultures. The whole problem of the formation of the individual's habit-patterns under the influence of traditional custom can best be understood at the present time through the study of simpler peoples. This does not mean that the facts and processes we can discover in this way are limited in their application to primitive civilizations. Cultural configurations are as compelling and as significant in the highest and most complex societies of which we have knowledge. But the materal is too intricate and too close to our eyes for us to cope with it successfully.[18]

THE BIOLOGICAL BASIS OF DIVERSITY

However, even in the most homogeneous primitive society, individual personalities would never be the same. In the first place, no two biological systems are exactly alike. Differences in bodily structure, in the functioning of internal glands, in thresholds of visceral drives, and in the structure of the nervous system provide a range of difference in salience of biological need, level and type of gratification, scope of possible modification, and so on. This means that the impact of similar socialization may vary for different biologies. We cannot go into detail concerning the relationship here, but the reader should not lose sight of the significance of individual biological differences in our focus upon culturally induced similarities.[19]

THE SOCIAL BASIS OF DIVERSITY

In the second place, no two individuals can experience socialization in precisely the same way, even in the same family. Order of birth, number

[18] Ruth Benedict, *Patterns of Culture* (New York: Mentor Books, The New American Library of World Literature, Inc., 1950), pp. 50–51.
[19] These matters are discussed and documented in detail in such sources as Gardner Murphy, Lois B. Murphy, and Theodore M. Newcomb, *Experimental Social Psychology* (rev. ed.; New York: Harper & Brothers, 1937), particularly Part II.

of siblings, and aging of parents between births present different socializing environments for different children in the same family. In addition, people always receive some socialization from systems outside the family. To the extent that these systems reinforce values learned within the family, social elements of personality are not greatly differentiated. However, such socialization presents each individual with different constellations and sequences of socializers and, hence, different socialization experiences.

IMPACT OF THE LARGER SOCIETY

In all societies, then, there is an irreducible minimum of diversity to which children are exposed. Their siblings and their playmates are almost bound to have different biological structures that make other people in the society respond to them differently (thus giving them special self-images) and that lead them to respond differently to the same socialization experiences. Furthermore, a child's siblings and playmates, also, are almost sure to have had slightly different socialization experiences. Complete consistency of expectations and of rewards and punishments is therefore impossible.

In some societies this irreducible minimum of diversity becomes greatly expanded. When the societal system increases in size and division of labor, when the culture tolerates variety and divergencies, and when the environment is subject to rapid change, the chances for exposure to diversity are greatly increased. Families become distinguished according to economic position, ethnic origin, regional location, rural or urban location, occupational specialization, and so on.

The existence of occupational or ethnic or other subcultures in a society, however, only expands the *possible* diversities to which an individual may be exposed. Actual exposure is made highly likely to the degree that integrative and adaptive mechanisms encourage movement from one subsystem to another. In India, for example, where there is considerable diversity among subsystems, any one person may still have very little exposure to diversity. The major statuses learned within the family tend to be retained throughout the individual's life, and he may come in contact with no one outside his village.

In our own society, by contrast, although such statuses as sex, kinship, and citizenship remain relatively stable, a wide range of movement in and out of other statuses is permitted on the basis of individual choice. Since the diversity of cultural patterns is great, the heterogeneity of socializing influences any one person may experience is expanded as he freely moves from one to another social system. This offers the possibility of considerable differentiation of personality structures and diminishes the scope of the modality of personality types, insofar as culturally defined characteristics are concerned. It also permits the development of autonomy. At the same time, it presents problems for both the social system and the individual. The social system is presented with the problem of integrating people of diverse background and orientation into its division of labor, and the individual is faced with the problem of reconciling and integrating the diverse and often conflicting definitions contained in the various statuses to which he is socialized. Furthermore, as individuals become more differentiated, the common bonds of shared values and experiences may be weakened, on the one hand; and on the other, individuals may tend to feel isolated, psychologically speaking, from one another.

Our own society, then, permits of considerable variation in the development of the social self. In addition to the fact that no two people can possibly develop exactly the same personality structure because of unique biology and socialization, societal members are subject to differentiating experience within subcultures. At the same time, they are all subject in varying degree to somewhat similar socialization through a common educational experience, mass media of communication, and other societal sources of socialization. Thus a person's social self becomes a synthesis of his unique experience, his socialization to his subculture, and his socialization in the societal system. In this way, people, although "unique," assume values and behave in ways associated with their class, region, rural or urban setting, and the like; and they also assume values and behave in ways associated with the larger society. It is for these reasons that, as Clyde Kluckhohn and Henry A. Murray have succinctly put it, "Every man is in certain respects

    a. like all other men,
    b. like some other men,
    c. like no other man."[20]

The point to be emphasized is that despite the fact that each individual is unique, he also shares with some other people common characteristics. These shared characteristics are a consequence of groups of people being socialized in a common culture and are as much a part of the individual as are his unique attributes. These *socialized similarities* have been referred to variously as "basic personality structure" (Kardiner), "national character" (Gorer), "modal personality type" (Parsons), "social character" (Fromm), and "communal aspects of personality" (Kluckhohn).

[20] Clyde Kluckhohn and Henry A. Murray, "Personality Formation: The Determinants," in Kluckhohn and Murray (eds.), *Personality in Nature, Society, and Culture* (New York: Alfred A. Knopf, Inc., 1948), p. 35.

THE PERSISTENCE OF SOCIALIZATION

The presumption is that these basic features of the personality are laid down relatively early in the socialization experience through the mechanisms of identification and internalization. This implies that the basic identification patterns developed in early childhood are relatively stable and unchangeable. At the very least, they would seem to provide the foundation that sets the general outlines for the subsequent building process of socialization, and gives to the development of "personality" the impression of an inevitable, biogenic unfolding. The significance of this view of the person, in relationship to his environment, has been cogently stated as follows:

> Although personality is a product of the social environment of the past, it is not, once it has developed, a mere object of the contemporary environment. What has developed is a *structure* within the individual, something which is capable of self-initiated action upon the social environment and of selection with respect to varied impinging stimuli; something which though always modifiable is frequently very resistant to fundamental change. This conception is necessary to explain consistency of behavior in widely varying situations, to explain the persistence of ideological trends in the face of contradictory facts and radically altered social conditions, to explain why people in the same sociological situation have different or even conflicting views on social issues, and why it is that people whose behavior has been changed through psychological manipulation lapse into their old ways as soon as the agencies of manipulation are removed.[21]

Some analysts of culture and personality have suggested that the basic personality traits themselves influence the nature of culture and set the limits within which change or alteration of the cultural pattern takes place. Abram Kardiner, a psychiatrist and anthropologist, has hypothesized that the basic personality structure, developed in what he calls "primary institutions" (principally the specific pattern of interrelationships and early child-rearing practices of the family), creates a constellation of needs, tensions, and orientations that tend to dictate the structure of "secondary institutions" (systems of taboos, religious belief, ritual, thought). By the same token, the basic personality structure is seen as conditioning the direction and limits of adaptation of a people.[22] Such ideas, although stimulating and fruitful for detailed research, are still

[21] T. W. Adorno, Else Frenkel-Brunswik, D. J. Levinson, and R. N. Sanford, *The Authoritarian Personality* (New York: Harper & Brothers, 1950), pp. 5 ff.

[22] Abram Kardiner and Ralph Linton, *The Individual and His Society* (New York: Columbia University Press, 1939) and Abram Kardiner, *et al.*, *The Psychological Frontiers of Society* (New York: Columbia University Press, 1945).

largely in the realm of speculation and frequently based on assumptions that cannot be or have not been subject to empirical verification. Furthermore, it should be remembered that "basic personality structure" is only one aspect of the total person, and that some variation of and deviation from the modal type is inherent in socialization.[23]

In addition, it is probable that there is a good deal more flexibility to the personality than is sometimes assumed. Frequently, ideas of rigidity of the basic structure of personality are built upon observation of isolated, homogeneous, primitive cultures and upon analysis of somewhat extreme types or even upon pathological case studies. This may bias our conclusions in the direction of rigidity and fixity, since both are more likely to be encountered in such sources of analysis. At the same time, the impact of social structure upon the person over time may be underestimated.

The utility of the "culture-personality" concept is that it provides an empirical basis for analyzing the linkage between human beings and social structure. Put another way, it gives a basis for understanding the uniquely human relationship between man's subjective world and his object world as it has developed at different times and in different places. On the one hand, it takes the abstract concept "culture" and lodges it firmly in empirically identifiable units; for, after all, human beings express and transmit cultural patterns. On the other hand, it shows how human, biological potentialities are mediated by the social experience of interaction with other human beings in a cultural context that exists outside the organism. On the basis of a wide-ranging survey of the literature, A. Irving Hallowell has probably stated very well the present condition of our knowledge in these respects:

> We may say, I think, that the general hypothesis underlying culture and personality studies has been confirmed. Moot points, such as how early personality structure is set, what reorganization is possible after the initial years of childhood, and what are the most crucial determining factors involved, concern personality theory itself rather than the fundamental hypothesis. That human personality structure is a product of experience in a socialization process and that the resulting structure varies with the nature and conditions of such experience can scarcely be doubted.[24]

[23] Talcott Parsons analyzes the significance of these features of socialization and their relationship to basic personality structure in *The Social System* (New York: The Free Press of Glencoe, Inc., 1951), pp. 229–235. See also Talcott Parsons, R. F. Bales, and E. A. Shils, *Family, Socialization, and Interaction Process* (New York: The Free Press of Glencoe, Inc., 1955).

[24] A. Irving Hallowell, "Culture, Personality, and Society," in A. L. Kroeber (ed.), *Anthropology Today* (Chicago: The University of Chicago Press, 1953), p. 608. Copyright 1953 by the University of Chicago.

Consistency of Socialization

Our discussion of diversity of socialization might well lead to the conclusion that consistency of socialization is almost totally absent in a diversified and differentiated society such as our own. However, the structure and relationships of subsystems, developed without any apparent design or intention, are such that some consistency in socialization is present, despite great and often conflicting differences.

Socialization within the family is usually facilitated by the fact that family members tend to share some relatively similar statuses. The wife is ascribed the general social position of the husband and the economic, prestige, and power statuses associated with it. Mate selection tends to result in the uniting of persons of similar race, ethnicity, education, income, religion, political affiliation, and the like. This is true particularly when the differences that flow from such statuses are defined as conflicting by the culture and by the individuals mating. In addition, mates are likely to share similar or possess complementary personality characteristics, as well as very general "bridging" values more or less common to all members of the societal system. For reasons such as these, the child may be presented in the family with a relatively consistent pattern to be learned, despite the differences that exist in the larger societal system.[25]

However, in cultures such as our own, once the individual moves from the immediate family as a source of socialization, he is confronted with a wide variety of social definitions—some simply additive and consistent with those already learned, some almost completely new and unrelated to previous socialization, and some conflicting and inconsistent with what has been internalized. As he interacts with his age group, the church, the school, and the job, and as he comes into contact with mass media of communication such as radio, television, books, and magazines, the range and variation of meanings open up drastically. This confrontation might prove overwhelming were it not for two characteristics of the systems in which he is beginning socialized.

First, the family members tend to screen and sift the definitions experienced by the child by interpreting and rationalizing them for him in terms of their perceptions and by shielding him from sources of deviant values and guiding him toward those that reinforce parental values. Mother says, "Don't play with those naughty children!" or "Good girls

[25] For detailed discussion and documentation of these patterns see Chapter 7, "Marriage, Family, and Kinship."

don't go out with that kind of boy." Father says, "Those politicians don't know what they are talking about," and tells the child that "what the teacher really means is . . ." and then proceeds to interpret in the light of his own perceptions. Both turn off television sets and confiscate forbidden literature. They also lay down rules and regulations concerning the child's interaction with others outside the family; sometimes subtly, "We had something else planned for the week end"; sometimes more drastically, "You can't have the car tonight"; or even, "I will not permit you to see him again." In addition, Catholics, Jews, and Protestants are likely to send their children to their respective places of worship for religious instruction and even to schools that support their religious point of view. Parents are likely to socialize their children to their own political party or guide them in the "right" direction (their own) concerning judgments on political and economic matters.[26] In similar ways, they tend to see that the child is exposed to socializing experiences that will not deviate too greatly from their own values, attitudes, and opinions. Such procedures are not always deliberate and domineering, but are traditional and often unconscious on the part of parents. They receive the support of the larger culture and are defined as part of the parental roles. Of course, the degree to which they are observed and the manner in which they are handled varies greatly from family to family. This variation itself may have significant consequences for the child's development.

Second, the position of the family in the societal system tends to be such that children are selectively introduced to outside socializing agencies in such a way that the various definitions with which they come in contact reinforce one another with some consistency. The general economic position of the family, for example, tends to determine the kinds and amounts of cultural resources available. Access to mass media, extent of education, amount of travel, attendance at concerts, lectures, and the like, are to a considerable degree determined by family economic resources; and the content of such experiences tends to be geared to family culture.[27] Families are distributed geographically and socially so that people of similar backgrounds are likely to interact with one another.

Studies of human ecology, which focus upon the spatial distribution and interrelation of differentiated groups or categories, have shown how people of different race, nationality, income, marital status, age, sex, and even degrees of conformity tend to cluster together in geographical pat-

[26] See Herbert Hyman, *Political Socialization* (New York: The Free Press of Glencoe, Inc., 1959), for an analysis of a wide range of evidence on the role of the family in transmission of political and economic orientation.

[27] Chapter 11, "Social Stratification," will discuss the pattern of "class" socialization.

terns. The proximity of culturally similar peoples provides the opportunity for a pattern of socialization relatively isolated from the larger
culture or from influence by dissimilar groups.[28]

Similarly, studies of voluntary association demonstrate that people of
relatively similar orientation tend to interact informally with persons of
similar cultural background and join formal organizations that bring together persons of similar cultural orientation.[29]

The consequence of these conditions for the person being socialized is
that his status-sequence and his status-set are prone to some consistency;
and therefore, the cultural aspects of his personality, to some degree of
integration. However, as we have seen, this structuring toward consistency is likely to be countered by other features of the societal system.
Geographic and social mobility, occasioned by free occupational choice
and free mate selection and other dynamics of an industrial society, inevitably introduce the individual to meanings he has not encountered
previously. The educational system, in part, is specifically structured to
introduce children of diverse home backgrounds to a universal cultural
experience. Mass media by their very nature cut through the barriers of
home, church, and neighborhood. Complexities of social organization and
the changing and shifting nature of such organization demand that people
meet new and often conflicting role-expectations.

One consequence of this is that one subsystem may be faced with a
problem of fitting to its statuses persons who were socialized in different
systems. The problem arises from the fact that, although previous socialization may have been relatively consistent, and hence functional for
learning, the definitions internalized may be inconsistent with the new
role-requirements. People moving into the system may resist the new
demands because they are inconsistent with ones already internalized.
This creates the necessity for some mechanism for handling recruitment
and processing of new members. Such mechanisms include selective
recruitment, so as to procure members adaptable to the system, or re-

---

[28] For some representative studies see Clifford R. Shaw and Henry D. McKay,
Juvenile Delinquency and Urban Areas (Chicago: The University of Chicago Press,
1942); Ernest R. Mowrer, *Family Disorganization* (Chicago: University of Chi-
cago Press, 1927); Samuel C. Kincheloe, *The American City and Its Churches* (New
York: Friendship Press, 1938); and Calvin F. Schmid, *Social Trends in Seattle*
(Seattle: University of Washington Press, 1944).

[29] For an example of this pattern among young people in a small community see
A. B. Hollingshead, *Elmtown's Youth* (New York: John Wiley & Sons, Inc., 1949).
The adult pattern has been described by W. Lloyd Warner and Paul S. Lunt in *The
Status System of a Modern Community* (Yankee City Series, Vol. II; New Haven,
Conn.: Yale University Press, 1942). Mirra Komarovsky, among others, has shown the
pattern of voluntary association in a large urban center in "The Voluntary Association
of Urban Dwellers," *American Sociological Review*, 11:686–698 (1946).

socialization, so as to fit nonadaptive members to system requirements; as well as mechanisms for handling the disruptive effects of neophytes or for the ejection of those too disruptive to be contained.

The point to be emphasized here is that resistance is lodged in the person. Socialized people are not just passive receptacles into which new system definitions are poured. It makes a difference what is "in" the person, and it makes a difference that people may resist new expectations. Understanding how people react to subsequent socialization, once some socialization has taken place, not only furthers our knowledge of socialization but gives us a basis for understanding some of the aspects of deviance and social control to be discussed later. These matters will be taken up in the next chapter.

SUMMARY

In order for human social existence to take place, people must learn to cognize the statuses in which they act and be motivated to conform to them. By means of socialization, they learn to define conformity as intrinsically or instrumentally gratifying, as necessary for the favorable response of others, or as a means of self-approval. By means of social conditioning of biological needs and through the processes of identification and internalization, people learn to define social objects and to respond to them in ways more or less consistent with the systems in which socialization takes place. A social self emerges that is built upon a person's individual biological characteristics and the cultural patterns to which he is exposed. This gives rise to both a unique self and a social self that reflects the modal pattern of the subsystems and larger systems of social organization. Deviant types may develop as a consequence of atypical biological factors and atypical group experiences. In addition, socialization itself may be atypical as a result of resistance to or control of the socialization process on the part of the socializee.

The development of the individual into a mature, socialized human being is a continuous process, taking place in stages, and resulting in successively higher levels of complexity. What is meant by "higher level of complexity" is simply *a greater range of "others" who are internalized, identified with, and responded to differentially.*

In short, "becoming socially more mature" means, for one thing, expanding one's repertoire of statuses, by learning imaginatively to take the role of a greater range of others and thus being able to interact with them confidently on the basis of one's ability to understand their symbolic definitions. But "becoming socially more mature" also means that the repertoire of roles one can play and respond to, while complex and varied, is *organized* into a coherent whole. "Social maturity"—the product of effective socialization—is, in other words, neither such flexibility as to make behavior unpredictable nor such intense specialization as to make it highly limited. Social maturity is the possession of many, many facets of a self, which, however, *are* an *organized* self. Social maturity, then, may be deviated from in either of two directions: (1) by overrestriction of the others with whom one can identify; (2) by underorganization of one's identities and identifications.

4

THE STRUCTURE
OF SOCIALIZATION

Once beyond the stage of infancy, the child has had established by his family certain cognitive, cathectic, and normative orientations. However, some further socialization is always necessary as the child moves out from his family into the school, the church, the play group and on into the wider range of group memberships of adult life. The same may be true as people change status within a group. Even in a family, a child must give up his infantile pleasures, and a youth must surrender his "childish ways." Frequently, socialization to new groups or new statuses does not involve any great change in the definitions already internalized, even though the behavior required may be different or more exacting and difficult. However, particularly in a highly differentiated, mobile, and changing society such as our own, socialization may involve considerable alteration or change in cognitive beliefs, cathectic tastes, or values already internalized, if people are to become integrated members of new groups. For reasons such as these, once some socialization has taken place, the problem of further socialization becomes one of providing a structure that motivates people to give up or modify their old definitions and accept new ones.

In the last chapter, we pointed out that people act in certain ways because they find it intrinsically pleasurable or instrumental to intrinsic pleasure, because they desire the approval of others, or because they desire self-approval. These are the basic rewards that motivate their behavior. People try to act in ways that will give them the most pleasure, approval, or self-approval in the long run, and that will cost them the least pleasure, approval, or self-approval in the long run—as they define these rewards and as they define "long run." In other words, people try to maximize their "profits." "Profits" are rewards minus costs, and costs are forgone rewards.[1]

If, then, people are acting in certain ways, we assume that it is because, so far as they can see, any other way of acting they know of would cost them more rewards than it would gain them. That is, changing would certainly cost them some of those rewards, and so far as they can see, it would not produce greater compensatory rewards. If they are to change, there must be some incentive to do so. They will have an incentive to change if something happens to their situation that (1) *reduces the rewards they are receiving from their present behavior* (which is the same as reducing the costs of changing) or (2) *increases their estimate of the rewards they will receive from the new behavior*, or both.

Given these conditions, people will have an incentive to change. But having an incentive to change is still not changing. They must know in what way they are expected to change;[2] they must have the capacity to behave as they are expected; and means for making the change must be provided. They must be physically and intellectually able to engage in the new behavior; there must be facilities present to help them learn it; there must be opportunities to practice; there must be a clear definition of what the new and more rewarding behavior is. Without these further conditions, their old behavior will no longer be rewarding, but there will be no way of achieving satisfaction in terms of the new expectations. Their old adaptation will be disorganized without any reorganization in terms of new expectations, or their behavior will be reorganized in a way that deviates from rather than conforms to the new expectations.

The satisfaction of these conditions of change depends upon the way in which the process of socialization is structured. Without denying the importance of the psychological make-up of persons being socialized, the sociological focus is placed on the structure of socialization rather than on the psychology of particular individuals. The assumption underlying this focus is that, holding individual psychology constant, effective socialization may be facilitated or impeded by the structure of the socialization situation. In other words, if people are to be socialized to new definitions,

---

[1] Without our taking up the complexities of unconscious motives, the reader should be aware that we do not mean to imply that in "estimating costs" and "maximizing profits" people are always consciously aware of what they are doing (or that their estimates, in fact, result in what they are seeking). We are assuming that human behavior, consciously or unconsciously, is motivated by a desire to seek gratification and avoid its absence or its opposite in punishment, broadly speaking.

[2] Let us emphasize that we are here dealing with socialization. That is why we speak of people's knowing what they are "expected" to do. Often, people also must learn new definitions that are not "expected," as when totally new situations confront everyone in a group. "Nature" may then be the socializing agent, but the same principles will apply.

the structure of socialization may be relatively functional or disfunctional (either manifestly or latently) for providing the incentives and conditions necessary for change. In this chapter we want to discuss and illustrate in some detail different ways in which social structure may facilitate socialization.[3]

Reducing Rewards from Prior Behavior

We have said that one way of providing an incentive to conform to new expectations is to reduce or eliminate the rewards of conforming to old expectations. If rewards are consistently denied whenever behavior fails to conform to expectations, socialization is facilitated. There is some reason to suppose that consistent *denial* of rewards for the "wrong" behavior is more important than consistent *granting* of rewards for the "right" behavior. What seems to be important is that the socializee be unable to obtain a reward *without* successful performance in the new status.[4] Since the rewards for conformity to old expectations consist of approval of others, self-approval, and intrinsic gratifications, we must examine some mechanisms that might be functional for reducing these rewards.

APPROVAL OF OTHERS

Often one of the deterrents to acquiring new ideas or values or tastes is that the individual's associates continue to give approval for conformity to their *existing* definitions. As we pointed out in the preceding chapter, people come to identify with others in the process of socialization and to desire their approval, which is conditionally granted on the basis of conformity to their standards. However, if a new group makes its acceptance contingent on conforming to different standards, the old source of approval may be disfunctional for socialization to the new group. One structural way of reducing or eliminating this old source of reward is to

[3] A useful discussion of the problems and techniques associated with the study of socialization is contained in Robert K. Merton, George G. Reader, M.D., and Patricia L. Kendall (eds.), *The Student-Physician* (Cambridge, Mass.: Harvard University Press, 1957).

[4] For impressive evidence of this in experimentation with animals under laboratory conditions, see B. F. Skinner, *Science and Human Behavior* (New York: The Macmillan Company, 1953).

separate the person from prior associates. This has the effect of denying him gratification for the old behavior, and at the same time it frees him from conflicting expectations so that his status-set is consistent.

The importance of such isolation has been highlighted by an instructive study carried out by Theodore M. Newcomb in a college setting.[5] In the college where the study was made, it was determined that one important index of assimilation to the community was the attitude of students toward public issues. The dominant pattern was one of nonconservatism with respect to certain political, social, and economic issues; and individual prestige in the college was associated with this nonconservative orientation. It was further determined that most students underwent a rather marked change in such attitudes. The general pattern was a movement away from freshman conservatism to senior nonconservatism. Although most students were successfully socialized to this new (to them) value orientation, some seniors were more conservative than the average student and some were less conservative. An intensive study of a sample of the most and the least conservative of three graduating classes was made. Students who retained their prior conservative orientation were all similar in one important respect: their major source of group identity with respect to attitudes on public issues *remained outside the college community*. In other words, the group whose approval was sought on the issues under consideration was not the college community. The following quotations from interviews of these most conservative students are revealing:

> "The things I really care about are mostly outside the college."
>
> "I'm all my mother has in the world. It's considered intellectually superior here to be liberal or radical. This puts me on the defensive, as I refuse to consider my mother beneath me intellectually, as so many other students do."
>
> "Family against faculty has been my struggle here."
>
> "All that's really important that has happened to me occurred outside of college."
>
> "Politics and that sort of thing I've always associated with home instead of with college."

Among the conservative students, several different sources of their failure to make the college community their reference group were discovered. First, there were those students who eagerly sought acceptance but

---

[5] Pertinent discussion, based on an original study, is reprinted in "Attitude Development as a Function of Reference Groups: The Bennington Study," in G. E. Swanson, T. M. Newcomb, and E. L. Hartley, *et al.* (eds.), *Readings in Social Psychology* (rev. ed.; New York: Holt, Rinehart and Winston, Inc., 1952), pp. 420–430.

felt rejected by the college community. They were unable to get the approval they sought and, in defense, rejected the college values and sought support from other conservative students or from the original source of their conservatism—their families or other groups outside the college. Second, there were students who, fearing rejection, did not seek acceptance from the college and relied upon approval from a small circle of conservative students and from their home and family. Third, there were students who retained their allegiance to parental attitudes of conservatism but sought and managed to gain approval and respect in other valued activities in the college. Strong parental ties inhibited acceptance of nonconservative values, but these students managed to maintain a divided allegiance in which they yielded to the college influences on all attitudes except those that brought them into conflict with their parents. Fourth and finally, there were students who maintained family conservatism because their participation in college life was so limited that they were largely unaware of the nonconservative college values, although they were neither hostile to the college nor fearful of rejection.

The comments of the most nonconservative girls are equally revealing:

> "I started rebelling against my pretty stuffy family before I came to college."
>
> "I accepted liberal attitudes here because I had always secretly felt that my family was narrow and intolerant, and because such attitudes had prestige value."
>
> "I came to college to get away from my family."
>
> "Social security is the focus of it all with me. I became steadily less conservative as I was needing to gain in personal security, both with students and with faculty."
>
> "It's very simple. I was so anxious to be accepted that I accepted the political complexion of the community here."

In contrast to the most conservative students, these least conservative students did not seek approval of their orientation to public issues from conservative, noncollege groups. Some apparently had rejected these groups, their values, or both. Others were seeking approval from some group, and the college served as a source of approval, which could be earned by accepting the nonconservative norms of the college community.

As this college study suggests, the separation of the socializee from prior sources of approval may not be a deliberate practice or policy. Most separation comes as a structural consequence of status-transition. As a person moves from one group to another, he usually is separated physically from those in the group from which he moves. Even where contacts remain, new group affiliations necessarily diminish the frequency of contact and interaction in previously established relationships. This means

that the old group has less opportunity to support and reinforce its values
and protect its members from conflicting or different values.

Using the waning influence of parents on their children as a model,
Herbert H. Hyman has analyzed a wide range of research that has shown
how the *relative* influence of one group declines as its members come
under the influence of other groups.[6] In our society, as age brings greater
independence from parental authority, attitudes and values are altered by
other agencies of socialization. The studies that Hyman cites show, for
example, that such varied orientations as preference for parental authority, idealization of parents, discussion and communication with parents,
and agreement with parents on ideological preferences and moral values
diminish with age, even while the child remains a member of the family
group. In a number of these studies, the range of drift from parental influence is greater for males than females, suggesting a relationship between degree of independence based on sex (as well as age) and change
or alteration of orientation. The factors of age and sex are of particular
sociological significance because they point to *social* sources or structures
that are instrumental in the *psychological* changes that take place. Because, in our society, independence from parental authority is granted
with age but somewhat differentiated by sex, socialization tends toward
a pattern in which change from parental orientations takes place with
age but, in some respects, is likely to be greater for males than for
females. From the point of view of the socializing agencies outside the
family this means that the separation of the socializee from his old reference groups, either by deliberate intent or by fortuitous social structuring,
enhances socialization to new groups, particularly where there is a discontinuity in status-transition.

An extreme case of isolation that is formally organized is found in the
so-called brain-washing practices reported as taking place in the Soviet
Union and Communist China. Attempts are made to isolate a person completely from reinforcement of old definitions by the use of solitary con-
finement and the absence of any verbal or written communication. Even
self-reinforcement—singing, reciting poems, setting up countertension by
physical activity, and the like—are prevented so far as possible. At the
same time, the "socializee" is permitted access only to people who possess
the new definitions and are the only possible source of response and interaction. Since socialized persons appear to have developed a need for
interaction with other human beings, this structure places them in a
position of intense psychological dependency upon the socializing agents.
This isolation and dependency then sets the stage for a series of un-

[6] Herbert H. Hyman, *Political Socialization* (New York: The Free Press of Glencoe,
Inc., 1959), pp. 98–109.

predictable, but not entirely unwelcomed, encounters with "socializers" who vary their responses and demands to compound confusion and uncertainty. Although, no doubt, there are individual differences in capacity to resist, there seems little wonder that many people yield to these pressures; just as they apparently return to their old ways when they escape to the freedom and security of their old environment.[7]

One final example may further illustrate the point. One of the goals of modern penology is the rehabilitation of the offender, which, for some offenders, involves a process of socialization to conventional societal norms. However, studies of prison social systems have revealed a basic structural weakness in the process of socialization.[8] Prison authorities do not have anything like a monopoly of rewards in the prison situation. One vital source of reward they do not control is the approval prisoners extend to one another. Since the values of prisoners frequently are in conflict with those held by prison authorities, the recalcitrant may be rewarded by fellow prisoners because he *fails* to conform to the expectations of the prison administration. The criminologist Lloyd E. Ohlin has described the situation in the following terms:

> In the majority of prisons throughout the country the leaders among the inmates are those who embody in clearest form anti-administration and anti-conventional values. Inmate cliques tend to form about such men, who serve as models of opposition to the administration. Positions of status and prestige sentiments are accorded those members of the inmate community whose behavior embodies an aggressive disregard for administrative interests and conventional values. Such inmate leaders form cliques of other inmates who regard themselves as "right guys" and who define themselves as "cons."[9]

The prison represents a striking example of a situation in which the informal organization of subgroups circumvents and inhibits the goals of the formal organization. In most prisons, the staff is totally unable to consistently deny inmates rewards for the "wrong" behavior. As long as an inmate's reference group is the dominant inmate clique and he is able to get the rewards of approval and prestige from them by conforming to

[7] For a discussion of such indoctrination techniques based on medical and psychological examination and interview of persons who have experienced "brain washing" or participated in it, see Lawrence E. Hinkle, Jr., M.D., and Harold G. Wolff, M.D., "Communist Interrogation and Indoctrination of 'Enemies of the States,'" *A.M.A. Archives of Neurology and Psychiatry*, 57:115–174 (1956).

[8] Two outstanding studies of prison social systems and prison life are Donald Clemmer, *The Prison Community* (New York: Holt, Rinehart and Winston, Inc., 1958), a reissue of the 1940 edition, and Gresham M. Sykes, *The Society of Captives* (Princeton, N.J.: Princeton University Press, 1958).

[9] Lloyd E. Ohlin, *Sociology and the Field of Corrections* (New York: Russell Sage Foundation, 1956), p. 18.

their standards, the staff cannot socialize him to conventional values. Even when the inmate identifies with conventional values, he may find it impossible or very difficult to withstand the pressures exerted by fellow prisoners to conform to their deviant standards.

This difficulty is aggravated by the relative social distance between a prisoner and the staff, in contrast to that between other prisoners. In maximum security prisons, where inmates with established criminal orientations and identities are confined, it is the policy to maintain strict, formal relations between prisoners and staff. Fraternizing is not permitted on the assumption that it will lead to lax custodial practices, endanger security, or result in the subversion of the formal authority of the administration. Although this may be functional for maintaining security, it may be disfunctional for socialization, as Ohlin points out:

> This policy . . . is detrimental to the reorganization of the inmate value system along conventional lines, for it permits an inmate to relate in different ways to other inmates and the administrative staff. In short, it permits the inmate to segmentalize his relational system and to protect himself against the potential conflict of exposure to competing value systems and identifications. He is thus enabled to present himself in a conventional light to officials so as to secure early release on parole, and at the same time to censure the officials when conversing with other inmates in order to reassert his solidarity with the inmate body.[10]

This is simply a special instance of the principle that separation from a reference group may facilitate socialization. In this case, it is a matter of social rather than physical distance. The alternatives for effective socialization in the prison are to reduce the prisoners' social distance from the officials, increase the physical separation among prisoners, or change the orientation of inmates *as a group* to conform to those of conventional society. It should be pointed out that, although sound, these are not necessarily "practical" alternatives, since the goals of maintaining security and a low operating budget may be in conflict with the goal of socialization.

The alternative of changing the group orientation is worth some further consideration at this point because it represents a very special case of reducing the cost of disapproval by changing the reference group itself. Very little systematic analysis and even less research has been made of the process of changing the values of individuals by means of altering those of other individuals with whom they associate in a group. Several different sources of experimentation and research are instructive, however. While we are still in the discussion area of penal correction, one promising experiment should be mentioned.

There has developed in recent years a practice known as "group ther-

---

[10] *Ibid.*, p. 20.

apy" in which each individual in the group plays a role in mutual social-ization. This technique has received a special application in a correctional institution in New Jersey, where the term "guided group interaction" is used to indicate the nature of the institutional program. Details of the program cannot be developed here, but the general nature of guided group interaction is indicated in the following comment.

> Guided group interaction has the merit of combining the psychological and the sociological approaches to the control of human behavior. The *psychological* approach aims to *change the self-conception of the boy from a delinquent to a non-delinquent.* But this process involves chang-ing the mood of the boy from impulses to lawbreaking to impulses to be law-abiding.

> To accomplish rehabilitation, the *sociological* approach is also needed. The insight of sociology is to *reverse the process by which the group in-ducts a boy into delinquency* and compels him to continue in it. In guided group interaction, the *influence of the group is directed to free the boy from being controlled by delinquent association* and to give him the desire and inner strength to be autonomous.[11]

The point of leverage in the socialization to conventional values is the delinquent boys themselves. The institution is structured to reverse the process described above in the prison situation so that the delinquent reference group becomes a means for altering the delinquent's self-conception, for giving him a new definition of his problems, and for mak-ing progress toward their solution. Within the group, prestige is accorded the boys making progress, so that group approval is linked to progress in socialization rather than to conformity to the delinquent culture.

SELF-APPROVAL

The socializing group is not always able to control the interactions of its members with other groups so as to decrease rewards from these groups. Furthermore, people may be able to receive rewards for resisting socialization, even though they are isolated from those who would give them approval for resisting. They may resist because to conform would violate their *self*-conception. In other words, self-approval is a source of reward; and frequently, if a person is to be socialized to new behavior, he must change or alter his self-conception.

Since a person's present self-conception may stand as a barrier to social-ization to new definitions, suppression of prior statuses upon which it is

[11] Ernest W. Burgess, Foreword in Lloyd W. McCorkle, Albert Elias, and F. Lovell Bixby, *The Highfields Story* (New York: Holt, Rinehart and Winston, Inc., 1957), pp. iv–viii. Emphasis added.

based may be functional for the development of a self-image consistent with the new expectations. Sanford M. Dornbusch has provided an excellent illustration of a structured suppression of status in the socialization of cadets at the United States Coast Guard Academy.

> The new cadet, or "swab," is the lowest of the low. The assignment of low status encourages the cadet to place a high value on successfully completing the steps in an Academy career, and requires that there be a loss of identity based on pre-existing statuses. This clean break with the past must be achieved in a relatively short period. For two months, therefore, the swab is not allowed to leave the base or to engage in social intercourse with non-cadets. This complete isolation helps to produce a unified group of swabs, rather than a heterogeneous collection of persons of high and low status. Uniforms are issued on the first day, and discussions of wealth and family background are taboo. Although the pay of the cadet is very low, he is not permitted to receive money from home. The role of the cadet must supersede other roles the individual has been accustomed to play. There are few clues left which will reveal social status in the outside world.[12]

What these practices seem to involve is a structure calculated to mute prior identity, minimize its reinforcement, create a new status of low rank, establish equal rank among socializees, and provide rewards for status-transition in a new status-sequence within the military group. The suppression of prior statuses and the substitution of low but equal rank among the socializees appears to provide a situation favorable for the introduction of new values and orientations. The similarity of function, rank, and symbols of rank has a leveling effect that strips the person of both prior statuses and ranks. These practices not only have their individual impact on the person, but may operate collectively so that no one person can know very readily what the other's previous positions were. Thus, the structure that supported the web of prior interactions in civilian life is dramatically and visibly transformed.

Suppression of prior statuses may be facilitated by peer support. Peers, it will be remembered, are people of relatively similar status or rank. Because of the similarities of peers, mutual identification, or at least empathy (sympathetic understanding of others), tends to develop in the process of their interaction. The common leveling that characterizes the cadet status and that is found in initiation into a wide range of different groups creates a peer group based on a novice or neophyte status. In such a group the changing identity of each member is supported by all the others. No one member need feel he is "going it alone." In addition, maintaining identity with the peer group entails moving with it through the process of socialization, and the strong pull exerted by the group

[12] Sanford M. Dornbusch, "The Military Academy as an Assimilating Institution," *Social Forces*, 33:316–321 (1955).

works in the same direction as the efforts of the more direct socializing agents. Furthermore, mutual support may be exchanged within the peer group so as to make bearable the extended frustration that may accompany intense socialization. Ruth Benedict has indicated the nature of peer support as it is instiutionalized in age-graded cultures:

> Age-graded cultures characteristically demand different behavior of the individual at different times of his life and persons of like age-grade are grouped into a society whose activities are all oriented toward the behavior desired at that age. Individuals "graduate" publicly and with honor from one of these groups to another. Where age society members are enjoined to loyalty and mutual support . . . an individual who at any time takes on a new set of duties and virtues is supported not only by a solid phalanx of age mates but by the traditional prestige of the organized "secret" society into which he has now graduated. Fortified in this way, individuals in such cultures often swing between remarkable extremes of opposite behavior without apparent psychic threat.[13]

Frequently a status-transition may be facilitated by reducing the feelings of guilt that a person may experience as a cost of change, rather than demanding a change in his self-conception. The established self-image then may be used as a mechanism of socialization to new attitudes, if the socialization structure is somehow arranged to gear the new to the old. An example of a potential cost of change is found in the transition from civilian to military service during wartime. If, for example, people have learned to respect themselves for their independence of judgment, their "refusal to take insults," and their respect for life and property, then the acceptance of military regimentation, a sergeant's scathing dressing down, or the idea of killing and destroying may be very difficult. Their innermost integrity, as they have come to define it, may be violated if they conform to the new definition.[14]

In such a situation, one way in which the cost of changing might be reduced is to emphasize the linkage between the old and the new and attempt to de-emphasize the discontinuity. Thus, in the military case, the "ability to take it" may be emphasized, so that the recruit is encouraged to perceive the new learning situation, not as a violation of his manhood, but as a confirmation of it. Such a perception is usually further aided by devaluing all previous inconsistent statuses. Military service, for example, "makes men out of boys," or "separates the men from the boys." Civilian status is demeaned by such terms as "slacker" or "draft dodger."

In similar ways, attempts may be made to turn the respect for life and

[13] Ruth Benedict, "Continuities and Discontinuities in Cultural Conditioning," *Psychiatry*, 1:161–167 (1938).

[14] A vivid glimpse into one aspect of this problem in another setting is provided in Rocky Graziano's autobiography, *Someone Up There Likes Me* (New York: Simon and Schuster, 1955).

property into a positive reason for killing and destroying, which are defined as instrumental means for legitimate ends. Thus, war becomes a "war to end war," a "police action," or a means to "make the world safe for democracy." Institutionalized rationalizations and justifications may be stressed in order to foster a consistent self-conception on the part of socializees and overcome the feelings of guilt or resentment that might inhibit effective socialization.

INTRINSIC PLEASURE

Socialization to a new status or group frequently requires that people relinquish certain behavior patterns or relationships that are gratifying in themselves. This may be necessary for two reasons. First, pleasures legitimate in one status may not be legitimate in another, and, second, some kinds of pleasurable behavior may impede the process of socialization.

How might situations be structured so as to prevent the socializee from "keeping his profits high" by continuing to derive pleasure from his old habits, thus reducing his incentive to change? One way is to raise sharply the cost of his doing so by making another reward, the approval of others, contingent on his giving up the old pleasures. Thus, although at one age the child gets both pleasure and approval for drinking from a baby's bottle, at a later age he may continue to get the pleasure but at the price of *dis*approval. So also with such substitutes for the nipple as thumb-sucking. As the child grows older, the price of refusing to "put away childish things" is the acceptance and respect of his peers and socializing agents.

Closely related to this mechanism is the structuring of the situation so that the old pleasures are physically inaccessible. Both conditions—the physical removal of opportunities for old pleasures and the making of respect contingent on giving them up—depend for their effectiveness on arrangements for controlling the socializee's environment and keeping him highly visible to the socializing agents. This is another function of isolating the socializee from his past environment. Giving up the short-run but powerful pleasure of alcohol or drugs, for example, often requires isolation of the socializee (who would here be called a "patient") from access to his supplies and keeping him under constant surveillance. Similarly, however different the context, the isolation of cadets in military academies makes it easier to prevent them from receiving their old pleasures. Although there is no evidence on the subject, it seems reasonable to speculate that such military colleges probably are more effective in teaching students than is the usual liberal arts college, because the liberal arts faculty has nowhere near the same monopoly of sources of pleasure or of approval as has the military school.

One source of intrinsic gratification that may impede socialization and the integration of people into new groups is the cathexis they have established for members of old groups in prior statuses. Status-transition often involves physical mobility that removes people from one group and places them in another. Such transition usually requires that established interpersonal relations be relinquished and new ones formed. Feelings of identification and ties of loyalty to the old group must be given up or modified. When a worker moves from one occupation or business organization to another, a student from one college to another, or a family from one neighborhood to another, old group ties may be disfunctional for socialization of the person and integration of the new group. This is particularly true when old ties are strong, and the new group is faced with socializing a considerable number of people whose loyalties lie outside it.

Robert K. Merton and Alice S. Kitt have pointed to this problem in their discussion of a possible function of the replacement depot during the last war.[15] Replacement depots were organized to accommodate men who had completed their basic training and were awaiting assignment to established units. These men had recently made a transition from civilian to military status in basic training, which was facilitated by establishing ties to training groups that would help to support and reinforce the military status. However, the established ties to the training group are broken by the transfer of newly trained personnel to militarily active units that have neither the time nor the facilities to begin the process all over again. Here is where the replacement depot may intervene as a mechanism to ease the transition. Merton and Kitt discuss this function in the following way:

> Thus from the perspective of the replacements' eventual ease of absorption into a combat group, new to them, as well as from the point of view of their potential effect upon the group they enter, there may well be a functional requirement for their *not* being transferred immediately from the training outfit to the outfit with which they will shortly serve in combat. One alternative is that which was in fact the practice utilized during the war years: filtering the newly trained soldier through replacement depots. This suggests the latent function possibly performed by the replacement depot: it may serve to loosen the soldier's previous army group ties, thus making him more amenable to ready absorption into his combat outfit. In much the same way that the sand-hog adjusts to normal atmospheric pressure at the end of a day's work under water

[15] Robert K. Merton and Alice S. Kitt, "Reference Group Theory and Social Mobility," in Robert K. Merton and Paul F. Lazarsfeld (eds.), *Continuities in Social Research* (New York: The Free Press of Glencoe, Inc., 1950), pp. 95–99.

by going through de-compression chambers, so the soldier is *degrouped* by passing through replacement depots. This would seem all the more important in view of the speed with which replacements were actually sent into combat upon joining a combat outfit.[16]

A somewhat similar function has been ascribed to "romantic love" in societies where it has become an institutionalized basis for marriage. It has been hypothesized that in societies where very strong attachments between parents and their children are established, "falling in love" becomes a necessary condition for relinquishing these ties in favor of the ties of marriage. Being in love with an age peer motivates the youth to loosen the strong attachments he has formed with his parents so that he can assume effectively the rights and obligations of a marital status.[17] As in the case of the replacement depot, a structure is provided that helps to reduce the cost of giving up old pleasures and facilitates the establishment of new attachments instrumental in socialization to the new group.

Increasing Rewards for New Behavior

In the preceding discussion, we have focused attention on some social structures that help to reduce, alter, or eliminate rewards for prior behavior so as to decrease the cost of change. The complement to decreasing rewards for old behavior is to increase rewards for the new, as we have pointed out. To do this is not as simple as it may seem upon first consideration, for there are all the sources of resistance we have discussed that are inherent in successful socialization that precedes the required change or alteration. If prior socialization has been successful, salient needs have presumably been gratified, at least through the termination of the socialization process. This poses the necessity of increasing gratification even further, creating new needs, activating latent ones, or in some other manner structuring the socializee's reward system so as to provide incentive to change. All this demands careful and coordinated, although not necessarily formally organized, structuring. Attention, therefore, should be directed to some mechanisms that are functional to this end, for which we have some scattered evidence in a variety of socialization situations.

[16] *Ibid.*, pp. 97–98.
[17] Some of the functional and disfunctional consequences of love in marriage have been discussed by William J. Goode in "The Theoretical Importance of Love," *American Sociological Review*, 24:38–47 (1959).

ANTICIPATORY SOCIALIZATION

Anticipatory socialization refers to socialization in one status or group that is functional for occupancy of another status in the same or in a different group. The functionality of such socialization lies in the fact that people begin to acquire the values and orientations of groups or social categories of which they are not members, but in which membership is desired or anticipated. Such socialization appears to facilitate the movement of the socializee to the new status and aid his adjustment to the new group. (Such is the case if, in fact, the movement is made. If it is not made, then such anticipatory socialization may be disfunctional for both the individual and the group in which he remains.) At the same time, it is functional for the new group by providing a source of reward for learning to conform to the group structure. The new rewards flow from membership rights and prerogatives and the sharing of common values to which the person has been previously socialized in other groups. Several mechanisms that operate in different contexts to produce these consequences seem to be involved in anticipatory socialization.

RANKED STATUSES

When statuses, groups, or social categories are ranked, anticipatory socialization involves progressive raising of aspirations so that people are not only favorably disposed to the values of higher rank but urgently desire to acquire the rank. In a relatively open social structure, where there is some assurance of movement up the rank system, rewards to which all or most people are socialized are progressively increased as they move up in rank. In anticipation of increasing their profits, people are motivated to learn and conform to the structure of each successive status.

In our own society, this kind of motivation is structured for a considerable number of people. Families and individuals are ranked by such indices as prestige of occupation and amount of income or wealth; but whatever may be their point of origin in these respects, people tend to be socialized from childhood to the desirability of progressively moving upward into the higher positions in the rank system. Such socialization usually involves creating some anxiety about present rank, providing a strong positive orientation toward higher rank, and acquiring the techniques and skills necessary to attain it.[18]

---

[18] Further discussion and documentation of these comments on "class" and those that follow will be presented in Chapter 11, "Social Stratification."

GRADED STATUSES

Although ranked statuses involve unequal distribution of prestige, graded statuses involve statuses that are organized in a sequence but are equally prestigeful, even though rewards may differ in kind. Age grading is a typical example. In anticipatory socialization to this sequence, people are socialized to the expectation of relinquishing one status and taking on another, so that *different* behavior is seen as appropriate and rewarding as they move through the sequence. The separation of different rights and obligations in different statuses in the sequence permits a changing evaluation of the statuses that compose it. Thus, behavior appropriate in one status can be downgraded in another without demeaning the former status for those presently in it. Support for appropriate behavior is provided in the role-set of each status in the sequence. The child is admired for his cute ways in childhood but admonished for them in adolescence. Similarly, the adolescent is cautioned to refrain from adult ways, but reminded that these pleasures may be indulged at a later time. Anticipatory socialization and structured support for each status in the sequence may induce a continuity in status-transition that otherwise might seem sudden, capricious, and unrewarding.

CONTINGENT REWARDS

Contingent rewards are neither fortuitous nor quality-based, but are granted conditionally on role performance or assumption of a status. We have spoken of such rewards as they operate in initial socialization, but to some extent they operate whenever people are socialized to new statuses. In a status-transition, use is made of contingent rewards through anticipatory socialization so that people are socialized to goals in one status that are available only in another. Desire for the goal provides incentive to make whatever change is required to assume the status where the goal may be legitimately realized. To a considerable extent such structuring is present in both ranked and graded statuses. However, the mechanism is by no means restricted to these structures. Whenever self-approval, approval of others, or intrinsic gratifications are made contingent upon conformity to a status, this mechanism operates in socialization.

In our society, as in others, marital status provides an example. Marriage offers a relatively stable and readily available sexual union. In some primitive societies particularly, this is not so significant because premarital or extramarital sexual relations are legitimized. However, in these instances, most adult prerogatives are contingent upon family membership. In our culture, it is somewhat different, since many, if not all, adult rights may be obtained by the single person. However, many people eye, "single blessedness" with some suspicion, antagonism, and even pity. Celibacy is regarded as at least a rather curious state for adults, unless it is protected by a very special status, such as the priesthood. In addition, children, held with some regard in all societies, cannot ordinarily be reared in great intimacy outside the marital structure. Beyond this, marriage and family in adulthood provide one of the few primary group relationships in a society where so many of our interactions are secondary. Furthermore, romantic love is highly institutionalized, and the legitimate culmination of this love is marriage. In sum, we collectively hold the expectation that most people ought to get married, and we provide significant and rewarding experiences that cannot be obtained easily outside the marital status.

An unusual case of the use of contingent rewards to help bridge a severe discontinuity is found in the introduction of polygyny (plural wives) into the religious dogma of the Church of the Latter-day Saints. The sociologist Kimball Young, himself a descendant of a father of the Church, Brigham Young, points out that this ran counter to some of the deepest values of the Latter-day Saints when it was first announced by the Mormon prophet Joseph Smith in 1843.[19] However, in a relatively short time, the pattern was accepted by nearly all members and practiced by a small but significant number of them. It seems likely that this was a consequence of the very special structuring that accompanied this transition. In the first place, a higher glory was available to the male through plural wifehood and the reproduction of many children. Polygynous women were also assured of such rewards. This was based on earlier religious dogma that granted males the status rights of priesthood and assured that women who married them and bore children would share the male's status in life and after death. At the same time a puritanical spirit regarding the sexual aspects of marital relationships was maintained and romantic love attachment in courtship and marriage was muted. This functioned to play down jealousy and envy within the plural family. These patterns worked toward a certain degree of status-consistency for the female, particularly, where it was most needed. Her status as a woman, a wife, a mother and her religious status fitted together. In addition, conversion to Mormonism involved an intense, emotional experience with full acceptance of the divine mission of the Church founders, and

[19] Kimball Young, "Variations in Personality Manifestations in Mormon Polygynous Families," in Quinn McNemar and Maud A. Sherrill (eds.), *Studies in Personality Contribution in Honor of Lewis M. Terman* (New York: McGraw-Hill Book Company, Inc., 1942).

conversion to the faith meant transition to and acceptance of polygyny. Here, then, we have a status-transition that was supported by a system of supernatural rewards that could not be obtained without full acceptance of polygyny, where the practice of plural wifehood accorded to both men and women greater rewards than the monogamous status, and where the transition was supported by intensely religious ritual and ceremony in a setting of relative cultural isolation. Although polygyny was by no means a completely stable pattern among the Mormons, it stands as a remarkable example of a discontinuity that was bridged with some success.

DEFERRED GRATIFICATION

Deferred gratification refers to the postponement of immediate satisfaction in the anticipation of future rewards. In its psychological sense, it involves "impulse renunciation" rather than gratification. Its psychological opposite is implied in the phrase "leaving the field," which refers to a tendency to withdraw from frustrating situations rather than sustain frustration and master its source. Sociologically, deferred gratification is referred to as a "pattern" because it tends to involve a wide range of interconnected behavior and appears to be a consequence of specific socialization, embracing categories of persons, rather than being an idiosyncratic attribute of specific persons.[20] It is contended, for example, that the deferred gratification pattern is found more frequently among middle-class than lower-class persons in our society. This distribution seems to be partly a consequence of differences in socialization between the classes. In part, it probably is also a consequence of the different positions of the classes in the larger social structure, which gives relatively greater assurance that middle-class people, in fact, will be able to realize rewards if immediate gratifications are deferred.

Deferment of gratification frequently is necessary for socialization to a new status or group, and a person's success may depend upon his being previously socialized to this pattern. In turn, this may have important implications for selective recruitment on the part of the socializing group when socialization is conditional on severe or prolonged deprivation. The effectiveness of this mechanism seems to depend on a structure that provides some reasonable assurance that rewards will follow deferment. In

[20] For an indication of the pattern and a preliminary research on it in American society see Louis Schneider and Sverre Lysgaard, "The Deferred Gratification Pattern: A Preliminary Study," *American Sociological Review,* 18:142–149 (1953).

such a structure, some immediate gratification flows from anticipation of rewards and helps to compensate for the deprivations that may be involved in socialization. This helps to reduce the "cost" of change while the person seeks to increase his "profits" by means of deferring gratifications.

RELATIVE DEPRIVATION

Relative deprivation refers to the fact that felt deprivation or satisfaction does not depend on the objective situation alone, but is related also to the state of the reference group used as a basis of comparison. If the members of a socializee's reference group are as deprived as or more deprived than he, he is likely to feel relatively satisfied with his situation; if they are more favorably positioned than he, he is likely to feel relatively deprived. In other words, how a person will estimate his "costs" of changing and appraise his "profits" will depend importantly on the structure of his reference groups and their visibility to him.

Although the socializing group cannot readily control the structure of the socializees' reference groups, it may counter their effects by instituting some of the mechanisms previously mentioned. For example, it may decrease their visibility by physical separation from them. By means of leveling and "putting all the swabs in the same boat," it may diminish invidious comparisons among socializees. The reference group basis of feelings of deprivation may be neutralized by linking the socializee's favorable self-image to a willingness to suffer deprivation or by defining the suffering as a validation of his right to the new status or membership in the group. Thus, practices that otherwise are seen as frustrating and depriving may be redefined as tests of self-worth or as legitimate obstacles to be overcome.

In addition, more positive structuring may vest the new status or group with greater prestige, so that in relation to prior reference groups, they are more rewarding. Although the status of socializee, itself, may rank low within the socializing group, the group as a whole may rank higher than prior membership groups that are used as points of reference. Speaking of the socialization of cadets, Dornbusch asserts, "An increase in the cadet's self-esteem develops in conjunction with identification of his new role. Told that they are members of an elite group, respected by the community, most cadets begin to feel at ease in a superordinate role. One may be a low-ranking cadet, but cadets as a group have high status."[21]

[21] Dornbusch, "The Military Academy as an Assimilating Institution," p. 320.

Structural Facilities

Earlier in our discussion, we pointed out that the reduction of rewards for prior behavior and the increase of rewards for new behavior were instrumental in facilitating socialization. We called attention to the fact, however, that they were not sufficient for effective socialization and that other conditions also may affect the success of socialization. The structure of both the statuses to be learned and the situation in which the learning takes place may be either more or less conducive to socialization. On the one hand, the content and the relationship of statuses to be learned may present the socializee with a relatively formidable or an easily manageable set of definitions to learn. On the other hand, the learning situation, as distinguished from what is to be learned, may be structured so as to facilitate or retard socialization. In the remainder of this chapter we shall briefly discuss ten such conditions that may affect the success of socialization procedures, the first referring to the nature of the statuses to be learned, and the other nine referring primarily to situational factors.[22]

STATUS-CLARITY AND CONSISTENCY

"Status-clarity" points to the utility of having a pattern of expectation sharply defined, so that people being socialized to changing situations will know what is to be learned, what the appropriate responses are, what can be expected, and the like. "Consistency" points to the utility of structuring a status so that the expectations will not conflict with one another. A lack of consistency places the persons being socialized in the position of having to learn one expectation that is in conflict with another in the same status. Both a lack of clarity and a lack of consistency tend to place people who are being socialized under considerable strain, which may result in their regression to old statuses, in their improvisation of behavior that may impede socialization, or in problems of adaptation when the new status is assumed.

Of the many instructive discussions on this matter that may be found in the anthropological and sociological literature only two examples may be mentioned here. In analyzing adolescence in primitive and modern

---

[22] Leonard S. Cottrell, Jr., has postulated a series of tentative propositions concerning socialization to age and sex roles in "The Adjustment of the Individual to His Age and Sex Roles," *American Sociological Review,* 7:617–620 (1942). We are indebted to this article in the following discussion.

society, Margaret Mead contrasts the highly structured support and clarification accompanying puberty changes in some primitive societies, with their relative absence in our own.

> We have kept a large enough amount of Victorian prudery so that menstruation seems salacious to men and shameful to girls. We still have many girls who *do not know* of menstruation until they attain puberty. . . . The physical facts have been relegated to the backstairs, and our girls are taught the *need for lying and circumlocution* to account for their backaches and headaches and refusals to play tennis. . . . The California Indians, the Thompson River Indians, the Gilbert Islanders, prescribed a ritual, a series of definite, easily comprehended acts, often exacting, often boring, but *not baffling*.
>
> We prescribe no ritual; the girl continues on a round of school or work, but she is constantly confronted by a *mysterious apprehensiveness* in her parents and guardians. . . . Such an attitude begets its own offspring —self-conscious nervous unrest in the adolescent.[23]

In this same age and sex status, Mirra Komarovsky has provided an example of a lack of consistency. In studying college undergraduates, she found that a considerable number of young women found themselves faced with inconsistent goals and attitudes in their families. These inconsistencies were reinforced by their male age peers. To cite but one example:

> A senior with a wide acquaintance among men in service reports their reactions, as well as those of her parents, to her plan to become a newspaperwoman. The girl is bewildered to discover that after having been stimulated to excel in certain areas of endeavor she is now censured for her very success in meeting those challenges. She, as it were, awakened one morning to find her world upside down: what had hitherto evoked universal praise now suddenly arouses criticism. Some of her male friends are also confused in their attitudes. Admiration and sympathy for her aspirations is mixed with apprehension and, then, a sense of guilt about that very apprehension.[24]

CONSISTENCY IN EXPECTATIONS OF SOCIALIZERS

Consistency in socialization seems to be an important condition of success in at least two respects. Not only must the status be consistently defined by any one socializer but different socializers must not hold different definitions of the same status. If, for example, a mother's con-

---

[23] Margaret Mead, "Adolescence in Primitive and in Modern Society," in *Readings in Social Psychology* (rev. ed., 1952), pp. 536–537. Emphasis added.

[24] Mirra Komarovsky, *Women in the Modern World* (Boston: Little, Brown & Company, 1953), p. 69.

ception of how a boy should act conflicts with the father's, the child is placed under the strain of trying to meet these conflicting expectations, even though each parent's definition of the status is clear and consistent. Ordinarily, of course, system members tend to hold relatively similar definitions of a given status, and this is particularly true of the immediate socializers. Probable differences in expectations may be found in mixed marriages involving marriage across religious, racial, ethnic, or class lines. Similarly, children of immigrant parents may encounter sharp conflicts between their home and the school or their age peers.[25]

A variety of studies has shown that people tend to accept new definitions or alter old ones to the extent that others in the system to which they are exposed uniformly and firmly hold to the same definition. In such a situation it is difficult for the socializee to retain assurance of the validity of his old perceptions and evaluations in the face of a solid phalanx of denial and the absence of any assurance but self-assurance. This has been demonstrated in experiments in the effects of the group upon individual perceptions and judgments, which have shown that there is a greater tendency to conform to group definitions, even though distorted, if they were unanimous.[26]

CONSISTENCY OF STATUSES LEARNED SIMULTANEOUSLY

Frequently, people are socialized to more than one status at the same time. A boy, for example, is socialized to the expectations that govern the male status in his culture. At the same time, he is also socialized to the status of son to his father and mother. If there are other children in the family, he is socialized to the status of brother. Although each of these

[25] One consequence frequently associated with this situation is the production of the "marginal man," one who has abandoned the values of one group but is not fully accepted or is rejected by another. See, for example, E. V. Stonequist, *The Marginal Man* (New York: Charles Scribner's Sons, 1937). The consequences of inconsistencies within the family or between the family and other socializing agencies for the fostering of delinquency have been treated in numerous studies and speculations. See Edwin H. Sutherland and Donald R. Cressey, *Principles of Criminology* (5th ed.; Philadelphia: J. B. Lippincott Company, 1955), Chaps. 8 and 10, for summary discussion and documentation.

[26] We mentioned the work of Sherif and Asch in this regard in the first chapter. Also, see, for example, Morton Deutsch and Harold B. Gerard, "A Study of Normative and Informational Social Influences upon Individual Judgment," *Journal of Abnormal and Social Psychology*, 51:629–636 (1955). See also S. E. Asch, "Effects of Group Pressure upon the Modification and Distortion of Judgments," in H. S. Guetzkow (ed.), *Groups, Leadership, and Men* (Piitsburgh: Carnegie Press, 1951), pp. 177–190.

statuses has a set of expectations that distinguish it from the other, all tend to mutually support and reinforce one another. Note, similarly, the consistent pattern that accompanies the female, daughter, sister status-set. Such consistency of a status-set to which people are socialized is similar to the internal consistency of a single status mentioned earlier. To our knowledge this structural condition has not been the subject of systematic research but appears to be an important condition that merits more focused attention.

CONSISTENCY IN A STATUS-SEQUENCE

Socialization to a sequence of statuses may be facilitated by structuring each successive status so that it is relatively consistent with what has been learned in each prior status. Such structuring produces a continuity and gradation that reinforces prior socialization and prepares the way for change. If a student, for example, has been well prepared in high school (and preparation is concerned not only with course content, but techniques of learning, attitudes toward intellectual activity, and motives governing scholarship), he is better able to meet the expectations of college.

A number of analysts of American society have asserted that some aspects of its youth culture stand as a barrier to adequate adjustment to adulthood, particularly among some middle-class people.[27] Adolescence is said to be characterized by a pattern of relative submissiveness, non-responsibility, emphasis upon quality rather than performance, rejection of interest in adult ways, and stress on having a good time and enjoying glamour. Although such characteristics are not absent from the adult status, they generally are less significant and may be entirely inappropriate. Since behavior based on these qualities frequently is a major source of gratification in youth, it is not easily abandoned in adulthood. This produces a discontinuity in the age sequence that may be disfunctional for socialization to adult roles.[28]

[27] For example, see Talcott Parsons, "Age and Sex in the Social Structure of the United States," *American Sociological Review*, 7:604–616 (1942); Benedict, "Continuities and Discontinuities in Cultural Conditioning," and Arnold W. Green, "The Middle Class Male Child and Neurosis," *American Sociological Review*, 11:31–41 (1946). These articles are reprinted in Logan Wilson and William L. Kolb (eds.), *Sociological Analysis* (New York: Harcourt, Brace & World, Inc., 1949).

[28] See Kingsley Davis, "Adolescence and the Social Structure" and "Causes of Parent-Youth Conflict" in Kingsley Davis, Harry C. Bredemeier, and Marion J. Levy, Jr. (eds.), *Modern American Society* (New York: Holt, Rinehart and Winston, Inc., 1949), pp. 627–646.

CLARITY OF STATUS-TRANSITION

In any social system, statuses are not always clear and consistent, nor can they always be so. Consistency in status-sequences and -sets are subject to the flux and flow of time and to the differentiation that accompanies specialization. Therefore, some strain is likely to exist in most socialization; discontinuities and inconsistencies in social systems are by no means an unusual state of affairs. However, these barriers may become less threatening or inhibiting to the process of socialization if special structuring is introduced.

One thing that may be disfunctional for socialization in a status-sequence is a lack of clarity concerning the *transition* from one status to another. What needs to be made clear is the timing of the transition and the fact that old gratifications and expectations must be renounced for new ones. Traditional mechanisms for clarifying status-transition are ceremony and ritual.

Rituals of transition have been highly developed among primitive peoples and have been referred to as "rites of passage." In the article mentioned earlier, Ruth Benedict describes a ceremony that appears to support and clarify status-transition where certain cognitive and normative definitions foster discontinuity:

> In such societies it is believed that men and women have opposite and conflicting powers, and male children, who are of undefined status, must be initiated into the male role. In Central Australia the boy child is of the woman's side and women are tabu in the final adult stages of tribal ritual. The elaborate and protracted initiation ceremonies of the Arunta therefore snatch the boy from the mother, dramatize his gradual repudiation of her. In a final ceremony he is reborn as a man out of the men's ceremonial "baby pouch." The men's ceremonies are ritual statements of the masculine solidarity, carried out by fondling one another's *churingas,* the material symbol of each man's life, and by letting out blood drawn from their veins. After this warm bond among men has been established through the ceremonies, the boy joins the men in the men's house and participates in tribal rites. The enjoined discontinuity has been tribally bridged.[29]

In our own society, marriage ceremonies seem to illustrate similar transitional functions. The timing of the transition and the fact that old expectations and gratification should be renounced are symbolized and dramatized by various ceremonies and rituals leading up to marital status. Progressive commitment to the status is crystallized by the engagement.

[29] Reprinted in Wilson and Kolb, *op. cit.,* p. 229.

Showers for the bride-to-be link her to future roles. Sometimes the ceremony of a bachelor party takes place, where the prospective groom presumably takes his last fling and is admonished to make the most of it, since those days are gone forever, once married. In the wedding ceremony, the bride and groom are joined in marital vows and their status is solemnized and supported by religious ritual and the authority of the state. The wedding usually is followed by a honeymoon, which separates the couple from familiarities of persons and place before they return to the community to assume their roles together.

TENSION MANAGEMENT[30]

Since socialization may involve considerable strain, people being socialized are faced with the problem of somehow handling the tensions and anxieties that may accompany socialization. Individual or group techniques, devised by those being socialized, may be functional psychologically or socially for *them,* but disfunctional for the group to which they are being socialized. Such practices may interfere seriously with system processes or inhibit adequate socialization to the group. Therefore, the socializing group usually provides some normatively sanctioned means for handling strain that are less disruptive or more subject to control than those that may be improvised by socializees.

In the crying and fretting of the infant we see what seems to be a primitive form of tension management. Such activity appears to diffuse, temporarily, hunger tensions and other discomforts and helps the infant to sustain them until he is cared for. The child may handle his tensions at a somewhat higher level by setting up countertensions, as when he hops up and down while his mother prepares him for the toilet. Ordinarily, these forms of diffusion are permitted and may become highly patterned by parents or other socializers to accord with the needs of the family and other contingent groups.

In more complex situations, social systems may provide the novice with elaborate means for tension management. These tension management devices have an approved pattern just as does the role being learned. Various forms of play as manifested in physical exertion, pranks, jokes and humor, controlled brawling and thrill seeking, and the like, are usually tolerated and expected in youths as they are not in adults. It seems likely

---

[30] Since tension management operates in the context of social control as well as socialization, further discussion of it will be found in Chapter 6, "Social Control." We reserve, until that chapter, detailed illustration and reference to research literature.

that one function this pattern performs is to provide a socially harmless outlet for the strains that may be produced in the process of socialization —an outlet that can be controlled by adults and is not too far removed from the adult culture to which youths are expected to conform eventually.

PERMISSIVENESS

Flexibility in the extent to which conformity to role expectations is demanded usually accompanies socialization. The novice is expected not to conform precisely to expectations, and some socially controlled regression is tolerated while he learns his role. Permissiveness differs from tension management in that the novice is permitted to deviate from expectations or return to behavior no longer appropriate. Tension management, on the other hand, tends to hold the novice to the expectations, but allows him to handle tensions by releasing them in socially approved ways. Permissiveness is, of course, both conditional and controlled. Permission to deviate or regress is granted on the condition that the novice continue to try to meet role-expectations, and the extent to which he may deviate or regress is culturally specified. In particularly difficult socialization, the novice may be granted special consideration in the form of relief from certain status-obligations or extensive gratification of certain of his needs. These permissive conditions are revoked later when he has learned the status. In this way, the denials sustained in socialization are counterbalanced by rewards outside the immediate socialization process. In the armed services, for example, the quality and quantity of food offered him is often especially stressed while the recruit is in training; or during preparation for difficult examinations, the student may be relieved of normal responsibilities and duties.

ROLE REHEARSAL

Opportunity to act out behavior required in future statuses before they are occupied may ease transition to them. This has the advantage of providing opportunity to acquire the cathectic and normative orientations of future statuses as well as the more cognitive aspects. Role-rehearsal may be provided relatively early in a status-sequence. In such cases, practice of future roles is part of the legitimate expectations of these earlier statuses in the sequence. For example, little girls are given dolls, learn to "play house," dress and groom themselves in ways defined as attractive to males, and in other ways rehearse the culturally prescribed behavior of their future roles as wives and mothers.

Sometimes the practice period is incorporated in or extended to include the status being learned. This is particularly true where practice in prior roles cannot possibly be sufficient to meet the expectations of new roles. In our society, for example, young people do not practice or may not legitimately practice some of the expectations that confront them as wives and husbands or as parents. This is particularly true of the sexual side of marriage, but may be found in other aspects as well. In such cases, the practice period is extended into the initial introduction to the role. The term "newlywed" refers to what amounts to a special status that allows the marital partners to "adjust" to one another and to practice and perfect the behavior that is defined in their marital roles. Sometimes there is very little if any prior opportunity to practice a role by means of a status-sequence. In this case, the practice period is incorporated in the role to be learned and usually is highly structured and intensive. The mass induction of civilians into the armed services in the last war is a case in point. During the practice period, permissiveness usually is extended to reduce the strain of failure as the novice strives to conform to role-expectations. The culinary disasters of the bride, the yardbird antics of the army recruit, and the "greenery" of the freshman are forms of behavior during the practice period that later are not taken so lightly.

MODELS

The provision of appropriate models during the period of socialization appears to have important implications for effective acquisition of the patterns to be learned. Models supply the symbolic and concrete reference point for the behavior that is structured in the new status. The effectiveness of a model seems to hinge upon the extent to which the socializee identifies with him and the position of the model in the social system.

A positive cathexis for the model provides the socializee with incentive to learn the status-expectations and vests them with prestige and value. In addition, the model becomes a source of support during the strains of socialization and a source of reward for encouraging deferment of gratification in the form of favorable approval for mastering the status. Parents usually act as models for a range of statuses such as those linked to age, sex, and occupation. The initial identification that may be established in early socialization gives such models particular saliency for the child.

The position of the model in the social system affects both his visibility and his saliency. Anthropologists and sociologists have noted the relative lack of visibility of a model of adult male roles for young boys in our society. Talcott Parsons's comment illustrates the point:

> There is really no feminine equivalent of the expression "bad boy." It may be suggested that this is at least partially explained by the fact that it is possible from an early age to initiate girls directly into many important aspects of the adult feminine role. Their mothers are continually about the house and the meaning of many of the things they are doing is relatively tangible and easily understandable to a child. It is also possible for the daughter to participate actively and usefully in many of these activities. [Note, here, incipient role-rehearsal.] Especially in the urban middle classes, however, the father does not work in the home and his son is not able to observe his work or to participate in it from an early age. Furthermore many of the masculine functions are of a relatively abstract and intangible character, such that their meaning must remain almost wholly inaccessible to a child. This leaves the boy without a tangible meaningful model to emulate and without the possibility of a gradual initiation into the activities of the adult male role.[31]

Position of the model is likely to affect saliency where statuses are ranked or otherwise differentially evaluated. People in the more important or prestigeful statuses in the system tend to epitomize the dominant expectation pattern and their response to the socializee is likely to have greater impact. Individuals of low prestige, of little seniority, or of junior office tend to conform to those above them. Thus, exposure of socializees to models who are positively evaluated by the group may help to strengthen the structure of socialization.[32]

FACILITIES APPROPRIATE TO EXPECTATIONS

If the novice is to be socialized to status-expectations, the physical facilities necessary to carry out the expectation should be available. This includes the capacities of the individual as well as the instruments required to learn the behavior expected. Ordinarily, status-requirements are geared to the biological maturation or the individual biological differences of the novice. A familiar example in American society is the recent concern about toilet training of the young child and the admonition to institute the training when he is sufficiently mature biologically to handle

[31] Parsons, "Age and Sex in the Social Structure of the United States." Reprinted in Wilson and Kolb (eds.), *op. cit.*, p. 593. Brackets added.

[32] A vivid example of the salience of leadership roles has been documented in the study of boys' gangs, where it is found that changes are instituted by gang leaders and then internalized by the other members. See, for example, William F. Whyte, *Street Corner Society* (Chicago: The University of Chicago Press, 1943).

the necessary muscular control and coordination, rather than to try to force him to learn the pattern before he is physically capable of mastering it. Biological differences, real or assumed, are usually provided for by special role-expectations. Sometimes, very special roles are created for the mentally retarded, the physically handicapped, or the aged. Frequently, the difference may be assumed rather than real, as in the case of certain assumed differences based on sex, race, or family lineage; and one of the problems of gearing expectations to capacities is to determine just what the capacities are.

Serious strains may be developed if the expectations are set below people's capacities, as well as if they are set too high. Whether the "set" is "too high" or "too low," in turn, may depend upon other characteristics of the social structure. In the previously cited discussion of the work of Mirra Komarovsky, comment is made on the discrepancy between expectations and capacities.

> As long as women were brought up and educated very differently from men, as long as their whole mode of life was different, it was safe and suitable to uphold the traditional beliefs as to certain mental sex differences. But as the differentiation in the education of the two sexes lessened so have the actual differences in their abilities and interests. Today the survival of some of these stereotypes is a psychological strait jacket for both sexes. Witness the fact that some 40 per cent of women undergraduates have confessed (the proportion was confirmed in two studies on widely separated college campuses) that they have occasionally "played dumb" on dates; that is, concealed some academic honor, pretended ignorance of a subject, "threw games," played down certain skills in obedience to the unwritten law that the man must be superior in those particular areas. If he *were* superior, the stratagem would not be necessary.[33]

Provision of physical facilities necessary to learn new statuses is an obvious requirement, but one that is not always met by the social structure. Sometimes differential access to facilities is structured so that groups or categories of people are placed at a relative disadvantage in socialization to statuses. In our own society, for example, children from widely varying economic and social backgrounds are all socialized to a relatively similar pattern in the public schools. One important function of such socialization is to provide a fairly uniform orientation at the societal level among persons and groups of diverse social and psychological make-up. However, facilities functional for successful socialization in the structure of formal education are not equally accessible to all. Setting aside differences in family and peer group attitudes and values and focusing only upon physical facilities, we find that some children are disadvantaged be-

[33] Komarovsky, *op. cit.*, pp. 76–77.

cause their home cannot or does not provide the physical facilities functional for success in the schools. Indeed, one index of "class" differences in our society is the amount and type of reading material, "cultural" activities, private music or dancing lessons, participation in clubs and organizations of an "educational" nature, and the like, that are provided by the family. As a consequence, children in the lower reaches of economic and social rank have difficulty adapting to a school system that is largely geared to facilities more available to children in higher positions.

SUMMARY

Once some socialization takes place, further socialization involves some change, alteration, or modification of what has been internalized. This requires that some incentive to change be structured in the socialization to new statuses. Such structure involves reducing rewards for old behavior, increasing rewards for new behavior, and providing the conditions functional for making the change. Rewards for old behavior may be reduced by (1) separating socializees from former associates so as to minimize their approval for resistance to change; (2) enlisting peer group support and suppressing prior statuses in order to minimize self-approval for resistance to change; (3) emphasizing the linkage between the old and the new and deemphasizing the discontinuity so as to maintain consistency in self-conceptions; (4) downgrading previous sources of gratification; and (5) "de-grouping" so as to diminish the saliency of old associations. Estimates of future rewards may be increased by (1) developing anticipatory socialization in a structure of ranked or graded statuses; (2) making desired rewards contingent on conformity to new statuses; (3) socializing to a pattern of deferred gratification; and (4) structuring or countering reference groups so that estimates of relative gratification and deprivation decrease conceptions of costs and increase conceptions of profits. Provision of functional conditions includes having (1) clearly and consistently defined statuses; (2) socializing agents that hold out consistent expectations; (3) consistency among statuses learned simultaneously; (4) consistent status sequences; and (5) clear status-transitions. Other facilitating conditions include (6) tension management mechanisms, (7) permissiveness, (8) role-rehearsal, and (9) models. Finally, (10) transition may be aided by gearing expectations to the capacities of those being socialized and providing the physical facilities necessary to learn the new status-requirements.

5

DEVIATION FROM
CULTURE PATTERNS

In this chapter we shall explore some of the reasons why people might deviate from institutionalized expectations.

In discussing deviance, we want to emphasize that we are not discussing what is "good" or "bad" in evaluative terms. We are not even discussing what is functional or disfunctional for the social system or for the individual. We are discussing only the *fact* that sometimes some people under some conditions do not conform to the expectations of other people, or perhaps even to some of their own expectations. Very often it is a good thing that deviation or nonconformity occurs. There are some expectations that we (the authors) would say, from our own ethical point of view, *ought to* be violated. There are some situations to which individuals ought *not* to be "well adjusted"; they ought to deviate for the sake of their own sanity or integrity. Furthermore, the institutional structures of some social systems are disfunctional for the system's own adaptation or integration, and therefore, it would be better off if its members did deviate from institutionalized expectations. *Successful* pattern maintenance in such conditions might well mean the end of the system. Still further, we would not hesitate to say—again, from the point of view of our own values—that some systems ought not to survive (some families ought to break up, for example); and therefore, if conformity would help the system, we would be all for deviance.

We should also note that in discussing deviance we are not necessarily discussing "social problems." Some "social problems" are a consequence of deviant behavior, and some consist of deviant behavior. But (a) not

all deviance is a "social problem" and (b) many social problems have
nothing to do with deviance.[1]

None of that is relevant to the business of this chapter, however. Here
we want to focus our attention only on the question of why people deviate from institutionalized expectations, regardless of whether their deviation is "good," "bad," "functional," "disfunctional," or a matter of indifference.

Let us begin by considering just what is meant by "deviance." As we
have said at several points in previous chapters, people always have some
conception of a state of affairs they would like to bring into—or maintain
in—existence. They may not be able to articulate their conception—indeed, they may be unconscious of it. Still there is some state of affairs
the existence of which seems to satisfy them and the absence of which
sets them in motion of some kind—either efforts to "correct" the situation
or expressions of protest. The state of affairs they want to bring into or
maintain in existence is their goal. Effort may be expended toward it
either because it is defined as intrinsically enjoyable, or because it is regarded as morally proper, or because it is believed to be instrumentally
useful for some other state of affairs that is positively cathected or
evaluated.

The goal an individual strives for may be one that other people think
is legitimate or one they think is illegitimate. If they think it is legitimate,
the individual is a conformist *in their eyes;* if not, he is a deviant *in their
eyes.* (The individual himself also may think it is legitimate or illegitimate
and thus be a conformist or a deviant in his own eyes, quite independently of what he is in other people's eyes.) The point that cannot be
emphasized too strongly here is that there is no such thing as "deviance"
or "conformity." There is only deviance *from* someone's expectations or
conformity *to* someone's expectations.

Whatever the goal and whatever anyone thinks about its legitimacy or
illegitimacy, the individual engages in some kind of action to achieve it.
That action also is defined by other people and by the individual himself
as either legitimate or illegitimate. If it is defined as legitimate, there is
conformity (in someone's eyes); if it is defined as illegitimate, there is
deviance (in someone's eyes).

[1] For an excellent discussion of the general issue, see Robert K. Merton, "Epilogue:
Social Problems and Sociological Theory," in Robert K. Merton and Robert A. Nisbet
(eds.), *Contemporary Social Problems* (New York: Harcourt, Brace & World, Inc.,
1961). For an analysis of social problems that either consist of or result from deviance, see Harry C. Bredemeier and Jackson Toby, *Social Problems in America* (New
York: John Wiley & Sons, Inc., 1960).

Forms of Deviation

Viewing deviance as a failure to conform to norms governing goals and means provides a classification by offering four logically possible types of deviance.[2]

First, people may strive for the prescribed goals, but use proscribed means. They may either devise new means that violate the norms or make use of deviant means already available. This form of adaptation Merton has called "innovation." The student who cheats on an examination to pass a course, the businessman who infringes a patent to gain competitive advantage, or a thief who steals to buy a car are all innovators in this sense.

Second, people may conform to the institutionalized means, but fail to strive for the prescribed goals. They derive satisfaction from their conformity to means and, at the same time, are freed from the strain of goal striving. Their behavior is deviant because they are expected to strive, at some specified level, for institutionalized goals. Merton calls this form of adaptation "ritualism." "Bureaucrats" who have lost sight of the function of the practices they so meticulously observe are ritualists. Students who give up trying to understand a subject and content themselves with the mechanical and faithful reading of assignments are behaving ritualistically, as are people who give up "success" goals as prescribed in American society, but pride themselves on their devotion to "hard work" and their thriftiness.

Third, people may reject or may fail to internalize both the institutionalized goals and the institutionalized means. Their physical presence in the system is accompanied by neither a commitment to its values nor social conformity to its demands. They fall far short of the ideal adaptation, but they make no effort to close the gap by either proper or improper means.

[2] This classification is another of the contributions of Robert K. Merton. See *Social Theory and Social Structure* (rev. ed.; New York: The Free Press of Glencoe, Inc., 1957), Chaps. 4 and 5. Talcott Parsons has devised a similar analysis of deviance. See *The Social System* (New York: The Free Press of Glencoe, Inc., 1951), Chap. 6. The following discussion has drawn upon these sources, with some modification. For an analysis of subtypes based on this classification, see Robert Dubin, "Deviant Behavior and Social Structure: Continuities in Social Theory," *American Sociological Review*, 24:147–164 (1959). See also Robert K. Merton's instructive comments on this article in "Social Conformity, Deviation, and Opportunity Structures: A Comment on the Contributions of Dubin and Cloward," *American Sociological Review*, 24: 177–189 (1959).

They are in they system but not of it. Merton labels this form of deviance "retreatism." Among a society's retreatists might be found some types of alcoholics, drug addicts, psychotics, and such social outcasts as vagrants and bums.

Fourth, people may deviate from cultural prescriptions defining both means and goals by *excessively conforming* to each. Rather than relinquish or lower goals, they step up their efforts in excess of that expected, or they hold aspirations above those culturally specified, making extreme demands upon themselves and others. Adhering strictly to means and with their eyes fixed firmly on goals, they are at the ready to take inordinate risks, to push themselves to the breaking point, and to seize upon every legitimate means and exhaust every legitimate advantage. They are overscrupulous in their insistence upon conformity of others, lest they lose advantage or so that they may gain leverage by instrumental use of such compliance. The prototype may be found in some upwardly mobile people in our own society. It may be seen among those "newly arrived" who, as they strive to validate their status, are "more royal than the royalists." The deviant character of overconformity lies in the fact that convention is adhered to more rigidly and goals are sought more zealously than institutionalized expectations either prescribe or favor.

Each of these four types of deviance may be further distinguished in terms of whether the deviant person *attempts to get his deviance accepted as the proper way of behaving,* or, on the other hand, *covertly deviates from the institutionalized definitions without seeking to change them.* We must distinguish, in other words, between the innovator who steals in order to obtain money, and the innovator who attempts to get the new means of collective bargaining institutionalized in place of the old means of individualistic bargaining. Similarly, we must distinguish between the "ritualist" who simply gives up the goal of economic success while continuing faithful obedience to his job demands, and the person who promulgates the view that productive work *is* an end in itself and ought *not* to be engaged in simply as a means to economic acquisition.

In the same way, we must distinguish between the "retreatist" who abandons institutionalized definitions of goals and means without substituting anything in their place save the deep sleep of suicide or morphine, and the rebel who seeks a whole reorganization of the social system. Finally, in the same view, we must distinguish between the "excessive conformist" who anxiously drives himself to be more royal than the royalists, and the dedicated person who summons his fellows to renewed commitment to traditional values.

These distinctions are related to the observation made at the outset of this chapter: that deviance and conformity are relative to someone's expectations. From the point of view of those special kinds of "innovators," "ritualists," "retreatists," and "overconformers" *who seek to change the institutions*, it is not *they* who are "wrong"; it is the conformists. The *reforming* "innovator," for example, may see himself as a realistic pragmatist and the rest of society as blind slaves to tradition. The *reforming* "ritualist" may see himself as a man of righteousness and integrity and the rest of society as people seduced by the bitch-goddess Success. The *reforming* "overconformer" may see himself as a man of energy, dedication, drive, vigor, and ambition and the rest of society as lazy backsliders. The *reforming* "retreatist" may see himself as a prophet carrying enlightenment to benighted robots, or as "the vanguard of the proletariat."[3]

Clearly, the four types of deviance we have distinguished make analytical distinctions that may overlap and blur in the empirical situation. Furthermore, people may move from one to another adaptation and from any one back to conformity again. It is probable, also, that different types of deviance are not equally devalued by the conformist members of the system. Most likely, they are ranked on a continuum of disapproval based on the degree to which the deviance disrupts system processes and violates institutionalized expectations. On this basis, innovation probably would be most disapproved by the conformist members of a system; and retreatism, ritualism, and overconformity would follow in rank order. For example, it is probable that the average schoolteacher would most disapprove of the aggressive cheater in her class, would disapprove somewhat less of the child who daydreams and stares out the window, still less of the child who passively but faithfully does his homework but is uninterested in real learning, and least of all of the compulsively striving eager-beaver.

It should be kept in mind, then, that this scheme for classifying deviations is an analytical device. It permits the observer systematically to identify similarities and differences within a wide and apparently disparate range of deviance by focusing upon particular social factors (in this case, institutionalized means and goals and the relationship of system members to them). In addition, as we shall point out in what follows, it provides a means for locating both structural *sources* of deviance and structural factors making for one rather than another form of deviance.

[3] Readers familiar with Merton's analysis cited above will note that what we are doing here is to apply to *all* the modes of deviance the distinction he makes between the "rebel" and the "retreatist"—namely, the distinction between one who only violates the institutionally prescribed goals and means, and the person who both violates them *and* seeks to have new goals and means institutionalized. The full set of distinctions we are making here is similar to Merton's distinction between "nonconformity" and "other" forms of deviance developed elsewhere. For a more detailed discussion, see *Social Theory and Social Structure*, pp. 357–368.

Sources of Deviation

INADEQUATE AND INAPPROPRIATE SOCIALIZATION

The most obvious reason why people might not conform to cultural prescriptions or proscriptions is that they were not socialized to them. This might come about in either of two ways. Either socializing agents who tried to inculcate institutionalized definitions could not do so successfully because one or more of the favorable conditions of socialization were absent, or the socializing agents successfully inculcated deviant definitions. The first condition involves *inadequate* socialization to definitions *appropriate* to systems in which the socializee acts; the second involves *adequate* socialization to definitions *inappropriate* to systems in which he acts. Hence these sources of deviance might be called "inadequate" and "inappropriate" socialization, respectively. (The reader should note a significant implication of this distinction, which we shall not pursue further at this point: two sources of *conformist* behavior may also arise from socialization. The familiar source, of course, is adequate socialization to appropriate definitions. The less familiar possibility is inadequate socialization to inappropriate definitions. An example of the latter would be a boy who failed to be adequately socialized to a delinquent gang and whose failure to learn the gang's culture resulted in conformity to the larger middle-class values of the society.)[4]

These two sources of deviance pose no new issues, and we shall not dwell on them here. Inadequate socialization, as we have indicated, may result from the absence of one or more of the structural conditions favorable to socialization that were discussed in Chapter 4. Here we need only call attention to the fact that whatever factors prevent those favorable conditions are factors that tend to promote deviance. As far as inappropriate socialization is concerned, we need only note in the present context that this is simply calling attention to the fact of cultural diversity or inconsistencies in a status-sequence, such that what is learned in one system conflicts with what is expected in another. The lower class child may be the deviant in the middle class school situation; the civilian inductee, in the military establishment; and so on. These and other examples were called to the reader's attention in the preceding chapter.

---

[4] W. F. Whyte describes this situation among some boys in an underprivileged urban environment who fail to get socialized to the dominant "street corner society" and become deviant "college boys" in the slum area, but conformists to the middle-class pattern of the larger society. See *Street Corner Society: The Social Structure of an Italian Slum* (Chicago: The University of Chicago Press, 1943).

Socialization that is inadequate or inappropriate may be idiosyncratic and randomly distributed in a society. It is always possible for a *particular* individual to have a unique socialization experience that fails to impart the patterns to which he is being socialized or that socializes him to a relatively unique and atypical pattern.[5] The sociologically more germane case is that in which whole *groups* or *categories* of people are inadequately or inappropriately socialized because of their particular position in the social structure. Again, examples discussed in the preceding chapter may illustrate the point. The relative visibility of sex status-models may give rise to significant differences between boys and girls in compliance and adaptability to childhood roles; a lack of clarity and consistency of the adolescent status may result in problems of adaptation to it and to adult roles; or the urban middle-class female may encounter difficulties in meeting the expectations of the housewife and mother statuses because of inadequate or ambivalent socialization to them. Similarly, the lower-class child may be inappropriately socialized to the culture of the predominantly middle-class school system; the underprivileged worker may have failed to internalize the pattern of deferred gratification and striving for "success" goals that characterizes the larger society,[6] or the slum dweller may learn patterns of physical aggression or of sexual behavior that are acceptable in his immediate milieu, but defined as deviant by the laws that govern the total society.

Focus upon structured conditions that result in inadequate or inappropriate socialization is of particular sociological significance. It demonstrates how the societal system in which people act may affect them differently, depending upon their location in particular statuses or subsystems within it. Awareness of this fact helps to locate and identify conditions in the social structure that account for differential rates and types of deviance among various groups or categories of people. We know that rates of social deviance are distributed in a predictable pattern, rather than only randomly throughout the society. We are also aware of the fact that these rates change over time and vary among societies. Directing attention to the relationship between these "categorical risks" of deviance and the conditions in the social structure to which the high-risk categories

[5] It should be recognized, also, that an individual's biological system may be idiosyncratic in the sense that it inhibits or prevents socialization even under the most favorable circumstances. Little empirical evidence is available concerning the role of the biological system in predisposing individuals to inadequate socialization. Mental deficiency seems to be the clearest case of biological inadequacy, but other conditions may be pertinent as well.

[6] Deviant adaptations that are made by some underprivileged workers, particularly those who are isolated from the mainstream of middle-class values, are described by Allison Davis in "The Motivation of the Underprivileged Worker," *ETC: A Review of General Semantics,* 3:243–253 (1946).

are exposed, gives us a basis for understanding why these differential rates exist. As we shall see, the same proposition applies to other sources of deviance.

STRUCTURAL SOURCES OF STRAIN

A second major source of deviation arises as a consequence of exposure to strain induced by the organization of the social structure. Although people may be both adequately and appropriately socialized, they may find themselves, at one time or another, faced with conflicting expectation or with expectations that exceed their capacity. They may attempt to relieve the strain by deviation from institutionalized expectations. It should be understood, however, that inconsistencies need not produce strain, and that *motivation* to deviate need not result in deviation. Much depends on the effectiveness of mechanisms of social control and the existence of structured opportunities for deviation. How these operate to impede or facilitate deviation will be discussed later. At this point we simply want to inhibit the hasty assumption that inconsistencies necessarily produce strain or that motivation to deviate is always expressed in deviation.

There is, of course, always some real or potential strain in social action. Social structures are never so perfectly integrated or clearly and specifically defined that conflict is completely eliminated. Nor are human impulses and desires so tractable that they can be easily molded to the dictates of social structure. No doubt, too, there are individual differences in the degree to which people can tolerate ambiguities and conflict. What is sociologically significant, however, are those structural conditions that tend to produce strain sufficient to culminate in deviance among *groups and categories* of people; in other words, structures that tend to produce *differential rates* of deviation. What can be said of groups and categories, of course, also may apply to particular individual cases.

People are exposed to conflicts in social structure through their status-sets and role-sets. Since everyone occupies more than one status, and statuses are located in different systems, each with its own structural requirements, it is more likely than not that people will be subject to varying degrees of strain in attempting to reconcile and coordinate the various demands imposed by their status-sets.[7] Societies with a complex division of labor are especially subject to this problem. One familiar example in our own society is the potential conflict between familial and occupa-

---

[7] For a general analysis of strain induced in role-playing see William J. Goode, "A Theory of Role Strain," *American Sociological Review,* 25:483–496 (1960).

tional statuses. Some business and professional statuses, especially, may be so demanding that a male is unable to meet fully the status-expectations of husband and father, or vice versa. This poses the problem of allocating scarce resources among statuses in different systems. A somewhat different problem arises from the fact that statuses in different systems may impose conflicting standards of evaluation and behavior. Alvin W. Gouldner has analyzed this situation in a study of "progressive" trade-union leaders.[8] He found that the union norms governing leadership statuses were at variance with those in the larger society. Union norms that called for indifference to personal importance, that defined trade-union office as a "calling," and that demanded that union officials ascend from and maintain the culture of the rank and file were not supported by the societal values stressing individual competitive striving for high income and prestige. This potential conflict of values was activated for the union leader in marriage, where his husband and father statuses not only called for him to be a "companion" in his family, but to be a "good provider" and increasingly live up to middle-class standards. Such incompatibilities in a status-set may be sharply focused when people occupy conflicting statuses simultaneously. In our society, this situation is inherent in the combination of race and citizenship. For example, the restrictions of rights ascribed to a Negro conflict with those ascribed to his status as a citizen. More particularly, the Negro physician frequently is faced with the dilemma of reconciling, in his interaction with both Negroes and whites, the conflicting status-rights and -obligations afforded a physician and a Negro in our society.[9] Another rather special situation of strain may arise as a consequence of marginality, in which a person's position in one or another system is not clearly articulated in his status-set. Such marginality results from relinquishing position in one group or category without securing the status sought in another. A special case of marginality is found in the mulatto Negro, who may possibly lay claim to either white or Negro status, but finds difficulty in occupying either because he is likely to be rejected in both. The more familiar example is the immigrant who relinquishes his ethnic status in favor of becoming "Americanized," but is unable to get full acceptance because of his ethnic status.[10]

In addition to strains occasioned by conflicts among statuses in a status-set, any one status may demand more than particular individuals, groups,

[8] Alvin W. Gouldner, "Attitudes of 'Progressive' Trade-Union Leaders," *American Journal of Sociology*, 52:389–392 (1947).

[9] For a more detailed discussion see Everett C. Hughes, "Dilemmas and Contradictions of Status," *American Journal of Sociology*, 50:353–357 (1944).

[10] For an extended treatment of marginality, see E. V. Stonequist, *The Marginal Man* (New York: Charles Scribner's Sons, 1937).

or categories of people can give. Although statuses usually are defined so that most people can meet their expectations, some individuals may fall short of the physical, emotional, or intellectual requirements necessary to occupy a status they are required to fill. When statuses apply to whole categories of people who are biologically and culturally differentiated, some are very likely to feel themselves stretched or compressed on a cultural Procrustean bed. Among such people, strain may be experienced equally either by meeting successfully the status-expectations or by failing to live up to them. For example, to dichotomize people into males, on the one hand, and females, on the other, is to impose a rigid cultural division that does not correspond to biological facts; and to demand that all males conform to one model and all females to the other is to court disaster for some people who do not fit the models. When status-expectations are based on characteristics that only some possess, but to which all are expected to conform, some people either conform to the standards only at a cost of severe strain or cannot meet the standards and must experience a sense of defeat and failure.[11] The strain induced by failure may result in deviant adaptation to the status and the strain imposed by success may be expressed in deviant behavior in some other status.

This situation may apply to the many as well as to the few. It may be that the conformity required of people in order to entitle them to self-respect and the approval of others is set so high that most people, by definition, cannot conform. If, for example, the students who get admired or the businessmen who get praised or the professors who get recognition are the ones in the top 10 percent of their fields, then 90 percent of the people in those statuses are by definition failures, in a relative sense, at least. If, in other words, the social structure is such that most people aspire to be better than most people, most people have to be frustrated; and the sense of failure they experience can be as painful as the guilty conscience of Oedipus or the role conflict of Hamlet. Arthur Miller's modern tragedy, *The Death of a Salesman,* is an eloquent case study. This situation is compounded when there is a disparity between the number of rewarding statuses and the number of people who potentially are able to fill them. Prestige, for example, is enhanced by scarcity, and the statuses to which it is attached form a pyramidal hierarchy so that this reward is decreasingly available as one approaches the apex. Individual abilities and capacities, however, apparently are distributed in a form approximating the bell-shaped, normal probability curve. This means that not only are there fewer positions of relatively high prestige than there are candidates for them; there are fewer positions than there are *able* candidates for them. In this situation and in the absence of compensatory

---

[11] See the cases described in this context in Bredemeier and Toby, *op. cit.,* Chap. 2.

statuses or other alternative structuring, large numbers of people are likely to feel let down, dissatisfied, disaffected, or alienated.[12]

It may also be that the institutionalized means necessary to conform to status expectations are unavailable, ineffective, or differentially distributed. People may not be able to conform to the demands of one status in their status-sets because the necessary resources are not available in another contingent status. The familiar and dramatic instance of this in modern American society is the economic depression. Extended unemployment may result in a loss of self-respect, authority, economic resources, and the like that flow from an occupational status. This, in turn, may inhibit the capacity to conform to other statuses in a status-set. To cite but one example, it was found that during the depression, some men who experienced chronic unemployment were unable to maintain their position of authority in the family. In addition, work habits and skills gradually eroded away under extended idleness so that some workers became chronically unemployable or else adapted to unemployment as a status and lost a stable job-orientation entirely.[13]

The strain experienced as a result of "unemployment" is by no means confined to the "economic" case, nor does it consist entirely, or even most importantly, of a resulting inability to carry out other status-obligations. People whose jobs are made obsolete by technological inventions, aged people who find themselves "unwanted" because of compulsory retirement rules, women who have "nothing to do" after their children leave the family, adolescents who feel too old for the "kid stuff" of school but are not regarded as old enough for "serious responsibilities"—all these are cases in which people are placed under a strain that may lead to deviance. The strain they feel is not so much a result of inability to *procure* something they need to play other roles as it is a result of inability to *dispose* of services they want to dispose of. Human beings, as we observed earlier, need not only the satisfaction of getting things; they also need the feeling that they are *producing things that matter*. The adolescent who "has everything a child could want" may still be in a desperate state, because the one thing he does not have is something important to *do*. The problem is illustrated in a cartoon appearing in the *Saturday*

---

[12] The German sociologist George Simmel called attention to this dilemma some time ago. See Kurt H. Wolff (trans. and ed.), *The Sociology of George Simmel* (New York: The Free Press of Glencoe, Inc., 1950), pp. 300–303.

[13] Mirra Komarovsky analyzes some of the effects of unemployment on the family in *The Unemployed Man and His Family* (New York: Holt, Rinehart and Winston, Inc., 1940). For an excellent discussion of the effects of prolonged unemployment in Great Britain consult the Pilgrim Trust Study, *Men without Work* (Cambridge, England: Cambridge University Press, 1938). A similar analysis is contained in E. W. Bakke, *Citizens without Work* (New Haven, Conn.: Yale University Press, 1940).

Review.[14] The cartoon shows two small boys walking home from school. The less-studious looking one is saying to his faintly smug-looking friend, "O. K., so you grow up to be President, and you even get re-elected, that's still only eight years. What do you do with the rest of your life?"

The question is humorous coming from a child; but it may not be so amusing when confronted, for example, by men facing ten to fifteen years of retirement after a life built around the job, or women facing twenty years of life (probably ten or more of them as widows) after their children have left home. Its parallel among some teen-agers whose imaginations and energies the society has failed to capture, may be found in a kind of aimless drifting or worse. Sadism, violence, and hipsterism[15] may fill the vacuum in the lives of such youngsters (who may, of course, *chronologically* be adults).[16]

Not only special categories such as the aged or teen-agers, but whole societies may be in the position of not having any activity that can absorb their energies and that they can believe are "important" and "worth while." When this happens, there may develop on a wide scale various more or less frenzied efforts to find some "meaning" to life.[17]

It may be that the institutionally prescribed means are perfectly *accessible* but entirely *ineffective*. For example, someone who learns that "early to bed and early to rise makes a man healthy, wealthy, and wise," may discover, after a while, that in spite of his retiring and rising with the chickens, he is still sick, poor, and stupid. It may not be those means which, in fact, pay off. On the other hand, effective and legitimate means may be distributed differentially in the social structure. Where common goals are prescribed for statuses, but institutional means for obtaining them are differentially distributed, some people are relatively disadvantaged. This may result in different modes of adaptation on the part of people positioned differently in the social structure. Robert K. Merton has illustrated this situation in American society.[18] He contends that a common "success" goal (relatively high income, occupational prestige, and the like) is institutionalized for all members of our society, but that the means for attaining it (economic resources, education, social skills,

---

[14] *Saturday Review*, November 21, 1959, p. 18.

[15] Cf. Norman Mailer, "The White Negro: Superficial Reflections on the Hipster," in Bredemeier and Toby, *op. cit.*, pp. 476–481.

[16] Goallessness appears to be one dimension of *anomie*, or absence of clear and consistent social structure, upon which Émile Durkheim built his classic discussion of suicide. See *Suicide* (John A. Spaulding and George Simpson, trans.; New York: The Free Press of Glencoe, Inc., 1951). For a stimulating discussion of the "teen-age dilemma" see Paul Goodman, "Youth in the Organized Society," *Commentary*, 29: 95–108 (1960).

[17] See Bredemeier and Toby, *op. cit.*, Chaps. 3 and 15–17.

[18] "Social Structure and Anomie," in *Social Theory and Social Structure*, Chap. 4.

and the like) are differentially distributed. People lower in the socio-economic scale are under considerably more strain in goal striving than are members in the middle or upper reaches. This disparity between means available and goals sought may lead to one or another deviant forms of adaptation, such as innovating effective but illegitimate means or giving up goal striving and ritualistically conforming to means. It should be mentioned, also, that the cost the disadvantaged person pays who *legitimately* achieves his goals may be at the expense of family, friendship, or other statuses or may seriously cripple his capacity to con-form to such statuses.

Sigmund Freud has generalized the kinds of sources of strain discussed above to conclude that complex societies, especially, so inhibit certain basic drives that tensions and anxieties are the costs of civilization.[19] He has contended that fundamental "id" impulses, chiefly the drive for sexual pleasure and the expression of aggressive and hostile feelings, are neces-sarily inhibited by the demands of organized society. He further observed that it is impossible to inhibit them completely, and that cultural arrange-ments that rigidly proscribe them either are doomed to violation or are conformed to only at the price of crippling people and probably leading to deviance in other ways. Other analysts have placed less emphasis upon this kind of inevitable conflict between the nature of man and the nature of social life. They have contended that the conflict is not inevitable, but that its relative presence or absence depends importantly upon how the social structure is organized.[20] A final resolution of these contentions is still being sought; and, as is usual in such cases, the resolution will prob-ably be a synthesis of both views.[21]

We have said that sources of strain arise not only from the status-set but from the role-set as well. Often the different role-partners with whom an individual interacts in just one of his statuses may make inconsistent demands of him. This may be for either of two reasons. In the first place, the role-partners may occupy different statuses in the same system and, therefore, make inconsistent demands because of their different obliga-tions and commitments. A student, for example, has classmates, profes-sors, and administrators as role-partners in his status of student. If he conforms to the professors' expectations of hard study and active class

[19] Sigmund Freud, *Civilization and Its Discontents* (New York: Doubleday Anchor Books, 1958).

[20] See, for example, Karen Horney's *The Neurotic Personality of Our Time* (New York: W. W. Norton & Company, 1937) and Erich Fromm's *Man for Himself* (New York: Holt, Rinehart and Winston, Inc., 1947).

[21] For an example of the "argument" between the two views, see the exchange be-tween Herbert Marcuse and Erich Fromm in *Dissent*, 2:221–240, 342–349 (1955) and 3:79–83 (1956). See also Herbert Marcuse, *Eros and Civilization* (Boston: The Beacon Press, 1955).

participation, he may incur the wrath of his classmates or the disapproval of the dean of students, who may think he should engage in more extra-curricular activities. Similarly, the foreman in a factory may need the good will and cooperation of both the men under him and the supervisor over him, but the price of the men's good will may be bought at the cost of alienating the supervisor, and vice versa.[22]

In the second place, the inconsistent demands of role-partners may stem, not from the fact that they occupy different statuses in the same system, but from the fact that they occupy statuses in *other* systems that affect the demands they make in the first system. In other words, the role-partners have different status-sets. This is always so in marriage, for ex-ample. A husband and wife always occupy positions of son and daughter and perhaps brother and sister in different families. It may happen, then, that the wife with a sick mother or a lazy brother is forced to make de-mands on her husband that he cannot meet without great cost. It may also happen that, because role-partners have different status-sets, they have diverse attitudes and values that impinge upon their role-relations when they are acting in the same system. For example, the personnel of a hospital may be members of different religious faiths. A physician may be subject to conflicting role-expectations on the part, let us say, of Catholic board members and Protestant doctors, or a board member may have to struggle to reconcile somehow the conflicting expectations of Catholic and Protestant doctors. What is a legitimate medical procedure for one may be a violation of religious conviction for the other.

It should be noted that in such conflicts in the role-set, we are observ-ing potential conflicts in a status-set, also, but from the point of view of a different person. The wife who, because of her sick mother, makes de-mands on her husband in excess of his expectations or capacities has shifted to *him* the strain of a potential conflict in her status-set. Without this shift, she could be torn between her status-obligations as a daughter and those of her status as a wife, and we would analyze this situation in terms of a conflict in *her* status-set. Similarly, the doctrines of a doctor's religious faith and the medical judgments of his profession may pose a conflict for him. But when the conflict is resolved by adhering to one or the other side of the contending values, he passes it on to one or another of his role-partners.

Of the many sources of strain we have described it should be clear that it is the structure of statuses and roles that makes full conformity difficult or impossible and that produces strain. In such circumstances, it is quite beside the point to diagnose lack of conformity in terms of "weak char-

---

[22] For an instructive study of the strains imposed by the foreman status, see Robert Dubin, *Human Relations in Administration* (Englewood Cliffs, N.J.: Prentice-Hall, Inc., 1951), Chap. 9, "Foremen."

acter," "badness," "shirking duties," and so on. Except in the highly idiosyncratic case, the source of strain is not a consequence of the individual's
biological or psychological make-up, but a consequence of the organization of the structure in which he is acting.[23] People of diverse and individual "natures" may experience equally the strain of structured conflicts
and inconsistencies. As a corollary, it should be observed that because
people are distributed differently in the social structure they may be subject to quite different degrees and sources of strain, so that amount and
types of deviance assume a pattern. These patterns are expressed in differential rates of deviation and conformity among different categories and
groups of people in the society. We find in our society, for example, that
truancy and delinquency are higher among children who live in slums
than among those in the suburbs, that divorce is more frequent in urban
than in rural areas, that arrests and convictions for homicide are higher
among Negroes than among whites, that types and amount of mental illness vary with class position, that suicide is more common among men
than among women, and so on and on.[24] The search for the elusive causes
of these differences may lead in different directions, and one of the taxing
problems of the analyst is to untangle the threads of all possible sources.
The primary task of the sociologist in this search is to determine to what
extent, if at all, these patterns may be understood in terms of the structure of the social situation in which they take place.

Determinants of the Direction of Deviance

Thus far we have described four major types of deviation from institutionalized expectations: innovation, ritualism, retreatism, and over-

[23] For an excellent picture of this fact by a novelist who writes from a background
of sound professional experience, see David Alman, *World Full of Strangers* (New
York: Doubleday & Company, Inc., 1950). Other novels we recommend in this con-
nection include Pietro Di Donato, *Christ in Concrete* (Indianapolis: The Bobbs-
Merrill Company, 1939) and Willard Motley, *Knock on Any Door* (New York:
Appleton-Century-Crofts, Inc., 1947).

[24] We shall not attempt to cite all the relevant studies here but suggest the follow-
ing sources as useful statements of the correlations we have mentioned and attempts
to analyze them in sociological or social psychological terms. Albert K. Cohen,
Delinquent Boys: The Culture of the Gang (New York: The Free Press of Glencoe,
Inc., 1955); Carle C. Zimmerman, *Family and Civilization* (New York: Harper &
Brothers, 1947); John Dollard, *Caste and Class in a Southern Town* (New Haven,
Conn.: Yale University Press, 1937); August Hollingshead and Frederick Redlich,
Social Class and Mental Illness (New York: John Wiley & Sons, Inc., 1958); and
Andrew F. Henry and James E. Short, Jr., *Suicide and Homicide* (New York: The
Free Press of Glencoe, Inc., 1954).

conformity. We have pointed out that people may deviate in one or another of these four ways because they have been inadequately or inappropriately socialized or because strains have been created by the social structure. We have suggested, also, that deviance may be distributed at random or in a pattern in a social system. Now we want to note how certain social structures may canalize deviant motivation into one rather than another of the four types of deviance.

To do this we must begin by noting that people who are motivated to deviate may be faced with either an adaptive problem or an adaptive *and* an integrative problem. They are faced with only an adaptive problem when social structures simply stand as barriers to the realization of valued goals—barriers to be circumvented with no concern for any issues of "morality." They have both an adaptive *and* an integrative problem when barriers are not only outside them but also "inside" them; that is, when their adaptation involves violation of values they have internalized. Let us examine each of these problems separately.

THE ADAPTIVE PROBLEM

The student who has no scruples about cheating on an examination, the thief who has no compunction about stealing, the married man who feels no guilt in courting other women, or the laborer who is unrestrained in his Saturday night drunk are all faced with only an adaptive problem when denied access to the goals they seek. The conflict they are confronted with is a conflict between their desires on the one hand and other people's attitudes on the other. It is not a conflict within themselves. The problem is simply to find an expedient deviance to overcome or avoid the conflict they have with a structure external to them. The "others" who make contradictory demands on them or who fail to give them the responses they need are simply obstacles to be overcome, circumvented, manipulated, ignored, or abandoned. There need be no conflict in the individual over such deviance, for the internal control of self-punishment does not operate. There remains only the external restraint of social control to motivate him to conform.

Deviant adaptation that is free from internal conflict may be seen among people who are inadequately or inappropriately socialized. Deviant behavior does not involve internal conflict for them: it is consistent with their internalized norms. In such cases, the *direction* of the deviance will be influenced by the pattern of norms they have internalized. If they have internalized a system goal, but not the prescribed means, they will tend to innovate. If the means have been internalized, but not the goal, they are likely to be ritualistic. If they have internalized neither goals nor means, they may become retreatists. If they have been inappropriately socialized to a pattern of overconformity, they are likely to overconform.

People who have internalized system norms *autonomously* also may deviate without experiencing internal conflict. If the norms governing means are viewed merely as definitions of what is instrumentally useful, rather than as criteria of self-assessment, then their violation involves no problem of internal integration. The same is true of norms defining goals, except that even the autonomous person may be faced with the general human dilemma of being able to imagine the pleasure of goals that are forever beyond reach because of the inherent scarcity of means.

THE INTEGRATIVE PROBLEM

When people have *internalized* conflicting norms, or if they cathect the "others" who expect incompatible or frustrating actions of them, they are faced with an internal, integrative problem as well as an external, adaptive one. In such cases—perhaps as a result of perfectly adequate and appropriate socialization—they simply cannot subordinate one goal to another or cast about for any useful means as a solution to their dilemma. They cannot simply manipulate, ignore, or abandon the "others," for they judge themselves by their perseverance in goal striving, by their conformity to the prescribed means, or by their obedience to the demands others make upon them. There is, then, an additional cost to violating one or another of the norms involved in their conflict. Not only must they risk the potential cost of other people's sanctions; they also incur an unfavorable self-image—a sense of guilt, of "being a quitter," of being "less a man" or "less a woman," of being a "heel" or a "traitor."

In this case, not only must a person solve his immediate, adaptive problem; he has the problem of "living with himself" afterward. Short of the final retreat of suicide or possibly the temporary relief of drugs and alcohol, this latter problem requires him either to repress or to extinguish one of the conflicting norms he has internalized. *Extinction* seems to involve a process of "unlearning" what has been internalized so that it is no longer a constituent element of the person's social self. He no longer feels that he *should* conform to the standard. In contrast, *repression* simply banishes from consciousness one of conflicting standards; the conflict still remains in the person.

REPRESSION AND THE DEFENSE MECHANISMS

Since repression does not eliminate the internal conflict, a person is faced with the emergence of guilt-feelings that accompany violation of his internalized standards. Therefore, in order to facilitate repression and avoid guilt, he is contrained to use certain "mechanisms of defense."[25]

The essential function of defense mechanisms is to facilitate repression. The function is illustrated by the compulsive element in repression, which is the basis of the defense mechanism of *reaction formation*. In order to fortify repression, a person expresses the *un*repressed desire with double vigor—compulsively. For example, the student who is tempted to cheat but who resists the tendency may become extraordinarily meticulous about gluing his eyes to his own paper, violently condemning cheaters, and eloquently singing the praises of honesty. Another commonly used defense mechanism is *rationalization*. Rationalization may help the individual to violate one of his norms by reassuring him that the violation is justified. In other words, he thinks up a "good" reason for his deviance, a reason that is supported by institutionalized values and is consistent with the actor's internalized standards. Effectiveness lies in finding a value that is more lofty in the cultural hierarchy of values than the one that taboos the desired action. For example, the student who is confronted with the choice of studying for an examination or joining friends in a party may resolve the conflict by joining the party and rationalizing on the grounds that, after all, he needs the relaxation, and his health is more important than passing examinations. The fact that he could relax after the examination is ignored. Ignoring facts is one mark of defense mechanisms, since distorting reality aids repression. Rationalization may move on toward *projection*, which is a special form of it. Projection permits the violation of an internalized standard by attributing to others one's own tabooed motives and thoughts. For example, one may help himself to cheat by persuading himself that "everyone else really cheats, so I'm driven to it." Again, the person who is secretly envious of a friend may, by attributing envy *to the friend*, justify his hostility in a manner that his sense of fair play otherwise would not permit.

Even though the defenses of reaction formation, rationalization, and projection may help the frustrated individual to keep himself unaware of his ambivalence and his frustration, the frustration and ambivalence are still there. Often the result is a diffuse feeling of resentment and hostility that the individual cannot handle realistically, precisely because its *real* source has been repressed. Still, even though the individual is prevented by his internalized norms from getting at the root of his problem, he must do *something* with his hostility. It is in this situation that another defense

[25] An excellent analysis and research report on both the psychological and sociological dimensions of defense mechanisms is to be found in Daniel R. Miller and Guy E. Swanson, *Inner Conflict and Defense* (New York: Holt, Rinehart and Winston, Inc., 1960). Chapter 8 is a good overview of the defense mechanisms, classified slightly differently, though not inconsistently, from the way we treat them in the present text.

mechanism is likely to appear: *displacement.* The child who resents his mother's discipline may hesitate to give vent to the resentment by aggression against her, either because of her superior physical force or because he believes it "wrong" to dislike one's parents. He may repress his hostility toward her, compulsively insist to himself that he really loves, honors, and respects her, and *displace* the repressed hostility by destroying a toy, teasing his baby sister, picking a fight with a neighborhood child, or—on a more "adult" level—becoming anti-Semitic. For example, it has been reported that people who say they agree with the statement, "There is nothing lower than a person who does not honor and respect his parents," tend *also* to be the ones who are anti-Semitic, anti-Negro, and so forth.[26]

Although such mechanisms of defense as these are primarily psychological in nature, they are relevant sociologically for several reasons. In the first place, an understanding of the phenomenon of repression gives a clue to how the subsequent deviance will be expressed. If a person represses an institutionalized standard so he can violate it, he will be a compulsive innovator or ritualist, depending on whether goals or means are repressed. If both goals and means are repressed, deviance will be expressed in compulsive retreatism. The compulsive nature of the deviance emerges as a consequence of reaction formation. Similarly, if he represses a disapproved means or goal so that he can *conform,* he will express his deviance compulsively in overconformity. In other words, the direction of deviance is related to which side of an ambivalence a person in conflict represses.

In the second place, a social system may provide institutionalized structures that facilitate the use of mechanisms of defense and furnish socially acceptable aids to repression. For example, a lower-class delinquent gang may facilitate reaction formation by providing support and legitimation of aggression against middle-class persons and property. Similarly, certain categories of people, such as minority groups, may be so socially defined as to present a convenient focus for projection or displacement. Some of the violent anti-Semitic behavior in Nazi Germany very probably was a consequence of hostilities that arose from quite another source. Without such a scapegoat, conveniently fostered by Nazi ideology, the frustrations, anxieties, and hostilities of some people may well have been manifested in very different form. In the same way, rationalizations may be indigenous to the culture of groups and categories of people, so that repression is readily facilitated on the part of those who are ambivalent about violating social norms. The person who is ambivalent about his hostility toward Negroes, for example, may find ready-made rationalizations among some groups that will permit him to express that hostility

---

[26] See T. W. Adorno, *et al., The Authoritarian Personality* (New York: Harper & Brothers, 1950).

freely. Similarly, social situations may provide rationalizations that support deviance rather than conformity. Violations of sexual mores during wartime may be facilitated on the grounds of patriotism and justified as a "sacrifice" that the female is making for the morale of young men who face death. In such ways as these, position in the social structure or the circumstance of social situations may provide the structure that facilitates deviance and direct its expression into one or another type of deviation.

Third, the use of defense mechanisms may be an integral part of the pattern of social deviance. Recognition of this fact allows us to make a finer distinction among types and sources of deviance. It permits us, for example, to view alcoholism and drug addiction as neurotic patterns of retreatism and to differentiate them from other expressions of retreatism such as that resulting from the inappropriate socialization of underprivileged workers. Recognition of the nature of defense mechanisms also permits us to distinguish between such deviants as the alcoholic who is laboring under a compulsion to drink that is deviant in any system, and the Saturday night drunk who is following an institutionalized pattern that may be legitimate in his subculture, even if frowned upon in the larger society. Similarly, it points to the important distinction between the innovator who is motivated by neurotic or psychotic compulsions and the innovator who deviates in simple response to social structure or prior socialization. Such distinctions have important implications both for the analysis of deviance and for social action oriented to the treatment of the deviant.

Fourth, the use of defense mechanisms may be a direct consequence of a conflict that is built into the social structure, so that neurotic and even psychotic patterns of adaptation may be traced to the social rather than (or as well as) to the biological system. As we noted above, one traditional view of repression has been that it arises as a consequence of a conflict between biological "drives" and social constraints, familiarly illustrated in the repression of sexual urges in favor of conformity to cultural demands that impose restriction on their free expression. It seems just as likely, however, that serious conflicts may develop in the person as a result of inconsistent demands imposed by the social system. The inability to achieve a culturally defined goal without violating an institutional means, when both are internalized, is as likely to cause serious internal conflict as the incapacity to achieve sexual gratification without violating internalized social taboos.

Finally, it should be noted that it is necessary for the sociologist to be aware of the mechanisms of repression, projection, displacement, and so on; otherwise a good deal of the wanton destructiveness, violence, and irrationality of the behavior of some deviants is inexplicable. The intensity of hatred toward minority groups and the viciousness of some predatory juvenile delinquents cannot be understood apart from these mechanisms for coping with *internal* conflicts lodged in the persons of the deviants but stemming, in large part, from their social milieu.

EXTINCTION

Under certain structural conditions, the repressed norm may in time become extinguished. The basic conditions that seem necessary for this to happen have already been discussed in Chapter 4. If there are no external punishments for violating the repressed standard, and if there are consistent rewards for violating it (that is, for conforming to the other conflicting norm), then the repressed norm in time is likely to disappear altogether as a yardstick by which the individual judges himself. His deviance from the extinguished standard is then likely to be less compulsive and more instrumental. It becomes, in other words, like the deviance we discussed above—involving only an adaptive problem for the individual.

These conditions—instead of punishment, reward for deviance—are likely to be generated by several characteristics of a social structure:

1. If the norms are vague, people may gradually drift away from conformity to them, with no one being in a position to punish the drift until it is too late. Highly generalized and abstract social rules invite individual innovations, which may be more congenial to the individual than to system requirements. The loose fit of institutional means to the individual case provides the convenience of having one's cake and eating it too. In the eating, however, one is likely to move far from the banquet table. Even the highly specialized definitions embodied in formal legal language offer loopholes through which people may squeeze and violate the spirit of the law while maintaining a favorable self-image of honesty and incorruptibility. This is patently true where the general values of honesty and incorruptibility come to be seen exclusively as legal definitions. Perhaps quite unconsciously, morality becomes legality, and individual integrity is measured by conformity to the letter of the law.

An example of *overconformity* as a result of gradual extinction of limits is suggested in the observations of an economist of acute sociological insight, Thorstein Veblen.[27] Veblen has described a special case of vague goal structuring, where goals recede as they are attained, and the individual is never sure how much is enough. He illustrates this condition in terms of the acquisition of wealth, which confers honor and self-respect. In such a structure, the individual is motivated to strive for the goal but is never sure that he has strained hard enough, for the goal moves up-

---

[27] Thorstein Veblen, *The Theory of the Leisure Class* (New York: The Viking Press, 1931), Chap. 2.

ward as he attains it. One consequence is that people may overconform by redoubling their efforts so that there can be no possible doubt that they are striving adequately.

2. Second, the cost of the deviance even in self-approval may be reduced if the norm that is violated has received little *support* or *reinforcement* through ritual and tradition, one function of which is to support and periodically rekindle commitment to the norms. Another function of ritual and ceremony often is to symbolize in concrete objects the abstract values of moral judgment. Both are seen in religious practices that bring people together in the common affirmation and solemn testimony inherent in the liturgy and tradition of the church. Similar functions are performed by such varying practices as "occasions of state" and the simple family rituals that accompany eating, recreation, and even sleeping.[28] It is common practice today to scoff at the "old school tie" or the ritual and dress that are the trappings of high office, but in conjunction with other control devices, they may become important implements in keeping alive a dedication to norms.

Where reinforcement and support are inadequate or absent or when the forms they assume are practiced as mere formalities and lack vitality of meaning, commitment to values may gradually erode away. Whether the ceremonies foster goals, means, or both, their absence may facilitate extinction of internalized values and encourage deviance.

3. The path to the extinction of either goals or means may be smoothed by the presence of subcultures that give group support to the individual's motivation to deviate, and in some cases may even determine its direction. Some types of religious sects or some forms of bureaucracy, for example, may present a structure congenial to the ritualistic inclination. The other worldly orientation of the religious sect, its rejection of earthly goals, and its emphasis on strict adherence to rigid prescriptions tend to support and foster ritualism. Bureaucratic insistence on methodical conformity that frequently obscures the aims of its organization, the emphasis on seniority above performance, and institutionalized "buck passing" may serve the same end.[29] Similarly, the innovative pattern of the

[28] For a discussion of family rituals and their functions in American society see J. H. S. Bossard, *Ritual in Family Living* (Philadelphia: University of Pennsylvania Press, 1950).

[29] See, for example, Robert K. Merton's discussion of "Bureaucratic Structure and Personality," in *Social Theory and Social Structure*, Chap. 6, and Liston Pope's analysis of the sect in *Millhands and Preachers* (New Haven, Conn.: Yale University Press, 1942), pp. 117–140, particularly. It should not be concluded from these examples that religion or bureaucracy necessarily is ritualistic. For a discussion of varying types of bureaucratic organization that lead to different forms of action on the part of bureaucrats, consult Peter Blau, *The Dynamics of Bureaucracy* (Chicago: The University of Chicago Press, 1955).

delinquent gang or the criminal "organization" may offer the frustrated the bridge to deviance that he seeks. The structure of such deviant cultures as these provides social reinforcement of the individual's deviant tendency and facilitates the extinction of the conformist patterns that stand as barriers to his favorable self-conception.

For these reasons, the deviant adaptation made may be determined by which deviant subculture is most available to the person under strain. The fact that delinquent gang behavior is largely an urban, lower-class phenomenon is a case in point. The child who, for example, is alienated from a conforming family in such an area is more likely to find *delinquent* gangs a substitute source of the satisfactions denied him in his family. In the process of conforming to the delinquent subculture, he is likely to be molded to the delinquent status. In fact, his newfound source of satisfaction is contingent upon conforming to delinquent expectations.[30]

The middle-class child who experiences similar family deprivations is less likely to contact such gangs. He is just as likely to seek peer group support, but the behavior of his peers tends to embody the "youth culture" of the adolescent that is largely tolerated by the adult society. Furthermore, other avenues of conventional sources of satisfaction are more available to him. To put the point another way, the availability of deviant modes of adaptation may be distributed differentially within a population and be a determinant of the form that deviant motivation takes in behavior.[31] It may even determine whether or not the motive to deviate actually results in deviance.

4. The expression of motivation to deviate may be facilitated by the presence, in effective interaction, of a number of people who share a common problem of adaptation. The fact that they are thrown together in interaction, as a consequence of sharing similar positions in the social structure, provides a basis for the development of a *common* solution to their individual problems. Albert K. Cohen has described this situation in the case of the emergence of a delinquent subculture.[32] He suggests that a common problem exists among lower working-class youths that centers around their inability to meet the standards of the middle-class way of life. The delinquent subculture emerges as one alternative way of

[30] For a research study that explores the satisfactions received in delinquent behavior, but denied in the home, see William Healy and Augusta F. Bronner, *New Light on Delinquency and Its Treatment* (New Haven: Conn.: Yale University Press, 1936).

[31] For a detailed analysis of "differentials in availability of illegitimate means," see Richard A. Cloward, "Illegitimate Means, Anomie, and Deviant Behavior," *American Sociological Review*, 24:164–176 (1959). Also see Richard A. Cloward and Lloyd E. Ohlin, *Delinquency and Opportunity* (New York: The Free Press of Glencoe, Inc., 1960).

[32] Cohen, *op. cit.*

coping with this source of frustration. The delinquent solution offers group support for the repudiation of middle class values, the legitimation of aggression flowing from the hurt and humiliation of low rank, and possibly the expression of reaction formation occasioned by ambivalence toward the very values that are repudiated. At the same time, the culture of the delinquent group sets the standards of self-worth for its members and provides the recognition and response denied by the larger society. Thus the fact that a number of youths who share a common problem are brought together in interaction provides the basis for the emergence of a common solution and the structure for the support and legitimation of that solution. If each youth were separated from the other, each might work out independently quite different modes of handling his adaptive problems. Stripped of the stimulation of group interaction as well as of group support and legitimation of considered solutions, alternatives may never be conceived or, if conceived, may never be expressed in action.

A very similar structural condition appears to have operated among some unemployed men during the depression period of the thirties. We previously pointed out that some of the unemployed accepted their condition as a status, in a kind of retreatist adaptation. Research in England has shown that acceptance of the status of unemployment was related to the extent to which unemployed men were in association with one another, rather than simply to the length of unemployment, as might be expected. For example, among older workers, acceptance of unemployment was higher in those communities where the unemployed were more numerous. The long-unemployed man who was relatively isolated from others of his kind was less likely to accept unemployment. Those in close association in unemployment clubs, in friendships based on unemployment, in queues of men lined up for unemployment allowances, and the like, developed a culture and a community of the unemployed that supported and legitimized their acceptance of unemployment. Shared opinions developed as to the reason for their unemployment that protected them from the pain and humiliation of their status, patterns of behavior emerged to fill in their idle hours, and ways were innovated and exchanged to meet their reduced circumstances. Under the double impact of an economy that had no place for them and a subculture that provided some semblance of dignity and worth, the work disciplines of a lifetime were gradually extinguished.[33]

---

[33] For a detailed discussion of various types of adaptation to unemployment and some of the structural factors involved see the Pilgrim Trust Study, *Men without Work*, particularly Book II, pp. 143–176.

SUMMARY

Motivation to deviate arises from three primary sources. People may be inappropriately socialized, they may be inadequately socialized, or the structure of the system may present inconsistencies or impose demands that lead to frustration and motivate to deviance. Their deviance may take the form of innovation, ritualism, retreatism, or overconformity. If they have been inadequately or inappropriately socialized or have extinguished the internalized definition that inhibits deviance, they may resolve conflict and frustration by unambivalent, deviant adaptation. If, however, they have been appropriately and adequately socialized and are unable to extinguish some internalized definition, they are faced with the further problem of maintaining internal consistency; that is, they have an integrative as well as an adaptive problem. This they may handle by repression and resort to the mechanisms of defense. Which of the deviant modes of adaptation a given person or group expresses in a particular situation will depend upon a complex set of conditions in both the personality system and the structure of the social system or systems involved in the conflict. Setting aside biological factors, relevant personality considerations may be summed up in terms of the particular definitions people have internalized and the salience or degree of internalization of these definitions. Relevant considerations in the social structure include the extent to which a particular pattern of deviant adaptation is available, the degree to which conformity to system definitions is reinforced, the extent to which support for deviant behavior is present, and the clarity of and relative emphasis placed on social definitions. How such conditions as these will affect people depends, in turn, on their position within the structure. Similarly, the conditions that motivate to deviance impinge differentially on individuals and groups.

6

SOCIAL CONTROL

Early in Chapter 3 we observed that there are two major kinds of processes by which people are led to conform to one another's institutionalized expectations and thus are able to predict and rely upon one another's behavior. One is the socialization process; the other consists of social control mechanisms, which we briefly defined as the "trick" of "arranging things so that deviance cannot be engaged in even if motivated."

Now, on the basis of our analysis of various sources of motivation to deviance, we can refine that definition of social control. As we have seen, even if the socialization process is adequate and appropriate, people may be placed under such strains, as a result of their positions in the social structure, that they are under pressure to deviate from the norms. All the social arrangements that either *prevent such strains* or *prevent the strains from leading to deviance* are what we mean by "social control mechanisms."

Five different kinds of social control mechanisms may be distinguished. They might usefully be regarded as five different "lines of defense" against deviance (not counting the fundamental "line of defense" of the socialization process itself). The first line of defense is to *forestall the strain itself* by means of certain mechanisms that prevent *potential* strain from becoming actual. If this is not done successfully and strain is actually experienced by members of the system, a second line of defense is to drain off or canalize *responses* to the strain into socially sanctioned patterns of behavior. A third line of defense is a necessary adjunct to the second. It consists of arrangements that make socially disapproved responses either very *difficult* to express or very *costly*. In other words, not all strain is avoidable in any social system, but there may still be ways of deterring people from expressing their tensions in deviance and encouraging them to "manage" the tensions in accordance with certain "safety-valve" mechanisms.

However, these also do not always work; hence a fourth line of defense is to remove the deviant from the social system, through imprisonment, banishment, "excommunication," or execution. A fifth line of defense, sometimes coupled with removal, is to resocialize the deviant, for example, through psychotherapy.

We shall discuss each of these control mechanisms in this chapter. It should be clear at the outset that in our discussion of mechanisms of social control, we refer to devices that may or may not be collectively approved; that is, they may or may not be institutionalized. Any particular mechanism may be used illegitimately in the interest of a person or a subgroup in order to get others to conform to his or their private expectations. In such cases, however, the control is *deviant,* since it fails to conform to institutionalized definitions of the legitimate use of social control. The use of physical coercion in our society is a case in point. Except in self-defense, the threat or use of physical violence ordinarily is not permitted as a means of securing one's needs, even if those needs are legitimate. A monopoly of this means of control is vested in the authority of the state. Here, of course, it may be used legitimately, provided there is sufficient consensus concerning the institutionalization of power in the state. Under such a structure, use of physical coercion by private persons or groups is defined as deviant and a "crime" against the state, and physical coercion may be brought to bear against the offender. In a society such as ours, the law and the statuses designed to carry it out represent highly visible and formal structures of social control.

Mechanisms That Forestall Strain

In the last chapter we pointed out that strain may be induced by incompatibilities and inconsistencies in role-sets and status-sets. Although there is considerable variation in the complexity of status-sets within and among societies, the structure of society tends to counteract difficulties of adaptation to status-sets of even the most complex nature. As we have seen, people tend to be socialized to and to occupy relatively consistent status-sets either by the design of the social structure itself or through self-selection of statuses. Furthermore, people are aware of the fact that others occupy many statuses, and there usually is sufficient flexibility in role-relationships to accommodate the minor conflicts that may emerge between a person's status-set and the governing status of a particular social relationship. However, especially in highly differentiated societies, potential conflicts in status-sets cannot always be so readily accommodated. In such circumstances, mechanisms of social control may be institutionalized to inhibit potential conflict and reduce or eliminate strain. The following discussion will suggest three major ways in which this may be accomplished.

SEGREGATION

Structured segregation of statuses and role-players prevents strain by separating potential sources of conflict inherent in status- and role-sets. The pertinent function of such segregation is to prevent people from being confronted simultaneously with conflicting expectations. This may be accomplished in three frequently mutually supporting ways.

First, cultural definitions may allocate different times to different statuses that, if occupied simultaneously, would conflict. Take the simple case of a man who is a father, a husband, a golf enthusiast, a Christian, and a lawyer. From nine to five he is in the worker status; from six to nine, the father status; and from nine to eleven, the husband status. Sunday morning he occupies the religious status; Monday through Friday, the lawyer status; Saturday morning, the recreational status. Although, in reality, status-segregation is not so rigid or separate as we have indicated, some conception of the potential conflicts in these statuses may be seen in the occasional violation of time allocations. Note, for example, the strain induced when the wife decides to pay a visit to her husband's busy office while she is downtown shopping, when a small child accompanies his father in a round of golf with adult friends or business associates, or when the Sunday morning precept to lay not up treasures unto oneself on earth confronts the Monday morning exigencies of competitive economics that encourage one to lay up as much treasure as he legitimately can get his hands on.

Second, potential conflict may be avoided by *place* allocation. Shifting from one set of attitudes and beliefs to another may be facilitated if the place and surroundings in which each is appropriate are radically segregated. For example, being studious, amorous, gay, philosophical, and religious may be accomplished more easily if they are carried out, respectively, in a library, a parked car, a nightclub, a dormitory bull session, and a church or temple. The physical aspects of place not only segregate potentially conflicting activities but set the mood and provide the appropriate cues for action. The lofty reaches and stern serenity of a medieval cathedral evoke quite a different tone and feeling from that suggested by the trim efficiency of a modern business office. Winston Churchill sensed this relationship of mood to physical structure when he insisted, after the bombing of the House of Commons, that the room be restored in its original size, even though it could no longer accommodate all members of the House. His reasoning was that all members would be present only when the more serious matters of state were considered, and that the crowded assemblage would create the atmosphere of urgency appropriate to the occasion.

Third, segregating different *role-partners* with whom an individual interacts may forestall potential conflict. The discrepancy between the personality the student shows to his "date" and the personality he presents to his professors or his parents can be avoided by keeping these role-players apart. A moment's reflection will show that, even on a very informal level, one friend evokes one set of responses and another friend elicits quite a different kind of reaction, and that a person is likely to feel uncomfortable and under tension when he and his two friends are all together. Such strain is avoided by interacting separately with each of the friends. Similarly, polygynous societies sometimes handle problems of role-conflicts among wives by maintaining separate dwellings for each and requiring the husband to cohabit with each in rotation. Particularly in a society of great division of labor and differentiation, the congruity of a wide variety of personality types is likely to be moderate, at best. Each individual tends to interact with different and often conflicting personalities in order to meet his unique needs and play out his status-set. The socially sanctioned separation of role-players permits the individual to avoid the tension that would result were these people to interact among themselves as well as with him. In courtship the young man is not expected to bring home every date for parental inspection, nor is the businessman expected to invite every client to the supper table.

As we pointed out in the last chapter, sometimes strains in role-relationships arise from the fact that role-partners occupy statuses that conflict with the one governing their interaction in a particular system. This is likely to be the case, for example, when business associates are also close friends, particularly if one is in a subordinate position to the other. To use Parsons' terminology, the diffuse, affective, and particularistic character of friendship may be in sharp conflict with the specific, neutral, and universalistic relations structured in occupational statuses. This potential source of strain may be forestalled by formal or informal controls that canalize conflicting statuses in different persons. Peter Blau has described the operation of such informal controls in a bureaucracy. Commenting on the presence of friendly relations but the absence of close friendships among workers in the same department, he writes:

> The virtual absence of intradepartmental friendships was not fortuitous. A friend in the department could make unforeseen demands on his co-worker which would force the latter to choose between his friendship obligation and his official responsibility. Since most friendships were

*inter*departmental, between officials who hardly had any contact during office hours, such conflicts were avoided. The special character of *intra*-departmental relationships—personal interest in particular individuals, linked with clearly delimited social obligations—made them integrative and simultaneously assured that they did not interfere with bureaucratic operations in an unpredictable manner, as intimate friendships well might.[1]

Such controls may be stated directly in formal rules and regulations, such as those that prohibit husbands and wives from serving on the same teaching faculty, or they may be provided indirectly, as in the segregation of officers and enlisted men in separate living quarters. In the former case, there is no possibility of established statuses coming into conflict; in the latter case, the possibility of establishing intimate relationships that might conflict with official duties is minimized.

Structured segregation of persons may operate as a social control in still another context. To the degree that people who are under strain, occasioned by similar problems of adaptation, are out of touch with one another, the chances of their consolidating their forces, reinforcing their deviant motivations, and devising collective solutions are lessened. Isolated from one another, each may feel his problem is peculiar to himself; and although deviant means of adaptation may occur to each, no one receives sufficient support to express his solution in action. Even if expressed, the solution may pose more problems than it was designed to cope with, since it is likely to run counter to the moral sentiments of those who immediately interact with the isolated deviant. Given a structure that places potential deviants in communicative interaction, however, the spectrum of alternative modes of adaptation is greatly increased, and mutual support for an emerging pattern of deviance is provided. Once a subgroup solution has been established, it may also serve the needs of persons whose sources of strain are quite different from those who established the deviant subculture. Thus, a ready-made solution to adaptive problems of diverse sorts may be provided by deviant subgroups if structured avenues to such groups are available.[2]

INSULATION

A second set of devices for avoiding strain that might result from inconsistencies in a role- or status-set involves insulation, by which we

[1] Peter Blau, *The Dynamics of Bureaucracy* (Chicago: The University of Chicago Press, 1955), p. 142. Copyright 1955 by the University of Chicago.

[2] Albert K. Cohen has formulated this analysis in detail and applied it to delinquent gangs in *Delinquent Boys: The Culture of the Gang* (New York: The Free Press of Glencoe, Inc., 1955).

mean the *symbolic* segregation of times, occasions, or partners.[3] Often it is difficult or impossible to segregate statuses or role-partners so as to inhibit conflict. In this event, some mechanism may be necessary to support and reinforce the governing status in a particular relationship and to subordinate other statuses to it. Unlike segregation, insulation allows interaction among potentially conflicting role-partners and even permits potentially conflicting statuses to operate simultaneously; but people are protected from conflict by structures that withhold or diminish expectations that might conflict with those governing the relationship.

The difference between segregation and insulation may be illustrated by the operation of sex regulations among people who are related by blood or marriage. In order to enforce such taboos, males and females could be segregated physically. Indeed, this appears to be the case in some societies, where "avoidance relationships" are institutionalized among kinsmen of the opposite sex. For example, the rule may be that the husband must avoid interacting with his wife's mother or his son's wife. However, it is equally possible and sometimes necessary to permit relationships among family members, but inhibit interaction that may lead to violation of taboos on sexual relations. This may be facilitated by institutionalizing exaggerated respect between kinsmen of opposite sex. Thus, the husband may approach his wife's mother or his son's wife only with marked respect or reserve. Imposing this structure on the relationship provides external support for the maintenance of sexual taboos by emphasizing the social distance between these role-partners and muting the potential sexual attraction inherent in the interaction.[4] In this structure, kinship statuses clearly take precedence over sex statuses, and the nature of the permissible interaction reinforces the governing statuses in the relationship.

In such cases as this, if the legitimate relationship is not clearly symbolized as "the" appropriate one, the persons involved may be under pressure to act out their equally present but, in the existing context, illegitimate statuses. Similarly, in the military establishment, the differential rights and obligations of officers and enlisted men have been maintained traditionally by elaborate mechanisms of insulation at those points where

[3] We use this term in a different sense from that used by R. K. Merton, who confines it to insulation from observability by others, a phenomenon we intend to include in the concept of "segregation of role-partners." See his *Social Theory and Social Structure* (rev. ed.; New York: The Free Press of Glencoe, Inc., 1957), pp. 374–376.

[4] Our own society appears to rely primarily on a third alternative, wherein people are directly socialized to sexual taboos so that external structures of control, particularly in the family, seem less necessary. For a more detailed discussion based on a cross-cultural analysis see George P. Murdock, *Social Structure* (New York: The Macmillan Company, 1949), Chap. 9.

segregation cannot operate. Rituals of interpersonal contact, such as the salute, and the formalities of interpersonal interaction, such as formal forms of address and communication, use of the third person, and so forth, symbolize and reinforce the governing statuses in the interaction of people in their statuses as officers and enlisted men.

A special application of this insulating function is found in the maximum security prison, where the more serious and confirmed offenders are housed. Given the structure of contemporary penal practices, one of the pressing problems is the maintenance of discipline and the assurance that authority remains in the hands of the administration. The weakest link in the custodial chain is found where the prison population comes into daily, routine, and relatively intimate contact with the administration. This is found in the relationship between the prisoner and the guard. It is here that discipline and authority are apt to be dissipated. In his desire to be a good fellow and in his need to secure cooperation from prisoners, the guard may provide the opportunity for serious breaches of discipline and allow authority to slip into the hands of prisoners to the extent that they, rather than the administrators, are running the prison. Short of a complete revamping of the whole of penal practice, the only recourse is to institute insulating principles that provide social barriers between the prisoner and the guard. Such practices involve the very regimented, routinized, and rigid controls that reformers so frequently oppose.[5] It should be noted that insulation in this case also acts as a negative sanction, since the prisoners' way of life is more punishing with such insulation than without it.

The sociologist William Foote Whyte, in studying the social structure of the restaurant, observed frictions accompanying the interactions of workers of different age, sex, occupational position, and seniority. He suggested that one source of the friction arose from the fact that individuals of lower rank (waitresses) originated orders for those of higher rank (countermen or bartenders). The affront to the prestige of the latter resulted in a variety of deviant behavior, such as delaying orders, bickering among workers, and overt expression of resentment. He found that the tension frequently could be reduced or eliminated by such relatively simple measures as requiring waitresses to write out orders and put them on a spindle, placing a physical barrier such as a warming compartment between waitresses and countermen, or permitting bartenders to mix drinks in the order of greatest efficiency rather than on the basis of when the waitresses presented their orders. Devices such as these act as buffers

---

[5] For a detailed discussion of this problem in a maximum security prison in New Jersey, consult Gresham M. Sykes, *The Society of Captives* (Princeton, N.J.: Princeton University Press, 1958).

between workers and provide social insulation at those points where the potential for conflict and resort to deviant modes of adaptation are greatest.[6]

On a larger scale, a great many of the institutionalized relationships between Negroes and whites in the South of the United States perform the function of status-insulation.[7] One important function of insulation in this situation is to maintain the status-definition of Negro social inferiority and sustain the Negro status-obligation of deference to whites. Insulation protects both the white and the Negro from forms of interaction that, by assuming equality on the part of Negroes, would upset these definitions. Thus, an informal sexual liaison between a white male and a Negro female (note that the reverse is not approved) may be tacitly permitted, but sexual union in marriage is prohibited by statutory law; a Negro may not sit at a white's dining table, but may prepare and handle his food as a cook; or a Negro may not dwell in the same home as a white, unless he is a servant. Such prohibitions as these do not prevent intimate and often kindly relations between Negroes and whites, but status-lines are sharply drawn and clearly protected by devices of insulation at points where status-conflict is potential.[8]

Status-insulation may be accomplished at a less elaborate and somewhat more informal level. Manners and politeness have more than a moral or esthetic function, and these practices should not be written off as meaningless ritual or crusty tradition, although they may be in particular instances. Not only do they provide a clearly defined structure for interaction where initially the structure may be vague or has not emerged, more importantly for analysis of social insulation, manners and forms of polite intercourse frequently permit interaction among occupants of conflicting statuses that would flare up into open deviance without them. They provide a buffer zone in which roles may be played without violating the deeper commitments of the role-players. Similarly, banter and small talk keep people at arm's distance but permit orderly and coordinated activity. Mark Twain's assertion that "everybody talks about the

[6] William Foote Whyte, "The Social Structure of the Restaurant," *American Journal of Sociology*, 54:302–308 (1949).

7. Race relations in the United States involve role-segregation as well as insulation. Segregation in the public schools has been a notable example. However, since many areas of behavior cannot be segregated so conveniently, insulating mechanisms are frequently used to avoid strains in interpersonal relations.

[8] For a brief discussion of forms of insulation and the ambiguity inherent in Negro-white relationships see Allison Davis, "Caste, Class and Violence," *American Journal of Sociology*, 51:7–16 (1945), reprinted in Logan Wilson and William L. Kolb (eds.), *Sociological Analysis* (New York: Harcourt, Brace & World, Inc., 1949), pp. 479–488. The most detailed summary of Negro-white relations in America is contained in Gunnar Myrdal, *An American Dilemma* (New York: Harper & Brothers, 1944).

weather" contains more than a grain of truth. In talking about the weather or baseball or movies or "what good books have you read lately," we are assured that we will not poke through the surface to the core of inner values. (Beware, however, the assumption that these subjects constitute small talk to the devoted specialist or the rabid enthusiast.)

The very symbols we use in discourse may provide a cushion to join rough surfaces. The language of diplomacy is something more than high-flown phrases and vague formalities. It permits communication through the barriers of hostility and deep conflict. Similarly, "reading between the lines" and "hidden meanings" may alert without offending directly. A special case of insulation is found in the role of the intermediary. He stands between opposing forces in much the same way as the warming counter stands between the waitress and the counterman. As the exchange agent between contending parties, he has the added advantage of actively keeping the potential conflict within the confines of comfortable behavior. Parties do not directly confront one another or openly pierce defenses, so that neither is motivated to make the ultimate break toward deviance. Lawyers frequently perform this function in modern societies.

PRIORITY

A third device for preventing the strain of conflict is institutionalized status-priority. A clear social definition of what demands of which status are to take precedence relieves people of struggling for decision. Conflicting expectation then causes only minimum difficulty, since people legitimately may give priority to one rather than to another. Is a woman who has witnessed her husband engaging in an illegal act to violate the obligation of loyalty to her husband and testify against him, or should she remain silent and violate her status as a citizen? In Anglo-American law the role of wife is given definite priority over that of citizen, and the woman is exempted from testifying against her husband. On the other hand, in most colleges with an honor system, the status of "citizen" unmistakably is supposed to be given priority over the status of friend. In such cases as these, status-priority gives institutionalized support for action that otherwise would bring self-censure to the individual and disapproval on the part of others. By institutionalizing the choice, people are relieved of making a decision that involves deviation no matter what is done.

The socially recognized priority of the patient's welfare over the demands of the doctor's family life helps him to handle these sometimes conflicting demands. The businessman is not so fortunate and frequently labors under the strain of serving two masters, for priorities of business roles and family roles are not so clearly established. The difference in the two cases is precisely the difference between the presence or absence of role-priority.

One final example may further illustrate the function of structured priority. We have suggested how segregation of role-partners in poly-gynous families may help to avoid strain. Another mechanism frequently institutionalized is to allocate authority to one wife, usually the first. Her superordinate status is the basis for distribution of household tasks among wives, and conflicts centering around such duties are minimized. Kimball Young has suggested that the absence of such mechanisms of control in the Mormon polygynous family may help to account for the relative failure of this practice in the United States.[9]

Before discussing the next major mechanism of control, we should pause to consider again a point made earlier concerning the nature of social control. It should be clear that in our discussion of segregation, insulation, and priority, as mechanisms of pattern maintenance, we refer to devices that may or may not be collectively approved and practiced by system members. It is often the case that illegitimate practices are func-tional as social control mechanisms. For example, segregation of Negroes or "caste etiquette" that requires Negroes to address whites as "Mr." or "Mrs.," while whites address them as "boy" or "girl," may operate to prevent overt conflict, even though illegitimate in terms of national mores.[10]

Similarly, in our society, maintaining a mistress in separate quarters is a form of segregation that happens to be deviant; in other societies, such behavior might more accurately be called institutionalized segregation. In both cases, it seems to forestall conflict on the part of all the parties involved. Again, parental knowledge legitimately may be kept from chil-dren as a means of social control in order not to reinforce their deviant motivation, or information may be illegitimately withheld in negotiation as a means to forestall the motivation to deviate. Banter and small talk may be positively sanctioned in social occasions where intimacy is not appropriate, or it may be thoroughly disapproved as deviance in situa-

[9] Kimball Young, *Isn't One Wife Enough?* (New York: Holt, Rinehart and Winston, Inc., 1954).

[10] We feel impelled to repeat here our earlier warning, however, that there is noth-ing sacred about conformity or peace. Our own values would lead us to prefer devi-ance and conflict in the present instance. The situation in the United States may be contrasted with the traditional operation of caste in India, where caste-relationships are institutionalized in the total society. The rights and obligations of caste are gen-erally accepted and supported by the total organization of the society. Thus, segrega-tion and insulation are congruent with other institutionalized arrangements. Even here, however, caste structure is changing under Western and industrial influences.

tions where it is used as a manipulative device to talk down to or demean. In sum, when we are discussing social control, the question is not whether the mechanism is approved but whether it controls.

Tension Management

When structure fails to forestall conflict, and frustration and strain ensue, deviant adaptation may be prevented by permitting relief from tension in socially sanctioned ways. This procedure involves the mechanism of tension management. This mechanism was encountered in the discussion of socialization where tension management was described as a mechanism for handling strains that accompany learning and internalization of social definitions. Tension management as a form of social control parallels this function in the support and maintenance of definitions, once learned or internalized.

Tesion management may be institutionalized in essentially two ways. First, people may continue to play frustrating roles as prescribed and cope with their resultant tensions by *compensatory behavior*, either in the same status or in other legitimate statuses. Second, they may be permitted to withdraw from the frustrating status and assume *alternative* ones that are equally legitimate, but less frustrating. Each of these alternatives will now be discussed in some detail.

COMPENSATORY BEHAVIOR

Compensatory behavior that allows people to sustain or release tension may be of several different kinds, in terms of the degree of social approval attached to them. In these terms, we may speak of "safety valves" that are *culturally preferred*, those that are culturally *permitted*, those that are simply *tolerated*, and those that are *prohibited* (while still remaining effective safety valves).

Compensatory behavior that is *culturally preferred* is usually available in the status-set of most people. For instance, the worker who is frustrated in his occupational status may find compensatory satisfactions in his family roles. As husband and father, he may achieve sufficient esteem and approval to make bearable the frustrations of low prestige and impersonal relationships inherent in his job. By maintaining a home workshop, he may compensate for the obsolescence of skill on the assembly line. In family recreational activities and consumption of material goods and services, he may compensate for dull routine and hard labor.[11] Since playing these roles depends upon satisfactory performance of occupation, the motive to conform to the demands of the job become even more firmly institutionalized. For some males, of course, the job may serve as a compensatory status for the frustrations of family roles. In the same ways, many American women find release from the frustrations of the housewife and mother statuses in political, religious, and "social" activities.

The growth and development of the union in American society may be understood in part as an attempt of manual workers to acquire prestige and respect in the larger social structure that frequently were denied them in the performance of their economic and political functions.[12] The proliferation of social clubs, lodges, and fraternal organizations in America very probably has performed similar functions for people who have felt the isolation of rural farm life or the impersonal impact of urban life or who have been isolated from the "ingroup" and stigmatized as "outsiders."[13] What such compensatory statuses as these have in common and what sets them apart from other such devices is that the way in which the tension is managed is culturally approved and tends to be collectively conceived as important, significant, and legitimate. Therefore, it has equal rank with the status that presents conflict and gives rise to tensions.

Second, tension management may be *culturally permitted,* but not preferred. These activities are frequently incorporated in the status that frustrates. In industrial society, managers have found it wise to allow and even deliberately include tension management in the work status. Banter and a certain amount of free interplay among workers is permitted, coffee breaks are arranged, music is piped in, and routine, monotonous tasks are rotated. This is a far cry from the earlier industrial period when workers were fined for whistling and doors were locked lest workers waste valuable time getting a drink of water. Culturally permitted activities usually operate informally and contribute chiefly to the individual's tension management, rather than directly to the productivity of the status or to other social functions. Most statuses give the individual some relatively loose rein to act out his tensions and permit him to fit his own rhythm and

---

[11] For a discussion of compensatory role-playing among some American steel workers, see Warner Bloomberg, Jr., "The State of the American Proletariat," *Commentary,* 19:207–216 (1955).

[12] See Frank Tannenbaum, *The Philosophy of Labor* (New York: Alfred A. Knopf, Inc., 1951) for a discussion of some of the noneconomic functions of the labor movement.

[13] It should be noted that these organizations usually at least avow their intentions to do "good works" and support "moral uplift," thus gaining collective approval from the larger system in which they function. For a discussion of clubs and fraternal organizations in American society, see Charles W. Ferguson, *Fifty Million Brothers* (New York: Holt, Rinehart and Winston, Inc., 1937).

particular functioning to status-obligations. Conversely, statuses usually prescribe a boiling point at which the individual may let off steam and design the safety valve to do so. Such activity may appear to decrease efficiency of role-playing, but is permitted, nonetheless, because without it even more deviant motivation might develop and be expressed in still more deviant adaptation.

Societies sometimes permit behavior at specified times and places that under other circumstances would not be tolerated. Ancient societies, particularly, institutionalized "Roman holidays" and festivals where license was extended to behavior that ordinarily would be severely condemned. Remnants of such practices are found in the observance of Halloween and New Year's Eve, when mild pranks and excesses are permitted and even expected. Such devices as these may serve to release hostilities and aggression and relieve tensions in relatively harmless ways or in situations where they can be socially controlled.

Under conditions of unusual strain, special structures may develop to facilitate tension management. In many ways the ritual surrounding death in our society, as in most soceties, is more for the living than the dead. Similarly, after periods of extended strain, persons are often permitted relaxation and are not held to the normal demands of roles. One important social function of humor, involving as it does the very physical relief of laughter, is to manage tensions in situations involving strain. Murdock and others have commented on the tension management function of obligatory "joking relations" institutionalized in some societies among relatives of the opposite sex. It has been suggested that the rough and compulsive joking associations between siblings-in-law, for example, who also are permissible sex objects, may permit the socially sanctioned expression of latent hostility and aggression occasioned by ambivalence toward the primary sex object, one's spouse.[14] Similarly, the relief of weeping and lamentation may be socially patterned and permitted. It is significant to note, in this respect, that crying is permitted females more frequently than males in our society, in conformity with the different status-expectations of the sexes, and that the higher incidence of heart disease and ulcers among men has been attributed, in part, to the unavailability of this safety valve to men.

Although magic is not manifestly supported in the major values of modern society, it is still culturally permitted and informally practiced,

[14] Murdock, *Social Structure*, p. 282. For some of the psychological functions of humor see A. A. Brill, *The Basic Writings of Sigmund Freud* (New York: Random House, Inc., 1938), Book IV, pp. 633–803. A sociological analysis may be found in John H. Burma, "Humor as a Technique in Race Conflict," *American Sociological Review*, 11:710–711 (1946), and in Richard M. Stephenson, "Conflict and Control Functions of Humor," *American Journal of Sociology*, 56:569–574 (1951).

although usually under the guise of pseudo science. In American society, various forms of magic inherent in astrology, palmestry, crystal-ball gazing, and other assorted cult practices still consume a substantial portion of our income. Although partly devoid of the manipulative and instrumental aspects found in more primitive magic, these practices sometimes help to manage tensions accompanying uncertainty and fear. Indications of the more primitive forms of magic may be found in some hair oil jingles, soap operas, toothpaste slogans, and cosmetic advertisements. In their magic, boys will be pursued, problems will be solved, friends will multiply, and suitors will marry.[15]

A very important form of tension management is the satisfaction of frustrated wishes, or the escape from conflicting demands, by means of fantasy, both individual fantasy of the daydreaming (or night-dreaming, for that matter) type, and the "manufactured fantasies" of folklore, stories, movies, radio, television, magazines, novels, and so on. Whether these are to be viewed as "culturally preferred," "permitted," "tolerated," or even "prohibited" depends on the specific content of the fantasies; and, in the heterogeneous United States, at least, on the particular cultural subgroup doing the evaluating.

A particularly interesting research showing the differential appeal of manufactured fantasies to children who are differentially frustrated has been carried out by Matilda White Riley and John W. Riley, Jr. They first classified a sample of fifth- and seventh-grade children into those who were members of *both* a family group *and* a peer group, and those who were members only of their family groups. They found that for both boys and girls, those who were not peer group members were distinctly more likely to read and enjoy "little animal comics" such as Bugs Bunny than were the peer group members. The Rileys interpret their finding thus:

> Those children who belong in family groups but not in peer groups are offered a set of adult values by their parents. This usually means that they are expected to help at home, to do well in school, to learn to strive in order to achieve, and in general to prepare for a future life as adults. For many ten- and twelve-year-old children those goals may often seem difficult or even completely unattainable. Small wonder, then, that they love to read about little animals like Bugs Bunny, whom they perceive as the complete negation of the goals and conventions established by adults.[16]

[15] For a study that suggests the tension management function of the soap opera for some listeners, see Herta Herzog, "Psychological Gratifications in Daytime Radio Listening," in Theodore M. Newcomb and Eugene L. Hartley, *et al.* (eds.), *Readings in Social Psychology* (New York: Holt, Rinehart and Winston, Inc., 1947), pp. 561–566.

[16] Matilda White Riley and John W. Riley, Jr., "A Sociological Approach to Communications Research," *Public Opinion Quarterly*, 15:451 (1951).

Similarly, they found that "only" children in the family were more likely
to like radio and television programs of action and violence. The Rileys
summarize their findings with this general observation: "When the social
structure imposes undue strain upon the individual . . . we should expect
him to be highly productive of fantasies, and therefore to select a kind of
media material, such as little animals or violent action, which would foster
such fantasies."[17]

Third, in addition to tension management activities that are culturally
preferred and permitted, there are some that are only *tolerated*. These
are activities that are officially and collectively opposed in general, but
are tolerated and frequently practiced under culturally specified conditions. They border on deviant behavior, but usually are tolerated as long
as the behavior does not become a dominant or compulsive mode of
adaptation for the individual or sufficiently common in the group to impede orderly social processes or threaten established patterns. Tolerated
activity is typically found in gambling, drinking to intoxication, certain
deviant sexual behavior, rowdiness, and the like. The phrase "boys will be
boys" suggests the mood and tone of such tolerance. It is significant to
note that this license does not apply equally to women in our society.
Compensatory behavior that is culturally tolerated is usually specified as
to time, place, and person. This is one of the characteristics that gives it
its institutional quality and differentiates it from a completely deviant
mode of adaptation. The use of alcohol in American society presents a
particularly interesting case because of the ambivalence that still seems
to linger concerning it, particularly among that American minority that
has recently come to be called middle-class WASPS (White Anglo-Saxon
Protestants). Even within this group, social drinking, restricted by age,
frequently performs a tension management function at social gatherings.[18]
These occasions usually carefully restrict consumption up to the point of

---

[17] *Ibid.*, p. 455. For additional stimulating discussions of the tension management
functions of the mass media, see the following: James S. Plant, *Personality and the
Culture Pattern* (New York: Oxford University Press, 1937), Chaps. 6 and 8; Abram
Kardiner, *Psychological Frontiers of Society* (New York: Columbia University Press,
1945), pp. 367–373; Martha Wolfenstein and Nathan Leites, "An Analysis of Themes
and Plots," in Kingsley Davis, Harry Bredemeier, and Marion J. Levy, Jr., *Modern
American Society* (New York: Holt, Rinehart and Winston, Inc., 1949), pp. 559–566;
David Riesman, *The Lonely Crowd* (New York: Doubleday Anchor Books [abridged],
1953), pp. 141–148 and 184–186.

[18] For some of the social functions of alcohol, see Seldon D. Bacon, "Sociology and
the Problem of Alcohol," *Quarterly Journal of Studies in Alcohol*, 4:402–445 (1943–
44). For a cross-cultural analysis of preliterate peoples and folk societies, based on
the function of alcohol in reduction of anxieties occasioned by cultural practices or
other factors, see Donald Horton's "The Function of Alcohol in Primitive Societies,"
in *Quarterly Journal of Studies on Alcohol*, 4:199–320 (1943–44).

intoxication. However, intoxication may be tolerated under special circumstance, to "let off steam" or on occasions of high celebration. Males generally are permitted more liberty in this respect than females. However, if drunkenness becomes too frequent or drinking is compulsive, it is socially disapproved and no longer receives institutional support.

The line between tolerated and *prohibited* compensatory behavior sometimes is very thin, and "tension management" may blur over into outright deviation. This is particularly true of some forms of mob action, such as lynching, where the latent tensions being expressed frequently have little connection with the object against which they are directed. Collective sentiment allows the tensions to be displaced on objects that are commonly disapproved or devalued.[19] Some analysts have suggested that insistence upon harsh punitive measures against criminals may express this same function by providing a legally supported and culturally sanctioned focus for aggression.[20] In such cases, mechanisms of tension management supply institutionalized aids to the repression of disapproved impulses by providing socially acceptable rationalizations, displacements, and projections.

Such tolerated or even tabooed forms of tension management may be pattern maintaining even though they are deviant in respect to *some* of the values of the systems in which they take place. To the extent that the release of tensions receives some institutionalized support in one direction, it is probable that the tensions will not be expressed in another. Assaulting criminals may forestall wife beating; getting drunk may inhibit homicide; and committing aggression against minority groups may restrain aggression against the State. The elimination of marginal tension management mechanisms may raise more problems than it "solves." Strict enforcement of gambling laws, for example, may result in other more serious forms of social deviance. The roots of the problem are located in

[19] Durward Pruden's analysis of a lynching presents a useful illustration of the function of mob action for the management of tensions of some of its members: "A Sociological Study of a Texas Lynching," *Studies in Sociology*, 1:3–9 (1936), reprinted in Wilson and Kolb, *op. cit.*, pp. 335–343.

[20] Campbell's finding—that prejudice against Jews was found more frequently among individuals dissatisfied with their economic and political circumstance—suggests the "scapegoat" role that minorities may play in American society: "Factors Associated with Attitudes towards Jews," in Newcomb and Hartley, *Readings in Social Psychology*, pp. 518–527. For a more detailed study of the relationship of personality structure to ethnic prejudice, see Else Frenkel-Brunswik, Daniel J. Levinson, and R. Nevitt Sanford, "The Antidemocratic Personality," *ibid.*, pp. 531–541. For speculations concerning the displacement of aggressions on criminals, consult Paul Reinwald, *Society and Its Criminals* (New York: International Universities Press, 1950) and F. Alexander and H. Staub, *The Criminal, the Judge, and the Public: A Psychological Analysis* (London: George Allen & Unwin Ltd., 1931).

the sources of tension, rather than in the mechanism through which the tensions are expressed. However, removal of structural sources of tension may require abandonment of cherished norms that have been supported by the avowedly obnoxious but tolerated tension management mechanisms.

It should be clear in this discussion that the activities we have described as compensatory roles that are functional for tension management may also perform other functions. It is not contended that the family, for example, is merely a convenient device for managing tensions arising from work roles, and, thus, simply an appendage to the industrial process. Family roles, like work roles, have their independent functions. In the same way, prejudice and discrimination may function as coercive controls, punitive measures may be functional for resocialization, and love, laughter, and tears may play their separate roles in the satisfaction of a wide range of needs. However, in the analysis of tension management, the point to be understood is that any of these, under specified conditions, may be functional for pattern-maintenance by "managing" tensions that would otherwise result in pattern-destruction or in "more serious" pattern-destruction than is inherent in the mechanism. Indeed, one of the crucial and difficult tasks that confronts the analyst is to determine in specific cases under consideration precisely what the function of behavior is and to isolate out the elements of tension management and other functions or disfunctions that may be involved.

STATUS ALTERNATIVES

Where sufficient compensatory gratification is not built into a status or where other statuses do not permit adequate compensation, individuals may be permitted to withdraw from the tension-producing status in favor of some other conformist activity. The permission to withdraw from a status allows the individual to avoid the strains that it induces, and the obligation to assume another culturally approved status assures conformity and inhibits deviance. To the extent that alternative and satisfying statuses are available and individuals are permitted to move to them, they are less likely to resort to deviant adaptation. This is one of the advantages of an open occupational system and permissive geographical mobility. People are not held to a specified status or to particular role-partners, but may seek among alternatives until they find a status that meets their needs or role-partners that are congenial. Alternative statuses go beyond compensatory statuses in tension management, because they allow the person to withdraw from the source of tension or to seek a less tension-producing situation. Compensatory statuses, on the other hand, provide means for sustaining or releasing tensions without withdrawing from the source of strain.

There is a certain social danger in the provision of status alternatives, since people may move among them without sufficient commitment to any one to provide productive role-playing. This is typical of the worker who drifts from job to job; or of the husband (or wife), from marriage to marriage. Usually, therefore, some penalty or barrier to movement is institutionalized so as to make the move of some seriousness and consideration. Divorce in our society is a case in point. Some stigma is attached to the process and ordinarily it is not obtained without considerable effort and expense. In contrast, some primitive societies complete divorce by the simple expedient of allowing one partner to place the other's worldly goods on the doorstep. It is significant to note, however, that divorce in such cultures may be rare. Much depends on the support that marriage and the family receive from other institutional arrangements and on the functions of the marital system. This is but another way of saying that much depends on the amount of strain produced and the provision for release and compensation in the marital situation. It should be pointed out, also, that status-alternatives may provide as much tension as produced by the frustrating situation if people have no firmly established standards by which to judge their needs. The individual who does not know what he wants is under tension, partly because he does not play any role long enough to find out. Furthermore, it should be recognized that the controls exercised by a group are diminished to the degree that institutionalized avenues for withdrawal are present. One of the compelling factors in the structure of delinquent gangs is the fact that there are few if any alternative systems to which its members may turn. Even if the doors to "respectable" groups are not closed and securely bolted, as is frequently the case, their alien values are likely to repel or confuse. In addition, such groups are unlikely to offer the needed psychological or physical protection that is found within the gang, so that gang boys literally may have no place to go and are reluctant or unable to give up their membership even if they want to.

In some cases, special statuses may be created for particularly tension-provoking conditions. Where the individual finds it difficult or impossible to observe the normal requirements of a status, he may be allowed to assume an alternative one that provides equal or nearly equal self-respect. In the last decade or so, our own society has paid particular attention to such structuring by attempting to create productive statuses for the physically or mentally handicapped. A more general case is found in some present attempts to develop alternative statuses for retired members of the population. The institution of the *berdache* among the Indians of most of North America offers a dramatic example of a special status-alternative. Although homosexuality was not positively sanctioned as a status for males, men who were unable to assume the usual masculine status-specification were permitted to take on those usually reserved to females. They could assume the attire and occupation of women and sometimes married other males. They were granted the right to self-respect and social position on their own terms, as persons adept in the practices of an alternative status that received social support and recognition. This institution provided shelter for both sexual inverts and those who simply found the requirements of the males status too demanding.[21]

Mechanisms of Blockage

Thus far we have discussed two of the five major dimensions of social control: mechanisms to forestall strain and mechanisms of tension management. In a metaphorical sense, they may be thought of as the system's first and second lines of defense. They tend to function so as to prevent or suppress *motivation* to deviate. If the motivation cannot be prevented or suppressed, it may still be prevented from resulting in deviant behavior if the behavior can be made extremely difficult or costly.

MAKING DEVIANCE DIFFICULT

One way to ensure conformity despite deviant motivation is to structure situations so that deviant adaptation is very difficult or, if practiced, is relatively ineffective. At the same time, the negative sanction of disapproval of deviation and potential coercion of the deviator remain as background motives to conformity. The consequence of such mechanisms is that people conform "in spite of themselves." The advantage over purely punitive mechanisms of control (to be discussed below) lies in the fact that the potential deviator is not so subject to pressures that might alienate him completely from conformist values or motivate him to develop effective methods of circumventing them. In addition, reliance is not placed completely on the individual's conscience as an inhibitor of deviance. The ways of the devil are less tempting because they are less available. An

---

[21] Ruth Benedict, *Patterns of Culture* (New York: Mentor Books, The New American Library of World Literature, Inc., 1950), pp. 242–245. Other examples of special alternative statuses are discussed in this chapter.

example or two may serve to illustrate the special features of this mechanism.

Despite the "glory that was Greece," the Greeks were not unmindful of the foibles and temptations of the human kind. In Athens particularly, which fostered considerable individual freedom (in contrast to the rigid socialization processes and authoritarian controls of Sparta), the ancient Greeks were ingenious in devising mechanisms to undercut resort to deviance. With shrewd recognition of the deviance motivated by the desire to win in competitive situations, they devised mechanisms for controlling it. In the competition for selection of the annual plays to be presented in the public theater, for example, ten citizens were chosen by lot to act as judges. After they had reached a decision through ballot, five votes were selected at random and destroyed. The prize then was awarded on the basis of majority decision of the remaining five. This reduced the possibility of bribery except in the unlikely circumstance that the playwright could bribe all ten judges. Selection of judges by lot provided a further barrier, since no one could know beforehand who the judges would be. A parallel mechanism is used in the selection of a new pope in the Roman Catholic Church. Despite the lofty position and presumption of incorruptibility of participants, precautions are taken. When the cardinals convene to select a new pope, by tradition no one is supposed to vote for himself. However, the temptation is there, since a single vote might add the weight necessary for election, and the ballot is secret. To reduce if not eliminate the temptation, it was agreed that election would be by a majority, *plus one*. Thus, the chances of a cardinal hoisting himself to office by his single vote were somewhat reduced.

Contrasts in the structure of the British Parliament and of the American Congress may help to explain, in some measure, the differences in the amount of corruption that exists between them. In the first place, members of the House of Commons are relieved from the sometimes conflicting loyalties of local and national interests, since there is no locality rule in the British system. They are further protected from pressure by the fact that the Cabinet rather than members of the House initiates legislation. However, in standing committees, where an M.P. may play a role in drafting and amending legislation, he is potentially subject to direct pressure. This is forestalled by use of nonspecialists on committees, a nonpermanent chairman, and the selection of chairmen in no predetermined order by the Speaker of the House. By these devices, no one knows in advance who will be working on what legislation. Furthermore, a member of the House of Commons must announce his financial interest in any subject that he wishes to debate, and standing committee members must swear that neither they nor their constituents have any local interest in bills under committee consideration. Commenting upon such measures as these, Alistair Cook, the former British subject and present American journalist, has observed, ". . . . the Member of Parliament is protected from his worst self by the system, whereas some other systems tend to put a Representative on the receiving end of a cornucopia and then expect him to be a demigod."[22]

It is sometimes wise to set a thief to catch a thief rather than to rely on the unsupported integrity of a "disinterested" third person. With no offense to either political party intended, the American practice that allocates both Democrats and Republicans to election boards instead of appointing an impartial watchdog (but who watches him?) reflects this wisdom. The self-interest of contending parties for mutually desired objects may be controlled by having one party separate them into two piles and giving the other first choice. It has been reported, for example, that this is an effective technique for dividing archeological spoils between the host government and visiting archeologists. The simple expedient of deducting taxes at the source of income rather than attempting to collect from the individual receiving it, forestalls deviance where it is most likely to emerge. The opposite practice of reliance on individual integrity inherent in collecting taxes on interest and dividends tempts deviance.[23]

The largely private nature of the income tax suggests the utility of full and public disclosure in those situations where common decency permits, for secrecy is the curtain behind which deviant motivation may be expressed in action. Conformity, then, is partly dependent upon "visibility." Visibility or observability of both norms and role performances, in turn, is contingent on the structure of the social system. Merton puts the relationship of visibility to deviance and social control in the following way:

> The structural conditions which make for ready observability or visibility of role-performance will of course provide appropriate feed-back when the role-performance departs from the patterned expectations of the group. For under such conditions, the responses of other members of the group, tending to bring the deviant back into line with the norms, will begin to operate soon after the deviant behavior has occurred. Collaterally, when there are structural impediments to such direct and im-

---

[22] Reported in the New York *Herald Tribune*, October 28, 1951. For a popularized discussion of some of the problems in the American system, see Blair Bolles, *How to Get Rich in Washington* (New York: W. W. Norton & Company, Inc., 1952). For a more academic analysis, consult George A. Graham, *Morality in American Politics* (New York: Random House, Inc., 1952), and H. H. Wilson, *Congress: Corruption and Compromise* (New York: Holt, Rinehart and Winston, Inc., 1951). Our discussion does not carry the implication that we can transfer readily the practices of another system to our own, or even that we should.

[23] For an account of some of the vagaries and loopholes of the American tax structure, see John L. Hess, "The Gentle Art of Tax Avoidance," *The Reporter*, 20:12–17 (April 16, 1959).

mediate observability, deviant behavior can cumulate, depart ever more widely from the prevailing norms before coming to the notice of others in the group, and then often elicit an "over-reaction" which serves only to alienate the deviants, rather than to "correct" their deviations. These structural hindrances to the flow of information (which would appear to be the present-day counterpart of Simmel's concept of observability) will in this manner interfere with the relatively steady state of the group and produce fitful and irregular oscillations of social control.[24]

Such devices as these need not reflect world-weary cynicism, for in discouraging deviation, they may encourage conformity: it is easier to be moral in the absence of temptation. They give support and structure to morality that reliance on punitive action or individual conviction alone sometimes fail to provide. In assuring that deviance is difficult for all, they support the conformity of each.

INCREASING THE COST OF DEVIANCE

When roadblocks to deviance of the kind we have described are not present people may still be deterred from acting out their deviant motivations if the probable cost of deviance is higher than the cost of conformity. This is one reason why the punishment frequently does not fit the crime, but is all out of proportion to it.

As George C. Homans has pointed out, a wide range of controls that operate informally in any social group is simply a consequence of the nature of the organization of group life.[25] Since interdependence and exchange are implicit in the division of labor of a group, and complementary needs get met only by means of established patterns of interaction, departure from these regularities is likely to be met by resistance. The resistance results from the fact that a change in the established pattern on the part of one group member affects the other group members. If it does so adversely, resistance is probable, and is effected by withholding of goods, services, and attitudes. The deviant then is brought back to conformity to the degree that what is withheld denies him what is needed to occupy statuses he seeks or presently holds. Thus, the network of interpersonal relationships may operate informally, without specific design or intent, to penalize the deviant and to motivate conformity to the folkways and mores governing group activities.

Such controls as these are found typically in the primary group. Al-

[24] Merton, *Social Theory and Social Structure*, p. 320. A detailed discussion of the relationship of visibility to authority is given on pp. 336–352.

[25] George C. Homans, *The Human Group* (New York: Harcourt, Brace & World, Inc., 1950), Chap. 11.

though in a society such as our own, many goods and services are exchanged at the secondary level of interaction, the exchange of attitudes for behavior is basic to the small group and to direct, interpersonal relations. In such situations, the withholding of approval by members of a positive reference group becomes a powerful mechanism of control. Here the deviant is faced with direct confrontation and immediate punitive response. Persons in interaction are continually providing the cues to conformity by tone of voice, facial expressions or gestures, mild ridicule disguised in humor, tactful disagreement, and the silence that speaks in a loud voice. Within the family, among friends, within the immediacies of work and play associations, and in small villages or primitive groups, the response of each controls, in some measure, the behavior of all.[26] Some sociologists have made the further suggestion that there may be, in most groups, an informal division of labor by which this control mechanism operates. As Riley and Cohn have put it, the individual's ". . . . conformity may be noted by his friend, who in general is disposed to reward him for it; while, at the same time, enemies may be at hand to rebuke him at some other point where he seems to step over the line in the deviant direction. . . . Thus a composite of other persons may tend to divide . . . the labor of imposing the positive and negative sanctions which the support the individual's conformity."[27]

When the size and density of population increase, the effectiveness of social disapproval as a control mechanism tends to decrease. Social disapproval still operates and operates effectively. but it is likely to be segmental rather than total. On the one hand, people are set apart and restrict their cathexis of others to a limited range of interactions. On the other hand, the individual is more anonymous, his relationships more segmental, and his interactions with many other persons less enduring.[28] In such a social setting, deviants may be able to protect themselves from the scorn of the larger society by finding refuge in groups that support and reinforce their deviant motivations. The deviant group becomes their reference group, and they may act out their deviant motivations relatively immune from the impact of the larger culture. Their deviant behavior may receive tacit support, in turn, from members of the avowedly "respectable" society, who make *selective* use of their deviance to further

[26] For an analysis of the operation of informal mechanisms of social control in a small American town, see Albert Blumenthal, *Small Town Stuff* (Chicago: The University of Chicago Press, 1932), Part II, "Agencies of Social Control."

[27] Matilda White Riley and Richard Cohn, "Control Networks in Informal Groups," *Sociometry*, 21:30–49 (1958).

[28] For a discussion of some of the characteristics associated with population size and density, see Louis Wirth, "Urbanism as a Way of Life," *American Journal of Sociology*, 44:1–24 (1938).

their own goals. For example, people in the business and industrial sector of society may find it expedient to use organized criminal elements to consolidate and maintain competitive advantage in union or business activities, and those in the political sector may trade support for votes and financial contributions.

Nonetheless, it is doubtful that people are entirely free from the constraints of informal public disapproval even where expressed through secondary sources. In such relationships, social disapproval may still operate as a control mechanism if being of good repute is necessary to function in the system or to achieve personal goals. In this case, compliance is instrumental and the good opinion of others is sought, despite motivation to deviate. This is one of the social functions of "reputation," and is effective to the degree that individual behavior is open to public scrutiny.

In addition, the deviantly oriented person is faced with the cost of public derogation of deviant statuses. The deviantly motivated may inhibit their desire to deviate in order to avoid seeing themselves in the public stereotype of the nonconformist. Gilbert Geis, a criminologist, has provided an interesting example of this:

> Investigating shoplifters in Chicago's Marshall Field's Department store, Mary Beth Cameron grouped offenders . . . as either amateurs or professionals. She observed that store detectives, after apprehending amateur shoplifters, made strenuous efforts to break through their self-conceptualization in attempts to force them to re-define their behavior in terms which led inescapably to the conclusion that they were criminals. "Yes, I took the purse," one woman sobbed, "but that doesn't mean I'm a thief." Store detectives had to point out again and again to the amateur that she was in fact a thief, and had to reiterate that she was under arrest and would in the due course of events be taken in a police wagon to the police station, booked and fingerprinted, and then brought before a judge and sentenced. Cameron found this technique was so effective, though the procedures threatened were not often carried out, that the amateur shoplifters rarely repeated their offense either at Marshall Field's or elsewhere in Chicago.[29]

The stereotypes that characterize the public image of the deviant obscure the differences of person and circumstance and highlight the common sentiments of disapproval, scorn, loathing, and revulsion. People are reluctant to be identified in terms of the stereotype, even though they may rationalize their motivation to deviate or have no scruples about the deviance itself. They are loath to accept identity as "bureaucrats," "eager beavers," "bums," "pansies," or "jail birds." Such stereotypes are com-

---

[29] Gilbert Geis, "Sociology and Crime," in Joseph S. Roucek (ed.), *Sociology of Crime* (New York: Philosophical Library, Inc., 1961), pp. 26–27.

municated by jokes, cartoons, and caustic wit, and emphasized by the punitive measures applied to the deviant.

The efficacy of such controls is highlighted when seen in operation within a deviant group. Lloyd D. Ohlin, in commenting on a study of a North Carolina prison by Richard McCleery, describes how the "rat" concept operates as a mechanism of social control among inmates.

> Many actions of the administration are incomprehensible to the inmates, since very little effort is made in maximum security institutions to explain official actions. In the face of apparently whimsical and unpredictable official actions, inmates experience an increasing sense of tension, anxiety, and feeling of being powerless. The "rat" concept, according to McCleery, serves to explain all that is unpredictable or mystifying about official actions which affect inmate welfare. The free use of such a concept in a tight, maximum security institution breeds suspicion and distrust of anyone seen talking to an official unless other trusted inmates are within immediate hearing distance. The value of this concept as an effective informal control device is abundantly clear, since the inmate defined as a "rat" is automatically excluded from the society of "right guys," who exercise dominant control of inmate attitudes and behavior.[30]

It should be pointed out, however, that these same images may tend to foster deviation, once the break from institutionalized patterns has been made. One of the many factors in the motivation to deviance is the expectation that others have concerning the behavior of the deviantly oriented person. The social image that is publicly held of the innovator or the ritualist, for example, is composed of a set of patterned acts that are perceived to identify the deviant. The commonly shared definitions of what constitutes a "tough guy" or a "bureaucrat" provide the specifications of a status. Once identified, the deviant is contrained to act out this status. Deviations may perform no particular instrumental function, but serve to verify the deviant self-image, which is supported by the community. Simply put, the deviant says that if he is to be labeled a ritualist or a retreatist, well, then, this is how a "bureaucrat" or a "bum" act. In other words, he lives up to his reputation. He is expected to deviate; therefore he does. This is particularly well illustrated by some people who are publicly identified as criminals and delinquents. One of the barriers to the rehabilitation of a criminal deviant who has been motivated to change *his* self-definition is the difficulty of getting the public to change *its* definition of him as a deviant.

The potential deviant is the more likely to dread the high cost of deviance to the degree that actual deviants in his system have already paid the price. If he has witnessed the scorn, contempt, and hatred directed toward other violators of the norms, he may have a vivid picture of the

[30] Lloyd D. Ohlin, *Sociology and the Field of Corrections* (New York: Russell Sage Foundation, 1956), p. 21.

cost of acting out his own motivations. In this sense, paradoxically, a little deviance may be functional for pattern-maintenance by affording opportunities for the rest of the system members to reassert their commitment to the norms and thereby providing "horrible examples" to potential deviants! Contrariwise, if crime, fraud, violence, and other forms of deviance become widespread, if they are *not* punished and scorned, if public opinion becomes jaded with accounts of dishonesty, then the cost of deviance declines. Even if the reward remains the same, the *profit* goes up because the cost has been reduced.

Although mass society thus gives rise to many problems of social control, it may also increase individual choice of alternatives as well as foster tolerance of differences. In any case, the mechanism of social disapproval may be woven more deliberately and extensively in the fabric of some large-scale systems than in others. Military organization, for example, has seen the wisdom of fostering the intimacies of primary group loyalties. The simple desire to avoid letting the other fellow down coupled with a need for his good opinion may hold a man to the firing line as no amount of lofty exortation or repressive control can. Hence attempts are made to maintain integrity and structure at the squad level embracing a handful of men, and to build links of loyalty that move on up successively to encompass larger units. A study of the German Army's morale and fighting effectiveness during the last three years of World War II has revealed the degree to which conformity to the structure of the larger society is dependent on the maintenance of the integrity of primary groups. Most people are members of secondary groups by virtue of the identifications established and maintained in primary groups, which mediate and sustain the norms of the larger groups. Study of the German Army revealed:

> Where conditions were such as to allow primary group life to function smoothly, and where the primary group developed a high degree of cohesion, morale was high and resistance effective or at least determined, regardless in the main of the political attitudes of the soldiers. The conditions of primary group life were related to spatial proximity, the capacity for intimate communication, the provision of paternal protectiveness by NCO's and junior officers, and the gratification of certain personality needs, e.g., manliness, by the military organization and its activities. The larger structure of the army served to maintain morale through the provision of the framework in which potentially individuating physical threats were kept at a minimum—through the organization of supplies and through adequate strategic dispositions.[31]

The social structure of Athens suggests a somewhat similar but more complex form of organization. In the sixth century B.C., an outstanding

[31] Edward A. Shils and Morris Janowitz, "Cohesion and Disintegration in the Wehrmacht in World War II," *Public Opinion Quarterly*, 12:280–315 (1948), pp. 314–315.

statesman, Cleisthenes, reorganized the social structure of Attica. He created ten new and totally fictional "tribes." Each "tribe" was composed of a nearly equal number of "demes," roughly approximating a parish. These "demes" were scattered throughout three areas into which Attica was divided, so that each tribe contained "demes" in each district. Local affairs were handled in the "deme" and the tribe provided the larger loyalty: citizens voted by tribe, dramatic contests were by tribe, and the tribe was the citizen's regiment in warfare. This web of interrelationships was capped by an assembly of *all* citizens, which was the sole and final legislative body and the ultimate source of judicial power. This amazing fiction was compounded later by the apparent madness of selecting archons (political leaders) by lot. The apparent absurdity or folly of such measures can be judged, however, in the light of the century that followed, which we refer to today as "the golden age of Greece" and view as the peak of classic civilization.[32]

When the potential deviant is immune to public opinion, he still may be deterred by the threat of more extreme, physical punishment—imprisonment, exile, or death. In secondary groups, such means of social control are likely to be institutionalized in the formal mechanism of "law," with specialized statuses created to detect, judge, and punish deviants. The utility of specialization in such systems is born of necessity. Not only is it more efficient to separate out functions and train specialists to perform them; it is necessary to allocate the responsibility to do so, since the informal controls of social disapproval and the structure of role-relationships are less effective in carrying out social control. Coercive punishment, however, is likely to be an effective deterrent only under four conditions.

First, punishment must be severe enough to throw the balance of calculation in favor of conformity. Second, it must be immediate enough to link the punishment to the deviance. Third, it must be relatively uniform, applying to all persons who commit a particular deviance. Fourth, it must be relatively certain if any of the other conditions are to be effective. Because these conditions are so interdependent and their application is so dependent upon relational and value considerations, it is difficult, if not impossible, to determine the relative effectiveness of any one or to apply them all at their maximum level of efficiency. Therefore, very little precise empirical evidence exists concerning the effectiveness of punitive coercion. However, this should not lead the analyst of social control to the conclusion that coercion is ineffective, nor should he permit personal

---

[32] For an analysis of this structure and supporting elaborations, read the excellent summary discussion contained in H. D. F. Kitto, *The Greeks* (Baltimore: Penguin Books, Inc., 1951).

sentiments to obscure the fact that it may play a very real role in social control.

Besides the manifest functions of deterrence, reformation, and "protection of society," coercive punishment may function *latently* as a mechanism of social control. Particularly where the direct force of primary group interactions is absent, the application of punitive measures tends to be ceremonial and ritualistic. The ceremony and ritual attending such occasions serves to underscore the severity of the offense and to emphasize the public support and hence the legitimacy of the punishment. This, in turn, may reinforce the sanctity of conformity and symbolically support the hierarchy of collective taboos. Thus, periodic punishment of deviants may function to reaffirm and maintain the vitality of conformity in much the same way that any public ritual does. At the same time, the public nature of the punishment may foster solidarity among the conforming and close their ranks against the deviant. It is as if everyone plunged in the dagger or dipped his finger in the blood. Punishment itself becomes an instrument in developing and fostering common setiments against deviance. Furthermore, stigmatizing and isolating people on the basis of their deviancies prevents them from spreading their deviant attitudes and, more important, from laying claim to any legitimacy for their deviances. Such functions as these serve less to deter or reform specific deviants than to give collective expression of hostility toward deviance and public affirmation of conformity.[33]

So far as the deviant himself is concerned, as distinct from the potential deviant, this extreme of coercion represents the "fourth line of defense" listed at the beginning of this chapter. The deviant is removed, temporarily or permanently, from the social system.

The fifth "line of defense," we suggested, was resocialization, or "therapy" for the deviant.

Therapy

The use of social coercion tends to put the balance of the accent on deviance rather than on conformity. Repressive measures that isolate and exclude the deviant are likely to be used. Support is apt to be withdrawn

[33] A number of discussions of the social functions of punishment are available. See Émile Durkheim, *The Division of Labor in Society* (trans. George Simpson; New York: The Free Press of Glencoe, Inc., 1947) and G. H. Mead, "The Psychology of Punitive Justice," *American Journal of Sociology*, 23:346–359 (1918).

and severe punitive measures may be instituted. Reaction to these devices may reinforce the negative orientation of the deviant and drive the wedge between deviance and conformity deeper. This is particularly true when the deviance is conceived as a "crime" and the deviant assumes the role of "criminal." Some forms of modern penology attempt to inhibit this vicious circle by instituting therapeutic practices of one kind or another. The more deliberate program of therapy is found in modern psychiatry. Instances of a coupling of coercion with therapy are found in reports of "brain washing" that come to us from the Soviet Union and China. All these practices essentially involve resocialization and have met with varying degrees of success. We have only begun to explore the possibilities of the application of chemical and surgical techniques.

The first stage in the therapeutic resocialization of the deviant is a certain degree of toleration of deviance. Social tolerance of deviance is akin to permissiveness in socialization. Both seek to maintain the link to institutionalized structures while expressing disapproval of the person's deviant tendencies or acts. The link consists of a certain generalized "support" of the individual as a person, accompanied by a refusal to approve and thereby reinforce the deviancy. The desired effect is to prevent a complete break from institutionalized patterns and to inhibit the "vicious circle" effect that might move over into acceptance of deviant adaptation.[34] In order for this to be effective it is necessary that the individual be ambivalent about his deviance. Contemporary practices in psychotherapy represent a highly specialized application of tolerance of deviance as a mechanism of social control. The therapeutic situation allows controlled expression of hostilities and frustrations coupled with a manifest desire on the part of the therapist to understand the patient and to support him as a person. At the same time, the deviant nature of the behavior that brings the patient to the doctor is dramatically underscored by the very presence of the patient in therapy. The more familiar, less formal, specialized case is found in relationships within the family and among friends, where people "stick by" one another, tolerate deviations without approving them, and help each other overcome problems and difficulties.

Some contemporary measures for coping with criminality, especially youthful delinquency, have institutionalized toleration of deviance. First

---

[34] The "vicious circle" is a condition of interaction of two or more variables such that a change in any one will tend to alter the others in the same direction; and this change in the others, in turn, will feed back to further move the first changing condition in the same direction, and so on, as the variables interact. Gunnar Myrdal calls this the "principle of cumulation," pointing out that the direction of the change may be either desirable (and therefore not necessarily "vicious") or undesirable. See his discussion of the principle in *An American Dilemma*, App. 3.

offenders are treated more leniently than repeaters. Youthful offenders are not identified by name in newsprint, and closed court hearings are held. Offenders are placed on probation, which allows the individual to serve his sentence under supervision in the community rather than in prison. Such devices as these attempt to avoid branding the person as a deviant, thus leaving him open to public acceptance, or they place him in an environment where avenues to conformity are more readily available. Recognition of toleration of deviance is found in such common phrases as "give a man another chance," "don't kick him while he's down," and "give him a break." The essential idea is to keep the bridge to conformity open and to keep the balance of factors in favor of compliance for the person who has *not yet made the complete* break to deviance as an *established* pattern. As with permissiveness, these major questions are raised by this mechanism: How much toleration, under what conditions, and at what point does tolerance cease to motivate conformity and begin to reinforce deviance?[35] The balance between tolerance as social control or convenience for deviance is a delicate one, involving complex considerations and calculated risks.

Structured tolerance of deviance attempts to "nip in the bud" deviant motivation before it reaches the full fruit of patterned deviant adaptation. Its effectiveness as a mechanism of social control lies in the ambivalence of people concerning their deviant motivation, the support extended by conforming people, their simultaneous refusal to countenance the deviant behavior, and the provision of rewards for conformity. This last condition all too frequently is absent in many attempts at therapy. The basic difficulty in formal mechanisms of therapy is that rewards are difficult to control outside the therapeutic structure (the mental institution, the reformatory, and the like). Once the deviant has left the therapeutic situation, he is likely to return to the very structure that produced the strain and provided the rewards for deviance. This suggests that changing social structure may be a necessary condition for the success of therapy, in addition to attempts to change individual deviants. This consideration moves the focus from pattern maintenance to social change, for which deviance and deviant motivation may often be the stimulus. Some types of change in cultural patterns, in other words, may be brought about in the very effort to maintain them. It should be recognized, also, that patterns of deviance may spread until what was deviant becomes legitimate. In both cases, deviance is likely to be the prelude to change rather than an interlude in pattern maintenance.

---

[35] For a book that poses and discusses these problems in the area of criminal deviance, see Richard R. Korn and Lloyd W. McCorkle, *Criminology and Penology* (New York: Holt, Rinehart and Winston, Inc., 1959).

SUMMARY

Pattern maintenance is fostered by socialization and social control mechanisms. Social control consists of those social structures that either prevent strain or prevent deviance from resulting from strain. Potentially conflicting situations may be avoided by institutionalizing mechanisms of segregation, insulation, and priority. By allocating statuses and role-players by time, place, and person, the simultaneous impact of conflicting expectations may be avoided. By use of insulating mechanisms at those points where conflict is most likely to arise, motivation to deviance may be forestalled. By establishing a hierarchy of status- and role-obligations, people are relieved of potentially conflicting choice.

Where strain in role-playing is induced, it may be sustained, decreased, or eliminated by the institutionalization of compensatory or alternative activities. Compensatory activity provides socially approved patterns of behavior that hold people to positions of strain, but permit them to release tensions in ways that can be socially controlled. These activities are evaluated differently and range from behavior that is culturally approved to behavior that is tabooed (while still remaining functional for pattern maintenance). Alternative statuses permit people to withdraw from statuses that produce strain in favor of other conformable activities.

When motivation to deviance has been established, overt expression in deviant adaptation may be inhibited by structures that make deviance difficult to carry out or very costly. Making deviance difficult reduces the probability of rewards for deviant behavior. Making deviance costly, by withholding goods, services, and attitudes or by exerting punitive and coercive measures may reduce the profit of deviance.

Finally, therapy, embracing some tolerance of deviance, refusing to reciprocate deviance, and rewarding conformity, may motivate the deviant to relinquish his deviant adaptation and move back to conformity to institutionalized behavior.

7

MARRIAGE, FAMILY, AND KINSHIP

Marriage, family, and kinship offer particularly convenient structures for the analysis of social systems in an introductory text, where space and time limitation prevent extensive discussion of a wide range of social systems. The readers of this text will all have had some firsthand experience in these systems. However, they probably will be less familiar with the way in which these systems operate in other societies. One of the advantages of the comparative analysis of social systems (sometimes referred to as "cross-cultural" analysis) is that it permits us to see that all people everywhere are confronted with certain similar problems or dilemmas of social organization and to understand that it is possible to develop different social arrangements for handling them. By such analysis we are able to see how a wide variety of structures may perform similar functions. At the same time, such analysis gives a basis for observing certain functionally essential characteristics that lead to similarities in social arrangements among widely differing peoples. In addition, cross-cultural analysis of such structures as those that control sexual behavior, marriage, or family gives us an understanding of how a particular system in a given society is linked to other systems in that society and to the society's peculiar historical and cultural setting. In this way, we can see how institutionalized definitions that characterize the family or marriage or kinship in a specific society are, in part, a consequence of other institutionalized arrangements as well as how they affect these other arrangements.

In order to give the student a working understanding of these principles, we have divided this chapter into two major sections. The first section is concerned with an analysis of some commonly shared problems centering around sexual behavior, reproduction, and socialization of the young and the various ways in which different societies have developed structures for coping with them. At the same time, attention is directed to the way in which a particular "solution" is related to other structural characteristics of a particular society. In this discussion, some basic concepts for the analysis of marriage, family, and kinship in any society are developed. The second section is devoted to a discussion of these systems in American society, using the conceptual tools that have been developed in the first section. The purpose of this discussion is not only to acquaint the student with certain factual and descriptive characteristics of marriage, family, and kinship in the United States, but to show how these characteristics may be interpreted sociologically.

The Regulation of Sexual Gratification

The regulation of sexual gratification, the regulation of reproduction, and the patterning of in-group solidarity represent social structures that, although interlinked and reinforcing, need to be analytically distinguished because the ways in which they are actually combined in operating societies are quite varied. To begin with, the tight linkage, at least normatively, of sexual behavior and marriage in American society is not the usual arrangement. Understanding this may be facilitated by considering the two subjects separately, since they are, in fact, separate issues.

The fact that human adults are continuously sexual (that is, there are no periods of oestrus and anoestrus) means that sexual gratification is always something that any two persons (male or female) can seek to procure from and offer to one another. Unlike most other services that are exchanged, sex is something at which "anyone can play," in the sense that it requires no special training for anyone to be able to gratify anyone else sexually. The significance of this is that sexual gratification is an almost universally desired goal which is potentially available in almost unlimited supply.

Yet the striking fact is that in all societies the procurement and disposal of sexual pleasure is sharply limited. Why is this so? Are there certain characteristics of group life that are incompatible with completely "free sex"? There seem, in fact, to have been at least four such obstacles in most conditions of human life so far.[1]

---

[1] Because the following kind of functional analysis is often misunderstood, let us make it clear that we are not saying that if a cultural definition—for example, "sexual promiscuity"—is disfunctional, it will not develop. We say, on the contrary, that almost anything conceivable may be expressed in patterned behavior; but if it is seriously disfunctional, the group that institutionalizes it will fail to survive.

In the first place, survival of the species is dependent upon reproduction. This means that two sources of sexual gratification—autoeroticism and homosexuality—must not be evaluated more highly than—and certainly not to the exclusion of—heterosexual involvements, if system members are to reproduce themselves. We do not know to what extent a group may rely solely upon biological drives toward heterosexuality in order to assure reproduction. We do know that cultural circumvention of biological drives is possible. There are instances where homosexuality has been institutionalized (in adolescence among the Keroki of New Guinea, for example), and celibacy has been institutionalized among members of some religious sects. These examples, however, are rather special and limited cases, and, like the *berdache* of the Plains Indians, such statuses are not considered desirable for all members of the society. As a matter of fact, we know of no instance where other sources of gratification are not devalued relative to heterosexuality. Where sexuality in general may be devalued, as in some versions of Christianity, it still is regarded as a "*necessary* evil," and heterosexual relations for reproductive purposes are sanctioned as the legitimate expression of the "baser instincts."

In the second place, one necessity of group life is interdependence. Biological separation of the sexes in reproduction has the consequence of fostering interdependence, but autoeroticism may have the disfunction of reducing the dependence of individuals on other people. In a sense, it would permit people to be "too self-sufficient"—in the sense, namely, that if the reward of sexual self-gratification were readily available and had no cost attached to it, at least one important motive for establishing cooperative relations with others would be diminished.

The degree of normative devaluation of nonheterosexual relations varies in different societies over a long continuum—from acceptance as a partial outlet, through amusement and mild disapproval, to harsh condemnation. The only point we wish to make here is that heterosexual involvements cannot be devalued to the point of eliminating reproduction, and that usually they are evaluatively preferred to any alternative forms of sexual gratification.

A third necessity of group life, at least under certain conditions, is closely related to the disfunctions of autoeroticism. Even if sexual orientations were successfully directed away from the individual's self and from persons of his own sex, there appear to be some disfunctions of completely "free"—that is, unregulated—heterosexual gratification. Here we refer to the universally observed fact of the "incest taboo." That is, not only one's self and people of one's own sex are generally frowned upon as sources of gratification, but certain persons of the opposite sex are also tabooed: opposite-sex members of the individual's intimate in-group. Mother-son, father-daughter, and brother-sister sexual relations are almost always prohibited, and, as we shall see, those taboos may be extended to others of more distant relationship as well.

Why is this?

The efforts to solve the puzzle of the universal "horror" of incest have been numerous. We cannot review them all here, but shall simply call attention to one matter that seems probably a sufficient explanation.[2] First, though, let us note one "explanation" that is no explanation at all— namely, that people "instinctively" abhor incest.

In the first place, the argument that incest is "naturally" repugnant to human beings is much like the argument of racially prejudiced persons that racial miscegenation is "instinctively repellent." The reasoning usually is the self-contradictory reasoning that miscegenation is so hateful, especially (in the United States) to white women, that they must be sternly forbidden to engage in it. Similarly, the "horror" of incest can hardly be explained in terms of instinctive distaste; for if it could, there would be no reasons for stringent laws against it. In the second place, (again, much like the miscegenation example), it is a little difficult to account for all the incest that occurs (or all the mulattoes who exist) if there is such an instinct. In both cases, the obvious "instinct," if one wishes to use that language, is *not* to discriminate against relatives or against other races so far as sex is concerned; sexually, people seem to be pretty democratic. It is precisely the absence of a "natural" horror that makes prevention depend so much on normative and legal taboos. What needs explanation is the existence of the biologically *un*natural taboos.

In the incest case (we shall return to "miscegenation" and related taboos immediately below), the basic danger is much the same as the potential danger of autoeroticism—the danger of too much "self-sufficiency"—not, however, this time on the part of individuals but on the part of small groups. If the powerful drive for sexual gratification could be satisfied within one's small group, at least one important incentive for establishing close bonds with other groups, thus welding many small groups into a larger unity, would be absent. One of the major functions of the incest taboo, in other words, is to propel individuals out of the sanctuary of their immediate small groups, into the establishment of emotional ties with (opposite-sex) members of the larger community. To the degree that the females of one's intimate group are not available and to the degree that *other* females are available, to that degree any given male has an incentive to strike up cordial relations with other groups. This is

---

[2] The social functions of the incest taboo are discussed in detail by George Murdock, *Social Structure* (New York: The Macmillan Company, 1949), pp. 291–301. Chapter 10 also contains a discussion of the extension of this taboo. Elsewhere we have discussed a function of the incest taboo *within* the immediate family (see Chapter 2); here we are concerned with its function for the larger society.

the important function so sharply formulated in Max Gluckman's quotation of a Nuer tribesman: "They are our enemies; we marry them."[3]

But, in the fourth place, this cultural device for preventing too sharp and permanent cleavages between subgroups has the defects of its virtues. It may be necessary to dilute somewhat the emotional identification of small-group members with one another so that they can identify also with "outsiders." But there may also be, under certain conditions (namely, when the group defines itself exclusively in terms of qualities rather than of performances), such a thing as "too much" dilution—that is, a loss of commitment to a group that could spell its end as a distinct entity. Therefore, a fourth restriction on choice of sexual objects is widely institutionalized—the normative requirement *not* to become sexually involved with "outsiders." In other words, some women are tabooed to a man because they are "too close" and others are tabooed because they are "not close enough."

In these four ways, the "unlimited supply" of sexual gratification becomes sharply limited culturally. What without culture is "free" becomes, with culture, "costly."

Furthermore, there is another cost attributable to culture that still further diminishes the supply of sexual gratification, although this additional cost is more in the nature of a by-product of culture than a functional requirement of group life. We refer to the fact that, entirely apart from norms of *exogamy* (choosing partners outside one's group) and *endogamy* (choosing them inside), people develop esthetic standards of what is gratifying. Standards of feminine or masculine attractiveness develop, as well as standards of pleasant and unpleasant behavior, manners, interests, and so on. Men are not simply males to women; they are handsome or ugly, polite or rude, interesting or dull. The supply of *really* eligible men, then, for any woman becomes radically reduced, and vice versa (especially, of course, if a further institutional requirement of sex is marriage, an issue to which we shall return below). Since many of those standards are likely to be patterned rather than idiosyncratic, it turns out that a few men may be appealing sexual objects to many women, while all other men are not "really available." A good-looking white Anglo-Saxon Protestant woman from an upper-class family, with a Ph.D. and an intense desire to live on a ranch, for example, may find herself in a position where there are *no* available men. Her *cultural* definitions have restricted the supply of what is potentially unlimited to zero. In addition, there is the matter of propinquity. The social and the geographical distribution of peoples, particularly in populations of great size

---

[3] Max Gluckman, *Custom and Conflict in Africa* (New York: The Free Press of Glencoe, Inc., 1955), p. 13.

and density, tend to reinforce the normative and cathectic definitions of eligible mates, since people of similar social statuses tend to interact. At the same time, the number of potential partners is reduced by the cultural and physical distribution of people.

There still remains, however, a problem. Given that social necessities and cultural standards restrict the legitimate and acceptable sources of sexual gratification, why is sex usually not "free" at least as between men and women who are neither objectionable nor tabooed to one another on the grounds we have already discussed?

One reason for the universal occurrence of some institutional regulation is fairly obvious, but nonetheless of great importance. This is the fact that heterosexual gratification (and, for that matter, homosexual gratification) is a service people perform for one another. As such, it is always a possible focus of exploitation. Rape is the sexual instance of the war of each against all which occurs in the absence of normative regulation. The physical superiority of males over females makes rape an ever-present possibility. Add to this the fact that anything as relatively scarce (for the reasons discussed above) and desirable as sexually attractive and available women is likely to be fought over by men, and it becomes obvious that a human group that fails to institutionalize rules of the game is likely to be torn apart by the Hobbesian war.

Furthermore, there is another side of this coin that is perhaps too little examined. Women also may be both active seekers after and active disposers of sexual gratification. Being weaker and therefore for a long period subordinated, they have been predominantly seen in their disposer roles; but their procuring roles have probably never been absent, and have grown in importance as physical strength has become less important in human affairs and therefore a less possible basis of subordination. Normative rules of the game have been necessitated, therefore, not only because of male rivalry but also because of female rivalry. If men needed surcease from fighting off marauding males, they equally needed respite from hog-tying their roving females. Institutional regulation helps both, since, as we have seen, internalized norms are more effective barriers and chains than the real things.

The institutional substitutes for exploitation are, here as elsewhere, bargaining, legal-bureaucratic rights, and primary-group cathexes. Sex is regulated in all societies by one or another or some combination of those mechanisms. Thus, although social life demands control of sexual behavior, *alternative* structures may perform this function. Which structure is institutionalized is importantly conditioned by *other* institutionalized arrangements in a particular society.

Among most of the peoples of the world, the regulation of sex is not focused on sexual intercourse itself but on its relationship to some other activity or structure in which sex and reproduction play an important part. The normative restriction of sexual behavior to marriage in our society has led some people to the conclusion that ancient societies and primitive peoples were or are permissive and promiscuous. This is not the case, for all societies place restrictions of the order we have discussed, consistent with *other* institutionalized arrangements in each. Where premarital relations are permitted they frequently are the institutionalized prelude to marriage, and pregnancy is the crystallizing and, in some societies, the necessary condition of marriage. Similarly with extramarital relations. A substantial majority of societies permit *privileged relationship* among kinsmen in both premarital and extramarital relations. For example, the male may be permitted access to his brother's wife or his wife's sister. However, such privileged relationships are commonly linked to *preferential mating*. The most common linkage is found in the *sororate*, where a widower marries by preference the sister of his deceased wife and in the *levirate*, where a widow marries by preference the brother of her deceased husband. Thus the pattern of privileged relationships and preferential marriage involves a kind of anticipatory socialization, consistent with reinforcement of marriage and the family.

Even where sexual license is relatively indiscriminate, it may be linked to other structures and conditions in the society. Institutionalized prostitution, for example, seems to be associated with accessibility of females. Very generally speaking, prostitution tends to be linked to strong family organization, to the seclusion and surveillance of marriageable females, and to male authoritarianism. Kingsley Davis contends that "free intercourse for pleasure and friendship rather than profit is the greatest enemy of prostitution" and that where the family is strong there tends to be a well-defined system of prostitution.[4] In contrast to the alternative of extramarital relations, institutionalized prostitution, under certain conditions, may actually support the family structure. It usually frees the male from anything but an economic exchange, discourages strong emotional attachments, and is less visible to the spouse and the community. In our own society, it is probably tolerated most where there is a high ratio of males to females, such as is found in certain occupational complexes—military posts, isolated industrial areas, frontier regions, or the like. Similarly, such rare practices as "sexual hospitality," in which the wife's sexual services are available to family visitors, are frequently associated with other features of the society. For example, males on hunting expeditions may be separated from their families for long periods of time, or people may be scattered over wide geographical areas so that a traveler is isolated from

[4] Kingsley Davis, "The Sociology of Prostitution," *American Sociological Review*, 2:744–755 (1937).

his home. Sexual hospitality provides an institutionalized means for controlling sexual relations and sanctioning sexual outlets.

In some societies, relatively free access to sexual indulgence may be
institutionalized by ceremonial occasion or status-prerogatives in accordance with prevailing belief systems or with a social organization that are
not directly concerned with the control of sexual behavior. For example,
on the occasion of a great hunt, among the Thonga of Africa, important
hunters could have intercourse with their daughters, although that relation was normally taboo. Periods of sexual license institutionalized in
some societies during religious or magical ceremonies have had symbolic
significance in reinforcing and embodying religious and magical beliefs.
The well-known rule of *jus primae noctis,* according to which the feudal
lord or another male in authority has sexual rights, before her husband,
to a woman on the first night of her marriage represents an example of a
status-prerogative. In the Nayar caste of India, a husband is married to
his wife for only three days, and thereafter she is free to have sexual relations with other men. The Nayar claim that the three-day marriage is
functional for the male occupational role. They are a warrior caste, frequently hiring out as mercenaries, and it is thought best to free males
from the responsibilities and ties of marriage and family. The wife's
brothers perform the normal nonsexual functions of a husband, and children resulting from the extramarital relations of the wife are considered
the legitimate children of the male taken in marriage.[5] It should be noted,
also, that certain statuses, such as the priesthood or widowhood, may
taboo sexual behavior entirely, consistent with certain normative rights
and obligations of these statuses, with views concerning the nature of
sexual activity, or with ideas governing the sanctity of marriage.

The practice of restricting sexual relations strictly and exclusively to
marriage may also be geared to other institutionalized arrangements.
Such functional interlinkage is nowhere better illustrated than in rural
Ireland, where country people yield to no one in strictness of sexual
morality. Premarital chastity and marital fidelity are firmly bound to continuity of descent and ownership and to the procreation of children. To
"ruin" a young girl is to destroy the pattern of family and community life
by upsetting the possibility of an orderly change in farm succession.
Arensberg and Kimball have described this relationship between sexual
relations and social structure in the following way:

> Apart from the moral censure misconduct brings upon a young woman
> and the shame it inflicts upon the people of her "name," it brings as
> well the destruction of her social role. It makes an end to her potential-

---

[5] Ralph Linton, *The Study of Man* (New York: Appleton-Century-Crofts, Inc.,
1936), pp. 154–155.

ities, for these, too, are her "character": potential motherhood of a familist line on the one hand, and potential transmission of an advantageous alliance on the other. In a familistic order they are identical. They are both based upon her sex. They make of the unmarried girl a sort of symbol of familistic aspiration. To use the symbol for any but its proper purpose of procreation and alliance is to destroy not only its efficacy but the aspirations that are attached to it. Rural Ireland, indeed, provides a sort of archetype or "pure" form of this sexual outlook, the conventional western European ideal of premarital virginity. It is important here as a living function of a closely integrated social system.[6]

It is not our purpose here to condemn or condone any one of these patterns of sexual relationships. Rather, we would point to the principle that social norms are necessary for orderly group existence and that responsibilities and obligations accompany rights and freedoms. The neophyte in comparative cultural analysis might as well learn from the start that because "they do it in New Guinea" does not mean that it can be done in his own society. Although we must be wary of a rationalistic bias that ascribes logic and instrumental purpose to all social structures, the various patterns we have described are not entirely a matter of caprice or accident. Analysis of these patterns in the context of other institutionalized practices presents an excellent illustration of the relation of structure to function and the interrelationship of structures within and among systems. There are few isolated structures, if any at all, that have an existence independent of others; and if we are to enjoy the fruits of one, we must assume the burdens of othe others. It seems to be the universal state of the human condition that "costs" accompany "rewards" and rights beget obligations. In any social situation, the council of imperfection is wisely taken.

Marriage

The first point to be made concerning marriage is that it is not primarily a way of regulating heterosexual relations. It is primarily a way of regulating *sociological* reproduction, which is a different matter. Hence the analytical separation of "the regulation of sexual gratification" and "marriage."

In other words, although there is a wide range of variation among

---

[6] Conrad M. Arensberg and Solon T. Kimball, *Family and Community in Ireland* (Cambridge, Mass.: Harvard University Press, 1948), p. 218. See Chap. 11, "Familism and Sex," for an extended discussion of this complex.

peoples in the mores that govern sexual activity outside marriage, culmination of such relations in pregnancy and childbirth usually is legitimized only in marriage. Here, as elsewhere, there is structural variation. For example, in some societies pregnancy may precede marriage legitimately, or evidence of fertility may even be necessary for marriage; and where concubinage is institutionalized, children of both the concubine and the wife may be legitimate.

One essential function of the principle of legitimacy is to establish a linkage between an adult male and the child. Although the relationship between the mother and child is readily visible, the tie between the father and the child is not. Thus a *social* definition of fatherhood is established. The linkage of a male and a female in marriage and the rights to sexual relations that universally accompany marriage provide a relatively stable social group for the assignment of rights and obligations in the care and training of children. Thus the legitimation of childbirth in marriage provides the institutionalized structure necessary for the replacement of societal members. At the same time, the ascription of sociological paternity to a male is functional for the family and kinship, since it discourages dissipation of rights and resources through indiscriminate childbearing, for illegitimate children ordinarily do not acquire full rights in the family group or in kinship lines.[7]

The great variation in the structure of marriage and the relation of these structural variations to other systems may best be understood within the context of family and kinship organization and certain features of the larger society. We shall discuss family and kinship separately. Here we shall take up two major issues of the marital system: (1) the number of partners in the marital relationship, and (2) the ways of allocating people to marital statuses.

NUMBER OF PARTNERS

There are two basic types of marriage, so far as numbers are concerned: monogamy and polygamy. Monogamous norms restrict the individual to one spouse at a time. Polygamous norms permit plural marriage and take the form either of polygyny (one husband and two or more wives) or of polyandry (one wife and two or more husbands). There is a fourth type of marriage, usually called "group marriage," in which there are both plural wives and husbands in the marital unit. This last form is rare, and in all known cases the marital rights of one pair in the group

[7] For a sociological discussion of illegitimacy, see Kingsley Davis, "Illegitimacy and the Social Structure," *American Journal of Sociology*, 45:215–233 (1939).

take precedence over others. Monogamy is permitted in all societies, although polygyny is the preferred form in most societies. Murdock's analysis of 238 societies has shown that 193 were characterized by polygyny, 43 by monogamy, and 2 by polyandry.[8] In actual practice, monogamy is the most prevalent marital arrangement even where polygyny is permitted, since the economic burden of maintaining a large household or separate dwellings for wives prevents full participation in plural marriage. Furthermore, except in unusual circumstances, sex ratios are nearly equal; hence all eligible males and females could not possibly practice polygamy.

There are several variations on these basic types, and although all cannot be detailed here, some may be mentioned. In American society, as in many others, serial marriage is permitted with the death or divorce of a spouse. (This is by no means universal; some societies bind mates together until death and even after.) In some societies, successive mates are preferentially prescribed. The levirate, for example, rules that a widow marry by preference the brother of her deceased husband; and the sororate, that a widower marry the sister of his deceased wife. (The story of Onan in the Old Testament, whence comes the "sin of onanism" [*coitus interruptus* or masturbation] and the foundation of some religious prohibitions of birth control, is a story of a man who refused to follow the prescribed levirate.) Such preferential rules are found also in some polygamous societies where males marry their wives' sisters; and females, their husbands' brothers (sororal polygyny and fraternal polyandry, respectively).

These different kinds of marital arrangements frequently may be interpreted in terms of conditions outside the marriage structure itself.[9] Polygyny is often associated with a shortage of men, although this is not necessarily the case; multiple wives are sometimes a form of conspicuous consumption—a sign of affluence. Because of warfare and the more hazardous occupational pursuits of males, primitive societies often have a predominance of females. This, however, does not place the male in the enviable position that some (male) readers might assume. Ralph Linton has described the general situation in the following way:

> . . . there are few polygynous systems in which the position of the male is really better than it is under monogamy. If the plural wives are not

[8] Murdock, *op. cit.*, p. 28. Another study of 185 societies found that 154 were polygynous. See C. S. Ford and F. A. Beach, *Patterns of Sexual Behavior* (New York: Harper & Brothers and Paul B. Hoeber, Inc., 1951).

[9] Probably the most explicit and systematic structural-functional analysis of marriage and the family in a single literate society is contained in Marion J. Levy, Jr., *The Family Revolution in Modern China* (Cambridge, Mass.: Harvard University Press, 1949).

congenial, the family will be torn by feuds in which the husband must take the thankless role of umpire, while if they are congenial he is likely to be confronted by an organized feminine opposition. Among the sub-human primates the male can dominate a group of females because these females are unable to organize themselves. He can deal with them in detail. The human male cannot dominate his wives in the same degree, since they can and do organize for both defence and offence. If all a man's wives want a particular thing, they can work on him in shifts and are fairly certain to get what they want.[10]

Mechanisms of social control are usually institutionalized to minimize friction and to assure individual rights and obligations. Wives may occupy separate dwellings, or husbands may be required to rotate serially among them. The husband may have to secure permission of his first wife before taking another, a request that may be willingly granted where family burdens weigh heavily on the female. In sororal polygyny, wives are sisters and have previously been socialized together. In all cases, women's self-esteem and esteem of others is not contingent upon sexual or marital exclusiveness, and may even be enhanced by marriage to a male rich enough to afford many wives.

Plural mating may also be related to economic practices. Murdock suggests that this may partially determine the form of marriage.[11] Where women play a major role in family economy, polygyny is common. Where their contribution is insignificant, polyandry may be practiced. This latter state is frequently associated with a preponderance of males over females. Where economic conditions are poor, population may be controlled by female infanticide, and polyandry provides surplus males with a mate. Similarly, when rules of inheritance and differential disposition of economic holdings relegate a segment of males to very small land holdings, as in Tibet, wealth sufficient to sustain a family may be consolidated through polyandry. Social change may also occasion a shift in marital forms. The Toda of India, for example, who formerly were polyandrous, have developed an approximate group marriage. Under British rule, infanticide was discouraged, the number of females increased, but polyandrous attitudes remained, so that brothers came to take two or more wives in common, rather than one.

Whatever the form of marriage, within it the rule of mutual availability of sexual services is virtually universal. Even here, however, sexual relations are not altogether uncontrolled. Reproductive processes and the female menstrual period provide a basis for taboo in most societies. In addition, continence may be required before or after warfare, hunting, and other occasions, as well as during ritual periods and religious cere-

[10] Linton, *op. cit.*, p. 187.
[11] Murdock, *op. cit.*, p. 36.

mony. As we have noted, it is unusual for the marital relationship to involve sexual monopoly, as it does normatively in American culture. This is not to say that in most societies there is nothing recognized as fornication (illicit sexual intercourse among unmarried persons) or adultery (illicit relations involving married persons). It is rather to say that in most societies *certain* kinds of nonmarital sexual relations are permitted or sometimes prescribed, and certain others are only mildly disapproved. Beyond those certain kinds, some sexual relations are likely to be viewed as adultery or as fornication.

ALLOCATION TO MARRIAGE

Allocation to a marital status is like the allocation to any status. The issues are these: Who does the allocating? What criteria do the allocators use? Do the allocatees have a choice?

Allocators are typically either the spouses themselves or their parents. When parents select the mates of their offspring, the selection is sometimes made while the principals are children. Americans are likely to exaggerate the problems of marital adjustment that are thought to be inherent in such arranged marriages. Most people everywhere consider marriage a desirable arrangement, and some bond of affection and response is usually expected to develop between husband and wife. Accordingly, parents are not wholly unmindful of congeniality of mates when they arrange their children's marriages. Linton makes the following comment on arranged marriages:

> Even when marriages are arranged by the parents and the young people have no opportunity of knowing each other in advance, there is usually a sincere effort to bring together individuals who will have the potentialities of happy life together. . . . When the young people have opportunities for meeting each other, their wishes are almost always consulted even when marriages are, in theory, arranged by the parents. Many societies believe that the parents have better judgment in such matters, but very few of them approve the forcing of children into unions which are actively distasteful to them. Such forcing occurs mainly in societies which practise child betrothal with exchanges of property, but even here there are usually provisions for escape.[12]

We shall consider in more detail the case of self-selection of marital partners when we take up the American marriage and family systems toward the end of this chapter.

Whoever does the selecting, the range of different criteria used provides a fascinating example of cultural variability and, at the same time,

[12] Linton, *op. cit.*, p. 174.

of the linkage between different parts of a social system. In the first place, all the restrictions discussed above on the selection of *sexual* partners apply also to the selection of *marital* partners: if anything, more so. Some persons are "too close" and some are "too different" for marriage. In the second place, in all societies there is some notion of a "good match," which guides selection among the persons who are technically eligible for one another so far as the endogamy and exogamy rules are concerned. The criteria of a "good match" may range from the fantasy of a noble knight and a fair, fainting damsel, through the mysterious magic that is expected to afflict people on some enchanted evening, to the strategy of welding empires—of either the political or the economic kind—through marriage. In some cases, where kin groups are the chief economic units of the society, the negotiations among families to procure marriage partners for their marriageable young people may be very elaborate and involve elaborate economic exchanges as part of the marriage. Here, as well as in modern American marriages, where it is even more disguised, the "bargaining" mode of adaptation is readily observable, as the procurement of both sexual gratification and legitimate offspring becomes a counter in the struggle of men and women (and their families) for prestige, power, wealth, or security.

In some cases the cultural notion of a "good match" may be standardized to the point of prescribing the general category of persons from whom mates are to be drawn, or even specifying the ideal person. Among primitives in Australia, for example, as well as in Africa, certain kin groups have the obligation of supplying one another with marital partners. In ancient Peru, Hawaii, and Egypt, the otherwise universally tabooed brother-sister marriage was the preferred or even required one for the purpose of securing legitimate heirs to the ruling family. More frequently the preferred mate is specified as a cross-cousin (the child of a father's sister or a mother's brother) or, as noted earlier, a sister or brother of a deceased spouse.

Kinship

Marriage and biological reproduction form the basis of kinship systems. Coupled with the incest taboo, marriage and reproduction establish a series of socially recognized relationships of two types. Because people ordinarily do not marry and reproduce with their parents, children, or siblings, relationships based on marital ties are established. People related by such socially recognized linkages are classified as *affinal relatives,*

Because of the nature of biological reproduction, another set of relationships, based on blood relation and common ancestry, is established. These biologically interlinked persons are known as *consanguineal relatives*.

The number of possible relatives a person may have increases geometrically as the relationship becomes more distant. One of the functions of kinship is to limit these potential relationships to a manageable number by assigning a status to certain of them and ignoring the others. Although kinship systems are found in all societies, the number and type of relationships institutionalized vary enormously. Murdock found that all societies he analyzed recognized kinship at least through three levels of relationship. First are the primary relatives, who are a person's parents, siblings, spouse, and his own children. Next, secondary relatives may be distinguished who are the primary relatives of each of these persons. Then, there are tertiary relatives who are the primary relatives of each of the secondary relatives. At the tertiary level, 151 distinct relatives may be distinguished. The kinship terminology applied to these and more distant relatives that are socially recognized cannot be taken up here; we can merely note that there is a great variety in the way in which kinsmen are classified and in the status-rights and -obligations assigned to them.

DESCENT

The birth of children gives rise to the problem of social placement in the kinship system. From the point of view of the child, there is the problem of extending support and assistance beyond the immediate parents and establishing rights and obligations upon which his future may be built. From the point of view of kinsmen, there is the problem of deciding who shall bear these obligations to the child and how the established rights of kinsmen shall be affected by new members. The birth of a child in any society alters the prospects and relationships of others and raises questions of succession, inheritance, marriage, and the like, that must be culturally answered if uncertainty, conflict, and chaos are to be avoided. Therefore, in all societies, rules of descent are established that specify those kinsmen who are to assume reciprocal role-relationships. Rules of descent are culturally rather than biologically determined, for bonds of blood and marriage extend to an unmanageable number, even among socially recognized relatives, and restrictions must be imposed arbitrarily.

There are three basic types of descent. *Patrilineal descent* specifies that those kinsmen who are to assume reciprocal role-relations are the father's consanguineal kin group rather than the mother's. *Matrilineal descent*, in contrast, specifies the mother's kin group, setting aside the father's.

Bilateral descent—the form in our society—specifies by relating children
to a limited number of corresponding kinsmen of both parents. In addition, these rules of descent may be combined to form other less common
types.[13] Rules of descent are important in every society because they
provide people with a set of primary relationships and define a series of
reciprocal rights and obligations encompassing a wide range of social
behavior. Unraveling these sometimes complex interlinkages is necessary
to understand patterned behavior in many areas of life activity that extend beyond the family and kinship. In addition, descent determines the
pattern of family transmission that can have ramifications into religious,
political, economic, and other institutionalized structures. *Inheritance*, the
transmission of property rights along kinship lines, is determined by
descent. *Succession*, the family transmission of specific statuses, is also
based on descent. Whether, for example, a child is to be a king or a com-
moner, of high or low caste, or a freeman or a slave may be determined
by rules of descent.

KINSHIP GROUPS

Although kinship relations, *in toto*, do not constitute social groups, they
are the basis of a number of social groupings known as *kin groups*, which
are based on rules of descent. The basic kin group is, of course, the
family, which we shall discuss in some detail shortly. Although, in our
society, kin relations seldom form specific and enduring groups beyond
the immediate family, they are the basis of a number of extended group
relationships in other societies. Consanguineal kin relations are the para-
mount basis of these larger kin groups. Unilinear descent (either patrilineal or matrilineal) provides two kinds of consanguineal kin groups. A
lineage exists when the descendants of either a patrilineal or a matrilineal line can trace their exact genealogical relationships and are bound
by mutual kinship rights and obligations. A *sib* exists when members of
a unilinear kin group assume common ancestry even though they are
unable to trace their exact genealogical connections. Sometimes two or
more sibs are combined by convention to form a *phratry*. In societies
where only two sibs or phratries exist, so that people are necessarily
members of one or the other, the term "moiety" is applicable.

Unilinear, consanguineal kin groups are normally exogamous, and generally the smaller the kin group, the greater the tendency toward exogamy. Such groups are also prone to totemism, a fairly common feature of
which is the assignment of animal names to kin groups. Common ancestry

---

[13] For a discussion of these types, see Murdock, *op. cit.*, p. 45.

is linked to the totemic species, and many rituals, ceremonies, and taboos are associated with the totem. Because of the somewhat tenuous nature of the relations established in sibs and moieties, especially, it is likely that these patterns have developed because they are functional for maintaining solidarity among members of a kin group. Thus a group name is assigned, and members of the same kin group engage in similar practices that are often elevated to a level of great importance. Such mechanisms help to support social unity in the group, particularly where members are dispersed geographically. Similarly, exogamous rules perform functions similar to the incest taboo by preventing possible disruptive rivalries within the kin group and extending linkages outside the group through marriage.

Another important kin group is the *clan*.[14] A clan consists of a group of families and is distinguished by three criteria: (1) common residence, (2) unilinear rules of descent, and (3) organization of members in common activities and group solidarity. Because of the rules of residence governing the clan, families comprising it live in the same local area. Thus the clan includes affinal as well as consanguineal relatives. However, clans are exogamous; hence if, for example, a clan is based on the male line (is patrilineal), a female child belongs to the clan of her husband when she marries and moves to his clan locale. Clan organization has a long history and is found in many primitive societies. The most notable example of clans in literate societies was found in pre-Communist China. Clans still flourish in some areas in China although it is unlikely that they will withstand the impact of urban industrial culture, quite apart from the speeding up of those processes under Communism.[15]

The Family

Marriage ordinarily coexists with the family, but the two should be distinguished. Marriage, as we have pointed out, is a set of customs, laws, or both centering around a socially recognized sexual union legitimizing procreation and operating within the family. Marital norms set the pattern of establishing such relations, the mutual rights and obligations entailed,

[14] The term "clan," like many of the terms used to designate kinship groups, has been used variously by anthropologists and other social scientists. In distinguishing kin groups, we have followed the usage of Murdock, *op. cit.*

[15] See O. Lang, *Chinese Family and Society* (New Haven, Conn.: Yale University Press, 1946).

the restrictions of persons permitted to enter into this state, and the means of terminating it. The family involves a group of related kin, linked by blood and marriage, who occupy a common household, and are usually characterized by economic cooperation and solidarity.[16]

TYPES OF FAMILIES

The basic form of family organization is the *nuclear family*. It typically consists of a married couple and their children and is the common form in our society, to the virtual exclusion of all others. Two other family forms are built on the nuclear family and are found in many other societies. The first consists of the *polygamous family*, which affiliates two or more nuclear families by means of plural marriages. The second is the *extended family*, which unites nuclear families through the extension of the parent-child, rather than the husband-wife relationship, as in the polygamous family. The typical extended family includes three generations who live in a single dwelling or closely adjacent households.

The by-now-familiar incest taboo confines the nuclear family to two generations, since a spouse must be sought outside this family unit. Without this taboo, the family would be continuous over time by replacing its members through procreation within the unit itself. However, the fact that a spouse must be sought outside the nuclear family unites it with other families. As a consequence, reproduction extends through the generations in such a way that people are members of two nuclear families. One is the *family of orientation* in which a person is born. The other is the *family of procreation*, which a person establishes through marriage. This gives rise to the complex set of kinship relations we have already discussed, involving primary, secondary, and tertiary relatives, patrilineal, matrilineal, and bilateral descent, and affinal and consanguineal relationships of varying types.

RULES OF RESIDENCE

Because both the male and the female cannot remain with their respective families of orientation upon marriage, the question arises as to which household they should join. This is determined in all societies by rules of

---

[16] No single definition of "the family" seems adequate to cover all possible kinds of familial organization. These criteria hold in general, but the analyst may vary criteria as he turns to empirical examples in different societies, some of which, like the Nayar of India or the family in the collective farms (kibbutzim) of Israel, are atypical in some respects.

residence. Murdock found that all of the 250 sample societies he examined are governed, either alone or in combination, by five basic rules of residence. *Patrilocal* residence stipulates that the married couple take up residence with or near the household of the groom's father. *Matrilocal* residence requires that the groom reside in the bride's household or neighborhood. In some societies, the couple may live with or near either of their families of orientation. This rule is known as *bilocal* residence. Where the couple establish residence independent of either of their families, as in our society, the rule is *neolocal.* The final and least frequent type, *avunculocal* (from the Latin *avunculus,* "uncle"), prescribes that the bride and groom take up residence with or near a groom's maternal uncle.

Rules of residence are commonly linked to other structural features of the kinship system. The major effect of such rules is to bring together in one locale kinsmen and their families of procreation. Patrilocal residence congregates a number of patrilineally related males and their wives and children. Matrilocal and avunculocal residence accomplishes the same function for matrilineal kinsmen. Bilateral relatives are brought together by bilocal residence. Similarly, matrilocal residence is consistent with sororal polygyny, and this is the usual combination.

However, the structures of marriage, kinship, and family are not always functionally interrelated so as to foster integration and adaptation of social systems. Frequently, they may give rise to integrative problems within kin groups. Exogamous marriages that require a spouse to take up residence in a new place give rise to problems of adjustment to new surroundings and to new peoples. This is aggravated by the fact that kinsmen are likely to maintain an interest in those who marry out of the kin group. Where clans and sibs coexist, a dual allegiance is structured that creates status-set conflict. Such breaks and disjunctures may be smoothed by ceremonial occasions signifying alteration of rights and obligations, which parallel rites of passage in discontinuities of socialization.

Extended family organization creates a temporal continuity that gives rise to adaptive problems. With increased size, the extended family may outstrip resources and necessitate measures to control population or reorganize familial structure. Female infanticide may be practiced, or the extended family may break up into groups that settle elsewhere. Clan organization is a common consequence of population growth in the extended family. Similarly, the structure of the family may have consequences that extend into the larger society. This is notably illustrated in rural Ireland, where family organization affects demographic conditions, such as emigration, decline of population, delay of marriage, and rise of bachelorhood. By custom, one son is chosen by the father to inherit the land. He, in turn, marries a woman who can provide a dowry roughly equivalent to the value of the farm. As a result the other children are placed in a position where the males must migrate to acquire economic holdings and the females put off marriage until they are provided with a dowry, which has the demographic consequence mentioned.[17]

AUTHORITY IN THE FAMILY

Like any social group, the family must be provided with structure that fixes responsibility and allocates authority. Decisions must be made, rules enforced, actions accounted for, the use of force institutionalized, and the like. Typically, age, sex, and generation provide the basis for distribution of authority. There are, roughly, three very general ways of institutionalizing authority in the family. *Patriarchal* norms ascribe authority to the male head of the household, and are represented by the ancient Hebrew and the traditional Chinese family.[18] Traditionally, the unmarried as well as the married female is subordinate to some male, her father, brother, husband, or, theoretically, her son. The eldest male member of the extended family is the usual patriarch, although in some cases the female actually may play this role in event of the death of her husband. *Matriarchal* norms vest authority in the female head of the household, as among the Iroquois of North America. Curiously enough, an informal matriarchy exists in our own society among many lower-class Negro families. Probably because of the uncertain, irregular, and low economic status of the Negro male, coupled with a widespread pattern of geographical mobility on the part of the male, occasioned by the historical circumstance of slavery and his unfavorable competitive position, the wife is the dominant figure in the family.[19] A third general form consists of a roughly *equalitarian* distribution of authority among adult household members. Our own society approximates this form, particularly in

[17] We have put the relationship in brief. A full accounting is given in Arensberg and Kimball, *op. cit.*

[18] For description and analysis of marriage and family organization in these cultures, see David R. Mace, *Hebrew Marriage* (New York: Philosophical Library, Inc., 1953), and Levy, *op. cit.*

[19] See the discussion of the Negro lower-class family in St. Clair Drake and Horace R. Cayton, *Black Metropolis* (New York: Harcourt, Brace & World, Inc., 1945) and E. F. Frazier, *The Negro Family in the United States* (Chicago: The University of Chicago Press, 1939). There seems to be some tendency toward matriarchy in the upper-middle-class suburban family, also, where the husband's occupational role removes him from the home for a considerable part of the time. For an early recognition of this and other types in American society, see Ernest R. Mowrer, *Family Disorganization* (Chicago: The University of Chicago Press, 1927).

the middle class. Even here the child takes the father's name (patronymic) and in other ways male dominance tends to emerge, so that vestiges of the general rule of granting authority to the father and husband in independent nuclear or polygynous families remain. In polygynous marriages a special problem of authority arises among the wives. This is commonly solved by giving one wife, usually the first or "primary wife" authority over the other or "secondary wives."

FAMILY FUNCTIONS

Very generally speaking, family structure is organized around the reproduction, placement, maintenance, and socialization of children. We have seen the wide variety of structures that may accomplish these functions, and family structures present a good example of "structural alternatives" in social organization. Familial patterns vary greatly in the extent to which these functions are vested in the family. In some societies, these primary functions are extended to include such activities as economic production, political control, or physical protection. In others, these activities are carried out by other systems, and even those centering around children are shared with other social organizations. Urban industrial societies are notable in this respect, but the constriction of family functions is by no means limited to them. Some primitive societies assign a major role in socialization to age groups, training for economic or warfare skills may be allocated outside the family, the economy may be far larger than the family unit, or males may take all their meals outside the home. The frequently mentioned "loss of family functions" in modern industrial societies is a loss relative to the history of Western European cultures; paucity of family functions is not unique to them. But everywhere, reproduction, placement, maintenance, and socialization of children, in some form or other, seem to be basic to families.

The structure of the family unit appears to be particularly suited to these functions. At least, if any social group is to be assigned these functions *in combination,* it is difficult to think of a more appropriate one. The family is a biological group involving sexual relations among married adults and provides a unit of procreation. At the same time, it is the group that first encounters the infant, and socialization may be initiated immediately. It is a primary group, which permits the formation of identifications essential for cultural transmission, and the intimacies, spontaneity, and solidarity of the family tend to foster mutual identification. The relatively stable and enduring relationships in the family furnish a structure for extending intensive socialization over a considerable period of time. The family provides both age and sex differences for modeling and for authoritarian and equalitarian relationships within which the socialization process may operate. Age and sex also provide a basic pattern for the assignment of maintenance functions, both in terms of child care and economic cooperation. Finally, immediate social placement of the infant may be made in the status-structure of the family and extended on into the larger societal system. Biological care of the child is assured, and he may be trained early for his status-set and for future statuses he may later assume.

DIVORCE

Although divorce is an integral part of the marital structure, it usually involves the family as well. Where there are children, it always does; and when economic or other arrangements between the families of those married are involved, the families also have a stake in the divorce. In addition, there is the question of the placement of divorced persons, and this is frequently settled by their return to their families of orientation. Therefore we have chosen to discuss divorce at this time rather than include it with the discussion of marriage.

Divorce is an institutionalized arrangement whereby marriage may be terminated without the death of a spouse. Although all peoples place considerable emphasis on the maintenance of marital ties and none encourage divorce, divorce in some form is institutionalized in practically all societies. Most societies regard marriage as a contractual arrangement and when the contract is broken by either party, some institutionalized mechanism is necessary to terminate the relationship.

The conditions under which the bonds of marriage may be broken vary, of course, among societies. However, there seems to be no necessary connection between ease of divorce and divorce rates. For example, among the Zuñi, people of the Pueblo culture in the southwestern part of the United States, when marriage results in an uncongenial union, divorce is relatively casual and no great occasion for recrimination between the mates or on the part of members of the community. If a wife is unhappy with her husband, she may find another eligible man and divorce her husband by the simple expedient of placing his meager possessions on the door sill. Similarly, a husband who finds his wife's female relatives uncongenial is free to return to his mother's household. Yet, despite the casual structure of divorce (and marriage, as well), a very large percentage of marriages endure.[20]

[20] Ruth Benedict, *Patterns of Culture* (New York: Mentor Books, New American Library of World Literature, Inc., 1950), pp. 68 and 99.

A major problem that arises from divorce is the disposition of children. By chance or wisdom, this is settled in many societies by the extension of the family beyond the immediate nuclear group and by unilinear rules of descent. In such societies, children are not dependent solely on their biological parents for the satisfaction of their needs and they "belong" to one or the other of the blood lines. In case of divorce, there is no question of placement of the child. He is the property of the matrilineal or of the patrilineal kin group. Where rules of residence coincide with descent, the child remains in the family and locale where he is being reared, and the spouse departs to his or her kin group. Where the extended family is bilateral or residence and descent are at variance, a variety of arrangements may be institutionalized. But whatever the case, the essential point is that custody and rearing of children are not contingent on the maintenance of the nuclear kin group, and placement is determined before divorce. There usually is no great discontinuity in the socialization of the child, and the emotional shock that he may suffer through the loss of a biological parent is muted. Furthermore, there is no possibility of competition between parents for custody at the price of the child's emotional security.[21]

In many societies, marriage is ratified by so-called bride price or wife purchase, and this frequently figures in divorce. Contrary to popular conception, such arrangements rarely reduce women to the level of chattels. Often it is only a token payment, and its chief functions are to compensate the family for a loss of female services, assure that the female will be well treated (since the husband cannot hope for a refund at divorce), and to establish family rights in children of the marriage. In respect to this last function, the mother's family, in substance, relinquishes rights to children in return for the bride price. In some cases, in the unhappy event that there are no children, the wife may be divorced and the bride price returned or the husband compensated by claiming a limited number of children from a second marriage of the divorced wife.

In most societies, divorce, like marriage, is intimately linked to the family and other kinship structures. Thus, arrangements that are made for disposition of children, property, and other rights focus primarily on the kinship group rather than on the marital unit. In our own society, with its emphasis on the nuclear family, divorce is primarily a matter of settlement within the marital unit.

[21] For discussion and documentation of such arrangements, see Kingsley Davis, "Divorce and the Child," in Kingsley Davis, Harry C. Bredemeier, and Marion J. Levy (eds.), *Modern American Society* (New York: Holt, Rinehart and Winston, Inc., 1949), pp. 667–687.

Marriage and the Family in the United States

Because of the heterogeneity of American society, one cannot speak of "the American family" as a type that is found consistently in all classes, regions, races, or ethnic categories.[22] However, the urban middle-class family is probably the dominant type, and other forms seem to be progressively developing in this direction. It is this family type, therefore, that we shall discuss in very general terms in this section.

Industrialization and the institutionalization of science and technology probably have had a major impact on family and kinship organization everywhere, but nowhere is the impact more clearly seen than in the United States. The pertinent characteristics of industrialization are numerous, and only a few can be mentioned here. The factory system shifts major economic activities from the home and family, restricts family income to occupational earnings, and physically separates the breadwinner from the household. The stationary steam engine and later other sources of industrial power, coupled with centralized administration, the need for large supplies of labor, and highly efficient farming techniques have urbanized vast sections of society. Geographical mobility has been increased by shifting demands for labor and the development of new industries. Social mobility has been occasioned by relatively rational recruitment to the labor force and changing patterns of industrial organization and growth. Standardized machine techniques and the rise of clerical roles have broken down the traditional sex differences upon which a division of labor has been based. Increased specialization and growth of knowledge have intensified generational differences and decreased family functions. In association with these characteristics, or as a direct consequence of them, there has been a decreasing emphasis upon extended

[22] For some indication of the variety of family organization in the United States, see Frazier, *op. cit.;* J. K. Folsom, "Regional Family Patterns: The New England Family," *American Journal of Sociology,* 53:423–425 (1948); R. B. Vance, "Regional Family Patterns: The Southern Family," *American Journal of Sociology,* 53:426–429 (1948); Albert Blumenthal, *Small-Town Stuff* (Chicago: The University of Chicago Press, 1932); C. C. Zimmerman and M. E. Frampton, *Family and Society* (Princeton, N.J.: D. Van Nostrand Company, Inc., 1935), Part III, "American Studies"; Walter M. Kollmogen, *Culture of a Contemporary Community: The Old Order Amish of Lancaster County, Pennsylvania* (Rural Life Studies, No. 4; Washington, D.C.: U.S. Department of Agriculture, 1942) and others in this series; Allison Davis, B. B. Gardner, and M. R. Gardner, *Deep South* (Chicago: The University of Chicago Press, 1941). A historical perspective may be found in A. W. Calhoun, *A Social History of the American Family* (3 vols.; New York: Barnes & Noble, Inc., 1945).

kinship structures. The isolated nuclear family is the prototype in urban industrial society. Accompanying this essential feature are a number of other characteristics that are particularly germane to American society.

MATE SELECTION

Mate selection is relatively open and, ideally, marriage is based on love. The unique position of love in American marriage is that it is supposed to precede the marital bond. Romantic love attachments are not absent from many other societies, but few have made it the basis of selection of a mate in marriage. Since kinship ties beyond the family of orientation are muted, economic functions are focused on the husband in the family of procreation, family functions are less generalized, and inheritance and succession are relatively unimportant, it is perhaps understandable that considerable freedom in mate selection should be the norm and that love attachments should be the crystallizing agent. Preferential mating on a kinship basis is absent, and married couples are not incorporated into existing kin groups. Therefore, there is minimal structural imperative for vesting marital choice in the family rather than in the couple contemplating marriage. Furthermore, geographical and social mobility occasioned by extended education and occupational placement frequently separate parents and children both in space and on social and psychological levels. On the other hand, it is undoubtedly oversimple to say that romantic love is the "only" basis left for marriage choice, since family socialization and informal endogamous norms governing race, ethnicity, religion, education, and social class, as well as the propinquity of these characteristics, lead to a "preferential" pattern within which love attachments are formed.

Earlier patterns of progressive commitment in courtship have given way to casual dating. Because marriage is put off for an extended period of time after puberty, and yet the sexes are not segregated and other forms of control of social interaction are relatively absent, transitory, frequent, and noncommitting sex-paired relations have developed. Succession of dating partners militated somewhat against premature failling in love, provided a range of prospective marital partners, and sanctioned social interaction without marital commitment. Left largely on their own, youths developed a code of ethics and a patterned procedure for interaction of the sexes, buttressed by the older norms of the virtue of chastity and the dire consequences of premarital pregnancy. In its erotic aspects, this has placed the locus of responsibility primarily on the female, and sexual adventure short of intercourse is a not uncommon feature of dating. The frequency and types of dates are often a source of ranking in the peer group, and the search for romantic love attachments sometimes becomes a source of adolescent strain and anxiety.[23]

More recently, probably since World War II, a pattern of "going steady" has been introduced into the dating complex. This pattern appears to shift the emphasis back to earlier courtship behavior, consistent with a trend toward earlier marriages. Marked differences between males and females appear to exist with respect to sexual aspects of dating and courtship. In contrast to the more generalized erotic impulse of the male, the female tends to yield most when love is involved in the relationship. The male tends to make the greater demands on the girl he does not love, who, in turn, is moved to resist if she does not love him. The female tends to yield to the male she does love, who, in turn, tends to resist if he loves her. Margaret Mead has made the following comment on this new pattern:

> It is a better and certainly a more honest code than that of the 1920's and 1930's. The search by today's young people for a mate is conducted under different conditions; going steady is no longer reserved for the wall flowers and athletic failures; indiscriminate dating is no longer the highest aim of the popular; a boy or a girl must offer more than the good "line" which once was all the adolescent needed to fill in the hours with a procession of partners. Yet in more ways than one it is a sorry picture, where both boys and girls are offered exploitative roles, the boy playing on each girl's hope of permanence and early marriage to get cheap and immediate and unsatisfactory sexual compliance, the girl playing on the vulnerability of the boy who begins to court her by entangling him in a sexual intimacy which will propel him towards marriage.[24]

Significant differences in sex codes exist between the male and the female and among males, giving rise to problems of communication and placing strains on interaction. Present arrangements are probably not wholly satis-

[23] For representative studies see Willard Waller, "The Rating and Dating Complex," *American Sociological Review*, 2:727–737 (1937); August B. Hollingshead, *Elmtown's Youth* (New York: John Wiley & Sons, Inc., 1949); Clifford Kirkpatrick and Theodore Caplow, "Courtship in a Group of Minnesota Students," *American Journal of Sociology*, 51:114–125 (1945); Samuel H. Lowrie, "Dating Theories and Student Responses," *American Sociological Review*, 16:334–340 (1951). William F. Whyte discusses some patterns among lower-class slum youths in *Street Corner Society* (Chicago: The University of Chicago Press, 1943), and Arnold W. Green sketches an atypical pattern among Polish youths during the depression in "The 'Cult of Personality' and Sexual Relations," *Psychiatry*, 4:344–348 (1941).

[24] Winston Ehrmann, *Premarital Dating Behavior* (New York: Bantam Books, Inc., 1960), Introduction, p. xviii. This is a detailed study, by questionnaire and interview, of over 1,000 college students and probably represents the most careful and complete study of precourtship and courtship behavior to date.

factory and are likely to move into some new direction, the outlines of which are not clear at this time.

MARRIAGE

With the major exception of the early Mormons and minor experiments among a few isolated "utopias," monogamy has been and is the only morally and legally approved form of marriage in our society. The closest we come to plural mating is a kind of "serial polygamy" occasioned by frequent divorce and remarriage and transitory liaisons of the type found among some lower-class Negro families. Premarital chastity and marital fidelity are prescribed, but sometimes honored more in the breach than in the observance.[25] Consistent with urban industrial organization, neo-local residence is the common rule.

It has been charged that romantic love is an unsound basis for marriage because it is unrealistic in terms of prosaic marital and family functions, leads to hasty and ill-considered marriage, mismatches mates, and sets expectations that cannot be realized in marriage. Actually, the influence of romantic love is easily exaggerated. We have already pointed out how love attachments tend to be made within groups and categories of relatively similar social characteristics and corresponding values and attitudes.[26] Parents play some role in guiding and controlling selection, and youths are not entirely unaware of the responsibilities and realities of marriage. Beyond these considerations, love attachments may be functional for the maintenance of marriage ties in a situation where there are few structural incentives for permanent union. The establishment of strong personal ties before marriage may help to sustain marriage itself. In addition, recent research has uncovered a pattern of "complementary needs" in mate selection. In a society where marital relations are viewed as an important source of gratification, where mate choice is voluntary and bilateral, and where premarital interaction between sexes is encouraged, selection tends to be based on each meeting some need of the other —either different needs or similar needs of different intensity. For example, the boy needs recognition and the girl needs to respond or defer

---

[25] The most comprehensive, although it is by no means complete, analysis of sexual behavior in American society is contained in the familiar works of Kinsey and his associates. See A. C. Kinsey *et al., Sexual Behavior in the Human Male* and *Sexual Behavior in the Human Female* (Philadelphia: W. B. Saunders Company, 1948 and 1953).

[26] See, for example, E. W. Burgess and P. Wallin, "Homogamy in Social Characteristics," *American Journal of Sociology*, 49:117–124 (1943), for a study of 1,000 engaged couples.

or the boy needs to dominate and the girl needs to be dominated. This mutual satisfaction of needs may bring together compatible youths and function to maintain their union.[27]

The United States maintains a relatively high rate of marriage. Roughly, about 90 percent of American men and women are married or have been married by the age of 49.[28] In 1951 the median age of first marriage was 22.6 for males and 20.4 for females and has been decreasing gradually since 1890.[29] Rates of remarriage are consistent with the high marital rates, and age for age the marriage rate of divorced persons is higher than that for either the single or the widowed. Over half of these marriages take place within two years of divorce.[30] Contrary to the prophets of doom and gloom, marriage is still very much a going concern in American society.

The marital relationship itself tends to involve a high degree of personal, subjective feeling on the part of mates, and the permanence of the union is likely to depend on maintaining intimate, affectional ties. Released from the structural demands and social controls of kin and community, the married couple are relatively free to express affectional and companionate inclinations. It has been suggested that the institutionalization of affect in courtship and marriage has arisen as a functional substitute for previously institutionalized supports; and that a central and specialized function of the urban industrial family is the provision of a structured source for intimacy, affect, and tension management.[31]

Authority approaches the equalitarian model, and the female status is less sharply differentiated in important respects than in many other societies. With the rise of "feminism" in the past hundred years, the female is far less constrained by ties of marriage and family. Formerly, marriage stripped women of many property rights, including their earnings; the wife was largely subject to the authority of her husband; guardianship laws favored fathers, and divorce laws favored husbands; marriage voided women's legal rights in various business capacities; and even

[27] See Robert F. Winch, *The Modern Family* (New York: Holt, Rinehart and Winston, Inc., 1952), Chap. 15, for an exposition of the theory of complementary needs.

[28] Metropolitan Life Insurance Co., *Statistical Bulletin*, 28:9 (February, 1947).

[29] "Some Statistics Concerning Marriage and the Family in the United States," in Robert F. Winch and Robert McGinnis (eds.), *Selected Studies in Marriage and the Family* (New York: Holt, Rinehart and Winston, Inc., 1953), p. 97.

[30] Reported in Paul C. Glick, *American Families* (New York: John Wiley & Sons, Inc., 1957), pp. 136 and 139.

[31] Talcott Parsons, *Essays in Sociological Theory, Pure and Applied* (New York: The Free Press of Glencoe, Inc., 1949), Chap. 11, and Talcott Parsons and Robert F. Bales, *Family, Socialization and Interaction Process* (New York: The Free Press of Glencoe, Inc., 1955).

a wife's criminal acts were chargeable to her husband if committed in his presence. In addition, she was denied voting rights, played no direct role in lawmaking, holding of public office, or sharing in jury duty. All this has changed in the direction of equality with the male.[32]

FAMILY AND KINSHIP

The organization of the family is focused on the nuclear unit, composed of husband, wife, and children. Descent is bilateral and residence is neo-local. For all practical purposes, extended kin groups of any sort are absent, including the extended family. Primary loyalties lie with the nuclear family and extend bilaterally to the spouses' families of orientation. Consistent with these patterns, primary relatives are distinguished terminologically and in function from all relatives outside the nuclear group in which they are positioned. Aunts do not stand as "mothers," cousins as "brothers," wife's sisters as "co-wives," uncles as "fathers," and so forth. In the absence of preferential, kinship mating, each marriage brings together two unrelated kinship groups and results in a dispersion of consanguineal lines of descent. In further consistency with the total pattern, rules of inheritance are optional, favor no one line of descent, and vest children with equal rights. As Parsons has put it, "This relative absence of any structural bias in favor of solidarity with the ascendant and descendant families in any one line of descent has enormously increased the structural isolation of the individual conjugal family. This isolation, the almost symmetrical 'onion' structure, is the most distinctive feature of the American kinship system and underlies most of its peculiar functional and dynamic problems."[33]

The size of the family unit is further constricted by fertility controls and the maintenance of separate households for related individuals. In 1790, there was an average of 5.7 persons per household. By 1955, this number had dropped to an average of 3.4. Whereas fully 50 percent of the households in 1790 contained six or more members, only about 10 percent have this number today.[34] A great part of this decrease is the result of bearing fewer children. Fertility rates (number of children born) in

---

[32] *The Legal Status of Women in the United States of America as of January 1, 1948* (U.S. Department of Labor, Women's Bureau; Washington, D.C.: Government Printing Office, 1951).

[33] *Essays in Sociological Theory, Pure and Applied*, p. 238. This essay should be consulted for a systematic treatment of what can only be touched on here.

[34] Reported in William F. Kenkel, *The Family in Perspective* (New York: Appleton-Century-Crofts, Inc., 1960), pp. 200–201, and based on U.S. Bureau of Census data.

the United States conform to the general pattern of decline in Western European countries. In our society, reproduction rates have decreased by more than 75 percent in the last 150 years. Beginning around 1940, there has been a marked reversal of this downward trend, but it is too early to tell whether this shift indicates a permanent trend. The major differentials in fertility rates are by rural-urban residence and by class. Generally speaking, rural and lower-class people have the higher reproduction rates, and farm families, by far, are the major contributors to our expanding population.

All of the complex of factors involved in these trends, even if they were thoroughly understood, cannot be dealt with here, but some may be mentioned. With the growth of science and technology and their application in the field of medicine, death rates have been cut drastically. As vastly greater numbers of children lived to reproduce themselves, world population took a sharp upward turn. With greatly improved agricultural techniques, generalized industrialization, and innovations in transportation and exploration, which opened whole new territories for migration, there was provided the wherewithal to support large populations. A shift was made from a pattern of high death and fertility rates, which resulted in a stable or slow growth pattern, to low death rates and a decrease in fertility. This latter pattern was accompanied by a sharp expansion of population, for the decrease in deaths more than countered the decrease in births, and the former decreased more rapidly than the latter.[35] Most of this appears to have taken place in the past three hundred years, and there is no immediate indication of a world-wide reversal. However, with the application of rational techniques to procreative potentials and the constrictions of urban life on family organization, a new demographic balance seems to be emerging in which the relation of births and deaths may again result in a relative stable population, but in a much more efficient equation than formerly.[36]

Economic productivity within the family unit has been sharply curtailed and is restricted largely to farming households. With mechanization

[35] There is some evidence that fertility may have increased in Europe, with the breakdown of institutionalized inhibitions to procreation, before the decrease set in, thus further propelling growth in the upward trend. See William Petersen, "The Demographic Transition in the Netherlands," *American Sociological Review,* 25:334–347 (1960).

[36] Because of the complexities involved and gaps in our knowledge, long-range predictions concerning population change are hazardous at best. For a more detailed treatment in terms of this general outline, consult Kingsley Davis (ed.), "World Population in Transition," *Annals of the American Academy of Political and Social Science,* 237:1–203 (1945). A popular treatment is contained in Warren S. Thompson, *Plenty of People* (New York: The Ronald Press Company, 1948). A continuing series of excellent studies may be found in *The Milbank Memorial Fund Quarterly.*

of the farm, it is greatly curtailed even in rural areas. Economic productivity is lodged in the male head of the household and removed from the family locale. The role of the female in the family economy has shifted from production to consumption functions. At the same time there has been an expansion of the employment of women outside the family, especially in urban areas.[37] Although the proportion of single women in the labor force is higher than that of married women, it is notable that the proportion of married women has increased more rapidly than that of either the single or the widowed. In 1890, approximately 5 percent of married women were in the labor force; by 1950, this number had increased to about 25 percent. Since World War II, by actual number, married women outnumber single women in the labor force by several million. In conformity with the central procreative and socialization functions of the family, married females with children under ten years of age work less. Consistent with the income of the husband, poorer wives work more.

With a decrease or dilution of traditional family functions, there appears to be an increase in the concentration of socialization and psychological security functions within the isolated nuclear family. Thus, the family appears to be more specialized than formerly, but no less important. The small size of the unit and the sheering off of kinship interactions probably has intensified emotional attachments and interactions between parents and children, as well as between husband and wife. At the same time, if children are to marry and assume adult roles, there must be an emancipation from close parental ties. This transition may result in tensional problems among adolescents, give rise to a "youth culture" in which to handle them, and propel toward romantic attachments and marriage. The sharp separation of economic and family functions in the male status-set conforms to the occupational demands of the larger society, for they require instrumental evaluation, specialization, mobility, and concerted direction apart from an unhampered by considerations of family and kin. The primary function of the wife still centers around her status as mother and "housekeeper." In the former, her task has been intensified by the absence of female kin to share the burden of caring for very young children. In the latter, the burden has been lifted with mechanical aids and the advanced or complete stage of preparation of consumers' goods. This has freed her, after the children have entered the school system, for wider participation in community life beyond the family and immediate neighborhood. This is likely to increase with the extension of higher edu-

---

[37] For this and other generalizations that follow, consult details in J. D. Durand, *The Labor Force in the United States, 1890–1960* (New York: Social Science Research Council, 1948).

cation for females and result in a further breakdown of traditional division of labor based on sex. At the same time, it may increase her specialized function as socializer of children and intensify her identification with her husband's roles outside the family. Withal, the American family remains a basic social system and is likely to persist—in altered form, perhaps, but not to "disintegrate" as has sometimes been predicted.

DIVORCE

In view of the sweeping and rapid changes that have taken place in marriage and in family organization in American society, it is not surprising that adaptive and integrative problems have arisen and frequently are resolved by dissolution of marital ties. Divorce rates are unquestionably high, and since they are viewed as a major social problem, some extended discussion here seems called for. There has been a steady increase in divorce rates since 1870. Starting with a low of about 3 divorces per 100 marriages, a high of 27.5 was reached in 1944. By 1956, this had fallen slightly to 24.[38] Hence comes the well-known headshaker that "one out of every four marriages ends in the divorce courts." These rates are differentiated by a number of social factors. The interrelated conditions of low occupational status, income, and level of education appear to be linked to the higher rates of divorce. Urban rates are generally higher than rural. Racially, Negroes have higher rates than whites. Divorce is also associated with early marriages, absence of children, short engagements, and heterogamous marriages (marriage across occupational, religious, and educational lines).[39] In general, studies of marital "happiness," "adjustment," and prediction of marital "success" are in accord with the factor of homogeneity, socioeconomic position, length of courtship, and age of marriage. In addition, happiness in marriage is also associated with happily married parents, amicable relations with parents, parental approval of marriage, childhood happiness, and moral conservatism.[40]

---

[38] Reported in Kenkel, *op. cit.*, and based on census data. Caution is warranted in the interpretation of statistics on divorce, since they should be corrected for variation in population size and rates of birth and marriage over time.

[39] A number of studies documenting these patterns are reviewed and analyzed in William J. Goode, *After Divorce* (New York: The Free Press of Glencoe, Inc., 1956). The major focus of the book is on an original study of postdivorce adjustment of a group of women with children.

[40] These studies, which attempt to correlate stated degrees of marital happiness with social variables, have been subjected to criticism on the grounds that samples are small and selective, involve only married people, and evidence a middle-class bias; and verbal reports of "happiness" are not validated. For a general introduction to this field see sample articles in Winch and McGinnis, *op. cit.*, Chaps. 16 and 17.

Although these general and specific rates no doubt are linked to structural conditions, the precise relationship has not been thoroughly researched. There is every reason to believe that the structure of marriage itself and its relationship to kinship and the larger society are conducive to divorce, at least in the transitory period in which we now find ourselves. On the one hand, the intensity of affect and the importance attached to emotional happiness in marriage have increased, while the moral imperatives of maintaining the union have decreased. On the other, strong structural supports of kinship and community have diminished. These changes are accompanied by general cultural values that emphasize individuality, freedom of choice, and the pursuit of individual happiness, and articulate them as a right. The relatively open structure of marriage, family, and kinship seems well adapted to these values, but the cost may involve frequent divorce.[41]

Differentials in divorce rates are interlinked and difficult to separate. Early marriages and short engagements are associated with low socioeconomic position and so is race. Presence or absence of children in marriage is associated with rural-urban residence and length of marriage. Such complexities discourage conclusions, but warrant informed speculation. In general, these variables seem to have significance in terms of the larger structural conditions we have mentioned in the preceding paragraph. The occupational position of the male is strategic in our society in many ways. It is linked to education and income, places the male and his wife and children in the class structure, affects stability of employment and income, is associated with employment of wives, gives rise to different styles of life, and so on. In their *social* aspect, economic factors of occupation and income appear to bring structural pressure on marriage in different degrees at different levels. For example, the higher levels tend to place people in a position of low mobility, high community control, greater job satisfaction, and stability of income and employment. Structural sources of support may thus be more available and economic strains that may be displaced in marriage may be less frequent. In rural areas, we tend to have larger families, greater homogeneity, stable occupational roles, expansion of family functions, and greater community controls—all of which would seem to produce a condition conducive to family stability.

Although divorce frequently is viewed as a major social problem in the United States, it is easy to exaggerate its impact on the society. Almost every social pathology from delinquency to mental illness has been laid

---

[41] The functional interrelationship of these values and the structure of marriage and family is well described by Ruth Benedict in "The Family: Genus Americanum," in Ruth Anshen (ed.), *The Family: Its Function and Destiny* (New York: Harper & Brothers, 1949). It is recommended for those who insist on having their cake and eating it too.

at its door. This preoccupation has arisen as a consequence of a focus on divorce rates to the exclusion of other sociological variables involved in these rates and to a nostalgic yearning for the assumed perfections of earlier family patterns. A reasonable assessment of divorce must be made in historical perspective and in terms of total societal organization. In an eagerness to exalt the old and condemn the new, we may fail to make a total accounting of functions and disfunctions of present marital and family arrangements.

Two problems directly associated with divorce are the adjustment of the divorced spouses and the disposition of children. As we have seen in our discussion of divorce in other societies, both are related to the nature of our kinship system. In our society the problems of postdivorce adjustment center around the relative absence of position and support for the parted couple. In general, their status is ambiguous. No clear or imperative lines are drawn for economic or emotional support on the part of kinsmen or even friends during or after divorce. Similarly, there is an absence of any clear structure that would draw the divorced into new group relationships. The aid and council extended by the family of orientation in the first marriage is withdrawn or muted in search for a second. Proper behavior of divorced persons with respect to others and between themselves is not clearly defined.[42] This places divorced persons in a situation of strain that is often severe. Earlier attitudes toward divorce already have been tempered, and it is likely that some clearer patterned arrangement for the divorced will develop.

The problem of children in divorce centers around their placement and the consequences a broken family may have for the socialization process. The emotional strain may bear as heavily on the children as on the adults, and the isolated nuclear family provides little alternative structure for its functions when it is dissolved by divorce. Since the same is true of the death of one of the spouses, our social accounting might well begin at this point. Although rates of divorce have increased greatly, we are likely to overlook the fact that death rates have decreased. As a consequence, the number of children in broken families today is no greater than it was sixty years ago. In fact, we are somewhat better off since the upswing in divorce has more than been offset by the downward trend in mortality rates.[43] Apart from this, the effect of high rates of divorce on children is mitigated somewhat by the fact that the preponderance of divorce takes place in the early period of married life and, therefore, does not involve children. Actually, the presence of children in marriage apparently is not the powerful deterrent to divorce that it is sometimes assumed to be,

[42] Goode, *op. cit.*, pp. 12–14.
[43] Paul H. Jacobson, "Differentials in Divorce by Duration of Marriage and Size of Family," *American Sociological Review*, 15:235–244 (1950).

when durations of marriage, separation before divorce, and the relation of fertility and divorce rates are properly taken into account. The impact of divorce on both the parents and the children also may be lessened by an increasing tendency toward remarriage, particularly since World War II. This recent development has increased remarriage, especially among men and women with children under eighteen, among rural-farm people, older persons, and those in the higher socioeconomic levels. Although it is too early to determine whether the general and specific upswing in remarriage is permanent, the over-all pattern suggests something more than a momentary adjustment to the dislocations brought about by the war.[44]

In a more general appraisal of divorce in the United States, consideration should be given to rates in other societies. Among some primitive peoples, divorce appears to be at least as frequent as in our society. Among contemporary literate societies, we are high on the list, but have been topped in the recent past. Japan was considerably higher in the late nineteenth century, and Russia, Palestine, and Egypt were higher in and around the 1930's.[45] Perhaps of more significance is the fact that other urbanized industrial societies are approaching our rates. In fact, divorce in the United States has increased less in the past forty years than in most other industrialized countries, particularly Canada, Great Britain, and Sweden. This suggests that divorce is closely related to the structure of industrial society, and certainly is not an exclusive American phenomenon.

Although these considerations cannot gloss over the problems raised by divorce in our society, they set it in proper perspective and give us a more realistic understanding of the problem and solutions toward which we may reasonably expect to work. It is unlikely that sheer moralistic exhortation or utopian schemes based on earlier agrarian structures will suffice. Divorce appears to be indigenous to modern social structure, and while it may be decreased (we see possible models in differential rates within the society), it is unlikely that it will drop spectacularly. Perhaps one fruitful development would be in the building of appropriate structure to accommodate divorce and diminish the traumas associated with it. Ruth Benedict's comment on the situation of marriage and the family in America today seems appropriate:

> The family in the United States is an institution remarkably adapted to our treasured way of life. The changes that are occurring in it do not

[44] For detailed discussion of remarriage see Jessie Bernard, *Remarriage: A Study of Marriage* (New York: Holt, Rinehart and Winston, Inc., 1956); Glick, *op. cit.*, Chap. 6; and Goode, *op. cit.*

[45] These are rough comparisons at best since comparable cross-cultural data are very difficult to obtain. See Ernest W. Burgess and Harvey J. Locke, *The Family* (New York: American Book Company, 1945), pp. 627–628.

mean that it is decaying and needs to be saved. It offers a long array of privileges. It needs more consideration in political tax-supported programs, by means of which many difficulties that beset it could be eradicated. Finally, Americans, in order to get the maximum happiness out of such a free institution as the family in the United States, need to parallel their privileges with an awakening responsibility. It is hard to live up to being so privileged as we are in the United States, but it is not impossible.[46]

SUMMARY

The structure of marriage, family, and kinship center around procreation and the care and maintenance of children. The structures institutionalized to accomplish these functions vary greatly among societies, although a limited number of types may be distinguished. Particular structures are functionally integrated with the systems of marriage, family, and kinship, with other subsystems, and with the larger societal organization. Familial structures may have consequences for the organization and development of the larger society and, in turn, societal developments may have direct impact on the organization of the family.

Urban industrial society evidences a tendency toward the emergence of the isolated nuclear family as the dominant form. In the United States, this form has been accompanied by an open system of mate selection, high rates of marriage and remarriage, and a decrease in the age of marriage, particularly in the recent past. Family functions are constricted but specialized, the number of children is relatively small, authority approaches equalitarianism, and divorce rates are high. The American family structure appears to be in a period of transition rather than "disintegration," and it is likely to emerge in a more stable and enduring form—the outlines of which are only dimly seen at present.

The major purpose of this chapter has been to acquaint the student with the structure of a particular system, illustrate the relationship of structure to function, demonstrate the proposition of structural alternatives, and show the relationship of structure to system adaptation and integration. In addition, the student should be able to isolate out specific examples of mechanisms of social control, and structures that motivate deviance, foster socialization, and give rise to the formation of groups.

[46] In Anshen (ed.), *op. cit.*, pp. 168–169.

8

ADAPTATION TO NONSOCIAL ENVIRONMENTS: INDUSTRIAL TECHNOLOGY

Social systems face the same kinds of adaptive problems in relation to their physical environments as they do with respect to their social environments. Energy and raw materials must be procured; viruses and waste products must be disposed of. In addition, the definitions of the situation in nearly all social systems include a world of supernatural beings to be adapted to. We shall consider adaptation to the supernatural environment in the next two chapters when we discuss magic and religion. Our concern in this chapter will be with the development of industrialism, and especially with the integrative problems of modern societies that result from industrialism.

Industrialism, man's extraordinarily productive method of bending nature to his will and pouring forth a flood of consumers' riches, has three central characteristics, each of which has far-reaching implications for other aspects of societies. These are the implications with which we shall be chiefly concerned. The central characteristics of industrialism are

1. a high ratio of capital to labor,
2. a factory system of production, and
3. an elaborate division of labor.

The Ratio of Capital to Labor

THE PROBLEM DURING INDUSTRIALIZATION

Industrialism is often referred to as "the roundabout method of production." Instead of labor's being devoted entirely to the production of food or other things that people consume, part of it is devoted to the production of tools. The tools then increase the productivity of the labor devoted to producing goods and services that are consumed directly rather than devoted to further production. In other words, people devote more time, energy, and material to the fabrication of tools in order to have more goods and services for consumption.

This, of course, has been a characteristic mode of man's adaptation to nature ever since the first cave man took time out to chip a point on a piece of flint. It is what the most primitive agriculturalists do when they make a plow. But the industrial mode of production does it to such an enormously greater degree as to amount to a difference in kind. In addition, industrialism has added a fundamentally critical tool—nonhuman and nonanimal energy. Steam power and electric power have so multiplied the productivity of labor as to warrant the much-used term "industrial revolution."[1] And atomic energy and solar energy, together with automation, promise to revolutionize the revolution.

The tools that add so much to man's control over nature are often called "producers' goods," in contrast to the food, clothing, automobiles, and so on, that are produced by the tools. These latter are called "consumers' goods." Producers' goods, in other words, are the "goods" (tools) that producers of consumers' goods *use* in producing consumers' goods. Producers' goods include factories, milling machines, hydroelectric plants, steam shovels, freight cars, hammers and nails, and so on—all goods that are used by people *in order* to produce other goods or services that are consumed for their own sake.

Producers' goods are also sometimes called "capital." This terminology may cause confusion because people are sometimes led by it to think of "capitalism" as a synonym of "industrialism"—the toolmaking mode of adaptation. "Capitalism," however, refers to a particular set of mechanisms institutionalized as the mechanisms of integration of a social system —namely, competition, bargaining, and self-reliance. Capitalism is a way

---

[1] One statistic will illustrate the difference in this respect between industrialized and unindustrialized societies. In 1953, total energy consumption per person from solid fuels, oil, gas, and hydroelectric and nuclear power was eighty times as great in the United States as in India. United Nations, *Statistical Yearbook*, 1954, Table 125.

of "running" an industrial organization; but, as we have seen, there are other mechanisms of integration by which it can be "run."

The tools, factories, tools to make tools, generating plants, and atomic reactors, then, we shall refer to as "producers' goods" or "capital." *Once produced,* they increase the output of consumers' goods many, many times over.

But the problem is to produce them. Industrialization requires that labor be diverted into producing tools and away from fabricating raw materials into the relatively small supply of consumers' goods that can be produced without tools. The immediate effect of the diversion is to reduce still further the already limited supply of consumers' goods. The workers who are left to produce consumers' goods, therefore, must not be permitted to consume all they produce: those who are producing capital must be supported out of the available supply of consumers' goods while they are devoting their time to the production of tools.

This is one of the problems of industrializing so-called underdeveloped countries—as all countries are, by definition, before industrialization. When the countries are already straining every resource to produce just enough to keep the existing population alive, as are most underdeveloped countries today, the problem of reducing the supply of consumers' goods still further becomes extraordinarily difficult.

The problems involved in industrialization, and the mechanisms for solving them, may be understood in terms of our earlier discussion of the processes of adaptation of subsystems to one another—which are also the processes of system integration. The relationship between subsystems that produce capital equipment or tools (including energy), and those that produce consumers' goods is like that of any two subsystems with respect to their procurement and disposal problems. This particular relationship is shown in Table 8–1.

TABLE 8–1

Relationship between Producers of Capital Equipment and Producers of Consumers' Goods

PRODUCERS OF CAPITAL EQUIPMENT	PRODUCERS OF CONSUMERS' GOODS
Seek to procure consumers' goods	Seek to dispose of consumers' goods
Seek to dispose of tools	Seek to procure tools

The producers of capital equipment and the producers of consumers' goods are adapted to one another when

1. producers of capital (tools, buildings, machinery) obtain as much consumers' goods (food, clothing, shelter) as they want;

2. producers of capital dispose of all the capital they want to dispose of;

3. producers of consumers' goods obtain as much equipment as they want; and

4. producers of consumers' goods dispose of all the goods they want to dispose of.

This is the equilibrium situation that prevails both in the typically pre-industrial society and in the *stably industrialized* society. That is, (1) role-players engaged in making food and clothing are satisfied with the amount and quality of tools they receive from the toolmakers; (2) they find customers for all the food and clothing they want to produce. At the same time, (3) role-players engaged in making tools are satisfied with the amount of food and clothing they receive from food and clothing producers. (4) They find that the food and clothing makers are willing to accept the tools offered.

The beginning of industrialization consists of a special kind of disturbance of this equilibrium: role-players charged with production of consumers' goods begin to *want more capital equipment than is available* and the producers of capital equipment *need more consumers' goods than are available.*

The critical problem is the procurement problem of the would-be producers of capital equipment. *How can they get enough consumers' goods to support themselves while they are making tools?* How can they get the people who produce consumers' goods to abstain from consuming all of them—to contribute some of them to the tool producers? The general techniques available to solve this procurement problem are, of course, the same ones we have discussed before: calling on an institutional obligation of producers of consumers' goods to consume less than they might, "bargaining" with them, appealing to their love or loyalty, or using force.

The special forms that these procurement techniques take in the case of industrialization can best be understood if we first consider the significance of money.

Money becomes a necessity in a social system when there is even a fairly slight degree of specialization. The reason is that the individual member of the system procures different things from different specialists, and may dispose of different things to still different specialists. The costs and values of those different things would be extremely difficult to compare, if they had to be compared with one another, and the greater the degree of specialization, the greater the difficulty. Procurement and disposal among specialized role-players or groups is made much easier if all comparisons can be made in terms of *one common thing.* That common thing, whatever it is, is money.

For example, if the value of cattle, corn, blankets, baskets, pottery, horses, and so forth can be expressed in terms of, say, beads, then beads become money. It is then possible to dispose of cattle for beads and use the beads to procure baskets, pottery, and so forth. Without some such common unit of measurement and exchange, it would be necessary to dispose of cattle for a bunch of baskets, a bunch of blankets, and so forth, then lug the baskets around to someone who would take them in exchange for a horse, and so on. Given any great complexity at all, this would obviously become an intolerable burden.

Once something has developed as money—whether it is beads, shells, gold, silver, or green pieces of paper—it becomes a symbol of purchasing power. The green piece of paper that you call a dollar bill, for example, amounts to a certificate representing *a claim on a certain amount of all available goods and services.* With it, you have a claim on a dollar's worth of someone's time, or a dollar's worth of ice cream, or four twenty-five-cent magazines, and so on and on.

With this notion of money in mind, we may describe as follows the critical procurement problem of capital-producers when a society is attempting to industrialize:

The money cost of producing the available supply of consumers' goods is just what it requires to induce their producers to produce them. That is, the money cost of producing them is the sum of the amount paid as wages to workers, plus the amount paid as rent to landowners, plus the amount paid as interest to lenders, plus the amount paid as profits to entrepreneurs. But those costs, plainly, are also the *incomes* of workers, landowners, lenders, and entrepreneurs. Their incomes, in other words, *are just sufficient to buy back the total supply of consumers' goods produced*—which is precisely what they must not be allowed to do if the producers of capital equipment are to have a share in them. In money terms, the problem is that of transferring some of the purchasing power represented by the wages, rents, interest, and profits of the producers of consumers' goods to the workers, owners, lenders, and entrepreneurs engaged in producing tools. As we have pointed out, this might be done either by "bargaining" or through calling upon obligations of either a cathectic or a "bureaucratic" type.

The most obvious form of bargaining in this context is the payment of interest or the promise of shares in future profits. Entrepreneurs—or government agencies—may, for example, sell stocks or bonds to the consuming public, exchanging, in effect, a *promise* of a future reward for present purchasing power. When people buy stocks and bonds, they surrender part of their claims on the existing supply of consumers' goods, and the money with which they pay for the stocks or bonds may then be paid to the producers of capital. The latter—workers, landowners, and so forth, who are engaged in producing tools—then can use the money to purchase that part of the supply of consumers' goods that the bond or stock purchasers have relinquished claim to.

Would-be producers of capital may, in addition, procure the purchasing power they need by appealing to various sentiments. The consuming public may be exhorted to be thrifty, as a virtue in itself, or to "save for a rainy day." Or they may be urged on the grounds of patriotism to consume less than they have the power to consume. A particularly vivid example of this aproach was provided in the campaign of the United States government to sell war bonds during World War II. (Here, of course, the aim was not to industrialize—the United States was already highly industrialized—but it was very similar. The aim was to produce tools of war, rather than tools with which to produce consumers' goods; and the problem of getting people to share the existing supply of consumers' goods with those tool-producers was essentially the same as in the industrialization case, except that it was not nearly so severe.)

Robert K. Merton has analyzed the appeals made by Kate Smith, a popular radio entertainer, during a twenty-four-hour "marathon" campaign to sell war bonds.

> The attempt to fan into active flame the readiness of listeners to sacrifice for the war effort followed [these] lines. . . . Foremost was the sacrifice which the boys were making "over there . . ." The listener was urged to do as much for them as they were ready to do for us.

> "Now they are braving swamps and jungles, risking illness and wounds, pain and death . . . staking their lives so that you and I may never know the horrors of a blitz or a bombing . . . nor the tragedy of torture and deliberate starvation. Because our boys' hands are at the throat of the enemy far from home, you and I can sleep in our beds with little fear of sudden death from the skies. Because our boys pin the enemy down far across the world, strange ships do not enter our ports and enemy guns and tanks do not rumble through our streets and across our fields."

> Generalities fail to promote empathy and vicarious experiences. To induce these, the Smith broadcasts moved quickly from the abstract to the concrete, from the general to the specific individual.

> "Could you say to Mrs. Viola Buckley . . . Mrs. Viola Buckley whose son Donald was killed in action . . . that you are doing everything you can to shorten the war . . . that you are backing up her son to the limit of your abilities?"

> The second sort of appeal was based upon . . . the sacrifices which other civilians were making.

> "This mother has given one son, and she knows each night when she goes to bed that the other son is doing the same tough job and running the same terrible risk. She knows too that her youngest will soon go away and leave her to fight for his country. . . . What are you doing compared with what this mother has done? . . . Are you backing the attack? Are you really, honestly now, in your heart, are you really seeing

to it that her sons have the best fighting equipment and plenty of it? Are you buying luxuries or are you turning those dollars you don't need into war bonds?"[2]

Similar appeals to patriotism and national pride are an important part of the efforts of many governments today to industrialize. The Russian and Chinese Communists' use of international crises to fire their peoples' willingness to sacrifice is notorious. General Nasser's cultivation of nationalistic fervor in the Middle East and the similar appeals of many African leaders are additional examples.

Western nations were aided in the solution of this difficult problem by a rather special circumstance. As the sociologist-historian Max Weber has shown, the ascetic spirit of early Protestantism provided an incentive for abstinence from consumption and dedication to work that helped considerably in the transition to industrialism. Among the early Lutherans and Calvinists frugality was a virtue in itself, and consuming as much as possible was a sin. Weber, in his *Protestant Ethic and the Spirit of Capitalism*, discusses the early Protestant feelings concerning these two sentiments.

> The peculiarity of this philosophy of avarice appears to be the ideal of the honest man of recognized credit, and above all the idea of a duty of the individual toward the increase of his capital, which is assumed as an end in itself. Truly what is here preached is not simply a means of making one's way in the world, but a peculiar ethic. The infraction of its rules is treated not as foolishness but as forgetfulness of duty. . . . It is not mere business astuteness, that sort of thing is common enough, it is an ethos.[3]

> Wealth as such is a great danger; its temptations never end, and its pursuit is not only senseless as compared with the dominating importance of the Kingdom of God, but it is morally suspect.[4]

Cultivation of those sentiments, then, was at least as effective as the present-day cultivation of nationalistic sentiments.

But neither sentiments of duty nor bargaining has ever been enough, either in the early days of Western industrialization or in the current days of Eastern and African industrialization. The massive amount of capital needed to industrialize a nation requires a greater amount of "belt tightening" than any people have ever been persuaded to undergo voluntarily. Force has been necessary also; and the faster a nation tries to industrialize—and the poorer it is to start with—the more does force seem to be necessary.

---

[2] Robert K. Merton, *Mass Persuasion* (New York: Harper & Brothers, 1946), pp. 52–53.

[3] Max Weber, *The Protestant Ethic and the Spirit of Capitalism* (London: George Allen & Unwin Ltd., 1930), p. 51.

[4] *Ibid.*, pp. 155–156.

The consumers' goods needed to support capital producers might be procured forcefully either by governments or by private entrepreneurs. Governments, of course, may confiscate consumers' goods directly, as the Soviet government confiscated wheat from Russian peasants and used it both to support urban workers and to export in payment for imports of capital equipment and engineering talent.[5] Similarly, by government coercion, workers may be forced to labor at construction projects for little or no pay. Governments may, and always do, simply take money through taxation, all or part of which may be used for production of capital goods.

Private entrepreneurs do not usually have the governmental option of confiscation, but they may use exploitative techniques that are just as effective. English and American industrialization, for example, was accomplished in part by working ten-year-old children twelve to fourteen hours a day, not to mention the extremely hard wage bargains they managed to drive with adult workers.

In addition to these relatively crass types of force, there is a more subtle method of forcing people to abstain from consumption. This is simply to create additional *symbols* of purchasing power, indistinguishable from those given to the producers of consumers' goods. These additional symbols may then be used to pay the producers of producers' goods. This, as we have seen, is what money is—a symbol of the power to purchase, a certificate representing a claim on the available supply of goods and services. If *more* such certificates are manufactured, so to speak, the result is that each certificate is worth less—its power to purchase has declined because it now has to compete with more certificates just like it.

The simplest way of adding to the supply of purchasing power is literally to manufacture additional certificates. Simply roll the government printing presses longer or faster and turn out more dollar bills. This is sometimes done. In a capitalistic system. however, with its cultural definition that government activity is bad and private activity is good, this is ordinarily frowned upon. (Not because it doesn't work, but because it works too well—in other words, it gives the government "too much" influence.)

In a capitalistic system, there is another, "private enterprise" method of accomplishing the same result—through the expansion of bank credit. This operates in the following manner: If A deposits $1,000 in Bank No. 1, Bank No. 1 may lend, say, 90 percent of it, or $900, to B. It does this not by giving him dollar bills but by giving him a checking account—a credit on the bank's books that entitles him to *write checks in payment for his*

---

[5] See Warren B. Walsh, *Russia and the Soviet Union: A Modern History* (Ann Arbor: University of Michigan Press, 1958), pp. 420–421, 448–450; and Bernard Pares, *Russia* (Baltimore: Penguin Books, Inc., 1941), p. 141.

purchases. Suppose he buys something from C and pays for it with a check for $900. (Notice that purchasing power is here clearly operating; yet no "money" is involved.)

C deposits the check in Bank No. 2, which now has an additional asset of $900. It may lend 90 percent of it, or $810, to D by giving D a checking account. D writes a check for $810 in favor of E, who deposits it in Bank No. 3, which may now lend 90 percent of $810, or $729, to F. F writes a check for $729 to G, who deposits it in Bank No. 4, which may now lend $656.10 to H, who . . . , and so on.

Notice that as far as we have traced these transactions (and they can go on for a long time), A's original $1,000 of purchasing power has been expanded into $3,095.10 ($900 + $810 + $729 + $656.10). This expansion of purchasing power is possible as long as those who have a claim on it do not all lay claim to it at once. The individual saving and spending habits of people operate collectively so that this does not happen ordinarily. The familiar exception is a "run on the banks" during an economic panic.

Far and away most business transactions take place through the banking system, so that the expansion of bank credit is a fundamentally important method of transferring purchasing power from producers of consumers' goods to producers of capital equipment.[6]

However the producers of capital receive their purchasing power—whether as a result of government printing or through the private banking system—they spend it, or part of it, on consumers' goods. So far as the retailer is concerned, there is no difference between the money offered to him by producers' goods workers and that offered by consumers' goods workers; all he knows is that the demand for his goods suddenly exceeds the supply. He raises prices, the consumers' goods producers can't afford to buy all the consumers' goods, and there are some left over for capital producers. The consumers' goods workers have been *forced* to "save"— that is, not consume.

There is, finally, one more way in which a society may procure the capital necessary for industrialization. That is to receive it from an already industrialized society. The United States, for example, might export to India either consumers' goods to compensate for the withdrawal of Indian workers from consumers' goods production, or, more usually, capital equipment and engineering skills. The exports might be gifts or

[6] The creation of additional symbols of purchasing power, whether by the government or by the banks, contributes to inflation; and inflation always represents a transfer of purchasing power from one group to another. The group receiving the additional purchasing power, of course, need not be producers of capital. They may be the aged (as when social security benefits are increased by inflationary means), the underprivileged, retired generals, and so on.

long-term loans to be repaid out of greater productivity later. The construction of American railroads was significantly aided in this manner by
English investors; and—as is not unusual in such cases—the aid was made
even more significant by Americans' subsequently defaulting on the
loans.[7]

The subsidization of American industrialization by (technically speaking) the exploitation of British investors is one example of the fact that
industrialization—the process of becoming industrialized—always requires
subsidization. This is simply another way of putting the fact that producers of capital must be supported out of the available and necessarily
limited supply of consumers' goods and services. Until the railroads, electric power plants, atomic reactors, or years of technical training begin to
pay off, the people engaged in their development have to be subsidized
at the expense of others. *Later on* (which may be generations later) the
early sacrifices pay off—although by no means necessarily for the same
persons who did the sacrificing.[8]

American industrialization was subsidized not only by British investors
but also in many other ways. We have already mentioned the exploitation
of—that is, hard bargaining with—workers. A further important source of
subsidy for American industrialization was the importation of adult workers with already developed skills. The support and training that went into
their growth and acquisition of skills was paid for out of the supply of
goods in their home countries. When they were old enough to pay off,
they migrated by the millions to the United States. An examination of
immigration tables shows that between the years of 1830 and 1900, an
average of 68.9 percent of the immigrants each year fell between the
ages of fifteen and forty, the most productive work years.[9] They carried
with them occupational skills mainly in the fields of agriculture, industry
and mining, transport and commerce, domestic service and general labor,
although there was some representation from the liberal professions and
public services.[10] No doubt the words inscribed on the base of the Statue

[7] Approximately $150 million of American railway securities were in default in
1873—of which $74 million were held in foreign countries, mainly Germany, Holland,
and England. John F. Crowell, "Railway Receiverships in the United States: Their
Origin and Development," *Yale Review*, 7:319–330 (1898).

[8] Let us note again, here, that the deferment of consumption may not be *felt* as a
"sacrifice." People may have autonomously internalized a Puritan ethic or a patriotic
zeal that makes the deferment pleasurable, or at least ego-gratifying, in itself.

[9] Walter F. Willcox (ed.), *International Migrations*, Vol. II, *Interpretations* (New
York: National Bureau of Economic Research, 1931), Table 33, Classification of
Immigrants by Age, at Ten-Year Intervals, 1820–1930, p. 114.

[10] Walter F. Willcox (ed.), *International Migrations*, Vol. I, *Statistics* (New York:
National Bureau of Economic Research, 1929), Table 8, Distribution of Total Number
of Passengers Arrived from 1820 to 1867 and of Immigrant Aliens only from 1868 to
1924, by Occupation, pp. 399–400.

of Liberty were felt—by many persons and under various conditions—
genuinely:

> Give me your tired, your poor,
> Your huddled masses yearning to breathe free,
> The wretched refuse of your teeming shore,
> Send these, the homeless, tempest-tossed, to me:
> I lift my lamp beside the golden door.

But the mine owners and other businessmen who advertised in Europe
for migrants and offered to lend them passage money were helping to
perform a different function—that of subsidizing American industrialization—and not, if they could help it, with any "wretched refuse."

In similar ways, but more rapidly and with more central direction,
Russia became industrialized after World War I—ruthlessly and at the
expense of millions of Russian people. China and India today, to take the
two largest societies, are beginning the same process, China with a forced
collective effort unparalleled in history; India with a similar, but more
democratic, centralized direction. Russia and the United States are now
in the position of being able to facilitate the industrialization of the remaining areas by subsidizing them. But this, of course, requires some
sacrifice of American living standards, and it remains to be seen whether
Americans are willing to make it.

To summarize, then, there are three possible ways of accumulating a
sufficient "surplus" of consumers' goods to support producers of capital:
voluntary savings, forced savings, and outside help. All three of these
possibilities are obviously made more difficult to the degree that the
population of the society attempting to industrialize is expanding. Any
"surplus" of consumers' goods that does arise is then needed to support
the additional members of the society, and the amount of surplus needed
to support capital-equipment producers becomes still greater. It is for
this reason that continued high birth rates in underdeveloped countries of
large population (without correspondingly high death rates) is a serious
deterrent to industrialization.

THE PROBLEM AFTER INDUSTRIALIZATION

In a fully industrialized society, the problem of equilibrium between
capital producers and consumers' goods producers becomes radically different in nature. In fact, it becomes just the opposite. The problem is not
that capital producers have difficulty in procuring consumers' goods,
while consumer's goods producers have trouble procuring capital; it is
that capital producers have trouble *disposing* of all the tools they can

produce, and people cannot find borrowers for all the money they want to invest.

The problem, in other words, is not the scarcity of consumers' goods but their staggering abundance; it is not that people might save too little but that they might save too much. In a phrase, the problems of a fully industrialized society are not problems of increasing production; they are problems of increasing consumption—or *decreasing* production.

The thrift that is so functional for industrializing a nation may be highly disfunctional when that nation is industrialized. If people do not spend all their money on the flood of consumers' goods that pour off the assembly lines, some goods must remain unsold. This, as we have seen, may be functional if the unspent money is transferred to producers of capital, who then spend it on the remaining consumers' goods. But suppose that no one wants to produce any more tools. Suppose, in other words, that the consumers' goods industry is already so fully tooled up that no more tools are needed.

Then the savings will *not* be transferred to capital producers to be spent on consumers' goods. Some consumers' goods will remain unsold; dealers will cut down their orders to manufacturers; manufacturers will have to discharge workers; with unemployment increasing, there will be less money spent on consumers' goods; more goods will remain unsold; dealers will cut their orders still further; manufacturers will discharge more workers; and so on, in a deflationary spiral toward depression.

What are the mechanisms for preventing this kind of disequilibrium?

They fall, of course (by definition of the problem), into two types. One consists of ways of *compensating* for thrift by taking up the surplus income that consumers fail to spend on consumers' goods; the other consists of ways of *reducing* thrift by increasing people's "propensity to consume."

Among the ways of taking up the incomes that otherwise would be withdrawn from the stream of purchasing power, the most vivid and spectacular way is war or preparation for war. In the United States in 1960, for example, about 12 percent of the national income was spent for the national defense program.[11] If a disarmament program were to be put into effect, the problem would inevitably arise as to how the resources presently invested in armaments could be invested in something else.

There are, of course, many *possible* answers. Instead of investments in bombs, there could be investments in schools, hospitals, libraries, slum clearance, foreign aid, cancer research, space exploration, and so on and on. The *possibilities* of investments alternative to armaments are limited only by the fertility of the human imagination.

---

[11] See Bureau of the Budget, *Federal Budget in Brief, 1961* (Washington, D.C.: Government Printing Office), pp. 18–22, 44.

An interesting and important restriction, however, is the fact that none of those investment outlets is "profitable" for private enterprise. Neither, of course, is investment in bombs. Only the government—the agent of the society-as-a-whole—can afford to purchase bombs or long-range missiles; and only for the government is investment in hospitals or cancer research "profitable." The difficulty is that "national defense"—preparation for war —is a more politically palatable reason for government expenditure than is, say, slum clearance or a war against cancer. Although it would be *possible*, therefore, to find outlets, other than military ones, for disposing of the immense purchasing power generated in an industrial society, it might be politically difficult in a society that values private enterprise and devalues government enterprise.

What about the other major kind of social defense against deflation—increase in the propensity to consume, or decrease in thriftiness? The outstanding mechanism to be understood in this context is advertising. As David M. Potter has put it:

> . . . advertising is not readily needed in an economy of scarcity, because total demand is usually equal to or in excess of total supply, and every producer can normally sell as much as he produces. It is when potential supply outstrips demand—that is, when abundance prevails—that advertising begins to fulfill a really essential economic function. In this situation the producer knows that the limitation upon his operations and upon his growth no longer lies, as it lay historically, in his productive capacity, for he can always produce as much as the market will absorb; the limitation has shifted to the market, and it is selling capacity which controls his growth. Moreover, every other producer of the same kind of article is also in position to expand output indefinitely, and this means that the advertiser must distinguish his product, if not on essential grounds, then on trivial ones, and that he must drive home this distinction by employing a brand name and by keeping this name always before the public. In a situation of limited supply the scarcity of his product will assure his place in the market, but in a situation of indefinitely expandable supply his brand is his only means of assuring himself of such a place.[12]

The primary social function of advertising, in other words, is to stimulate consumer demand. To the degree that consumers can be made dissatisfied with last year's model of automobile, refrigerator, or bathing suit, to that degree the immensely productive machinery of the industrial system can be kept running.

The size of the American effort to stimulate demand in this way is readily seen in the size of American outlays for advertising. In 1951, over $6.5 billion were spent for advertising, as compared to a little over $5 billion for all primary and secondary public education in 1949.[13] A more

---

[12] David M. Potter, "Advertising and Abundance," *Yale Review*, 43:55–56 (1953).
[13] *Ibid.*, p. 60.

specific comparison may be even more illuminating: "In 1944 the major political parties spent $23,000,000 to win the public to the support of Mr. Roosevelt or of Governor Dewey; in 1948, Procter and Gamble, Colgate-Palmolive-Peet, and Lever Brothers spent more than $23,000,000 to win the public to support one or another of their products."[14] Whether or not it would be possible to speed up the obsolescence of goods sufficiently to compensate for the ending of investment in armaments remains to be seen.

The Factory System

In discussing the problem of consumer demand, we have actually turned to another type of equilibrium problem of industrial societies. This second kind of problem stems from the second characteristic of industrialism we mentioned at the beginning of this chapter—a factory system of production.

Whereas in a preindustrial society, a household (a family or a kinship unit) is likely to be both the consuming unit and the producing unit, in an industrial society, there is a sharp differentiation. The household remains the major consuming unit, but the factory emerges as a specialized producing unit. People step out of their familial statuses and into their occupational statuses at certain specified times and places. The two kinds of statuses are sharply segregated.

The household and the factory—or "firm"—remain highly interdependent, but the equilibrium of that interdependence becomes rather more precarious in the industrialized society. Households and business firms become two different kinds of subsystems, with the households supplying labor and seeking to procure goods and services, and the firms supplying goods and seeking to procure labor. Their relationship is shown in Table 8–2.

TABLE 8–2

Relationship between Business Firms and Households

FIRMS	HOUSEHOLDS
Seek to procure labor	Seek to dispose of labor
Seek to dispose of goods	Seek to procure goods

[14] *Ibid.*, p. 61.

The four general equilibrium conditions apply here as usual. That is, there is equilibrium when

1. members of households are able to dispose of all the labor they want to dispose of (they can find jobs);
2. they procure all the consumers' goods they want;
3. firms are able to sell all the goods they produce; and
4. firms can obtain all the labor they want.

When societies are going through the transition to industrialism, the critical problems here, again, are the procurement problems. Household problems of procuring consumers' goods have already been discussed: there simply are not enough to go around, partly as a result of the low level of productivity that prevails in preindustrial societies and partly as a result of the fact that some labor has been diverted from producing consumers' goods into producing capital.

The problems of business firms in recruiting labor are similarly acute in the early period of industrialization. The basic reason for this is the fact that the industrial work discipline is completely different from the rhythm of work and life in preindustrial societies. The segregation of occupational statuses from other statuses in terms of time, place, and content requires the learning of wholly new ways of life. Life can no longer be governed by the rhythms of the seasons, the weather, or the earth's rotation. It must be governed by the clock, by fluctuations in demand, by the necessity for precise synchronization and dovetailing of thousands of specializations, and by the nature of the machines that set the pace and demand maintenance.

Consider, for example, the astonishing degree of routinization and standardization of living schedules of millions of Americans today, which we ordinarily simply take for granted. Every morning at six (let us begin with) in hundreds of thousands of homes hundreds of thousands of people start going through exactly the same motions. Hundreds of thousands of alarm clocks (set the night before with hundreds of thousands of identical motions) go off. Hundreds of thousands of people flick on electric switches, confidently expecting a current to be there; hundreds of thousands of garage doors slide open, hundreds of thousands of engines turn over, and hundreds of thousands of cars begin converging on railroad stations and factories. At six-thirty another wave of thousands and thousands of alarm clocks goes off and the identical motions are repeated by another category of workers. And so it goes.

Such precision, punctuality, and predictability are both essential and fantastic, if one lets his mind dwell on them for a moment. They rest on an extraordinary set of cultural definitions that were by no means easy to cultivate in the initial period of industrialization, much as we take them for granted today. The transition to industrial discipline was made still more difficult, of course, by the sheer impossibility of motivating people to undergo it by offering them rewards for doing so. They had, in fact, as we saw above, to accept *lower* levels of rewards.[15]

The alternative to the carrot of rewards in such cases is the stick, and it is to the exploitative force of the stick that no little part of American and English present-day riches and efficiency are owed. A concrete reminder may help to give some perspective on contemporary developments in countries going through their industrialization agonies:

> The fourteen or fifteen hours' confinement for six days a week were the "regular" hours: in busy times hours were elastic and sometimes stretched to a length that seems almost incredible. Work from 3 a.m. to 10 p.m. was not unknown; in Mr. Varley's mill, all through the summer they worked from 3:30 a.m. to 9:30 p.m. At the mill aptly called "Hell Bay," for two months at a time they not only worked regularly from 5 a.m. to 9 p.m. but for two nights each week worked all through the night as well. The more humane employers contented themselves when busy with a spell of sixteen hours (5 a.m. to 9 p.m.).
>
> It was physically impossible to keep such a system working at all except by the driving force of terror. The overseers who gave evidence before Sadler's Committee did not deny that their methods were brutal. They said that they had either to exact the full quota of work, or to be dismissed, and in these circumstances pity was a luxury that men with families depending upon them could not allow themselves. The punishments for arriving late in the morning had to be made cruel enough to overcome the temptation to tired children to take more than three or four hours in bed. . . . In some mills scarcely an hour passed in the long day without the sound of beating and cries of pain. . . . In the afternoon the strain grew so severe that the heavy iron stick known as the billy roller was in constant use, and, even then, it happened not infrequently that a small child, as he dozed, tumbled into the machine beside him to be mangled for life, or, if he were fortunate, to find a longer Lethe than his stolen sleep. In one mill . . . some of the slubbers tried to keep the children awake . . . by encouraging them to sing hymns. As the evening wore on the pain and fatigue and tension on the mind became insupportable. Children would implore any one who came near to tell them how many more hours there were still before them.[16]

Those days of transition are far behind contemporary North America—indeed, for most people out of sight. The equilibrium problem of more concern to present-day Americans is rather the opposite: not the problem

[15] For a valuable and well-written review of a great amount of research on the recruitment of labor in industrializing societies, as well as a report on his own original research, see Wilbert E. Moore, *Industrialization and Labor* (Ithaca, N.Y.: Cornell University Press, 1951).

[16] J. L. Hammond and B. Hammond, *The Town Labourer, 1760–1832* (New York: David McKay Company, Inc., 1920), I, 159–160.

of procuring enough labor but of disposing of all the labor available. (And, as we have already seen, not the problem of producing enough consumers' goods but of disposing of all that comes pouring out of the amazingly productive industrial machine.)

The difficulty of disposing of labor results from the extraordinarily greater productivity of labor when it works with modern industrial tools. As productivity per worker increases, it obviously requires fewer workers to produce the same amount of goods. This in itself, of course, does not necessarily mean that there are "surplus" workers whose labor cannot be disposed of; the same number of workers, or even more, can be used to produce not the same amount of goods but many more. This is the basic fact that lies behind the extremely high living standards of Americans.

One difficulty, however, is the fact that "labor" is not a homogeneous entity. Although it *may* be true (we shall express doubt about it below) that human wants are indefinitely expansible, it is certainly not true that there is an unlimited demand for any specific product—say, corn or wheat or steel or coal. When the productivity of farmers increases as a result of gains in technological efficiency, or when plastics or aluminum replaces steel, or when one coal miner can produce as much coal as a dozen coal miners of an earlier day—then for farmers, steel workers, and coal miners there is a serious problem of disposing of their labor. The fact that there are thousands of people who may be satiated with wheat, steel, and coal, but still have an unsatisfied wish for swimming pools in their backyards or air conditioners in every room—this fact is of little significance to the unemployed farmers, steel workers, or coal miners. They are farmers, steel workers, and coal miners—not air-conditioning producers; and there is no one in *their* neighborhoods ready to employ them to dig swimming pools.

A second difficulty concerns the idea of indefinitely expansible human wants for material goods. There is, as Paul Goodman has said,[17] *some* limit to the number of television sets a family wants or the number of cars it makes sense to have. If there is a limit, then the strain of stimulating consumer demand enough to keep employed a possibly growing number of more and more productive workers may become enormous. Beyond this, the question must become more and more insistent: Does it make any sense to spend so much ingenuity on finding ways to increase materialistic desires so that more people can be put to work satisfying them?

Finally, there is a third difficulty of disposing of labor in a fully industrialized society. This difficulty stems from the fact that most people do

---

[17] Paul Goodman, "Youth in the Organized Society," *Commentary*, 29:95–108 (1960).

not simply want jobs; they want jobs that *matter*. That is to say, one determinant of people's self-images is the *worth-whileness* of their statuses. If workers understand that they are not really needed to satisfy existing wants, but are, rather, surplus unless advertisers can create new wants for them to satisfy—are they likely to derive much self-respect from this?

Elaborate Division of Labor

OCCUPATIONAL SPECIALIZATION

The problem of finding a sense of satisfaction in occupational statuses is further complicated by the third characteristic of industrialism we cited at the beginning of this chapter—the extreme specialization of occupational statuses.

One of the prerequisites of the conscientious carrying out of status-obligations, as we have seen in earlier chapters, is that a favorable self-image result. But this means the conviction that one's status is *important*. In other words, if one is to carry out status-obligations conscientiously and with enthusiasm, one must get some ego-gratification for doing so. This is well illustrated in a famous study made at the Hawthorne plant of the Western Electric Corporation in 1927.[18]

One group of workers studied was composed of women engaged in assembling telephone relays. The work consisted of putting together a coil, armature, springs, and insulators. Six average women were selected for experimentation to see what factors contributed to or impeded their productivity, as measured by the number of relays they could assemble in a given period of time. The women were put in a special test room, and factors that the investigators thought might influence productivity were systematically varied. First, a midmorning and a midafternoon five-minute rest period were introduced; second, the rest periods were extended to ten minutes; third, the women were given six five-minute rest periods; fourth, light snacks were provided for them; fifth, the workday was shortened; sixth, the workweek was shortened. In between the introduction of those innovations, working conditions were occasionally returned to an

---

[18] See F. J. Roethlisberger and W. J. Dickson, *Management and the Worker* (Cambridge, Mass.: Harvard University Press, 1939). Also see George C. Homans, "The Western Electric Researches," in Committee on Work in Industry of the National Research Council, *Fatigue of Workers: Its Relation to Industrial Production* (New York: Reinhold Publishing Corporation, 1941), Chap. 4.

earlier stage to see what the results would be. Finally, all the innovations were eliminated, and the group returned to the working conditions prevailing at the start of the experiment.

The rather staggering result was that *every* time a change was introduced, including the changes *back* to earlier conditions, production went up! After the working conditions were returned to their *original* state, ". . . daily and weekly output rose to a higher point than ever before."[19]

It was not, then, the actual physical changes that mattered so much; it was, rather, as the reader should now be prepared to understand on the basis of Chapter 1, the *meaning* of those changes to the people involved. What they meant to the Western Electric employees was several things. One was that working in the test room was "fun"; second, they were participating in an important and interesting experiment—their work "mattered"; third, *they* mattered—they were consulted and "let in on" all the changes.

By contrast, it was discovered through study of another group of workers in the same plant—a group of twelve men engaged in wiring and soldering units for telephone exchanges—that, in spite of a carefully worked out wage-incentive plan by which the men's pay was determined by how much they produced, production was kept at a very steady level, much below what the group could have produced without fatigue. Furthermore, this wage-incentive plan was so devised that if any member of the group produced more than the others, not only he but the *entire group* profited. In effect, the group "sold" its weekly output to management, and the greater the output, the more money was available to divide up among the men. It was thought, plausibly enough that this would result in the development of group pressure on individuals to work at their peak efficiency, since anyone who "goofed off" hurt everyone else's financial position.

In fact, however, the opposite occurred. There was indeed group pressure, but it took the form of forcing fast workers to slow down. Why? George Homans offers a succinct explanation:

> Once the responsible officer has decided that a certain change ought to be made, he gives an order and this order is transmitted "down the line," appropriate action being taken at every level. The question in which the investigators were interested was this: What happens when the order reaches the men who are actually doing the manual work? Roethlisberger and Dickson made the following observations: "the worker occupies a unique position in the social organization. He is at the bottom of a highly stratified organization. He is always in the position of having to accommodate himself to changes which he does not originate. Although he participates least in the technical organization,

---

[19] Homans, *op. cit.*, p. 62.

he bears the brunt of most of its activities." It is he, more than anyone, who is affected by the decisions of management, yet in the nature of things he is unable to share management's preoccupations, and management does little to convince him that what he considers important is being treated as important at the top—a fact which is not surprising, since there is no adequate way of transmitting to management an understanding of the considerations which seem important at the work level. There is something like a failure of communication in both directions—upward and downward.

The worker is not only "asked to accommodate himself to changes which he does not initiate, but also many of the changes deprive him of those very things which give meaning and significance to his work." The modern industrial worker is not the handicraftsman of the medieval guild. Nevertheless, the two have much in common. The industrial worker develops his own ways of doing his job, his own traditions of skill, his own satisfactions in living up to his standards. The spirit in which he adopts his own innovations is quite different from that in which he adopts those of management.[20]

The more people feel that their parts in the division of labor are worthy significant parts, the more likely are they to take pride in their responsibilities and in the effort to meet them fully. The less the worthiness of their statuses in their own eyes, the less is the possibility of getting a favorable self-image from carrying out its responsibilities; and, therefore, the less is the incentive to do so.

Now, one difficulty for the occupants of many occupational statuses in an industrial society is the simple fact that it is hard for them to see that their parts in the division of labor are "important." This is true for two reasons, both resulting from the sheer fact of extreme specialization. One is the fact that it is hard to define the simple monotonous repetitive fraction of, let us say, automobile production in which the average worker engages, as very important. The other is the fact that if one *is* to regard his job as important, other people must support the definition; and this support is made difficult to secure because most other people are simply ignorant about any given specialization other than their own.

Both difficulties are dramatically illustrated in the case of a West Coast airplane manufacturing plant during World War II. Production was low because of high rates of absenteeism and labor turnover. In an effort to improve the situation, a bomber that had been produced in the plant and that had completed several successful bombing missions over Germany was brought back, together with its crew, and put on exhibition. The workers were invited to inspect it. The bomber crew explained to them how their lives had been saved time and again by the good workmanship

[20] *Ibid.*, pp. 84–85

that had gone into the thousands and thousands of specialized parts of the plane.

The experience of seeing so vividly the importance of their work apparently so improved the moral of the workers that absentee and turnover rates dropped radically.

This lesson, of course, has not been ignored by plant managers and sociological and psychological advisers to industry. But it is in fact very rare that circumstances can be arranged so dramatically to *persuade* workers of the importance of their work. A story told by Chris Argyris, an associate professor of industrial administration at Yale University, eloquently reveals the bedrock difficulty:

> Here is a young boy named Dick. Dick works on an automobile assembly line. "Hello, Dick." "Hello, Doc." "Can you give me an idea of what you do?" "Sure—I put four bolts into the right rear end of a car." "You do?" "You see that barrel there?" "Yes." "There are 10,000 bolts in there, and you know what I'll do when I finish those 10,000?" "What will you do?" "I'll get another barrel." "But, Dick, you sound a bit discouraged." "Wouldn't you be?" "But isn't your job an important part—" "Now, wait a minute; you're not going to hand me the same old stuff I get from management, are you?" I became a bit embarrassed. "But isn't it true, Dick, that if those four bolts didn't go in correctly, the whole car would fall apart?" Then he said something I won't forget: "You know, Doc, that's what hurts. How would you like to live in a world where you could say that the most important thing you could do with your life was put four bolts in the rear end of a car?"[21]

The difficulty is increased to the degree that the values of the society at large place major emphasis on occupational statuses as *the* primary basis of self-respect, and to the further degree that occupational statuses are themselves ranked in a hierarchy of prestige. That is to say, if a person's self-image is primarily defined by his occupational status, and if his occupational status is defined as lacking in prestige, then there is simply no escape from the punishment of an unfavorable self-image.

There is no escape, that is, except along the route of one or more of the mechanisms of deviant adjustment or social control. Either the person is likely to deviate by compulsive conformity, ritualism, innovation, or retreatism, or he may be motivated to conform by recourse to compensatory satisfactions, tension management activities, or some other form of control. In the extreme, but not unusual case, he may conform to the work role from sheer coercion; that is, fear of hunger and economic depriva-

[21] Chris Argyris, "The Individual and Organizational Structure," *Personnel Practice and Policy: The Changing Picture* (Personnel Series, No. 168; New York: American Management Association, 1956), pp. 3–11. Reprinted in Keith Davis and William G. Scott (eds.), *Readings in Human Relations* (New York: McGraw-Hill Book Company, Inc., 1959), pp. 60–69. Quotations from pp. 62–63.

tion. He works only to exist—which then raises the question of what the benefits of industrialization are to *him*, beyond a higher "standard" of existence (consumption).

This is connected with a third factor that complicates the problem of deriving a favorable self-image from one's occupational status. This third element is the fact that the level of occupational performance expected of people—and hence the level they expect of themselves—depends on certain qualities. That is to say, *how* worthy a job must be in order to be worthy enough for self-respect depends upon a person's *non*occupational identity.[22] For example, there is still a tradition that men should be "better" than women, in the sense of being able to outcompete them in virtually everything not culturally defined as "women's work." Men should be smarter, more dominant, stronger, and so on. Similarly, "whites" should be "better" than Negroes; older people more competent than younger people; college graduates more able than high school graduates.

The trouble is that these preindustrial, nonrational traditions that survive into the industrial period are incompatible with the rational performance-orientation of industrialism. In the market and in the firm there is a steady pressure to allocate people to statuses on the basis of their competence, not on the basis of their qualities; and there is also a pressure to reward statuses with prestige and income on the basis of relative scarcity of the competence needed to occupy them.

As a result, men may find themselves receiving less pay and prestige than do women; whites may be in jobs that Negroes are equally competent to fill; college graduates may not find themselves as highly rewarded and as highly regarded as their educational status requires them to be (in their own eyes); and so on. Older people, in the same way, often—and perhaps increasingly in today's and tomorrow's world—must experience a sense of failure and deprivation when they view their occupational displacement by younger people from the perspective of their self-expectations as older people.

In view of these conditions faced by specialists in most industrial societies, several characteristics of those societies become understandable. Lack of commitment to jobs and "featherbedding" may be seen as predictable reactions to lack of respect for the jobs. Lack of commitment to the status of "woman" may be seen as a predictable reaction to lack of respect for any but occupational statuses; and the same phenomenon makes predictable a lack of commitment to the status of "student." Simi-

---

[22] See, for a slightly different way of conceptualizing this difficulty, A. Zaliznik, C. R. Christenson, and F. J. Roethlisberger, *The Motivation, Productivity, and Satisfaction of Workers* (Boston: Harvard University Graduate School of Business Administration, 1958), p. 202. This work also reports evidence from a research program bearing on these points and illuminates some of the difficulties involved in measuring the variables of rewards and costs. See especially p. 295.

larly, if adolescents are denied self-respect until they assume occupational roles (which they are prevented from assuming by the requirements of education), then their efforts to find substitute ego-gratification in the "youth culture" are readily understandable.

If, for the reasons just discussed, the carrying out of status-obligations cannot be motivated by the reward of a sense of pride and commitment, then how can they be motivated? Two possibilities remain: coercion and *material* reward.

Coercion, as we have seen, was widely used as the motivating device during the early period of Western industrialization and is reported to be widely used in the Soviet Union and China today. Where unions are weak or corrupt, coercion may be used to some extent in the United States today.[23] Much more extensively relied on in the United States, however, is the incentive of monetary reward.

The meaning of work for most industrial workers lies in its *instrumental* utility for providing an income with which they and their families can then go about "living." Consistent with this is the finding by the Survey Research Center of Michigan University that older married men tend to be more productive on their jobs than younger single men:[24] the former have more of an instrumental stake in their occupations.

One "lives" when consuming; when producing, one merely endures.[25] Inevitably, then, the overwhelming interest of industrial workers in their jobs is to make them as *remunerative* and as *endurable* as possible. Hence, the annual or biannual round of efforts by unions to secure wage increases and more control over their members' working conditions, and, hence, the pressure on workers to canalize a large part of their ingenuity and creativity into finding ways of *not* working hard. For them, the "profit" from the job consists, as it does for everyone, of its rewards minus its costs; but in the average industrial case, effort is strictly a *cost*.

By contrast, in an occupational status that the individual can regard as important and worthy in itself, and that is compatible with his expectations of himself, the same amount of effort, or even more, is not a cost: it is a reward in itself. A physician, a teacher, a lawyer, or a scientist, for example, can derive personal satisfaction from working hard; and so

---

[23] See Sidney Lens, "Little Labor: The Forgotten Unions," *Dissent*, 6:454–461 (1959).

[24] Robert I. Kahn, "The Prediction of Productivity," *Journal of Social Issues*, 12: 41–49 (1956).

[25] This would seem to be one of the major reasons why the wives of physicians do not put the pressure on their husbands to "stay home more" and "be like other men" that the wives of progressive trade union leaders do. Cf. Alvin W. Gouldner, "Attitudes of Progressive Trade Union Leaders," *American Journal of Sociology*, 52:389–392 (1947). See also Logan Wilson and William L. Kolb, *Sociological Analysis* (New York: Harcourt, Brace & World, Inc., 1949), pp. 575–579.

could a skilled carpenter, let us say, in preassembly-line days. What we witness here is the same phenomenon we observe in the case of a typical high school boy, for whom the effort of learning historical dates or the rules of grammar is a distinct cost, but for whom the same or greater "effort" of learning the batting averages of every player in the National League or the complex rules of baseball is not a cost at all.

Our point here is that when industrial workers attempt to restrict the effort they invest in their jobs, they are behaving exactly like the most classical of entrepreneurs: they are seeking to maximize profits. The difference is a difference in their sociological positions, rather than in either the nature of their motivation or the orneriness of their nature.

The situation of workers in these respects has been made clearly understandable by Donald Roy.[26] Roy took a job as a machine operator in a factory, and kept a diary of his day-to-day experiences and feelings and of the conversations and attitudes of his fellow workers. After describing in detail the ways in which the men deliberately kept their output low, in spite of the fact that they were constantly complaining about their need for more money (which they could have earned with the piece work incentive system set up in the plant), Roy asked in effect, "Why?" He also noticed that at *some* times he and his fellow workers would in fact exert their maximum effort to achieve their quota of production, and he asked, "Why?" about this also.

So far as quota restriction was concerned, Roy communicates the basic attitude of the men in a vivid fashion. When he was hired, he was told that radial drill operators were averaging $1.25 an hour on piecework. For the first few days, he was assigned to watch an experienced radial drill operator in order to learn. Roy reports his initiation as follows:

> One of Starkey's first questions was, "What have you been doing?" When I said I had worked in a Pacific Coast shipyard at a rate of pay over $1.00 an hour, Starkey exclaimed, "Then what are you doing in this place?" When I replied that averaging $1.25 an hour wasn't bad, he exploded:
>
> "Averaging, you say! Averaging?"
>
> "Yeah, on the average. I'm an average guy; so I ought to make my buck and a quarter. That is, after I get onto it."
>
> "Don't you know," cried Starkey angrily, "that $1.25 an hour is the *most* we can make even when we *can* make more! And most of the time we can't even make that! Have you ever worked on piecework before?"
> "No."

---

[26] Donald Roy, "Quota Restriction and 'Gold-Bricking' in a Machine Shop," *American Journal of Sociology*, 57:427–438 (1952), and by the same author, "Work Satisfaction and Social Reward in Quota Achievement," *American Sociological Review*, 18:507–514 (1953).

"I can see that! Well, what do you suppose would happen if I turned in $1.25 an hour on these pump bodies?"

"Turned in? You mean if you actually did the work?"

"I mean if I actually did the work and turned it in!"

"They'd have to pay you, wouldn't they? Isn't that the agreement?"

"Yes! They'd pay me—once! Don't you know that if I turned in $1.50 an hour on these pump bodies tonight, the whole God-damned Methods Department would be down here tomorrow? And they'd retime this job so quick it would make your head swim? And when they retimed it, they'd cut the price in half! And I'd be working for 85 cents an hour instead of $1.25!"[27]

Nonetheless, there were times when Roy and his associates drove themselves hard to produce as much as possible. Under what conditions did this occur? Roy describes them as follows:

It would seem that the attainment of quota marked the successful completion of a task or solution to a problem in which the outcome was largely controllable by the operator, although chance factors were also important determinants of results. Making quota called for the exercise of skill and stamina, and it offered opportunity for self-expression. The element of uncertainty of outcome provided by ever-present possibilities of bad luck made quota attainment an exciting game played against the clock on the wall, a game in which the elements of control provided by the application of knowledge, ingenuity, and speed, heightened interest and lent to exhilarating feelings of accomplishment. Although operators constantly shared their piecework experience as a chief item of conversation, and always in terms of making money or not making money, they could, in reality, have been communicating game scores rather than financial successes or disappointments. It is doubtful if any quota-attaining operator ever believed that he had been making money in the sense of improving appreciably his financial status. Had anyone been able to communicate accurately such a conviction, he would have been laughed out of the shop.

It could be said that playing the make-out game had its negative as well as its positive values. It broke the monotony of repetitive work and made the long day pass. Although on day work the operator had only the pause at lunchtime to break up the meaningless flow of time, he had in his piecework game an hour-by-hour series of completions that served to mark his position in relation to the larger completion of the day's work. For the operator engaged in a good piecework job, time moved in a rapid succession of intervals toward the final hour of quitting the plant. But operator interest in quota piecework seemed to have its diminishing returns. McCann, for instance, expressed feelings of bore-

[27] Donald Roy, "Quota Restriction and 'Gold-Bricking' in a Machine Shop." *American Journal of Sociology,* 57:427–438 (1952), p. 430. Copyright 1952 by the University of Chicago.

dom on one job that was a never-failing source of premium pay; his claim was that he performed this particular operation so much that he could do the work in his sleep. His experience suggests that making out on piecework could be a stimulating game only as long as the job represented a real challenge to the operator, only as long as the element of uncertainty was present in the activity's outcome.

If making out lost its value as a game when operator control over the job became so complete that winning degenerated into mere routine, it also lost such value if the element of uncertainty became too predominant over the element of control; that is, if bad luck became too frustrating to the application of skill, the job became nerve-wracking. For instance, on one operation the work involved such a high rate of tool breakage at unpredictable intervals that quota attainment seemed to be more a matter of luck than of skill. The nervous strain suffered by the writer and other radial drill men who shared this operation made the job assignment a thoroughly unwelcome one.[28]

The pressure to define many productive statuses as instrumental tools, to be evaluated strictly in terms of their usefulness for the "real business" of consuming, has two important consequences. One is the fact that it becomes much easier—even normal—to define "proper" behavior as that which "pays off." Television quiz shows are readily "rigged," butchers cheat customers on the weights of meat while market inspectors accept bribes to overlook the practice, and so on.[29] "Deviance" as described in Chapter 5 becomes almost the norm.[30]

The second consequence is closely related. The public may come to have less and less trust and confidence in the conscientious role-playing of those on whom they are dependent. Cynicism and suspicion may become widespread, and a sense of futility may develop. Something corresponding to economic depression may become chronic.

We may schematically show this possibility by again turning to our model of subsystem equilibrium.

TABLE 8–3

Relationship between Status-occupants and Their Publics

STATUS-OCCUPANTS	THE PUBLIC
Seek to procure public recognition, respect, prestige	Seeks to dispose of respect, recognition, prestige to statuses
Seek to dispose of conscientious role-playing	Seeks to procure conscientious performance of status-obligations

[28] Roy, "Work Satisfaction . . . ," p. 511.

[29] See almost any issue of *The New York Times* during the month of November, 1959.

[30] See Harry C. Bredemeier and Jackson Toby, *Social Problems in America* (New York: John Wiley & Sons, Inc., 1960).

Equilibrium exists when

1. statuses receive the recognition and prestige their occupants desire;
2. status-occupants find people willing to accept their performances;
3. the public is satisfied with the quality of performance of status-occupants; and
4. the public has respect for the statuses comprising the social structure and defines them as important.

When the public fails to give respect to many statuses, the occupants of those statuses cannot have favorable self-images. If they cannot derive self-respect from conscientious performance of their roles, they lose an important incentive to perform conscientiously; and when they fail to carry out their obligations conscientiously, the public becomes dissatisfied with the role-services being received. When this happens, the public is still less able to give respect to many statuses, which makes it more difficult for those status-occupants to have favorable self-images, which makes it less likely that they will "take their jobs seriously," which . . . , and so on, in the familiar spiral downward.[31]

What mechanisms are there for preventing the interruption of this circular flow of respect and conscientious role-performance? Two kinds of mechanisms must be sought by the analyst: those that function to increase appreciation of the importance, the difficulty, and the needs of various status-occupants, both on the part of the status-occupants themselves and on the part of their various publics; and those that function to make receipt of that respect contingent on conscientious role-performance.

Mechanisms potentially making for mutual respect and appreciation are of two major kinds. One is the structuring of status-sets and role-sets in "cross-cutting" arrangements so that one's opponents in one contest are one's allies in another. When an individual's religious identity, for example, makes him an ally of someone else with a different occupational identity, he may be more likely to appreciate the latter's occupational status. On the other hand, to the degree that subgroups are homogeneous with respect to all their identities, their ability to empathize with others may be curtailed. For example, if white Anglo-Saxon Protestant businessmen live only with "their own kind," and marry, play, vote, and have clubs only among themselves, their inbredness may reduce their appreciation and understanding of others.[32]

[31] Leo Srole has developed a scale that measures one part of this process—the feelings of what we have called "the public" toward the quality of role-performances it receives. See Leo Srole, "Social Integration and Certain Corollaries: An Exploratory Study," *American Sociological Review*, 21:709–716 (1956). We should note that Srole does not conceptualize his study in the terms we have used in the text—that is, in terms of our analysis of equilibrium.

[32] For an excellent discussion of this and related issues, see Melvin Tumin, "Some Consequences of Institutional Imbalance," *Behavioral Science*, 1:218–223 (1956).

Notice one thing we are *not* saying here. We are not saying that simple "contact" with others breeds respect and understanding. This is a widespread fallacy that no one ought to fall into who understands the elementary principle we emphasized in Chapter 1: people do not respond to situations (or "contacts" with others); they respond to their *definitions* of those situations. This is why it is important to specify that if contacts are to result in enhanced appreciation and respect, they must be *contacts in which the different persons are allies.* The more contact our hypothetical WASP businessmen have with Chinese Buddhist laborers in which they are not allies, the *more* hostility they are likely to feel toward them.

Striking evidence of this point was provided during World War II by the reactions of white soldiers to the idea of incorporating Negroes into their army units. In a nutshell, the observations made by social scientists in the Army Information and Education Division, who studied the situation, was that the closer to the front lines the white soldiers were, the more favorable were their atitudes toward Negroes. The more pronounced the recognition that one needed these "different" people, the greater the tendency to accept them.

The second major kind of mechanism for increasing respect and appreciation across status-lines is one that operates directly on this critical factor of "definitions." Mass media of communication are at least *potentially* able to contribute to empathy and mutual respect by dramatically cutting through the barriers of status-differentiation and stimulating identification with others. People who have seen such effective moving pictures as "The Defiant Ones," "Come Back Little Sheba," "Porgy and Bess," or some of Edward R. Murrow's television productions of "See It Now" know what a powerful instrument these can be, at least temporarily, for carrying the individual beyond his own circumscribed experiences. Indeed, as Irwin Edman says, this is precisely the function of art: "To render experience by rendering it alive."

> For most people most of the time life is a heavy lethargy. They have eyes, yet they do not, in any keen and clear sense, see. They have ears, yet they do not finely and variously hear. They have a thousand provocations to feeling and thought, but out of their torpor comes no response. Only the pressure of some animal excitement, instant and voluminous, rouses them for a moment to an impulsive clouded answer. Life is for most of us what someone described music to be for the uninitiate, a drowsy reverie, interrupted by nervous thrills![33]

Art changes this:

> That passing face is not something to be persuaded or conquered or forgotten. . . . It ceases to be an incident or an instrument; it is not . . .

[33] Irwin Edman, *Arts and the Man* (New York: W. W. Norton & Company, Inc., 1939), p. 13.

a signal to anger or to lust. It is a moment crowded with vitality and filled with order; it is . . . beautiful, as we say, to look at, and its beholding is a pleasure.[34]

When they convey "art," then, the mass media may perform the function of enhancing the identification of specialized role-players with one another.[35] The leaders of the Soviet Union have for most of their history been so impressed with this potential function of art that artists of all kinds have had their work rigidly reviewed almost entirely in terms of political standards. Artistic "deviationists" have been as bitterly assailed as political "reactionaries."[36]

In the more loosely integrated, leisurely, and competitive bargaining structure of the United States, it is more difficult for the mass media to perform that function. The directors of mass media are constrained by the same cultural mechanisms as are all other role-players: they must "make it worth the while" of their audiences to read, listen, or view their wares, and this, especially in view of competitive pressures, means that they must cater to the audiences' existing attitudes and opinions, not attempt to change them.[37] Violation of an audience's existing prejudices means that the audience will simply switch the dial, subscribe to another magazine, buy another paper, or stay away from the movies *en masse*. What people read or see, then, tends to reinforce what they already think.[38] This means that if there is equilibrium of the kind we are discussing, the mass media may help to maintain it; but if there is widespread distrust, suspicion, and hostility, the mass media tend also to maintain that.

[34] *Ibid.*

[35] We do not mean to imply that this is the only, or even the most important, function of art. "Experience" that is "rendered alive" by art includes very much more than the experience of other people. This, however, is *one* of the things it includes. We are saying, then, that *a* function of art is to lead to identification, not *the* function. It has, perhaps, come close to being *the* function of art in the Soviet Union.

[36] For a fascinating account of this pressure on art, as seen and felt by a Soviet artist, see "On Socialist Realism" (anonymously written), *Dissent*, 7:39–66 (1960).

[37] This pressure has been observed and commented on in a variety of contexts. See the following for excellent analyses and descriptions: Robert K. Merton and Paul F. Lazarsfeld, "Mass Communication, Popular Taste, and Organized Social Action," in Guy E. Swanson, Theodore M. Newcomb, and Eugene L. Hartley *et al.* (eds.), *Readings in Social Psychology* (rev. ed.; New York: Holt, Rinehart and Winston, Inc., 1952); Bernard Berelson and Patricia J. Salter, "Minorities in Magazine Fiction," in Milton L. Barron (ed.), *American Minorities* (New York: Alfred A. Knopf, Inc., 1957); Ralph Ross and Ernest Van den Haag, *The Fabric of Society* (New York: Harcourt, Brace & World, Inc., 1957), Chap. 15, "Popular Culture"; and Hilde T. Himmelweit *et al.*, *Television and the Child* (London: The Oxford University Press for the Nuffield Foundation, 1958), especially Chaps. 9, 10, 12.

[38] See Paul F. Lazarsfeld *et al.*, *The People's Choice* (New York: Duell, Sloane & Pearce–Little, Brown, 1944).

CONSCIENTIOUSNESS AS NECESSARY FOR RESPECT

Recall that we said above that it is necessary to look for *two* kinds of mechanism that might prevent interruption of the circular flow of respect and conscientious role-playing. One kind, which we have just been discussing, consists of mechanisms making for understanding and appreciation across status-lines; the second, of mechanisms that function to make receipt of respect *contingent on* conscientious role-playing.

The problem here is that human beings are not only likely to "goof off" if their best efforts are not appreciated; they are also likely to do so if they receive appreciation *without being productive or conscientious*. This is simply a restatement, in the context of industrial occupations, of a point we made earlier in our analysis of socialization. We pointed out then that the socialization process might fail in either of two ways: (1) through failure to reward the socializee for adequate performance; (2) through failure to *withhold* rewards for *in*adequate performance (the "spoiled child" phenomenon).

Moreover, as we have seen before, both of these dangers—unconscientiousness as a reaction to lack of appreciation and unconscientiousness as a reaction to too-easy demands—tend to be intensified when bargaining and competition are institutionalized. Competitors, it will be recalled, reduce one's chances of getting his needs met. Therefore, it sometimes becomes advantageous to deflect one's attention from the productive carrying out of status-obligations to protecting oneself against competition. Two research projects have supplied important evidence of this tendency.

Nicholas Babchuk and William J. Goode studied a group of salesmen in a men's clothing department of a large department store.[39] At one period of their study, the salespeople were paid on a commission basis, so that their "take-home pay" was dependent on the sales they made. Therefore, the authors report,

> . . . the sales personnel began to use a number of expedients for achieving [high sales records] . . . . "Sales grabbing," for example, was a common accusation, and covered a number of practices such as taking a customer who seemed to be heading for another salesman. A salesman might be busy with one customer, but attempt to prevent a second customer from going to a second salesman—a practice called "tying up trade."[40]

[39] Nicholas Babchuk and W. J. Goode, "Work Incentives in a Self-Determined Group," *American Sociological Review*, 16:679–686 (1951).

[40] *Ibid.*, p. 683.

In addition, everyone was reluctant to spend time in preparing displays or in sorting, arranging, checking, and ordering merchandise; such activities, necessary as they were, were costly in that they prevented the salesman doing them from being available for customers. " 'High pressure' selling was common, and there was considerable bickering and quarreling during and after consummation of a sale."[41] After some time, the salesmen themselves (with the permission of management), developed an informal pooling system. "The members decided to cooperate with one another by dividing the stock work equally. Soon . . . [they] agreed to cooperate in all work areas. *However, this forced them to equalize sales volume among themselves, so that as a consequence each might receive equal pay.*"[42] The management of the store finally adopted this plan officially; and Babchuk and Goode report, "In terms of total group sales, 'production' has increased since the plan was finally put into effect."[43]

> Since the individual earns the same amount as his fellow-workers each week even if his sales tally is low, he can devote more attention to tasks which he likes. There is no economic loss for seeing to it that good displays are made or that sizes and types of merchandise are adequate. . . . Since each individual will be affected equally if sales are poor [or if] bottlenecks develop [or] unsatisfactory merchandise is bought, etc., there is some pressure on everyone to contribute to the needed solutions.[44]

Peter Blau, a sociologist at the University of Chicago, made very similar observations in his study of placement officers in a government employment bureau.[45]

The duties of the workers here were to interview job seekers, file their applications, take requests from employers for workers, and then match the requests with the appropriate job applicants in the files. Blau studied two different groups of these workers, Section A and Section B. In Section A, the supervisor, in evaluating the interviewers under him, emphasized the number of placements each had made; in Section B, the supervisor evaluated his subordinates more leniently and placed much less emphasis on *quantity* of placements. Furthermore, the workers in Section B "received their training together after World War II, at a time when intensive counselling had been stressed, since many returning veterans needed occupational advice."[46] In Section A, on the other hand,

---

[41] *Loc. cit.*
[42] *Ibid.*, p. 684. Emphasis added.
[43] *Ibid.*, p. 685.
[44] *Loc. cit.*
[45] Peter Blau, "Competition and Cooperation in a Bureaucracy," *American Journal of Sociology*, 59:530–535 (1954).
[46] *Ibid.*, p. 532.

no opportunity had existed for the development of such a group professional code of emphasizing *quality* of placements rather than quantity.
Further still, nearly al the members of Section B had tenure—that is,
could not be dismissed except "for cause"; whereas the members of Section A were more insecure. Most of them ". . . . had been appointed to
temporary civil service positions during World War II . . . [and] were on
probation pending permanent appointments. . . ."[47]

These three different structural conditions led to very different behavior in the two sections. The members of Section A (insecure, evaluated quantitatively, nonprofessionally trained) tried to improve their
individual placement records by hiding incoming orders so that no one
else could fill them, by falsifying the job description (for example, writing
"experience needed" when in fact experience was not needed), and by
refusing to cooperate with others. The members of Section B, however,
shared their information, consulted one another, and helped one another
to make the "best" placement possible.

Blau then compared the actual production records of the two sections.
He found that "the group most concerned with productivity (Section A)
was less productive than the other group. Fifty-nine per cent of the job
openings in Section A were filled, in contrast to 67 per cent in Section B."[48]

Not surprisingly, in short, what the Babchuk-Goode and Blau studies
show is that people tend to do what the structure of their situation rewards, and they tend to avoid doing what the structure penalizes. If a
person is penalized for turning a customer over to a colleague or for
putting the stockroom in order, he tends to avoid it. If he is rewarded for
making more job placements than his associates make, he is scarcely in-
clined to cooperate with them. People are likely to invest their ingenuity
into productive and conscientious role-playing to the degree that that is
what the structure rewards; they are likely not to do so to the degree that
that is what the structure punishes.

As Blau's study hints, the occupational statuses that are defined so as
to encourage conscientious role-playing are statuses that at least to some
degree have been "professionalized." Not only are professional statuses
likely to be regarded as important and justified, as we have already noted;
they also are likely to involve long periods of socialization into the service
traditions and ethics of the profession—teaching, science, the law, or
medicine. Moreover, the professions, more than other occupations, usually
include some formal mechanism by which the members of the profession
discipline other members who fail to discharge their duties conscien-

---

[47] *Ibid.*, p. 533.
[48] *Loc. cit.*

tiously. The American Bar Association and the American Medical Association, for example, have formal committees to try lawyers or physicians who are accused of violating professional standards.

Among scientists, there is no such formal committee; but the demand for the publication of research and the insistence on replication of experiments tend to serve the same purposes. Among teachers, perhaps especially at the college level, neither formal committees nor full publicity is to be observed as formal mechanisms, but it seems warranted to suggest that the tradition of devotion to status-obligations is here so strong that punishment of a teacher who abuses his academic privileges is fairly swift and certain. Moreover, of course, the long period of apprenticeship a teacher serves before acquiring tenure, with yearly and, later, triennial reviews of his performance, is itself a fairly stiff protection against anyone's deliberately getting off the track.

BUREAUCRACY

Clearly implicit in both the Blau and the Babchuk-Goode studies is a further technique for ordering relations among specialists—bureaucratization.

The term "bureaucracy" or, even worse, "bureaucrat," is close to a curse word in the minds of many Americans. It connotes rigidity, red tape, petty adherence to the letter of the rule book, insolence of office, uncooperativeness, frustration. Most Americans, we would guess, can readily imagine themselves saying, "Oh, don't be such a bureaucrat!" but few could imagine themselves saying, "Oh come on, be a little more bureaucratic."

And yet, realistically grounded as the negative connotations are, bureaucracy seems to be a functional necessity in a complex industrial system. Its necessity rests on the need to coordinate the thousands of occupational specializations into a coherent whole. What industrial specialization hath torn asunder, bureaucracy seeks to restore.

The basic prerequisites of coordination are no more and no less than the conditions we have met before as the conditions of integration or the conditions of subsystem adaptation. In other words, the problems raised to great importance by occupational specialization are those of ensuring the smooth disposal by the specialist of his special contribution and of ensuring his procurement of precisely what he needs from other specialists.

Within an organization of such specialists—for example, within the United States Army or the General Motors Corporation—it becomes apparent that to require each specialist to search around for someone to supply him with tools or paper or guns, then to dicker with the potential supplier on terms of exchange, meanwhile warding off competitive intrusions from others and calculating the advantages of taking over the roles of still others—this would be madness, as the Blau and Babchuk-Goode studies suggest. There would be very little, if any, time or energy left over for productive role-playing. And if the organization itself is confronted with adaptive exigencies from the outside, reliance on such expensive modes of internal integration would be suicidal.[49]

The bureaucratic mode of integration is an alternative to these. Each specialist's role is precisely and specifically defined, and he is trained to stick narrowly within its limits. The function of this, of course, is to prevent "invasion" by other role-players and an imperialistic attitude of the role-player in question. For every need, there is a role with the obligation to fill it and a specified way (requisitions in triplicate, for example) of getting it filled. Disposal is, similarly, simply no problem. The outbasket gets emptied regularly by a specialized messenger.

Bureaucracy, in other words, is man's closest approach so far to the integrative marvel of the termites. But perhaps Ralph Linton's pessimism was nowhere more justified than here. It is, after all, precisely these extraordinarily efficient mechanisms of integration that people are responding to when they say "Bureaucracy!" as if it were a synonym of "Hell and damnation!"[50]

For the rigid sticking to one's role which is so functional for internal integration may be disastrously *dis*functional for realistic adaptation—and

---

[49] Notice that the same realization occurs on a national level when adaptive problems become acute. In World War II, "bargaining" as a mode of procurement and disposal was promptly scrapped. Substituted for it were such strictly bureaucratic techniques as rationing, priority allocations, central planning.

[50] For superb literary and dramatic representations of the hell of bureaucracy, we recommend to the reader Franz Kafka's *The Castle* and Gian-Carlo Menotti's powerful opera, *The Consul*. Max Weber's classical analysis of bureaucracy is available in translation in A. M. Henderson and Talcott Parsons (trans.), *The Theory of Social and Economic Organization* (New York: Oxford University Press, 1947), pp. 329–341; and H. H. Gerth and C. Wright Mills (trans.), *From Max Weber* (New York: Oxford University Press, 1946), pp. 196–244. Robert K. Merton's essay, "Bureaucratic Structure and Personality," in his *Social Theory and Social Structure* (rev. and enl. ed.; New York: The Free Press of Glencoe, Inc., 1957), is an incisive close-up of bureaucracy in operation; and so is Philip Selznick, "An Approach to a Theory of Bureaucracy," *American Sociological Review*, 8:47–54 (1943). Peter Blau, *Bureaucracy in Modern Society* (New York: Random House, Inc., 1956) is a masterful synthesis of both the functioning and disfunctioning of bureaucratic structure, and his *The Dynamics of Bureaucracy* (Chicago: The University of Chicago Press, 1955), is an excellent case study. Another excellent case study is Alvin Gouldner, *Patterns of Industrial Bureaucracy* (New York: The Free Press of Glencoe, Inc., 1954).

maddening to the outsider being adapted to. Merton cites a perfect example:

> According to a ruling of the department of labor Bernt Balchen, Admiral Byrd's pilot in the flight over the South Pole . . . cannot receive his citizenship papers. Balchen, a native of Norway, declared his intention in 1927. It is held that he has failed to meet the condition of five years' continuous residence in the United States. The Byrd antarctic voyage took him out of the country, although he was on a ship carrying the American Flag, was an invaluable member of the American expedition, and in a region to which there is an American claim because of the exploration and occupation of it by Americans, this region being Little America.
>
> The bureau of naturalization explains that it cannot proceed on the assumption that Little America is American soil. That would be *trespass on international questions* where it has no sanction. So far as the bureau is concerned, Balchen was out of the country and *technically* has not complied with the law of naturalization.[51]

The frustrations produced by bureaucracy, it is important to remember, are often frustrations of the person not in it. In this sense it is meaningful to suggest that the remedy for bureaucracy may be more bureaucracy. The individual whose needs seem to be thwarted by impenetrable walls of proper procedure and the inscrutable blandness or insolence of clerks is an individual without adequate guarantees of his own. He is not integrated in the system; or, put the other way, the system does not extend its guarantees to him. Lacking a right matched by the bureaucrat's obligation, he is forced to bargain, appeal, or exploit; and he may not be a match for the bureaucrat, protected as the latter is by his complacent certainty that he is doing his job correctly.

SUMMARY

Industrialism is characterized by a high ratio of capital to labor, a factory system of production, and an elaborate division of labor. Each of these characteristics creates certain problems for the integration of industrializing and industrialized societies.

---

[51] Merton, *Social Theory and Social Structure*, p. 155.

One of the problems of industrialization is the development of capital, which may be accomplished through bargaining, legal-bureaucratic obligation, patriotic identification, and exploitation. Once a society is industrialized, the problem posed by the high ratio of capital to labor is that of disposing of all the goods produced. Mechanisms for coping with this problem consist of collective ways of taking up surplus productive capacity and ways of increasing propensities to consume.

The factory system of production poses the problem of "economic equilibrium," which in the period of industrialization centers around the problem of developing disciplines of routine work. After industrialization, the problem is in part that of keeping consumption high and in part that of compensating for occupational obsolescence.

The specialization characteristic of industrialism poses the problems of securing conscientious role-performance and maintaining understanding among specialists. Coercion and emphasis on material reward tend to be emphasized as motivating pressures. "Cross-pressures," "artistic" communication, and bureaucracy contribute both to motivating people to conscientiousness and to understanding among specialists, but each has certain shortcomings.

9

BELIEF-SYSTEMS
MAGIC AND SCIENCE

As emphasized in Chapter 1, and noted throughout this book so far, one important significance of culture is that it structures people's conceptions of "the way things are." Culture, in other words, is comprised partly of people's ideas about the nature and properties of the world around them, including other people as well as various aspects of themselves—their bodies, their capacities, and so on. Partly, also, culture is comprised of men's *moral* ideas of the world around them: how people should act, what is Right and Wrong, Good and Evil.

In Chapter 1 we analyzed culture into several different elements—pattern variables, folkways, mores, laws, and so on. Now, for another purpose, we want to analyze it in a different way, by putting together several aspects that we have touched on in previous chapters. We shall classify the undifferentiated and complex thing called "culture" into several different kinds of belief systems by focusing our attention on three aspects of culture. In the first place, we shall return to our distinction between cognitive and evaluative ideas.

In the second place, we shall distinguish between cultural symbols that refer to *empirical* things, and those that refer to *superempirical* things. Empirical things can be observed or experienced with one of the five senses—that is, they can be seen, heard, felt, smelled, or tasted. As it is often put, symbols with empirical referents are symbols that can be defined by *pointing* in some way. The symbol "F Sharp" can be defined by striking a certain key on a piano and saying, "The sound you now hear is what I mean by 'F Sharp.'" Or the symbol "red" can be defined by saying, "Go to the local fire station and notice the color of the trucks. Then go to any intersection with traffic lights and notice the color of the light facing the traffic that halts while traffic going at right angles to it is moving. Those colors are what I mean by 'red.' "[1]

In some cases, as this latter example merely begins to suggest, the "pointing" may be very complex. To define the concept "neutrino," for example, it may be necessary to say (much more specifically than we are capable of!) something like this: "First build a piece of equipment with such and such specifications; then perform the following operation, making sure that such and such conditions exist; then wait X seconds; then look to see whether there appears on your photographic plate a mark with such and such characteristics. If so, then that which left that mark is what I mean by a 'neutrino.' " Because of this complexity of the pointing, symbols with empirical referents are sometimes referred to as symbols that can be "operationally" defined. In other words, it is possible to specify some *operation* that the individual must perform, which results in some *observation,* which is then the "meaning" of the symbol—or rather, more accurately speaking, it is the thing that the speaker *means by* the symbol.

Superempirical symbols, on the other hand, are those for which it is impossible to specify an operation plus an observation that will point to what the speaker means by the symbol. For example, there is nothing that can be pointed to in order to define such symbols as "God," "Trinity," "Heaven," and so forth. These are superempirical symbols.

Finally, cultural definitions vary with respect to the way in which man sees himself related to the world. Following (with some modification) the anthropologist Florence Kluckhohn, let us distinguish among three different conceptions men may have of their relationships to things other than themselves—or three different "postures" or "stances" they may take. They may see themselves as *observers* of the world; they may see themselves as *manipulators* or controllers of it; or they may see themselves as *subordinated to* things outside themselves. (Florence Kluckhohn refers to these conceptions with the phrases, respectively, "man *in* the world," "man dominant *over* the world," and "man subjugated *to* the world.")[2]

We have now three kinds of distinctions: first, cognitive and evaluative ideas; second, symbols with empirical and those with superempirical referents; and third, man's stance as observer, as manipulator, and as subordinate. If we put these various distinctions together, we get the classification of idea systems shown in Table 9–1. We shall discuss these vari-

[1] This is an example suggested by S. I. Hayakawa, *Language in Action* (New York: Harcourt, Brace & World, Inc., 1941).
[2] Florence Kluckhohn, "Dominant and Substitute Profiles of Cultural Orientations: Their Significance for the Analysis of Social Stratification," in *Social Forces,* 28:376–393 (1950).

ous kinds of belief systems in more detail in the remainder of this chapter and in the next.

TABLE 9–1

Classification of Cultural Belief-systems

	COGNITIVE		EVALUATIVE	
	Empirical	Superempirical	Empirical	Superempirical
Man as Observer	Pure science	Theology (mythology)	Secular ethics	Religious morality
Man as Manipulator	Applied science (technology)	Magic	Liberal ideology	Religious activism
Man as Subordinated	Epicureanism	Fatalism	Conservative ideology	Religious passivity

Magic

Magic and technology are alike in that both consist of actions designed to produce some effect in the empirical world. One essential difference between them is that in technology, if a given act does not produce the intended result, the act is changed. In magic, however, if the act does not succeed, it is not changed. In other words, technology is viewed by its practitioners quite instrumentally: its effectiveness is judged by its results. In terms we used earlier, people have an autonomous orientation toward their technology. They have a heteronomous attitude toward their magic, however; if it does not "work," they still feel obliged to believe in it. They feel that it would be "wrong" or "dangerous" to tamper with the magic formula; and they "know" that it is the right way to do things. If there was a failure, then the magic was not done exactly right, or some taboo had been violated, or some countermagic had been at work. In that sense, magic is often "sacred"; it partakes of the "holy" and the "mysterious," which is what makes the difference between the "empirical" and the "superempirical."

There is, to put it another way, no way of disproving the efficacy of magic. This fact, indeed, can be used as an important clue to help determine whether or not a given practice is magic, or at least draws on magical beliefs. If the practice is believed to produce a certain result, and if there is no observation that would prove to its practitioners that it does not produce that result, then the belief involved is likely to be magical. From this point of view, the reader should be able to think of many practices in modern society that reflect some magical beliefs. We shall return to this point later, but before we do, it is necessary to distinguish among different *kinds* of magic.

TYPES OF MAGIC

Sociologists and anthropologists have made several different distinctions among types of magic.[3] We suggest that the most important distinction, for purposes of understanding the basic structure and functions of magic, is between two different kinds, distinguished in terms of the *mechanisms* by which the act is believed to produce the effect.

In one kind, the magical belief includes an explicit idea of a supernatural mechanism by which the magical act leads to the result (when all goes well); in the other kind, no such mechanism is postulated—the act leads to the result just because, as it were, "that's the way things are." The first kind is illustrated by beliefs such as the story of Aladdin and the magic lamp, which postulates a supernatural genie as the agent. It includes pacts with the devil or bargains struck with the gods, control over ghosts by appeasing them or warding them off with special charms, and so on. Many acts conventionally called "religious" are essentially magical in this sense. Prayers for rain or for success in battle or for cure of disease, for example, are magical *insofar as* a belief is involved that the prayer, if done right, will work—that is, will actually produce an empirical result.

This first type of magic involves anthropomorphism—imputing some human qualities to gods, devils, or inanimate objects, so that they can be "handled" in the same way that one handles other people—through supplication, threats, commands, bargains, and so on. Prayers or commands to the West Wind, for example, or to the seas, fall in this category.

In the second kind of magic there seems to be no explicit postulation of anthropomorphism. "Word magic" is often of this sort. In word magic, as Malinowski has said, "the most important element . . . is the spell." He

[3] The reader who wishes to examine more closely the extensive literature on magic is referred to the following major sources: Bronislaw Malinowski, *Magic, Science, and Religion* (New York: The Free Press of Glencoe, Inc., 1948); Ruth Benedict, "Magic," *Encyclopedia of Social Sciences* (New York: The Macmillan Company, 1933), X, 39–44; James G. Frazer, *The Golden Bough* (abr. ed.; New York: The Macmillan Company, 1944); and Reo F. Fortune, *Sorcerers of Dobu* (London: Routledge & Kegan Paul Ltd., 1932).

has described, on the basis of his study of magic among the Trobriand Islanders, two typical elements in the spell:

> There are, first, the phonetic effects, imitations of natural sounds, such as the whistling of the wind, the growling of thunder, the roar of the sea, the voices of various animals. These sounds symbolize certain phenomena and thus are believed to produce them magically. Or else they express certain emotional states associated with the desire which is to be realized by means of the magic. The second element . . . is the use of words which invoke, state, or command the desired aim. Thus the sorcerer will mention all the symptoms of the disease which he is inflicting, or in the lethal formula he will describe the end of his victim. In healing magic the wizard will give word-pictures of perfect health and bodily strength. . . . The sorcerer in tones of fury will have to repeat such verbs as "I break—I twist—I burn—I destroy," enumerating with each of them the various parts of the body and internal organs of his victim.[4]

What might be called "action magic," as distinct from word magic, also very often does not postulate any anthropomorphic mechanism. Ruth Benedict provides three examples: "A man desires his child to grow, therefore he chews the sprout of the salmon berry and spits it over the child's body that it may grow as rapidly as the salmon berry. . . . Fish hawk eyes are rubbed over a sleeping baby's eyelids to give him the fish hawk's sight. . . . One desires the death of his enemy, therefore he stuffs a bit of the enemy's clothing down a dead snake's throat. . . ."[5]

In nonanthropomorphic magic, the basic assumption ("feeling" might be a better word, since it need not be and probably is not consciously articulated) is that if you do something to an object that is even symbolically (verbally or otherwise) associated with the object you want to influence, that object will be influenced through some vague, perhaps mystical, certainly not-understood, relationship between the two. Thus you can kill a man by sticking pins into an effigy of him, improve eyesight with hawks' eyes, and stimulate growth with salmon-berry juice. Thus, also, "a treatment of the sword that has caused the wound will cure the wound . . . [and] milk can be made to sour properly by treating the sacred cowbell."[6]

It is tempting, as Malinowski has remarked, to look at magical beliefs "from far and above, from our high places of safety in developed civilization"; and from that perspective, "it is easy to see all the crudity and irrelevance of magic."[7] But to fall into that temptation would be to fail to understand this belief system, and it would be to underestimate the

---

[4] Malinowski, *op. cit.*, pp. 54–55.
[5] Benedict, *op. cit.*, p. 39.
[6] *Ibid.*, p. 40.
[7] Malinowski, *op. cit.*, p. 70.

prevalence of essentially magical beliefs even in modern societies. Indeed, a little reflection suggests that, at least from one point of view, the puzzling thing is not that human beings believe in magic but that they do not—that science-based technology has succeeded as far as it has in displacing magic.

The kind of cause and effect relationships that we in modern society think of as "real" or "empirical" relationships are, for one thing, extremely hard to discover. What is amazing is how man ever did figure out such a relationship as that between planting seeds, for example, and months later seeing crops grow. Or, for another example, the relationship between sexual intercourse and pregnancy. Certainly, there is nothing self-evident about those relationships. Often seeds are planted and crops do not grow; often intercourse is practiced and pregnancy does not result. Is it really any more "reasonable" to connect these crops with those earlier seeds than it is to connect them with that omen which some wise man remembered? Is it really very obvious that this birth is a result of that coitus nine months ago, rather than a result of the woman's prayers, or a result of the intercourse's having taken place in the dark of the moon?

Furthermore, people know from experience that they *can* get things from other people through pleading, flattery, cajolery, threatening, bargaining, promising, and so forth. Is it so stupid to think that those highly effective means will not work with animals or vegetables? And if one tries them and they do not work, does that so obviously disprove their effectiveness—have they not failed to work sometimes when applied to people too? People know also that very often their suffering or disappointment is a result of some other person's anger. Then what is so obviously silly about the speculation that sickness is a result of a dead ancestor's anger, especially since one remembers distinctly having wronged that ancestor? or the theory that one's sickness is a result of another living person's animosity? or the theory that if one feels and expresses his own anger at someone else vividly enough and strongly enough that other person *will* die? ("I burn—I twist—I break.")

The fact is that man's technology is never so effective as to guarantee the desired result. That the "best-laid schemes o' mice and men gang aft a-gley" is a fact experienced by everyone. This may create no problems for mice, perhaps because they do not realize the chances they are taking. For men, however, with their ability to remember past mishaps and their ability to imagine the future, it has always been a troublesome fact. Once men develop the idea, basic to science and technology as well as to magic, that events are caused by *something*, they are likely to think of a great variety of "somethings" that could be the causes. The "real" causes are, as we noted above, highly elusive under the very best of circumstances; and it readily "makes sense" to postulate as causes many antecedents that we would label magical.

Moreover, once a magical cause-effect is postulated, it may be extraordinarily hard to give it up. For one thing, if you plant a garden with a mixture of technology and magic, and if the garden grows, how do you know you did not need the magic as much as the technology? If the garden does not grow, which should you change—the method or planting or the magical incantation? Or, for that matter, why not think that there was nothing wrong with either—you just slipped up somehow in carrying *both* through *correctly*?

It ought not to be too difficult for the average reader to understand the reluctance to reject a theory simply because things do not work out as the theory says they should. When you perform an experiment in chemistry or physics to "prove" a theory, and the results contradict the theory, the odds are that your immediate reaction is the assumption that you "didn't do it right"—*not* that the theory is wrong. If you did it three times in a row and every time got the same "undesired" result, and if the "wise old man" who is your chemistry professor insisted, along with the sacred tradition written in the textbook, that the theory is right, we would still wager that you would tend to conclude that you were simply clumsy or stupid rather than trust the evidence of your eyes. And if this can happen to a member of the intellectual elite (which you are, comparatively, if you are in college), in the mid-twentieth century in a chemistry laboratory—the very citadel and shrine of the "scientific method"—there should be no wonderment at its happening to an illiterate savage.

THE FUNCTIONS OF MAGIC

So far in this discussion we have emphasized the *structure* of magical beliefs, in an attempt to suggest that they are, in a certain sense, natural. We may attempt to draw on the reader's own experience to suggest an additional and related point concerning the *functions* of magic.

Consider how it is, even among ourselves, when something we want desperately to happen may not, in fact, happen. *If* we know how to make it happen, then there is no problem: we simply set about in a matter-of-fact way to make it happen. But suppose its happening or not is something we cannot, at least with absolute certainty, control. There are many things, even today, that fall in that category: making someone fall in love with us, emerging from a battle alive, keeping a hitting streak going, having the play be a success, getting back from a motor trip without an accident, just plain living and not being sick (when we were children) until our birthday party was past, not having it rain until after the picnic —the list could be extended indefinitely.

Under those conditions—when the outcome is important but the technological control is inadequate—we are still prone to practice magic. Children, for example, attempt to bargain with God ("God, if you make everything go all right until my birthday, I'll never, never, never . . . ."), baseball players sometimes refuse to change their uniforms as long as the hitting streak is going for fear of upsetting *something* about the unknowable chain of events that is making things go well for the time being, soldiers carry amulets into battle ("there are no atheists in foxholes" is essentially a magical and not a religious phenomenon), motorists fix statues of the Virgin on their dashboards or carry St. Christopher medals, actors and actresses arrange their make-up jars in special inviolable ways, and so on.

It seems to be a striking fact that whenever people are confident of their ability to control or manipulate their environment by empirical technological means, they use those means and do not use supernatural ones. When there are aspects of the environment that they suspect are beyond the power of their technologies to control, they often turn to supernaturalism. The great anthropologist, Bronislaw Malinowski, has illustrated this vividly in the case of the Trobriand Islanders, part of the Melanesian peoples of the South Pacific:

> Magic is undoubtedly regarded by the natives as absolutely indispensable to the welfare of the gardens. . . . [But] if you were to suggest to a native that he should make his garden mainly by magic and scamp his work, he would simply smile on your simplicity. He knows as well as you do that there are natural conditions and causes, and by his observations he knows also that he is able to control those natural forces by mental and physical effort. . . . His experience has taught him also, on the other hand, that in spite of all his forethought and beyond all his efforts there are agencies and forces which one year bestow unwanted and unearned benefits of fertility, making everything run smooth and well, rain and sun appear at the right moment, noxious insects remain in abeyance, the harvest yields a superabundant crop; and another year the same agencies bring ill-luck and bad chance, pursue him from beginning till end and thwart all his most strenuous efforts and his best-founded knowledge. To control these influences and these only he employs magic. . . .[8]

> An interesting and crucial test is provided by fishing in the Trobriand Islands and its magic. While in the villages on the inner Lagoon fishing is done in an easy and absolutely reliable manner by the method of poisoning, yielding abundant results without danger and uncertainty, there are on the shores of the open sea dangerous modes of fishing and also certain types in which the yield greatly varies according to whether

[8] *Ibid.*, pp. 11–12,

shoals of fish appear beforehand or not. It is most significant that *in the Lagoon fishing, where man can rely completely upon his knowledge and skill, magic does not exist, while in the open-sea fishing, full of danger and uncertainty, there is extensive magical ritual to secure safety and good results.*[9]

Some writers have objected to Malinowski's interpretation of magic— that magic functions to allay anxiety in situations fraught with uncertainty and danger—and have observed that very often magical beliefs *create* anxiety where none existed before.[10] Radcliffe-Brown, for example, writes as follows:

> I think that for certain rites it would be easy to maintain with equal plausibility an exactly contrary theory, namely, that if it were not for the existence of the rite and the beliefs associated with it the individual would feel no anxiety, and the psychological effect of the rite is to create in him a sense of insecurity or danger. It seems very unlikely that an Andaman Islander would think it dangerous to eat dugong or pork or turtle meat [which he is forbidden to eat during his wife's pregnancy and for some weeks after she gives birth] if it were not for the existence of a specific body of ritual the ostensible purpose of which is to protect him from those dangers.[11]

Radcliffe-Brown's position, however, may reflect, in part, a misunderstanding of the theory reviewed above. Homans excellently puts it thus:

> Rightly understood, he [Malinowski] does not say that the natives feel anxiety in dangerous situations but that they would do so if the rites of magic were not performed. And the facts that Radcliffe-Brown cites, instead of supporting a theory opposed to Malinowski's, follows directly from it. To say that magic relieves anxiety, as Malinowski did, amounts to saying, as Radcliffe-Brown did, that if magic is not performed anxiety appears.[12]

In other words, it is true that magical superstitions sometimes frighten people, and this not only in the sense that Homans notes (that they are frightened by the idea of not doing the magic properly), but also in the sense that a superstitious person might be frightened by a black cat, or in the sense that he might be frightened by someone else's sorcery. Such fright and creation of *insecurity* is important to notice as a *dis*function of magic. We shall return to the issue of disfunctions below; but if we want to know what the attraction of magic is, we must note the *functions* it performs for those who believe in it. The function performed by the

[9] *Ibid.,* p. 14.

[10] See especially A. R. Radcliffe-Brown, *Taboo* (Cambridge, England: Cambridge University Press, 1939), and Ruth Benedict, "Magic," in *Encyclopedia of the Social Sciences.*

[11] George Homans, *The Human Group* (New York: Harcourt, Brace & World, Inc., 1950), p. 325.

[12] *Ibid.,* p. 327.

belief in black cats as omens of the future is that it at least takes some of the mystery out of the future. The function performed by sorcery for its user is to give him a feeling of control over events that his technology is inadequate to control.

Still, there can be little doubt that Malinowski's theory of the fear-allaying functions of magic is not the whole story. Radcliffe-Brown has two points that Homans does not entirely meet: that magic does not always allay anxiety even when it is used in anxiety-provoking situations, and that magic is often used in situations that are not apparently anxiety-provoking. Benedict puts it thus:

> The yam magic does not give agricultural security in Dobu; on the contrary, it emphasizes a danger spot in the culture and far from minimizing this stress in a community in which food is scarce it institutionalizes it. . . . Magic potency ascribed to menstruating women or to the dead has not generally inculcated social security in relation to those portents; it has rather indicated the situations which a culture regards as social hazards.[13]

The relationship between magic and situations of uncertainty, risk, or danger, then, is not so simple as to permit us to assert a general "law" to the effect that whenever there is uncertainty there will be magic, or to sum up the functions of magic by saying that it relieves anxiety. It is not so simple for at least three reasons.

In the first place, what is defined as "risky" or "dangerous" is itself culturally variable. You and I may be able to emphathize with the Trobrianders' anxiety about deep-sea fishing in frail craft and unable to empathize with the Andaman Islander's anxiety about his wife's pregnancy (or vice versa); but our empathic ability does not matter. The fact is that human beings are beset by an almost infinite number of things that they could worry about or define as risky or uncertain; and some cultures may evolve an emphasis on one, others on another. What Benedict has written in another place is relevant here too:

> In culture . . . we must imagine a great arc on which are ranged the possible interests provided either by the human age-cycle or by the environment or by man's various activities. A culture that capitalized even a considerable proportion of these would be as unintelligible as a language that used all the clicks, all the glottal stops, all the labials, dentals, sibilants, and gutturals from voiceless to voiced and from oral to nasal. Its identity as a culture depends upon the selection of some segments of this arc. Every human society everywhere has made such a selection in its cultural institutions. Each from the point of view of another ignores fundamentals and exploits irrelevancies. One culture

---

[13] Benedict, *op. cit.*, p. 43. Benedict goes on, as others have done, to observe that food magic, for example, may be found among people with apparently no food problem and may not be found among people with apparently severe food problems.

hardly recognizes monetary values; another has made them fundamental in every field of behavior. In one society technology is unbelievably slighted; in another, equally simple, technological achievements are complex and fitted with admirable nicety to the situation. One builds an enormous cultural superstructure upon adolescence, one upon death, one upon after-life.[14]

Whatever segment of the great arc of potentialities a culture emphasizes, its human carriers will have to find some means to achieve some ends. Given the difficulty of technological means-ends connections discussed above, some magical connections are more likely than not to be made. At what points they evolve (at the possible point of preoccupation with the eyesight of babies or the possible point of preoccupation with the pregnancies of wives, for example), is beyond prediction—except for the (not unimportant) statistical prediction that given indefinite time, *some* group at *some* time and at *some* place is likely to be preoccupied with the eyesight of babies and is likely to make the symbolic connection between the eyesight of people and the eyesight of birds. False analogies, in other words, are not difficult to make and, except under very special circumstances (to be described below), once made, are difficult to relinquish.

A second reason that the bald statement, "The function of magic is to allay anxiety," is, by itself, too simple is that once the false analogies underlying magic are institutionalized—that is, supported by group sentiments—they may perform many other functions as well. What function is performed depends on the nature of the magic institutionalized. Where magical ritual is a group practice, it may bring together diverse groups in a common activity so as to provide a source of solidarity. Magical ritual, like any ritual or ceremony, may function to maintain and reinforce the sense of community based on common beliefs, when these rituals are periodically performed in group situations. Special forms of magic may function as tension management or social control mechanisms, sustaining *other* cultural patterns. ("If you violate the mores a witch will put the evil eye on you.") Magical beliefs may provide the structure for tribal or clan membership, economic exchange, power arrangements, and the like. In other words, magical beliefs and practices may provide the basis for social organization in the everyday affairs of a people. When magic is deeply woven into the fabric of social life, to destroy it without replacing it with structural equivalents is to destroy that patterned way of life.

Finally, as just implied, in the third place the "magic-anxiety" formula may be too simple insofar as it ignores the possibility of *alternative* structures that might perform the same functions even better, or at least as

---

[14] Ruth Benedict, *Patterns of Culture* (New York: Mentor Books, New American Library of World Literature, Inc., 1950), pp. 21–22.

well. We shall consider structural alternatives to magic after we first
consider the place of magic in modern societies and some of the disfunctions of magic.

MAGIC IN MODERN SOCIETIES

The belief-systems of contemporary Western societies such as the
United States do not include, at least in institutionalized form, many examples of the kind of magic distinguished above as involving anthropomorphic elements. Such cases are not entirely lacking, however. Polterge-
ists and ways of exorcising them are believed in by some people, sacred
relics are believed to ward off accidents or disease, mediums are believed
to have the power to summon ghosts to give advice on worldly affairs,
and so on.

For the most part, however, the magical beliefs encountered in modern
America are of the second type—those which do not postulate an anthropomorphic element, but which occasionally still carry a connotation of
the occult and, even more frequently, are not subject to the critical and
experimental instrumentalism characteristic of technology. Beliefs in
astrology, for example, seem fairly widespread, judging from the advertisements in newspapers and magazines and from the sales of horoscopes.
Palm reading, fortune-telling through cards or tea leaves, beliefs in bad
luck attendant on walking under ladders, breaking mirrors, or having
black cats cross one's path—these are not totally absent, although we do
not know how widespread they are or how *seriously* people believe in
them.

One fact that must be noted in attempting to assess, even impression-
istically, the role of magical beliefs in modern society is that the *words*
"magic" and "superstition" are in bad repute. To some (unknown) extent,
they are like the word "prejudice." It is not respectable to be "prejudiced," so the most prejudiced people are likely to say indignantly, "I'm
not prejudiced, you understand; it's just that . . . ." In the same way, the
prestige of "rationality" and "science" are such that relatively few people
care to admit that they really believe in magic. But the tendency to perform acts in a stereotyped way, with the aim of producing an empirical
result, with no effort to test the effectiveness of the activity, with even
some horror at the very idea of experimenting, with anxiety about performing the activity "correctly," and with a reluctance to alter the activity
or belief even if it fails to "work"—this tendency, which we have suggested
is the essence of "magic," is very plain to see. It is often disguised as
"science," just as prejudice is often rationalized in terms of pseudo-

scientific notions of "race." Thus, as J. Milton Yinger has written, many "formulas"

> don't work, they have scarcely even been tested, but we rely on them. In international diplomacy, in the punishment of criminals, in education, modern men carry out activities which may allay their fears and feelings of helplessness, but which can scarcely be shown to be technically competent to achieve their avowed aims.[15]

Such belief-systems, as we noted above, may be very difficult to change, once they are part of people's thinking. In this respect they are like many other tension management mechanisms to which people become addicted, from neurotic symptoms to dope addiction or alcoholism. As Benedict has suggested, "The analogy [of magic] with neurotic behavior is striking; whether or not a culture has chosen to regard women or persons recently dead as supernaturally dangerous, the usual course has been to erect in a neurotic manner an associated edifice of ceremony by means of which displacement is achieved and the object of dread pushed off the scene or brought back in some more acceptable guise."[16]

Magic and neurotic symptoms *do* serve to give temporary relief from anxiety and fear; and even if the individual is intellectually aware that in the long run they are self-defeating, it may be impossible for him to sacrifice the assured short-term gains of "peace of mind" for the much more difficult "agonizing reappraisal" of his action that would be involved in a scientific technological approach. Especially, in the case of magic, is this likely to be true when, as noted, the outcome is important and *there is no certainty that an adequate technology even exists.* Thus people with "incurable" diseases, as well as people who are frustrated in love or feel themselves not to be getting ahead fast enough, may be fairly susceptible to such word magic as the power of positive thinking or "Eight simple formulas to say to yourself every day," and the like. How much difference is there between the sorcerer's effort to kill an enemy with the words, "I burn, I break, I twist" and the modern man's effort to ensure his success with the words, "Day by day in every way I get better and better"?

DISFUNCTIONS OF MAGIC

It is the heteronomous inability to give up magic or even to question its efficacy (for to question it is at once to destroy its functionality for giving security) that is the source of magic's *dis*functions. The faith in

---

[15] J. Milton Yinger, *Religion, Society and the Individual* (New York: The Macmillan Company, 1957), pp. 47–48.

[16] Benedict, "Magic" in *Encyclopedia of the Social Sciences*, p. 43.

the formula blinds people to alternative ways of realistically dealing with the anxiety and thus may perpetuate the uncertainty and fear. The belief that insanity must be cured by exorcising witches, for example, or the belief that criminality can be cured by increasing the severity of punishment, may prevent even consideration of alternative approaches.

Are there, perhaps, alternative approaches that can perform the positive functions of magic without the cost of its disfunctions? Even prior to that question is another: Are there conditions under which the functions performed by magic need not be performed at all?

It is not at all likely that scientific technology will ever be able to eliminate all the risk and uncertainly from life—or that anyone would want it to, for that matter. Accidents, unrequited love, possible failure—these would seem to be an inherent part of life. The question of the dispensability of magic and of all its functional equivalents, then, refers not to the removal of uncertainty but to the possibility of developing a high tolerance for uncertainty. And here, it must be said, not much is known as yet, although much interesting research is currently being done.[17] Some people, clearly, can face a great deal of risk and uncertainty without the need to minimize it magically. Other people seem to have a low threshold. The difference seems to lie importantly in different kinds of socialization experiences and probably in different degrees of status-set and status-sequence inconsistencies. But even biological sources of difference cannot be ruled out.

STRUCTURAL ALTERNATIVES TO MAGIC

Until it is possible technologically to control the social and/or other arrangements that increase people's tolerance of uncertainty, it may be wise for the social analyst to consider what substitutes for magic may be available to the members of a social system. Several such substitutes have been briefly alluded to above and described in a different context earlier (Chapter 5). Such modes of adjustment as overconformity, retreatism, or innovation may be reactions to strain and frustration that forestall the need for magic. On the other hand, it may be that the conformist mechanism of adjustment may depend on the availability of magic. "Ritualism," of course, comes close to being an essentially magical response in itself.

Tension management mechanisms as discussed in Chapter 6 may also be substitutes for magic, although some of them involve the very "formulistic" thinking characteristic of magic. Scapegoating, for example,

---

[17] See, for example, Milton Rokeach, *The Open and Closed Mind* (New York: Basic Books, Inc., 1960).

seems close to a simple substitution of minority groups for ghosts and demons. (It is worth noting, in this respect, that the original scapegoat was an actual goat, on which primitive tribesmen annually heaped all their sins and either drove from the village or killed in expiation.) Other tension management mechanisms, however, such as alcohol, Miltown pills, escapist television programs, vicarious expression of strain and hostility in sadistic literature, and the like may compete with magic. Whether or not such alternative devices are more or less disfunctional for realistic facing of issues is a question on which considerable research must still be done.[18] (We regret that we cannot offer a *certain* answer but use the impossibility of doing so as a further illustration of the ubiquity of uncertainty.)

Given the functionality of magical beliefs and the difficulty of uprooting them once they are established, the question may be raised concerning how such a very different way of viewing the world as science, on which technology is based, ever made headway. We shall turn to that question next.

SCIENCE

In all societies there is some body of knowledge about the observable world as well as some approved way of acquiring that knowledge. But, just as we observed in our discussion of industrialism that the difference between the use of tools in preindustrial and industrial societies is so great as to make a difference in kind, so we must now observe that the difference between the emphasis on knowledge and its acquisition in "prescientific" and "scientific" societies is so vast as to make a difference in kind.

The problem of "scientizing" a society (to coin a term for which we apologize but that seems useful) is very similar to the problem of industrializing it; and, as we shall see later, the problems of maintaining the equilibrium of "scientized" and industrialized societies are also similar. The similarities are readily seen in terms of our now-familiar model of equilibrium.

Let us begin by defining science as a systematic mode of discovering the nature of the environment, a mode that involves four essential steps:

1. Becoming curious about something.
2. Speculating about how it works.

[18] For one serious investigation of the issue, see Herta Herzog, "Psychological Gratifications in Daytime Radio Listening," in P. F. Lazarsfeld and F. N. Stanton (eds.), *Radio Research, 1942–1943* (New York: Duell, Sloan & Pearce–Little, Brown, 1944).

3. *Testing the speculation by some controlled observation.*[19]
4. Attempting to relate the tested speculation to other knowledge in a systematic and logical way.

Science, conceived in this way, is related to nonscientific subsystems of society as indicated in Table 9–2.

TABLE 9–2

Relationship between Scientists and the Nonscientific Public

SCIENTISTS	NONSCIENTIFIC PUBLIC
Seek to procure permission to be curious, speculate, test	Seek to dispose of permission and encouragement
Seek to dispose of knowledge	Seek to procure knowledge

Equilibrium obtains, of course, under the familiar four conditions: The public is satisfied with the knowledge scientists[20] produce and finds scientists who are willing to accept the encouragement to do research that the public wants to offer; scientists are content with the amount of permission and encouragement they receive and find acceptance of all the new ideas and knowledge they develop.

The institutionalization of science begins with the same kind of breakdown of this equilibrium as does the institutionalization of industrialism: dissatisfaction on the part of users of knowledge with the knowledge being supplied to them. What might happen to create such dissatisfaction?

For present purposes, we may note that either one of two major *kinds* of events may destroy satisfaction with the existing understanding of "the way things are" and "how they work." One is a change in the environment such that the old ways of doing things and the old predictions simply do not work any longer. Invasion by another group would be an obvious illustration or exhaustion of the food supply or a change in climate. A second source of dissatisfaction may be some endogenous development within the group itself, ranging from the inexplicable emergence of a genius (or a deviant crackpot), through the gradual immanent development of some already institutionalized custom, such as

---

[19] This is perhaps *the* critical step that distinguishes science from all the super-empirical belief systems.

[20] When referring to "prescientific" societies, we perhaps should use some term other than "scientists" to refer to those functionaries who in rudimentary form experiment and contribute knowledge—some such term as "savants," for example. We avoid doing so for the sake of simplicity.

astrology, let us say, to the point at which its own legitimate demands exceed the knowledge and understanding available in other parts of the culture.

THE DEVELOPMENT OF SCIENCE

The development of science in the Western world was stimulated by a combination of such factors. In the first place, the ferment created by expanded trade and cultural contact with the Near East and the attendant rediscovery of Greek culture proved to be a pregnant illustration of the force of a change in the environment. In the second place, needs increased for knowledge about navigation, astronomy, mining, shipbuilding, and energy sources as a result of the unfolding of the commercial and industrial revolutions.

The need for reliable guides to navigation prompted much astronomical observation and stimulated work in mathematics. Robert K. Merton writes that the problem of finding the longitude occupied the attention of such early scientists as Rooke, Wren, Hooke, Huyghens, Leibniz, Newton, Flansteed, Halley, and many others.[21] Work on magnetic attraction, hydrodynamics, and even botany was stimulated by the technical problems of navigation and shipbuilding. The problems of mining similarly inspired scientific developments in metallurgy, mineralogy, and hydraulics; and preoccupation with health lay behind studies of physiology and anatomy. In modern times, of course, the industrial and military encouragement to scientific research are so familiar as to need no listing at all.[22]

But problems of adaptation to death and disease, to minerals, and to uncharted distances have always existed. They are obviously not enough to account for science. Such "necessities" may *sometimes* be the mothers of invention; but in the first place fathers, too, are needed, and in the second place, the offspring might just as easily be magical techniques as scientific.

Abandoning the metaphor, the point to be emphasized is that the need for new knowledge is no guarantee that new—and especially new scientific—knowledge will be forthcoming. The problem at this stage is precisely analogous to the problem at the corresponding stage of incipient industrialization, when people become dissatisfied with the tools they

[21] Robert K. Merton, *Social Theory and Social Structure* (rev. and enl. ed.; New York: The Free Press of Glencoe, Inc., 1957), pp. 614–615.

[22] For extensive accounts of the beginnings of modern science, see *ibid.* See also Bernard Barber, *Science and the Social Order* (New York: The Free Press of Glencoe, Inc., 1952); and James B. Conant, *On Understanding Science* (New Haven, Conn.: Yale University Press, 1947).

are receiving. (Indeed, of course, the analogy is so precise because knowledge is itself a fundamental kind of tool.) Before more tools could be produced, as we have seen, a way had to be found to increase the supply of consumers' goods available to producers of tools. Analogously, before new knowledge can be produced, a way must be found to increase the supply of that which scientists are fundamentally dependent on—permission and encouragement to become curious, to speculate, and to experiment.

But scientific activities—becoming curious, speculating, and testing—are radical, costly, and potentially dangerous activities. This is the profound truth recognized in the story of the first eating of the fruit of the tree of knowledge. When man's ancestors changed from nonthinking creatures, at one with the rest of nature, to creatures whose adaptation to nature depended on *knowledge,* they changed from—what to what? from something just below angels to something much lower, as the legend of the "Fall" interprets it? from something no different from animals to something much "higher," as some interpretations of the theory of evolution have it? or from anthropoids content to live like anthropoids to anthropoids trying to live like termites and not doing too well at it, as Linton put it?

All such answers are poetry rather than sociology, but they all express (with slightly varying evaluations and cathexes) recognition of two facts: that the acquisition of knowledge is an important part of man's adaptive apparatus; and that the acquisition of such knowledge can be profoundly disturbing.

Why are curiosity, speculation, and experimentation potentially disturbing? The answer is not at all difficult. It is because they can be to man's life what excessive exposure to X rays could be to termites'—they could radically alter or even destroy the basic mechanisms of stability: beliefs in the one case, instincts in the other.

To become curious about something is to refuse to accept things as they are. It is to be dissatisfied with existing explanations. But dissatisfaction and refusal to accept things are a corrosive force that can threaten (or appear to threaten) the very foundation of a social structure. And to speculate about possible alternative answers is, almost precisely, heresy, for in order really to control men's actions, cultural definitions of the situation must be unquestioned and unchallenged. As soon as one begins to doubt, to say, "I wonder if it's really true that . . . ," or "If this is true, then how could that be true?" one is no longer completely controlled.

It is this "liberating" function of knowledge that makes us say that knowledge is freedom. "And ye shall know the truth and the truth shall make you free" is another way of putting the positive function of knowledge. But *curiosity* and *speculation* are not yet knowledge; they are only the necessary steps for getting rid of the old knowledge and preparing the way for new knowledge. "Emancipation" from the old beliefs means that one is no longer controlled by them, but it does not necessarily mean that one is free. One may be freed *from* the old beliefs, but, as the adage recognizes, to be freed *to* act with confidence requires more than emancipation: it requires *new* beliefs about how the world "really is."

Small wonder, then, that the heretic or the skeptic, the one who doubts and tries to spread his doubts, has throughout history been silenced, burned, crucified, given hemlock, or tortured. Small wonder that there are always some ideas that people try to protect against the contagion of doubt by censorship and iron curtains. "The truth" that "ye shall seek" and which "shall make ye free" has, much of the time, tended to be *"the"* truth—already possessed and to be protected against "error."

Permission to be curious and to speculate, then, is by no means readily forthcoming. It is something to be procured only under very special cultural circumstances. And the third step of science—to check one's speculations by controlled observation, preferably of an experimental kind—requires even rarer circumstances. For to be curious and to speculate, dangerous as they may be, are only mental and verbal activities, after all. But to experiment is to meddle with the unknown, to pry into nature's or people's secrets; it may even be to manipulate and treat instrumentally the sacred and the holy or the personal and the private. And to treat instrumentally the sacred and holy is almost a precise definition of sacrilege and profanation. We should not be surprised that some of the beginnings of science were in the "black arts" or that the origins of chemistry are in the mysteries of alchemy, and those of astronomy in astrology.

We are not, still today, so very far away from the antivivisection laws. And our own revulsion at the idea of biological experiments on human beings may enable us to understand somewhat the horror that our ancestors felt at the idea of questioning the sacred story of the Creation.

The encouragement and permission that are required, of course, are not permission and encouragement from all the nonscientific society—not, for example, from the masses of people. It is, rather, permission and encouragement from "those who count": from the scientists' *significant* others, from powerful persons who can protect them and support them while they work, or from both. And, as we briefly noted above, if science rather than magic is to develop, the permission and encouragement must be permission and encouragement to *test* speculative answers by controlled observation.

Such permission and encouragement came in the West from an unexpected source. It came as an unexpected by-product of the Protestant Reformation, particularly Calvinism, with its emphasis on "man's religious duty to order his 'this-worldly' activity of all kinds . . . in the most rational fashion possible."[23] The Calvinist theology encouraged men, furthermore, to show their respect for God by working to understand the complexity of His works in the natural world. Robert K. Merton, in a fascinating piece of historical research, has carefully traced the Puritan origin of most of the seventeenth-century English scientists, and shown the way in which their revolutionary scientific contributions were motivated and justified by their religious convictions. For example, Merton writes that Robert Boyle, discoverer of the relationship between the volume and pressure of air, petitioned the Fellows of the Royal Society in his last will and testament with these words: "Wishing them also a happy success in their laudable attempts to discover the true Nature of the Works of God; and praying that they and all other Searchers into Physical Truth may cordially refer their attainments to the Glory of the Great Author of Nature . . . ."[24]

The permission and encouragement supplied by Calvinism for breaking away from preoccupation with Holy Writ as the source of all wisdom and knowledge, were made even more effective by the banding together of the early seventeenth-century scientists into the Royal Society for Improving Natural Knowledge, organized in 1660. The Royal Society performed not only the function of providing support and encouragement to its members, but also the important function of facilitating communication among scientists, both personally and through publication of a journal. The Society also—as did the French Académie des Sciences—collected funds to help purchase experimental equipment.

But science is more than experimenting, important as that is. It is also *systematic* rational thought, and the roots of that tradition of thought go back even beyond Puritanism. A fundamental belief in the *orderliness* of the universe and in the power of reason to discover and understand that order was a critical underpinning of the development of science. Alfred North Whitehead has traced that conception to the theme of order in the classical Greek drama:

> Let me here remind you that the essence of dramatic tragedy is not unhappiness. It resides in the solemnity of the remorseless working of things. This inevitableness of destiny can only be illustrated in terms of human life by incidents which in fact involve unhappiness. For it is only by them that the futility of escape can be made evident in the drama. This remorseless inevitableness is what pervades scientific thought. The laws of physics are the decrees of fate.[25]

[23] Barber, *op. cit.*, p. 58.
[24] Merton, *op. cit.*, p. 576.
[25] Alfred North Whitehead, *Science and the Modern World* (New York: Mentor Books, New American Library of World Literature, Inc., 1948), p. 11.

But, as Whitehead continues, if science is to develop, more than a sense or order is required, essential as that is:

> It needs but a sentence to point out how the habit of definite exact thought was implanted in the European mind by the long dominance of scholastic logic and scholastic divinity. The habit remained after the philosophy had been repudiated, the priceless habit of looking for an exact point and of sticking to it when found.
>
> I do not think, however, that I have even yet brought out the greatest contribution of medievalism to the formation of the scientific movement. I mean the inexpungeable belief that every detailed occurrence can be correlated with its antecedents in a perfectly definite manner, exemplifying general principles. Without this belief the incredible labors of scientists would be without hope. It is this instinctive conviction, vividly poised before the imagination, which is the motive power of research:— that there is a secret, a secret which can be unveiled. How has this conviction been so vividly implanted on the European mind?
>
> When we compare this tone of thought in Europe with the attitude of other civilizations when left to themselves, there seems but one source for its origin. It must come from the medieval insistence on the rationality of God, conceived as with the personal energy of Jehovah and with the rationality of a Greek philosopher.[26]

For the Western world, then, the permission and encouragement to scientific speculation and experiment was given under the auspices of religion; and a special form of religion, Calvinism, provided the stimulus to focus that speculation on the empirical world, rather than on sacred texts or mystical signs.

SOME CONSEQUENCES OF SCIENCE

Once launched, the scientific mode of thought has proved such an enormously successful method of increasing man's knowledge of his empirical world that it now stands independent of religious justification. Indeed, as the reader well knows and as we shall discuss below, very soon after its emergence the thought-system of science began to turn its powerful thoughtways against its religious progenitor.[27] The new knowledge that science produces often threatens traditional thoughtways, and those threats have provided, and still provide, at least potential sources of resistance to the continued permission and encouragement for the scientific method.

[26] *Ibid.*, p. 13.
[27] It is tempting to continue our earlier metaphor of technological needs as the "mother" of science and Calvinist justification as its "father," by suggesting that in science's later history, we have a classical case of the Oedipus story!

The new knowledge that comes pouring out of the scientific laboratories, much as goods come pouring off the assembly line, is often threatening to nonscientists because it makes traditional ways of doing things obsolete. Three kinds of obsolescence are of special importance as possible sources of resistance to new scientific ideas: the obsolescence of *ideas,* the obsolescence of *status,* and what we shall call the obsolescence of *irresponsibility.*

As we noted earlier in this chapter, people's definitions of the situation may be so important to them that contradictory definitions appear as extremely disturbing threats. This is especially the case if the new knowledge appears to threaten their self-images in some way. Thus the scientific discovery that the earth is not the center of the solar system (let alone the universe); that men were not specially created but evolved from very simple forms of life, which themselves, it now appears, were the result of chance collisions of atoms; that their motives are largely unconscious and often highly unpleasant; that their very personalities can be radically changed by chemicals; that there may be millions of planets on which life exists; that the earth is doomed to extinction from an exploding sun— knowledge such as this has often struck at the very roots of men's conceptions of themselves and their world. And as the familiar cases of Galileo's forced recanting, the vehement attacks on Darwinism, and the angry repudiations of Freud show, people may refuse to accept such knowledge.

In addition to making ideas obsolete, scientific discoveries often render obsolete lifetime investments in occupational careers. Improvements in soil chemistry, for example, have made thousands of American farmers unnecessary, and automation promises to cancel out the jobs of hundreds of thousands of workers. (The fact that those same developments also create, in the long run, new occupational roles is, of course, scant comfort to the persons made obsolete today.)

Perhaps the most disorganizing of all the effects of new knowledge is one that is not as immediately apparent as the obsolescence of ideas and of statuses and, therefore, is not so likely to be a *conscious* source of resistance. This is the fact that new knowledge often makes necessary deliberate decisions that men formerly did not have to make. The most vivid illustration of this in the contemporary world is the case of population control.

Throughout most of man's history the struggle against death and disease has been so unequal that cultural values leading to high birth rates were functional for survival. Scientific discoveries leading to the control of death and disease were therefore eagerly welcomed and put to use. Now, however, so effective are the scientific methods of death control that a leading physician can say that if men succeed in winning the struggle against heart disease and cancer, it may be nothing short of a disaster, so overcrowded is the planet even now becoming. But the use of scientific methods to control birth rates continues to be resisted on both religious and nonreligious traditional grounds. The result is an extraordinary growth in the world's population, which in the long run simply cannot be maintained; and even in the short run can be maintained only at the cost of lowered living standards for everyone.

This means that whereas in the past the question of what size population to have was not a question men had to decide (it was decided for them by events beyond their control), now it is a question that must be decided deliberately. That is to say, once the power to control population size has been given to men by science, the decision must be made to use that power in one way or another. There is simply no escaping the fact that either there will be a decision to allow people to multiply to the point at which the pressure on living standards will generate widespread dissatisfaction, or there will be a decision to control births and deaths so as to maintain population at a level considered desirable. In either case, the important point is that there now must be a decision—and one affecting the heretofore highly private activity of reproduction.

Beyond this, the perpetual revolution in man's knowledge produced by science may provide the means to control the genetic structure of new generations and to control their thinking much more effectively than has been possible in the past. Then the decision must be made either to use the scientific power to ensure that people have the best possible genes and ways of thinking, or to refrain from using it, deliberately choosing to put some people at a physical and psychological disadvantage.

Scientific knowledge, in other words, gives control; but the possession of control means the acceptance of responsibility. When people can control their lives, they are responsible for the consequences of their actions; this is what we mean by the obsolescence of irresponsibility. The ability that men now have to wreck all civilization and perhaps all human life, as a result of their control over atomic energy, is only the most dramatic illustration of this vastly increased responsibility that modern science has thrust upon men.

FACILITATING CONDITIONS

These three possible sources of resistance to scientific knowledge—the fear of new ideas, the fear of becoming occupationally obsolete, and the fear of responsible decision making—point to certain further requirements of social systems if science is to flourish.

In the first place, if the fear of new ideas is not to be a source of resistance to scientific knowledge, leading possibly to a denial of permission to practice the scientific method, the dominant idea-system must be one that sharply distinguishes between empirical cognitions on the one hand and values, cathexes, and superempirical cognitions on the other. That is to say, conceptions of *what* things are and of *how* they operate must not be confused with questions of *why* they operate that way or what they are *for* or whether they should or should not be permitted to continue operating that way. What is "sacred," in other words, must not include ideas of what *is*—"must not," that is, if people are to avoid the fear that their important beliefs can be threatened by science.

As we have seen, the Puritan ethic made this separation possible by conceiving that *whatever* was discovered to be true simply gave further evidence of God's glory. Our point is not, of course, that the Puritan ethic is necessary; but rather that *some* ethic or belief-system is necessary that permits people to distinguish between existential, empirical propositions and evaluative, superempirical ones. Put otherwise, the important thing to understand is that all scientific propositions are in the indicative and they are about the empirical world. From them, no propositions in the imperative or about the superempirical world can possibly be derived.[28] Where this is recognized, the fear of new scientific ideas disappears; for it is then seen that all scientific ideas are irrelevant to the *validity* of evaluative or superempirical ideas. (Scientific ideas are, of course, highly relevant to the *implementation* of evaluative ideas, in the sense of pointing the empirical way to the realization of "shoulds.")

Where the distinction is not made, however, science suffers. And it is important to note that the blurring of the distinction may come not only from orthodox religious dogmas. Nazi confusion of evaluative myths concerning "Aryan supremacy" with scientific propositions led Hitler and his supporters to reject the scientific contributions of Jewish physicists, and the insistence of Russian Communists on the relative unimportance of genetics may have set Russian biological science back a good many years.

Just as the fear of the obsolescence of ideas depends on the nature of the society's other belief-systems, the fear of occupational obsolescence depends on its integrative mechanisms. When "bargaining" is institutionalized, as we have seen, an individual's procurement of what he needs depends on his ability to make it worth the while of someone else to give it to him. Occupational obsolescence threatens precisely this ability. The individual whose occupation has been wiped out cannot, by definition, make it worth anyone's while to give him what he needs. Such an individual has everything at stake and can naturally be expected to try to prevent the use or even the distribution of the new knowledge. Whether

---

[28] See Henri Poincaré, "Ethics and Science," in Kingsley Davis, Harry C. Bredemeier, and Marion Levy, Jr. (eds.), *Modern American Society* (New York: Holt, Rinehart and Winston, Inc., 1949), pp. 3–5.

he succeeds or not depends simply on his power. The new knowledge means ruin to him, and he will prevent its acceptance if he is powerful enough; he will be ruined if he is not.

Just as there are belief-systems that can reduce the fear of new ideas, so, of course, there are integrative mechanisms that can reduce the fear of becoming occupationally obsolete. The integrative mechanism most functional in this respect is probably the one we have called "lawful." If, for example, the obsolescence of one's occupational status did not mean that one's bargaining power was reduced to zero, but simply meant instead that one now had a right to be retrained, if necessary, for a different status, then an important cost of new knowledge would be eliminated. (More accurately—the cost of the new knowledge would be distributed over all of society instead of falling entirely on one person or category of persons.)

The cost of new knowledge that is most difficult to meet, or even, for that matter, to see clearly, is what we have called the obsolescence of irresponsibility. The fact that this cost is not so easy to recognize immediately as it is to recognize the obsolescence of ideas and the obsolescence of statuses does not, however, mean that it is any less disorganizing. We would say, in fact, that it has probably *the* most far-reaching disorganizing effects of all the consequences of modern science.

What is disorganizing about it is the same thing that disorganizes a small child standing before a candy counter with a nickel clutched in her hand, trying to choose among all the tempting candies spread out before her. The agony of indecision is sometimes so great that the child will willingly surrender her freedom to the nearest adult, saying, "You choose." The difference between the child and the adult is the difference between being free but without firm criteria for making choices and the possession of such criteria. The first is threatening;[29] the second is not.

Throughout the scientific period of Western Europe and America, until now, there has been no problem in this respect, because there was no lack of criteria. There was no ambivalence about the goals of improving navigation, prolonging life, raising health, increasing military efficiency, predicting weather, and so on. But the kind of control now coming to be offered by science, and in some cases demanded as a result of past scientific triumphs, raises questions about which there is not as much clarity. For example, probably few people would have any trouble deciding what to do with the knowledge that vitamins will improve a child's health. They would instantly choose to use the knowledge, and the alternative of deliberately withholding the vitamins would scarcely occur to them. But

---

[29] This is the theme of Erich Fromm's attempt to account for the rise of totalitarianism in Germany, aptly titled *Escape from Freedom* (New York: Holt, Rinehart and Winston, Inc., 1941).

suppose that the new knowledge is knowledge of how to improve a child's health and intelligence by scientifically controlling the genes he inherits. Now the fairly cruel dilemma is raised of deliberately withholding opportunities for good health and high intelligence on the one hand, or deliberately planning the nature of future generations by interfering with "natural" processes, on the other.[30]

It may be, of course, that such decisions will come to be made effortlessly (or rather to be elicited ineluctably) as a result of international competition. As Bertrand Russell has put it:

> When . . . methods of modifying the congenital character of animals and plants have been pursued long enough to make their success obvious, it is probable that there will be a powerful movement for applying scientific methods to human propagation. There would at first be strong religious and emotional obstacles to the adoption of such a policy. But suppose (say) Russia were able to overcome those obstacles and to breed a race stronger, more intelligent, and more resistant to disease than any race of men that has hitherto existed, and suppose the other nations perceived that unless they followed suit they would be defeated in war, then either the other nations would voluntarily forego their prejudices, or, after defeat, they would be compelled to forego them. Any scientific technique, however beastly, is bound to spread if it is useful in war. . . .[31]

Or, we might add, if it is in any way adaptively useful.

As Russell implies, it is not likely that any of the resistances to new knowledge we have considered will be strong enough to curtail science. The scientific method is too powerfully effective an adaptive mechanism for power-holders in modern societies to allow it to be interfered with. Its functions, in other words, outweigh its disfunctions. But the disfunctions are there, nonetheless; and the question is therefore raised of what mechanisms will develop, or be utilized, in modern societies to absorb them or mitigate them—or perhaps even turn them to positive advantage.

We briefly indicated above the kinds of cultural devices by which the first two costs (obsolescence of ideas and of statuses) might be reduced or eliminated. We suggested that a belief-system that sharply distinguished between empirical propositions about what *is* and evaluative or superempirical propositions, and that recognized that the former have no necessary implications for the latter, *could* enable people to accept all of the former with equanimity. We suggested, second, that the substitution of "lawful" mechanisms of integration for "bargaining" mechanisms *could* help to eliminate the fear of status-obsolescence.

---

[30] Cf. Jean Rostand, *Can Man Be Modified?* (New York: Basic Books, Inc., 1959).
[31] Bertrand Russell, *The Impact of Science on Society* (New York: Simon and Schuster, Inc., 1953), p. 28.

Reduction of the third cost—obsolescence of irresponsibility—requires, we indicated, a clear set of societal goals in terms of which decisions could be made as unequivocally as the decision to use scientific knowledge to reduce death rates.

The issue of "purpose" is closely involved in the cultural phenomena of religion and ideology. We can better discuss the impact of science in more detail, then, after we have considered further the nature and functions of nonmagical superempirical belief-systems, and the nature and functions of ideology.

SUMMARY

Systems of belief may be classified in terms of three characteristics: whether the terms used have empirical or superempirical referents; whether cognitive or evaluative elements predominate; and whether man's relation to nature is seen as that of observer, manipulator, or subordinate. Magic, a belief-system differing from technology in its use of concepts with superempirical referents, may or may not involve anthropomorphism. Magic may perform the function of relieving anxiety in situations that are defined as important but uncontrollable and unpredictable technologically. It may also, once institutionalized, contribute to pattern-maintenance and integration. The disfunctions of magic often stem from one of its central characteristics—the compulsive way in which adherents are likely to cling to it. Although it is unlikely that risk and uncertainty can ever be eliminated technologically, it may be that structural alternatives can perform most of the functions of magic. It is not certain, however, whether any of those alternatives would be more or less disfunctional than magic.

Science, the central characteristic of which is the testing of speculations by controlled observation, requires permission and encouragement from other sectors of society to develop and progress. Among the barriers to such permission and encouragement are the fears of the obsolescence of beliefs, of statuses, and of irresponsibility. Certain structural conditions are more conducive to overcoming those barriers than others. Modes of thought stemming from Greek philosophy, medieval Catholic theology, and Protestantism combined to provide such encouragement in the Western world; and the adaptive utility of science in modern society gives it an autonomous existence not likely to be surrendered whatever the strains produced by new scientific knowledge.

10

BELIEF-SYSTEMS
RELIGION AND IDEOLOGY

Religion

As the reader may have noted, the word "religion" does not appear in the classification of belief systems in Table 9–1. Rather, in labeling the various superempirical belief systems, we used the terms "theology," "religious morality," "religious activism," "religious passivity," "fatalism," and "magic." The term "religion" refers to varying blends and mixtures of those six different kinds of superempirical beliefs.

No doubt there are many who would instantly take exception to that sentence. Many people, including able scholars in this field, seek to reserve the term "religion" to refer to a complex that excludes magic, and some prefer to regard the relation between "religion" and "morals" as problematical.[1] The problem here is simply a problem of terminology—of how words are to be used—and the disagreement does not go deeper than that.

MAGIC AND RELIGION

A number of analysts have attempted to establish analytical distinctions between magic and religion. Distinctions frequently are made in terms of the goals sought and the means prescribed for their attainment.[2]

---

[1] See, for example, J. Milton Yinger, *Religion, Society, and the Individual* (New York: The Macmillan Company, 1957), esp. pp. 28–34.

[2] Cf. Bronislaw Malinowski, *Magic, Science, and Religion* (New York: The Free Press of Glencoe, Inc., 1949), Chap. 6; Kingsley Davis, *Human Society* (New York: The Macmillan Company, 1950), Chap. 19; and William J. Goode, *Religion among the Primitives* (New York: The Free Press of Glencoe, Inc., 1951), pp. 53–54.

Religion, it is sometimes contended, is concerned with ultimate goals, such as salvation, and the meaning of existence and death. Magic is concerned with more immediate goals, such as the control of weather, defeat of an adversary, or success in a love affair. Although both magic and religion involve supernaturalism, religion, some writers contend, seeks to achieve goals by nonmanipulatory means, such as supplication or sacrifice. The ends sought by magic, on the other hand, are achieved by means of manipulation and control of the supernatural.

These distinctions appear to break down, however, when applied to concrete social systems. In a detailed analysis of these distinctions, J. Milton Yinger has concluded that "there is scarcely a religion that does not have some magical aspects mixed with it," and that, in this sense, magic is an integral part of religion.[3] Yinger's judgment seems both valid and fruitful. Our suggestion in the opening remarks of this chapter carries it one step further: "religion" is best understood as a mixture of theology, magic, fatalism, morality, activism, and passivity. The "mix" of these simpler kinds of belief-systems varies considerably from one concrete religion to another, but they are all likely to be present in some proportion. In the rest of our discussion of religion, then, it must be understood that we use the term to refer to *all* the superempirical belief-systems differentiated in Table 9–1. We shall, however, throughout the discussion, try to be careful to specify just which element in "religion" we are dealing with at any given point. We shall, of course, have relatively little to say about the magical element, since we dealt with it at length in the previous chapter.

THEOLOGY

Theology, like science, is a set of cognitive beliefs about "the way the world is" and a way of discovering how it is. It is different from science in that it deals with a "world" not apprehensible by the five ordinary senses or any extension of them, such as microscopes, telescopes, cyclotrons, or sensitive photographic plates. Theological knowledge may be of two kinds. It may be knowledge of "how things work" in the empirical world, in the same sense as science, except that the forces, principles, mechanisms, or causes used by theology to explain the "hows" are supernatural. This category of theological knowledge is illustrated by such propositions as, "Eclipses of the sun result from the fact that there is an invisible dragon in the sky who periodically swallows the sun, gets nutriment from it as it passes through his stomach, and in a few minutes ex-

[3] Yinger, *op. cit.*, p. 42.

cretes it."[4] Or, "The reason there is light is that God said, 'Let there be light' and He can do anything." The conspicuous difference between this kind of explanation and the scientific explanation is (as we noted in connection with magic) that the above propositions have the advantage, in one sense, that they cannot be disproved.

It is precisely at this point that a considerable degree of conflict arises between "science" and "religion" that cannot be resolved except by the acceptance of one or the other's assertion of fact. The familiar example is the implication of Galileo's scientific findings for the theological assumption that the earth was the center of the universe. Galileo's empirical observations led him to challenge the theological assumptions concerning the relationship of the earth to the sun and to conclude that these assumptions, derived from superempirical sources, were wrong. Similar conflicts arose from the empirical investigations of Darwin concerning evolutionary development and variation of the species. Although these have been crucial conflicts in the past, they have been largely resolved in favor of the scientist rather than the theologian in the Western world.[5] However, note that these conflicts arise over statements of fact concerning the nature of the empirical world, not over why the world is the way it is or what is the nature of the supernatural. As far as we can see, these are not susceptible to scientific investigation and, therefore, are not scientific questions. They are questions, however, that the theologian may seek to answer.

The second kind of theological knowledge, then, is knowledge not of "how" things work, but of *why* they work the way they do, regardless of whether "the way they do" is taken in a scientific sense or in the sense of the first kind of theological knowledge. That is, whether the "how" proposition is one about invisible dragons or one about the moon getting between the earth and the sun, there still remains the question "why?" *Why* is there a dragon in the sky with such nutritive needs? *Why* do the moon and the earth have the relationships they do?

At the slight risk of belaboring an obvious point, it must be emphasized that this "why" question is not simply another "how" question in disguise. By "why," in the present sense, the speaker does not mean "how" or even

---

[4] This is an example used by Professor Merton in lectures at Columbia University.

[5] It is, however, quite possible to cling to the theological postulate by rejecting the premises of science or asserting, for example, that the devil had manipulated Galileo's telescope to confuse the nonbeliever. All of modern science, indeed, as well as the apparent success of the technology based on it, could be irrefutably challenged by contending that the devil systematically intervenes in each experiment to make it come out according to the scientist's theories, the devil's motive being to seduce men into the sin of pride. Science, then, is merely a continuation of the temptation with which Satan originally seduced Eve.

"how come"; he means, "Give me an explanation that makes me feel that the thing *should* happen at all. If you want to describe the process, tell me why that *is* the process in a way that makes it make sense for that to *be* the process." To use an effective illustration suggested by Talcott Parsons, when someone loses a loved friend or relative through an accidental, premature death, he tends to ask in a specially anguished way, "*Why* did it have to be him? Why *now*?" And he does not want an answer in terms of the physical law that two bodies cannot occupy the same space at the same time or in terms of the physiological process of blood circulation. Such an answer to a "why" question in this context would, indeed, be generally regarded as not only irrelevant but as insulting and callous.

It seems to be, in other words, an observable fact that sometimes some people want to know "how things work" in the sense of descriptions of regular and invariant cause and effect processes; and that sometimes some people want to know something different—namely, the *meaning* of their working that way, the *point* of it, the *sense* or *significance* of it.

Now the thing that people have in mind by "point," "meaning," "sense" is essentially *purpose*. What horrifies people, for example, is a "pointless" murder. If a man kills someone out of jealousy or for revenge or in self-protection, people may demand his punishment, but they do not feel the same sense of bewildered horror they experience at a wanton killing that has "no rhyme or reason."

"Understanding" of *why* things happen means comprehending a motive for their happening. It is, to illustrate the point in a different context, precisely the incomprehensibility of the motives of a "madman" that makes insanity such a particularly fearsome thing for many people. If people can get an idea of another person's motive and if it is a motive they have recognized in themselves, at some level at least, then they feel that they understand "why" he acts the way he does. They may condemn the action and the motive, but at least they understand it.

At the very least—the very minimum demand for "understanding," apparently—is the need for a conviction that there *is* or *was* a motive, even if one does not know what it was.

A theology is the system of beliefs that makes events "make sense" in this manner. It is a body of beliefs about why things happen, in the sense either of assertions that there *are* reasons (purposes, motives), or of assertions about what those reasons are. For example, in terms of the theology most familiar to readers of this book, either the assertions are assertions that God has a reason for every single thing that happens but He is inscrutable and unknowable; or else they are such assertions as that God's purpose is to punish people for the original sin of Adam and Eve.

UNIVERSAL RELIGIOUS THEMES

Many of the things that need explaining, and many of the kinds of "purposes" that make satisfactory explanations, vary from group to group, depending on the particular vicissitudes that beset the group and the motives or purposes institutionalized in their culture. But some of the things that need explaining and some of the kinds of purposes that make satisfactory explanations are common to all groups. They are universal, and this is what accounts for the universality of certain themes in all religions.[6]

Among the ubiquitous things that need explaining, three are of fundamental importance: injustice, suffering, and death.

In all societies there is a conception of justice. Its essence is that people should receive in proportion to their contributions, that if good fortune is "deserved," it must result from conformity to the norms and from some productive service rendered to the society or its members. The corollary notion is that bad fortune—failure—should result from violation of the norms and from an act of damage to the society and its members. Yet in all societies, cruel and unscrupulous liars and cheats not infrequently receive wealth, glory, and power, while gentle, considerate, honest, and conscientious men are exploited and fail. In no society, so far as is known, is there such a perfectly operating set of socialization and social control mechanisms that "deviance" fails to occur; and in no society do the mechanisms of integration operate so perfectly that people always get what they deserve. The "how" of this is fairly easy; but *why* should it be so? What is the sense of "wickedness" being rewarded and "virtue" being punished?

The ubiquity of the problem is matched by the ubiquity of certain human experiences and purposes that provide a theological answer—that *in the long run* the scales of justice balance. In a postulated next world, the first shall be last and the last shall be first; heaven awaits the virtuous, hell is the future home of the wicked. (This is the solution labeled by cynics as the doctrine of "pie in the sky by and by.") Closely related to that explanation is another possible one: life in this world is a testing ground. Men are put here by God so that He can see how they act, so that He can decide which ones are fit to sit in paradise with Him and which ones are not. "Testing" people for rewards is a familiar idea to men, so this explanation can "make sense" also.

[6] Note carefully that this way of "accounting for" the commonality of theological beliefs is an empirical mode of accounting. They could also be "accounted for" *theologically*, by postulating, for example, that the universal themes are universal because God has vouchsafed to all men certain truths; and the variation is a result of the fact that the devil has seduced some people into error.

The universal problem of suffering is similar in nature and in solution. Why should people be born blind or deformed? Even if cruel men will be punished in hell, why should innocent and helpless children, for example, suffer and die because of their cruelty? There are answers that "make sense" here too: they are being punished for sins committed in previous lives, or their suffering is a test of their own and other men's faith. Or, when the suffering is experienced by an apparently blameless adult, there is always the possible explanation that he was indeed only *apparently* blameless—that somehow, sometime, he transgressed and is being punished for that.

This last explanation is particularly important, and will bear some elaboration. Gilbert Murray has described the general phenomenon eloquently:

> Agriculture, for instance, used to be [almost] entirely a question of religion; now it is almost entirely a question of science. In antiquity, if a field was barren, the owner of it would probably assume that the barrenness was due to "pollution," or offense somewhere. He would run through all his own possible offences, or at any rate those of his neighbors and ancestors, and when he eventually decided the cause of the trouble, the steps that he would take would all be of a kind calculated not to affect the chemical constitution of the soil, but to satisfy his own emotions of guilt and terror, or the imaginary emotions of the imaginary being he had offended. A modern man in the same predicament would probably not think of religion at all, at any rate in the early stages; he would say it was a case for deeper plowing or for basic slag. Later on, if disaster followed disaster till he began to feel himself a marked man, even the average modern would, I think, begin instinctively to reflect upon his sins.[7]

Murray was writing as a scholar of ancient Greece. The same phenomenon is described by William Goode as it has been observed in modern times among the Manus, a contemporary preliterate Melanesian group. Goode begins by noting that . . . "the prime offense in Manus society [is] loose sexual conduct."

> Such conduct includes almost any sexual situation outside the marital relationship, not merely sexual intercourse, but even accidentally seeing someone of the opposite sex exposed during sleep . . . or obscenity between husband and wife. . . .
>
> The result of such loose sexual conduct is illness. This may occur in the house of the youth in question, or of the girl, or the house in which offense occurred. In each case it is the Sir Ghost of each house in question which causes the illness. The illness, in turn, may attack anyone of

[7] Gilbert Murray, *Five Stages of Greek Religion* (Boston: The Beacon Press, 1951.) Reprinted by permission of the Beacon Press. The present quotation is from the Doubleday Anchor Books edition, p. 5.

any of the three houses. This point is highly important, since it functions to interest everyone in the society in the transgression of anyone else. No one can be sure of safety through his own innocence. As a consequence, "the moment such an illness occurs the community is all suspicion. If the oracles have anything to go upon, and being older puritanical persons they are likely to have, they oracularly make the charge." That is, a diviner may remember having seen someone slip out of a house furtively a few days before a member of that house became ill, and therefore ask his Sir Ghost (through the [divining] bones) whether the cause of the illness is sexual sin. Since both question and answer[8] are public knowledge, there is no hiding from the charge of the oracle. The guilty one must confess in spite of the shame involved, else the ill person may die. If there is no confession, the public suspicion is that the ones charged have in effect murdered the one who died.[9]

The third universal frustration of human hopes and wishes is death, both the disorganizing loss of loved ones and the anticipation of one's own end. Here again, as we noted above, the "how" of death is not too difficult; but the "why," in the sense of giving some "point" to such a bitter defeat, is difficult indeed. For many people, death can have "meaning" only in superempirical terms, and again the terms that can give it meaning are readily available in men's empirical experiences with their own and others' motives and life cycles. The "testing ground" conception, as we have called it, is one way of projecting what is known and comprehensible empirically into a superempirical realm so as to "make sense" out of death. Another way is to extrapolate the status-sequences with which men are familiar in their lifetimes into the period after death. so that death can be regarded as analogous to moving from one age group to another.

The classic description of the social and individual functions of religious beliefs and their ceremonial reinforcement at the event of death has been made by Malinowski:

> Never does an individual need the comfort of belief and ritual so much as in the sacrament of the viaticum, in the last comforts given to him at the final stage of his life's journey—acts which are well-nigh universal in all primitive religions. These acts are directed against the overwhelming fear, against the corroding doubt from which the savage is no more free than the civilized man. These acts confirm his hope that there is a hereafter, that it is not worse than the present life; indeed, better. . . .
>
> After death, though the main actor has made his exit, the tragedy is not at an end. There are the bereaved ones, and these, savage or civilized,

---

[8] The bones "answer" in this way: The diviner throws two short pieces of bone, attached to a string, astride his shoulder, with one bone on his chest and the other on his back. If his left side itches, the answer is "yes"; if the right side, "no."

[9] Goode, *op. cit.*, pp. 66–67. Goode's quotation is from Reo F. Fortune, *Manus Religion* (Philadelphia: University of Pennsylvania Press, 1935), p. 40.

suffer alike, and are thrown into a dangerous mental chaos . . . torn between fear and piety, reverence and horror, love and disgust, they are in a state of mind which might lead to mental disintegration.[10] Out of this, religion lifts the individual by what could be called spiritual co-operation in the sacred mortuary rites . . . in these rites there is ex-pressed the dogma of continuity after death, as well as the moral atti-tude towards the departed. The corpse, and with it the person of the dead one, is a potential object of horror as well as of tender love. Religion confirms the second part of this double attitude by making the dead body into an object of sacred duties. The bond of union between the recently dead and the survivors is maintained, a fact of immense importance for the continuity of culture and for the safe keeping of tradition. . . . It must also be remembered that what the survivor goes through on such an occasion prepares him for his own death. The belief in immortality, which he has lived through and practised in the case of his mother or father, makes him realize more clearly his own future life.[11]

It should not be surprising that the common problems demanding "meaning," and the common experiences and hopes of mankind, have re-sulted in wide similarities in the theology of different religions. Yinger provides a set of appropriate examples in the following passage:

Historical research has shown that many of the elements of Christianity that were long thought by its adherents to be unique were common ideas, practices, and myths in the Ancient world. Some of its doctrines and practices were added, during the course of several generations, as it developed from a small Jewish cult into a dominant religion. Resur-rected gods had been worshipped in many societies for several centuries before the appearance of Christianity. The doctrine of virgin birth was familiar to pagans; and it is significant that the doctrine was not used by Paul nor by Mark, author of the earliest gospel, who said nothing about the early years of Jesus' life. A kind of eucharist meal was found in many pagan cults. And belief in miraculous powers was virtually uni-versal in the Ancient world. "Jesus turned water into wine, as did Dionysus on January sixth of every year; and multiplied loaves of bread as did Elisha. He walked on water like Orion, Poseidon's son. He raised men from the dead, as did Elijah and Elisha—this feat had once been so common that Aristophanes in *The Frogs* (ca. 405 B.C.) made Dion-ysus say of Hermes and Hermes's father, that performing resurrections was a family profession."

[10] Talcott Parsons has described the condition of the bereaved in somewhat less extreme, and we think better, terms, as follows: ". . . . in the case of bereavement, there may be a loss of incentive to keep on going. Ritual on such occasions serves to organize the reaction system in a positive manner and to put a check on the disrup-tive tendencies. . . . [Rituals] assert . . . the importance of the survivors going on living in terms of [the] value system, redefining the solidarity with the deceased in these terms: it is 'what he would have wished.' "—*The Social System* (New York: The Free Press of Glencoe, Inc., 1951), p. 304.

[11] Bronislaw Malinowski, *Magic, Science and Religion* (New York: The Free Press of Glencoe, Inc., 1949), pp. 42–43.

Many of the Christian holy days were blended with celebrations of ancient origins. The death and resurrection of Attis, the God of vegetation, had been celebrated in Rome on March twenty-fourth and twenty-fifth, the spring equinox being the appropriate time for his revival. It seems certain that the official dates for the commemoration of the death and resurrection of Christ were assimilated into this established custom; and the nativity of Christ was placed at the winter solstice in December —the date that was widely celebrated as the birth date of the Sun.[12]

An idea of the kind of anxiety that generated some of these common religious conceptions is provided by Gilbert Murray in the preface to the third edition of his *Five Stages of Greek Religion:*

Anyone who has been in Greece at Easter time, especially among the more remote peasants, must have been struck by the emotion of suspense and excitement with which they wait for the announcement "*Christos Aneste,*" "Christ is risen!" and the response "*Alethos aneste,*" "He has really risen!" I have referred elsewhere to Mr. Lawson's old peasant woman, who explained her anxiety: "If Christ does not rise tomorrow we shall have no harvest this year." . . . We are evidently in the presence of an emotion and a fear which, beneath its Christian colouring and, so to speak, transfiguration, is in its essence, like most of man's deepest emotions, a relic from a very remote pre-Christian past. Every spring was for primitive man a time of terrible anxiety. His store of food was near its end. Would the dead world revive or would it not? . . .

I hardly realized, when writing the earlier editions of this book, how central, how omnipresent, this complex of ideas was in ancient Greek religion. Attis, Adonis, Osiris, Dionysus, and the rest of the "Year Gods" . . . are different names given in different circumstances to this one being who dies and is born again each year.[13]

In addition to the problems of injustice, suffering, and death, there is another, somewhat more subtle but, we suggest, even graver and more important problem that men face, especially in complex civilized societies. We opened up this problem toward the end of the previous chapter, when we discussed the "obsolescence of irresponsibility," and also in Chapter 8, when we discussed the problem of "self-respect" in modern status-systems. The problem is that of "meaning" and "purpose" in a larger sense than the meaning and purpose of specific phenomena such as injustice, suffering, and death, although including them. Human beings, as we have observed, seem to need a conviction that what they are doing

[12] J. Milton Yinger, *Religion, Society, and the Individual.* Copyright, 1957, by The Macmillan Company. pp. 268–269. Reprinted with permission of the publisher. Yinger's quotation is from Homer Smith, *Man and His Gods* (New York: Grosset & Dunlap, Inc., 1956).

[13] Murray, *op. cit.,* p. v. Reprinted by permission of the Beacon Press.

is worth doing. They seem to need a feeling that they and their activities *matter*, are important; that the roles they play are significant roles.

One important basis for the conviction that one's statuses are important is, as we noted earlier, the effective communication to role-players of other people's appreciation of them—the communication and symbolization of respect and recognition. However, such communication alone is not likely to be a sufficient basis. It must in some sense be "true" that a status is important if its occupant is to believe that it is; for in the first place, other people are not likely to communicate respect if they do not really feel respect, and in the second place, even if they try to fake it, the status-occupant is not likely to be taken in.

Supernatural belief systems have also functioned to produce such a feeling, or at least to provide a feeling that is a fairly satisfactory substitute: that one's *lack* of importance is only temporary. Such sentiments as that they also serve who only stand and wait, or that all souls are equally precious in the sight of God, or that conscientiously serving out one's lowly status in this incarnation will ensure one a more important reincarnation—such sentiments may, for believers, compensate for the lack of significance in present roles.

Even more important, perhaps, supernatural beliefs have served to reassure believers that the whole process of life has some "point"—that there *is* a divine plan, however mysterious, even if people do not know it. The particular content of the theological description of that plan may range from the eschatological notion that at any moment Judgment Day will arrive, through the image of perpetual harp-playing (or perpetual torment for the damned), to the mystical feeling that the plan is unknowable but surely wonderful and surely *There*.

SOCIAL FUNCTIONS OF RELIGION

As the foregoing discussion suggests, religious belief-systems provide answers to questions that (1) seem to puzzle a significant number of people in all societies and (2) cannot be answered directly by empirical observation alone. Once institutionalized, answers to such questions may become a central basis for pattern-maintenance and the integration of a social group. Lest this generalization be misunderstood, it should be emphasized at the outset that religion may be divisive rather than integrative when divergent religious beliefs coexist within the same group: the very virtues that lend to religion its integrative power for believers also have the defects that set people apart in fierce and unreconcilable conflict. It should be understood, also, that the ascription of certain functions to religion does not explain its existence nor imply necessity.[14] Furthermore, the variety of religious belief is such that there is considerable variation in the degree to which any one performs the various functions ascribed to religion in general.

The *supernatural* character of religion has particular force for integrative purposes and is manifested in a variety of ways that may be functional for pattern-maintenance. In the first place, religion may provide an ultimate source and unquestioned authority for the norms of the group. As we have pointed out, answers to ultimate questions of morality and value cannot be derived scientifically or by any wholly rational procedure; moreover, in any case, man's knowledge is finite, incomplete, and, in the final analysis, only man's. The wisdom of the gods, however, can be infinite and all-embracing and may be vested with authority even beyond man's power to comprehend. Hence, the acceptance of re'igious authority makes an end to doubt and question and provides a stable and enduring source of validation of group norms—a justification for them and their primacy.

In the second place, religion may provide a certain and unlimited supply of punishment and reward otherwise unavailable in the mundane world. Thus, for the believers, a powerful mechanism of social control may be institutionalized in religion as an adjunct to secular mechanisms. Closely related to this pattern-maintenance mechanism is the function performed by the religious conceptions of the sacred and the profane. The general tendency is to make a sharp distinction between the holy and the unholy. To the holy or sacred is attached an attitude of reverence, respect, and inviolability. The sacred is accompanied by elaborate proscriptions and taboos that reinforce the special position of holy things. This division of forces and things into the sacred and profane lends to the former a quality of stability and primacy that protects them from an instrumental attitude. To challenge, question, or alter the sacred is a profanation that frequently is defined as a vile heresy and may bring down upon one's head the wrath of the group or of the gods themselves. Because there is a certain contagion to the sacred, this inviolability may extend to embrace a wide range of objects and beliefs; and many patterns may thus be maintained by protecting them against rational analysis of their validity or consequences.

Sacred objects and the religious rituals that surround them have a

---

[14] For a critical discussion of the traditional functional analysis of religion, see Allan W. Eister, "Religious Institutions in Complex Societies: Difficulties in the Theoretic Specifications of Functions," *American Sociological Review*, 22:387–391 (1957).

further significance for integration.[15] The sacred objects themselves present a concrete reference point for the intangible, supernatural order. Thus, these visible and tangible sacred objects give a symbolic "collective representation" of religious values and a common rallying point for those who profess the religious belief. Similarly, the rituals that are part of the practice of religion and frequently center around sacred objects or personages provide a periodic affirmation and confirmation of religious belief. When performed in common with other believers, ritual tends to strengthen and reinforce these beliefs and to unify in religious solidarity the members of the group.

ACTIVISM AND FATALISM

Although a variety of religious beliefs may be functionally equivalent for satisfying the hunger for reassurance that there is "a point," they are by no means equivalent in other respects. It makes a difference just *which* answer is given. Above all, it makes a difference whether the theology views man as an active agent in the world with the responsibility for transforming the empirical environment—including society—in accordance with the "divine purpose"; or whether, on the other hand, it defines man as a passive, essentially powerless part of the Scheme of Things, whose proper role is acceptance of the world the way it is. The best-studied examples of "the difference it makes"—that is, of the effect of theological beliefs on other aspects of human life—are the contrasting religions of Christianity, especially Calvinism, and Hinduism. Talcott Parsons has summarized as follows some relevant conclusions of Max Weber, the most famous of the students of the role of religious ideas:

> . . . on the basis of . . . the doctrines of Karma[16] and Transmigration, to seek salvation . . . through concrete achievement in worldly affairs would be meaningless. If such action contravened the traditional order, it would be reprehensible for that reason and [would] set the actor back

---

[15] A major contribution to the sociological analysis of religion and the significance of sacred objects is found in Émile Durkheim, *The Elementary Forms of Religious Life* (trans. J. W. Swain; New York: The Free Press of Glencoe, Inc., 1957).

[16] "Karma" in this theological system is a kind of net balance of virtue that people accumulate as a result of conscientiously carrying out the obligations of the statuses into which they are born, or not doing so. After death, people are born again, either into a higher or a lower status (including animal or insect forms and superhuman forms), depending on whether the Karma accumulated in their present lives was positive or negative. The aim of the believer is to be completely emancipated from the round of rebirths, and this can be done only by faithfully obeying the law of whatever station he occupies.

on his quest for salvation; if not, it could only generate more Karma and lead to endless rebirths. The only meaning of salvation is escape from the "wheel of Karma" in completely otherworldly mystical and ascetic exercises. For the Calvinist, on the other hand, mystical union with the divine is entirely excluded by the absolute transcendentality of God. He [the individual Calvinist] has been placed in this world to do God's will in the building of the Kingdom. His eternal fate is settled by Predestination; but he can become certain of salvation through proving his faith by active labor in the vineyard, by doing God's will.[17]

Both the Calvinist and the Hindu theologies, in short, can satisfy men's need for a sense of meaning, but with radically differing consequences. The Calvinist theology contributed to an intense preoccupation with improving this world, with results for science and industrialization that we have already seen; the Hindu theology contributes more to a passive acceptance of the world and a desire to be rid of it as much as possible.

RELIGION AND MORALITY

In pointing to the different consequences of differing theological solutions to the problem of "purpose," we have inevitably moved from pure theology to another but inextricably related dimension of "religions"— religious ethics or "morality." Indeed, as the reader may have noticed, it has been impossible at many points in the foregoing discussion to describe various conceptions of the theological "is-ness" of the supernatural without referring also to the ethical "ought-ness" mingled with those conceptions. In nearly all religions, the theology concerning the "nature of divinity" includes a description of how, "therefore," men "should" act. The situation here is similar to the situation we discussed above with respect to the concepts "religion," "theology," and "magic." Religions, we emphasized, are blends of superempirical elements, and most religions include *both* "theology" and "magic." In the present context we are making the same point: most religions include both theology and morality.

This *need* not be the case, however. The theological concern with man-God relations and the moral concern with man-man relations are logically independent and at times may be sociologically independent also, in concrete religions. Theological beliefs *may* contain the idea that the gods, or God, command obedience to certain "shoulds" concerning relations with other people, as is the case in most of the Ten Commandments of the Jewish and Christian religions. Alternatively, the theology may be a description of the superempirical world, with no implications at all for

[17] Talcott Parsons, *Essays in Social Theory* (New York: The Free Press of Glencoe, Inc., 1949), p. 159. Also see R. H. Tawney, *Religion and the Rise of Capitalism* (New York: Harcourt, Brace & World, Inc., 1926) and available in paperback edition (Baltimore: Pelican Books, Inc., 1947).

norms concerning interpersonal relations. The classical period of Greek religion was a good example of this, when the gods of Mt. Olympus went one way with their morals and the people went another.[18] Moreover, when the two are combined in a concrete religion, they may receive varying degrees of emphasis. One possibility is to place primary emphasis on morality, and relegate the relation of man to God to the background. As one Chinese scholar has described the nature of Confucianism, "Teaching a moral life is the essential thing; and the ways of the gods are merely one of the possible means of sanctioning the teaching. That is in substance the Chinese concept of religion."[19]

The other possibility is to reverse that emphasis. Yinger has described this position well:

> Correct belief and correct performance of ritual mark the religious man more certainly than does correct conduct. Religion [from the present point of view] is fundamentally the relation of man to God, and if moral behavior—the right relation of man to man—is religiously significant, it is only as a sign of the relation of man to God. In the history of Christianity, this assertion that morality is merely a subsidiary part of religion has often been made in reaction against the overinvolvement of the church in secular affairs. It is a protest against the "loss of religion," the loss of primary concern for man's salvation, which is felt by many acutely religious people to be the central problem of existence. One phase of Luther's protest, for example, was the emphasis on "justification by faith alone." Logically and consistently developed, this . . . led to the belief that concern with the affairs of this world, attention to good works and problems of justice, were not fundamentally religious questions.[20]

The shades of emphasis in these respects can become highly complex and subtle—more subtle and complex than we can justifiably treat in an introductory text. For present purposes, we must confine ourselves to calling attention to the possible variations and to the importance of discovering, in any concrete case, what the blending of theology and morality is, rather than assuming that it "must be" of one sort or another.

RELIGION AND SECULAR NORMS

In addition to the variations in emphasis on "salvation" and "morality" within religions, another kind of variation is of great importance sociologically. This concerns the relationship between superempirical ideas, both cognitive and evaluative, on the one hand, and *empirical* ethical systems, on the other.

[18] See Murray, *op. cit.*, esp. Chap. 2.
[19] Quoted by Yinger, *op. cit.*, p. 27.
[20] *Ibid.*, p. 24. Reprinted with permission of the publisher.

In fairly simple, especially "primitive" societies, there is likely to be only one homogeneous set of evaluative "shoulds," supported by secular and supernatural sanctions jointly. The division of labor is fairly limited, so that the determinants of one member's fate are the same as those for any other member; and since most people's experiences and frustrations are alike, the same theology can be satisfying to everyone. In such a case, the "shoulds" and "should nots" that comprise integrative and adaptive mechanisms can fairly easily be reinforced by identifying them with the will of the gods and by adding supernatural punishments and rewards to natural ones as incentives to conformity.

The more complex the division of labor becomes, however, the greater is the tendency for two things to happen that destroy this diffuse identity of religious and secular norms. In the first place, people in specialized statuses come to have different experiences, different risks, different frustrations, and different outlooks and aspirations from those of people in other specialized statuses. In the second place, the norms become specialized into "economic" "political," "educational," "familial," "recreational," and "religious" norms. The question is then raised—or at least is potentially raisable—as to the rank order of these normative subsystems, their relative priorities and interrelations. In other words, when a man in a primitive group plays his husband role he is likely at the same instant and inextricably to be playing his economic role, his teacher role, his religious role, and his political role. His status-set is so completely congruent, to put it in technical terms, that it is almost meaningless, except analytically, to try to dissect out its separate elements. In a complex society, on the other hand, there is likely to be one set of interests generated in one's occupational status, another set in one's religious status, and so on. While the need for integration of an individual's status-set and the need for integration of diverse, specialized persons become greater, the possibility of one *religion's* doing the integrating becomes less for two reasons. Different subgroups have less in common, and religion itself becomes one of the elements that *needs integrating* with the other elements.

The differentiation of society's members into subgroups, or at least subcategories, with differing problems and perspectives is likely to mean that the kinds of supernatural beliefs that are satisfying also become differentiated. So far as the relation of the religious beliefs to the empirical world is concerned, four different orientations may be distinguished, corresponding directly to the four modes of adjustment discussed in Chapter 5.[21]

In the first place, the religion may accept and endorse the secular institutional order without change or alteration, justifying it in supernatural

---

[21] Cf. Parsons, *The Social System*, pp. 372–373.

terms and either blaming those who are disadvantaged and deprived by it for their own misfortunes (they are being punished for their sins) or encouraging them to be patient and await their reward in the next world or in the next reincarnation. For example, the subordination of Negroes to whites has been justified in this way in American society by such arguments as that if God had not intended for there to be separate races, He would not have made them; and that Negroes are the descendants of Ham, destined by God to be the hewers of wood and the drawers of water. A vivid, if somewhat crude (to modern ears) example is provided in a sermon delivered by Henry Ward Beecher in 1877, a year of hard times and widespread unemployment. Beecher, with an income of $20,000 a year, said:

> God has intended the great to be great and the little to be little. . . . I do not say that a dollar a day is enough to support a working man. But it is enough to support a man! Not enough to support a man and five children if a man insists on smoking and drinking beer. . . . But the man who cannot live on bread and water alone is not fit to live.[22]

Put considerably less harshly and more appealingly, this religious view has been described by Gilbert Murray in the following words:

> Life [according to this view] is . . . like . . . a play, in which God has handed each man his part unread, and the good man proceeds to act it to the best of his power, not knowing what may happen in the last scene. He may become a crowned king, he may be a slave dying in torment. What matters it? The good actor can play either part. All that matters is that he shall act his best, accept the order of the Cosmos and obey the Purpose of the great Dramaturge.
>
> This . . . answer . . . accepts the Cosmos and it obeys the Purpose; therefore there is a Cosmos, and there is a Purpose in the world.[23]

In the second place, the religion may accept the secular order, in the sense of accommodating to "its rules of the game," but call for efforts to reform it and bring it closer to the ideal conditions of the religious values. The "Social Gospel" of American Protestantism, for example, has been the source of inspiration for many reform movements aimed at eliminating "abuses" and "injustices." As the historian Merle Curti has put it, speaking of certain clergymen of the 1890's:

> According to them, salvation is a matter not of individual conversion and atonement but of Christian nurture from infancy itself. But Christian nurture involves a Christian environment. . . . Salvation cannot be achieved without reference to the community of which the individual is a member and by which he is largely molded. The sacredness of every

[22] Quoted by Merle Curti, *The Growth of American Thought* (2d ed.; New York: Harper & Brothers, 1951). Originally in *The New York Times*, July 30, 1877.
[23] Murray, *op. cit.*, p. 93.

individual life can have little meaning in a society which fails to respect the most elementary prerequisites for the nurture of the divine spark through Christian social relationships and all-permeating fellowships....[24]

In the third place, the religion may reject the secular world completely, defining it as hopelessly sinful, beyond redemption, perhaps destined for extinction at any moment, but at any rate worthy only of true believers' contempt. The theology of Jehovah's Witnesses is a good example of this possibility. The Witnesses believe that the world is in fact ruled by the Devil and that God will redeem it in the Battle of Armageddon, which is very near. Meantime, one should have as little to do with it as possible, refusing, for example, to salute the flag or to serve in the army, and refusing certainly to play the world's game of politics, economics, science, recreation, art, or whatever.[25]

Finally, a religion may reject the secular order as wicked and immoral, but seek to redeem it through empirical, revolutionary means, instead of withdrawing from it. Some phases of the early Protestant Reformation provided examples of this,[26] but, significantly enough, there are no examples in contemporary life, to the best of our knowledge. Revolutionary movements of the modern day seem more frequently justified ideologically than religiously. It may be, however, that some of the nationalism now rampant in the Middle East is fired in part, at least, by religiously inspired revolt.

Each of the variant postures of religion toward the secular world is, of course, likely to appeal to different types of persons. The deprived are perhaps less likely to agree with Henry Ward Beecher than with the Jehovah's Witnesses;[27] the restless and aggressively ambitious are more likely to be attracted to a religion that calls for revolutionary change than one that insists that all is as it should be.

RELIGIOUS GROUPINGS: CHURCH, SECT, DENOMINATION, AND CULT

Religious belief-systems emerge, achieve their identity, and are expressed and maintained in social groups. Sociologists generally have rec-

[24] Curti, *op. cit.*, p. 631.

[25] See H. H. Stroup, *Jehovah's Witnesses* (New York: Columbia University Press, 1945).

[26] Emery Battis, in a forthcoming publication, *Troublers in Israel*, has shown how the "Antinomian Revolt" in the Massachusetts Bay Colony in the seventeenth century may be interpreted as a theological justification of the changing secular needs of prosperous Puritans.

[27] See Liston Pope, *Millhands and Preachers* (New Haven, Conn.: Yale University Press, 1942).

ognized four types of religious groupings: church, sect, denomination, and cult. Although this typology has developed in the analysis of Western religious life and its pertinence to Oriental or primitive religions may be questioned, it does help to understand something of the character of social organization of religion, at least as we in the West have experienced it. By means of such a typology, some basic differences among religious groups may be identified. These differences, then, may be related to some of the social factors that support the emergence of different religious groupings and their transformation over time. Such a typology also may aid in identifying some of the social differences among people who have membership in different religious groupings and in interpreting the relevancy of these social characteristics to the beliefs supported by the group. It should be recognized, of course, that there is some blurring and overlapping among these four types of religious groupings, and that the distinctions among them must be considered analytical. In the empirical situation, elements of the different types are likely to be mixed, and any given type is only approximated.[28]

Although there is some difference in terminology and concept, a major distinction between the "sect" and the "church" has been in wide use among sociologists and other analysts of religion.[29] The church is characterized as the sole possessor of the means of grace, which is dispensed only through the office of its ordained functionaries. Its members are born into the church, although conversion, sometimes by force, is used as a means to bring *all* peoples into its fold. The church adapts to the secular order when necessary, although ideally it has control of all secular life. The church type is most clearly represented by the Roman Catholic Church of the Middle Ages. In the sect, on the other hand, grace is not conferred automatically nor is it a possession of the sect. Its religious functionaries play no role in bestowal of grace, and the distinction between clergy and the laity is not sharply drawn, if at all. Membership is voluntary and exclusive; people must prove themselves worthy of grace or, at least, if grace is predestined or a pure gift it should be manifested in a proper life. Ideally, the members of the sect form a fellowship apart from the rest of society within which they live out their religious teaching. Sects tend to reject, be indifferent to, or withdraw from the secular

[28] For a useful overview of the variety of religions in the United States, see Leo Rosten, *A Guide to Religions in America* (New York: Simon and Schuster, Inc., 1955).

[29] The term "ecclesia" is sometimes used in place of "church." See Ernst Troeltsch, *The Social Teachings of the Christian Churches* (2 vols., trans. Olive Wyon; New York: The Macmillan Company, 1932), for a basic treatment of the sect-church distinction. Some of the problems inherent in this typology as it has come into common usage are cogently discussed in Benton Johnson, "A Critical Appraisal of the Church-Sect Typology," *American Sociological Review*, 22:88–92 (1957).

order, although they may sometimes attempt radical reformation of it. Sects are represented by such varied religious groups as Jehovah's Witnesses, the Amish, the Shakers, Seventh-Day Adventists, the Salvation Army, the Amana Community, Holiness movements, and many others.

The sect should not be regarded as more or less authentic than the church nor as a mere deviation from the church type. Indeed, the early Christians themselves formed a sect. Yet some sects have arisen in reaction to the "worldliness" of churches, for there is a general sociological tendency for the spiritual power of the church to lead to secular power, which may deflect the church from its religious mission. On the other hand, sects also seem to emerge in response to diffuse discontent with the social order and as a consequence of strain experienced differentially within the society. Rapid social change that dislocates the established position of groups and categories of people, marginal position in the social structure, economic deprivation, or the failure of a system adequately to integrate some of its members into the larger society are all occasions for the possible emergence of sects. For example, Daniel has shown how sects serve the needs of rural Negro migrants to urban Chicago, where established Negro religious groups fail to satisfy.[30] Similarly, Goldschmidt has analyzed the way in which sects may serve as compensatory mechanisms for unskilled laborers who are cut off from the dominant middle-class life of a community in California.[31] Liston Pope found a similar pattern among the poor millhands in North Carolina.[32]

It has been observed that some sects change certain of their basic characteristics over time and emerge as "denominations."[33] Generally speaking, denominations are less exclusive than sects, more tolerant of diversity of religious belief, more "worldly," less demanding of their members, more formal in liturgy, and more demanding in professional requirements for religious functionaries. The movement from sect to denomination seems to be a consequence of a combination of factors. The need to adapt to some degree to the secular world, the recruitment of new members and extension into the second generation through the family, the growth of membership with consequent bureaucratic elaborations, the emergence of a trained ministry, and the increased economic stake in the community on the part of both the sect and some of its members all seem to contribute to the transformation.

[30] V. Daniel, "Ritual and Stratification in Chicago Negro Churches," *American Sociological Review*, 7:352–361 (1942).

[31] Walter R. Goldschmidt, "Class Denominationalism in Rural California Churches," *American Journal of Sociology*, 49:348–355 (1943).

[32] Pope, *op. cit.*

[33] H. Richard Niebuhr, *The Social Sources of Denominationalism* (New York: Holt, Rinehart and Winston, Inc., 1929), and Pope, *op. cit.* Pope applies the term "church" to what we and others have called "denomination."

The emergence of the denomination is by no means inevitable or automatic, however, but depends on a number of factors both internal to the sect and external to it. Bryan Wilson has described some of these factors and linked them to a typology of sects, differentiating both the conditions under which each is likely to emerge and the extent to which each is vulnerable to denominationalism.[34] Wilson classifies sects on the basis of the type of mission particular to each as follows:

> The *Conversionist* sects seek to alter men, and thereby to alter the world; the response is free-will optimism. [The Salvation Army and the Pentecostal sects] The *Adventist* sects predict drastic alteration of the world, and seek to prepare for the new dispensation—a pessimistic determinism. [Jehovah's Witnesses and the Cristadelphians] The *Introversionists* reject the world's values and replace them with higher inner values, for the realization of which inner resources are cultivated. [Holiness movements and the Quakers] The *Gnostic* sects accept in large measure the world's goals but seek a new and esoteric means to achieve these ends—a wishful mysticism. [Christian Science and New Thought Sects][35]

Briefly put, Wilson contends that the conversionist sects are most subject to the denominationalistic transformation. Evangelism and revivalism require special training of religious leaders, inhibit isolation and insulation from the rest of the world, restrict adequate socialization of new members, dilute the imposition of strict and demanding standards of admission, encourage inclusiveness rather than exclusiveness, and retain an orthodox and fundamentalist tradition. Thus, the conversionist type of sect contains within it the seeds of the denomination, whereas the Adventist and introversionist types, particularly, are more protected from it by their greater exclusiveness, unique doctrines, special insulating mechanisms, and strong endogamous injunctions. The distinct and often bizarre nature of the beliefs of the Gnostic sect tend to isolate it and thus protect it from the transformation into a denomination.

Some of the religious groups that are included in what Wilson calls Gnostic sects have been called by some analysts "cults."[36] The cult is characterized by a special focus on one doctrine above all others, a loose organization and extreme openness of membership, dependence on emotional attachment to a leader, on special rituals and beliefs, and on a new and unique religious interpretation. The cult is represented by such

[34] Bryan Wilson, "An Analysis of Sect Development," *American Sociological Review*, 24:3–15 (1959).

[35] *Ibid.*, p. 5. The bracketed examples are those given by Wilson elsewhere in his article.

[36] Leopold von Wiese and Howard Becker make this distinction, along with the other major types we have discussed, in *Systematic Sociology* (New York: John Wiley & Sons, Inc., 1932).

religious groups as The Father Divine Peace Mission Movement, Bahia, I Am, and Buchmanism.

Urban areas, especially large metropolitan centers, seem particularly conducive to the formation of cults. The diversity contained in such centers, the exposure to this diversity, the relatively rapid and continual shift and change in the position of people, the loose social controls and the difficulty of maintaining traditional belief-systems, the rootlessness of many of the people who migrate to urban centers, and the complexities of the problems, coupled with the social distance from the sources of power to solve them—all seem to contribute to the emergence of the cult. In response to these conditions, cults are rather transitory and ephemeral, although they may achieve some enduring stability by transformation into sects and denominations.

A BRIEF RECAPITULATION

Let us pause here to recapitulate our discussion thus far. We have been noting that there is a tendency for people to extend their need to understand things in motivational terms, to nature and "life in general." That is, a tendency to ask why such frustrations as injustice, suffering, and death exist. Answers to such questions, we have said, can be found by projecting empirical experiences with motives and purposes that "make sense" onto a supernatural plane. This is theology.

In this sense, we have been "explaining" theology, or, as some might think, "explaining it away." That is what we want to pause about. In the first place, as we noted above, this is a "scientific" explanation in the sense that its explanatory terms all have empirical referents. A theological "explanation" is equally possible. For example, one could assert that ideas about God and the superempirical do *not* result from men's projective fantasies; they result from God's putting such ideas into people's minds. Or, even if our empirical explanation is accepted as "true," a theologian might still maintain that the *reason* it is true is that God planned it that way—that is, that God in His wisdom arranged for men to arrive at the Truth by the route of their projective efforts to solve their empirical dilemmas.

In short, to explain theological or "religious" ideas as we have done is not necessarily to "explain them away." As we pointed out in the previous chapter in our discussion of science, any scientific proposition whatsoever has no implication at all for the validity of a superempirical proposition. Put otherwise, nothing that can be said about the origins or the functions of any idea has any significance for the validity of that idea. We think it is important to emphasize this in order to indicate our disagreement *both* with those "believers" who think their beliefs are under attack by an analysis of religion *and* with those "nonbelievers" who think their nonbelief is justified by such an analysis. One can agree with Don Juan in Shaw's *Man and Superman* that "Nature *must* have a purpose," or one can agree with the Devil's rejoinder, "You think Nature has a purpose because you have a purpose. You might as well think that Nature has fingers and toes because you have them." Empirically, it is impossible to determine who is right.

All that can be said from an empirical point of view is that theological beliefs do, in observable fact, attempt to "make sense" out of many things that some people find disturbingly "senseless." Theology provides "meaning," for which many people feel a need. But even here it is important to be careful, and to say with Milton Yinger:

> We do not say . . . : "One of the functions of religion is to solve the personality needs that come from the fact of death [and other frustrations]," but rather, "religions everywhere struggle, sometimes partially successfully, sometimes unsuccessfully, with the problem of death [etc.]." The particular religious system may not "work" for some individuals; it may tend to break down for a whole social group that has been disastrously changed by some intrusive force (industrialization or great mobility or outside invasion . . .).[37]

In other, more general words, human beings often experience a peculiarly human anguish—the anguish of a brutal contrast between their sentiments of what "ought to be" and their cognitions of what is. Efforts are made to avoid such a dissonance; and *one* way in which *some* people avoid it is by harmonizing the ideal and the real through supernatural beliefs. This way of putting the matter is useful because it clearly, if implicitly, raises several questions:

1. Is it in fact necessary for there to be such a dissonance?
2. What *other* ways—what structural alternatives—are there to perform the functions sometimes performed for some groups by "religion"?
3. Are there any conditions under which people can simply adapt by accepting the dissonance instead of trying to avoid it?

So far as the first question is concerned, we shall answer, briefly, yes: from all the evidence, the problem of "meaning" is as inextricably a part of human life as water is a part of fish life. Even in Aldous Huxley's *Brave New World*, death and injustice need an enormous amount of rationalizing, and *some* people, at least, wonder what the point of the whole business is. It is no doubt true that in any society there are people who do not think beyond their physical sensations, but there are always others who do.

---

[37] Yinger, *op. cit.*, p. 76. Reprinted with permission of the publisher.

But for many of those who do, and perhaps increasingly in modern science-dominated societies, supernatural solutions to the problem of meaning are unacceptable. Although most people continue to profess a "belief in religion," there is some reason to suppose that this is a fairly superficial remnant of religious significance, and that supernatural beliefs are not really the structures relied on to supply "meaning" or to allay the anxiety of "meaninglessness."[38]

It is necessary, however, to be cautious in making such generalizations about the religious state of affairs in the present-day United States. The fact is that, although there has been considerable discussion about Americans' religiosity, or lack of it, there has been remarkably little systematic research on the subject and there is not much knowledge about it.

One of the problems has been, as we noted at the beginning of this chapter, that the term "religion" is used in so many different ways. Investigators who use it one way are likely to find that there has been a distinct religious upsurge in the United States since, say, World War II; those who use it another way may find that there has been no revival at all, but a decline; while still others argue that there has been no change in either direction.[39]

One common index of "religiousness"—common, no doubt, because so readily visible—is simply church membership; attendance at services held in churches, temples, or synagogues; or even contributions to churches. The difficulty with this, of course, is that, without anything more, one can know nothing about the significance of the membership, the attendance, or the contribution to the people involved. The view that membership in a church is, in modern society, simply a way to symbolize one's respectability in a community or to meet one's neighbors, and has nothing to do with man-God relationships, man-man morality, or theological explanations of purpose is as plausible as the opposite view (*as* plausible— neither more so nor less so). Similarly, the problem remains unanswered as to whether attendance at church or synagogue services is an empty ritual, an opportunity to show off one's clothes, or an effort to experience a one-ness with God. And there is little or no evidence to test the perhaps cynical theory that contributions are ways of lowering income tax payments.

[38] See, for example, the following: Will Herberg, *Protestant, Catholic, Jew* (New York: Doubleday & Company, Inc., 1955); Seymour M. Lipset, "What Religious Revival?" *Columbia University Forum*, 2:17–22 (1959); Sidney Hook, "Modern Knowledge and the Idea of God," *Commentary*, 29:205–216 (1960).

[39] Charles Y. Glock, Professor of Sociology and Director of the Survey Research Center at the University of California in Berkeley, has cogently reviewed the recent findings in "The Religious Revival in America?" (one of the papers in Jane C. Zahn [ed.], *Religion and the Face of America* [Berkeley: University Extension of the University of California, 1959]). We are indebted to Glock for the data in this section.

Thus, the report that church membership as a percentage of the population had increased from 49 percent in 1940 to 61 percent in 1957.[40] is impossible to interpret with assurance, one way or another. We may learn from a poll conducted by the American Institute of Public Opinion (the Gallup Poll) in February, 1939, that 41 percent of adults had attended church in the week preceding the poll, and from another poll in December, 1947, that 47 percent had done so;[41] but we do not know what they were doing there.

What part religion, or any of its manifestations, plays, then, in performing for Americans the functions that religion *might* perform, cannot be stated with any degree of certainty. The best that we can do in this introductory text is to consider what *other* kinds of structures might also perform those functions and await more research (perhaps to be conducted in a few years by one of the readers of this book) on the question of which ones do perform them, and for which kinds of people.

Two other kinds of structures help, more or less effectively (just as religions help "more or less" effectively), to perform the functions we have been discussing. One is the variety of tension-management mechanisms already discussed in Chapter 6. The second, which we shall discuss in the rest of this chapter, is ideology.[42]

Ideology

Talcott Parsons defines an ideology as a system of empirically oriented ideas that gives men an "interpretation of the empirical nature of the collectivity and of the situation in which it is placed, the processes by which it has developed to its given state, the goals to which its members are collectively oriented, and their relation to the future course of events."[43] Ideologies, in short, are *empirical* efforts to explain injustice, suffering, and death, and to supply the meaningful picture of the world that man seems to need in order to feel that he is a part, if not of the "Purpose of the great Dramaturge," at least of a great Drama.

[40] *Ibid.*, p. 33.

[41] *Ibid.*, p. 34.

[42] A third may also be distinguished—what might be called "distracting mechanisms." These are currently dealt with, in part, under the heading "mass culture," a subject we shall not take up in this text. See, for example, Ernest Van den Haag, "Popular Culture," in Ralph Ross and Ernest Van den Haag, *The Fabric of Society* (New York: Harcourt, Brace & World, Inc., 1957). See also Bernard Rosenberg and David Manning White (eds.), *Mass Culture* (New York: The Free Press of Glencoe, Inc., 1957).

[43] Parsons, *The Social System*, p. 349.

The problem least frequently and elaborately dealt with by ideologies is death. There is, after all, little that can be said about death in empirical terms, except to describe how it occurs; and that, as we have noted, is often unsatisfactory to people who want to know not "how" but *why*. There seem to be two major possibilities for coping with the "why" problem in ideological terms. One, corresponding most closely to the religious treatment, is to define the world in terms that come close to deifying some empirical entity, to which the individual is subordinated, in the service of which his life takes on meaning, and for the sake of which it is "glorious to die." The most familiar case, of course, is the ideology of nationalism and "patriotism." To regret only that one has but one life to give for his country, and to plunge exultantly toward death for the "Fatherland" or the "Motherland" or the "Party"—these are emotions that probably can for some people under some conditions remove the sting from death as effectively as religions do under other conditions for other people.[44]

It would not, however, seem likely that the high pitch of excitement and ardor that might operate in such cases can be sustained over the long pull. Moreover, it would seem to be difficult, to say the least, to make death meaningful in such terms when it comes not in the heat of battle but rather, as it comes to most people, slowly and only after a long period of physical and mental enfeeblement. To die gallantly for The Cause in the enthusiasm of conflict is one thing, but to romanticize as heroic and meaningful a death from chicken pox or malfunctioning of the liver is a rather more formidable task.[45]

The second ideological approach to the "why" of death is the answer that there is none. Erich Fromm has put this position in this way:

> The most fundamental existential dichotomy is that between life and death. The fact that we have to die is unalterable for man. Man is aware of this fact, and this very awareness profoundly influences his life. . . . Man can react to [such problems] . . . in different ways. He can appease his mind by soothing and harmonizing [ideas]. . . . He can try to escape from his inner restlessness by ceaseless activity in pleasure or business. He can try to abrogate his freedom and to turn himself into an instrument of powers outside himself, submerging his self in them. But he remains dissatisfied, anxious, and restless. There is only one solution to his problem: to face the truth, to acknowledge his fundamental

[44] Shakespeare's Henry V adroitly combines the religious and the ideological exhortation not to fear death:
> The game's afoot!
> Follow your spirit, and upon this charge
> Cry 'God for Harry, England, and St. George!' "

[45] An excellent performance of the task is Lael Tucker Wertenbaker, *Death of a Man* (New York: Random House, Inc., 1957).

aloneness and solitude in a universe indifferent to his fate, to recognize that there is no power transcending him which can solve his problem for him. . . . If he faces the truth without panic, he will recognize that *there is no meaning to life except the meaning man gives his life.* . . .[46]

Fromm's words, perhaps, appear stark. The same basic orientation lies behind the funeral address of the Ethical Culture Society, but the message may be somewhat softened in the way it is put:

> Death brings us into closer communion with each other. We are not singled out for a special judgment when we give up our dead; we but enter into a common sorrow . . . that tends to make the world one by dissolving all other feelings into sympathy and love.
>
> . . . And when death speaks to us, what does it say? It does not say: Fear me. It does not say: Wonder at me. It does not say: Understand me. It bids us think rather of life, of the privileges of life, of how great a thing life can be made.[47]

Most people find one of the other ways of handling death more appealing. Under what conditions and with what conseqences this answer would be acceptable to them is something about which there is not much knowledge at present.

INJUSTICE, SUFFERING, AND MEANING

Ideologies usually concentrate on the other problems of "meaning": injustice, suffering, and the more general problem of the significance of living. In this—as, of course, in the matter of death also—ideologies are competitive with religions, in the sense simply that they provide alternative ways of "explaining" the situations in which men find themselves and at the same time offer a program of what to do about it. The fact of this "alternativeness" or "substitutability" is rather dramatically evidenced in a study carried out in Sweden. Sven Rydenfelt compared two counties in Sweden—Vasterbotten and Norrbotten—which were similar in their social and economic composition. Both counties contained some of the poorest and most socially isolated groups in Sweden; and, other things being equal, one might expect them to be fertile recruiting grounds for the Communist party. In one of them, Norrbotten, this proved to be the case; there the Communists received an average of 21 percent of the popular vote in elections during the years 1924–1952. In the other, however (Vasterbotten), the Communists received only an average of 2

---

[46] Erich Fromm, *Man for Himself* (New York: Holt, Rinehart and Winston, Inc., 1947), pp. 41–45. The emphasis is Fromm's.

[47] Quoted by Yinger, *op. cit.*, pp. 77–78.

percent. Rydenfelt accounts for this by pointing out that in this county extreme radical tendencies were channelized into *religious* modes of expression: "The Communists and the religious radicals, as for instance, the Pentecostal sects, seem to be competing for the allegiance of the same groups."[48]

LIBERALISM AND CONSERVATISM

As Table 9–1 in the preceding chapter suggests, one fundamental basis for distinguishing among different ideologies is the conception they embody of the relationship between man and his social structure—that is, between man and the prevailing definitions of status-rights and -obligations, status-sets, status-sequences, integrative and adaptive mechanisms, and decision making. On the one hand, the institutionalized structure may be defended and justified by the ideological explanations of the world, with the duty of man being seen as adjustment and conformity to that structure. On the other hand, the social structure may be judged critically in terms of its consequences for the welfare of man—as defined, of course, by the ideology. Conservative ideologies are those that offer explanations of man's situation in terms that justify preserving the *status quo*. Liberal ideologies justify changing the social structure or some aspect of it.

The terms "liberal" and "conservative" are related to the concepts of "Left" and "Right" ideologies. The Left-Right terminology stems from the period after the French Revolution, when the delegates sat in a semicircle facing the presiding officer. The delegates arranged themselves from the left to the right according to the various shades of their political views. Those on the left favored the most extensive changes; those on the right were the most rigid about maintaining the *status quo*. Since that time, writers have distinguished politico-economic views in terms of Left, Center, and Right.

The term "liberal," as it is most often used, refers to those somewhere between the extreme Left and the Center. "Conservatives" are those somewhere between the Center and the extreme Right. The extreme Left and the extreme Right are variously labeled by different writers. The extreme Left used to be often referred to as "radical," and the extreme Right, as "reactionary"; but in recent years it has become more common to refer to both extremes as "radical." In the present introductory discus-

---

[48] Quoted by S. M. Lipset, *Political Man* (New York: Doubleday & Company, Inc., 1960), p. 108. See also the review of Rydenfelt's work by W. Phillips Davison in the *Public Opinion Quarterly*, 18:375–388 (1954–55).

sion, we shall not attempt to make these distinctions of degree, but speak only of the basic distinction between "left" or "liberal" ideologies of all shades, and "right" or "conservative" ideologies of all shades.

On the one hand, then, "liberal" ideologies tend to be based on a conception of man as a shaper and molder of his environment, particularly his social environment, in his own interests. "Conservative" ideologies, on the other hand, tend to emphasize the importance and value of existing social arrangements and the necessity of man's adjusting to them.

Objective discussion of "liberalism" and "conservatism" is made somewhat difficult at the present stage of American culture, because in one sense the dominant traditional orientation of American culture is toward a "liberal" ideology. At least, that is to say, it would be difficult to find spokesmen to defend the point of view that certain social structures ought to be maintained *even though* they may frustrate man's full development. Rather, most arguments tend to accept the premise that "man is the measure of all things," and then develop around the issue of whether the existing structures are (the conservative view) or are not (the liberal view) the best for men. The one area in which this is not the case is the field of race relations. There, of course, it is not at all hard to find spokesmen for the point of view that Negroes (or, depending on the region, Mexicans, Indians, Japanese, Chinese) ought not to be allowed to develop their full potentialities. In this version, "WASPS[49] are the measure of all things." Even in the area of race relations, however, the ideology of humanism is often strong enough to lead many bigots to attempt to rationalize their discrimination in humanistic terms: "This is really better for the Negroes, too; they're like children."

A second slightly complicating factor is the fact that much of present-day American conservatism was the liberalism of two hundred years ago. The spokesmen for free private enterprise, for "laissez faire," for self-reliance, and for competition and bargaining as mechanisms of integration were the innovators of the seventeenth and eighteenth centuries, struggling against the conservative ideology of state paternalism and a class system based on birth. But "free private enterprise" is the norm institutionalized in American capitalism, so that its defenders are the modern "conservatives." It must be emphasized, however, that the humanistic ideas referred to above exert influence here too; hence the conservative defense tends, more often than not, to be a defense of the *status quo* in terms of its instrumental efficiency in achieving the same goals as modern liberals espouse: the maximum opportunity for the largest possible proportion of people to develop their full potentials.

The most severely complicating element in contemporary discussions is

[49] White Anglo-Saxon Protestants.

the fact that two strands in the "liberal-conservative" ideological debate, which formerly seemed to be tightly interwoven into one ideological position, have been seen in recent years to be dissociated. These two strands might be labeled "politico-economic" liberalism-conservatism and "intellectual" liberalism-conservatism.

The political sociologist S. M. Lipset has summarily described some of the events which made the dissociation visible as follows:

> Before 1914, the classic division between the working class left parties and the economically privileged right was not based solely upon such issues as redistribution of income, status, and educational opportunities, but also rested upon civil liberties and international policy. The workers, judged by the policies of their parties, were often the backbone of the fight for greater political democracy, religious freedom, minority rights, and international peace, while the parties backed by the conservative middle and upper classes in much of Europe tended to favor more extremist political forms, to resist the extension of the suffrage, to back the established church, and to support jingoistic foreign policies.
>
> Events since 1914 have gradually eroded these patterns.
>
> . . . The poorer strata everywhere are more liberal or leftist on economic issues; they favor welfare state measures, higher wages, graduated income taxes, support of trade-unions, and so forth. But when liberalism is defined in noneconomic terms—as support of civil liberties, internationalism, etc.—the correlation is reversed. The more well-to-do are more liberal, the poorer are more intolerant.[50]

Economically, the conservative ideology defends self-reliance, competition, and bargaining as the most desirable kinds of integrative mechanisms. From this point of view, labor unions are wrong because they interfere with competition (among workers), public housing is wrong because it "weakens self-reliance" and violates the bargaining principle, federal health insurance plans are wrong for the same reason, minimum wage legislation is wrong because it violates the bargaining principle, and so on. These are all, in the phrase of one conservative spokesman, the "road to serfdom."[51]

The liberal ideology, on the other hand, sees it as a responsibility of the society as a whole to provide medical care, housing, employment opportunities, education, and secure and "decent" incomes to everyone, as a matter of "right." So far as this strand is concerned, the debate between "liberals" and "conservatives" is, as noted above, often a debate that, at least on its face, is over which will most effectively improve men's lives: the "welfare state" or "private enterprise."

---

[50] Lipset, *op. cit.* The first part of this quotation is from p. 99, the second part from pp. 101–102.

[51] Friedrich A. Hayek, *The Road to Serfdom* (Chicago: The University of Chicago Press, 1944).

In terms of "intellectual liberalism," or what might equally be called "civil liberties liberalism," the basic issue centers around the kind of liberalism associated with John Stuart Mill's famous essay *On Liberty*. The intellectually liberal ideology insists on maximum freedom of individuals to dissent and to express unpopular, deviant, even "wicked" opinions. The conservative tendency in this respect, on the other hand, is to prohibit the expression of "wrong" or "un-American" or "indecent" ideas.

In view of the clear cleavage between these two kinds of "liberalism-conservatism," the traditional conception of a single continuum of ideologies from left to right has become modified in recent years. The process of modification is itself an instuctive chapter in social science development and will merit review here.

The modification began with the publication in 1950 of *The Authoritarian Personality*, the result of a six-year study of prejudice, especially anti-Semitism, by a group of psychologists at the University of California at Berkeley.[52] The major conclusion of the study was that anti-Semitism and ethnocentrism in general were expressions of a more general kind of ideological orientation, one which the authors variously characterized as "authoritarian," "anti-democratic," "fascistic." Their conclusion was based on intensive clinical interviews with, and projective tests of, people who had scored extremely high and extremely low on tests of anti-Semitism and ethnocentrism. They reported that the "highs" (prejudiced) tended to be characterized by strong and rigid adherence to conventional values, a tendency to glorify and to accept uncritically the authorities of their ingroups, a punitive attitude toward all outsiders, preoccupation with power, and toughness, cynicism, and suspiciousness.[53]

The authors noted that some of their "low" scorers were also characterized by those very attributes; but at the time they were primarily concerned with the association between authoritarianism and "right-wing" ideologies, and paid little attention to this association between "left-wing" ideology and authoritarianism. (The reader should remember that this study was undertaken just after World War II, in which the major threat to democratic institutions was from the right, not the left.)

Four years after the appearance of *The Authoritarian Personality*, another book was published, entitled *Studies in the Scope and Method of "The Authoritarian Personality."*[54] One of the studies included in that work was an analysis by a theoretically and politically astute sociologist, Edward A. Shils, entitled, "Authoritarianism: 'Right' and 'Left'." Shils

---

[52] T. W. Adorno, Else Frenkel-Brunswik, Daniel J. Levinson, R. Nevitt Sanford, *The Authoritarian Personality* (New York: Harper & Brothers, 1950).

[53] *Ibid.*, pp. 227–228.

[54] Richard Christie and Marie Jahoda (eds.), *Studies in the Scope and Method of "The Authoritarian Personality"* (New York: The Free Press of Glencoe, Inc., 1954).

criticized the original study in the following words: "The entire team of investigators proceeds as if there were [a] unilinear scale of political and social attitudes at the extreme right of which stands the fascist . . . and at the other end what the authors call the complete democrat. . . ."[55]

Contrary to this picture, Shils listed nine "deeper tendencies of the authoritarian of the Right" as delineated by the Berkeley writers and showed that they have precise parallels in the authoritarian of the Left, as represented by the typical member of the Communist party.[56]

In short, Shils made explicit an insight of great importance: ideologies of any politico-economic content may be held in different ways—"authori-

CHARACTERISTICS OF THE AUTHORITARIAN LEFT AS FORMULATED BY SHILS	CHARACTERISTICS OF THE AUTHORITARIAN RIGHT AS FORMULATED BY SHILS
1. The demand for complete and unqualified loyalty to the party.	1. Extreme hostility toward "out-groups."
2. The insistence on the necessary conflict of interests between the working class of which the party is the leader and all other classes and the need for unrelenting conflict against these other classes, even in times of apparent truce and cooperation.	2. Extreme submissiveness toward the in-groups.
3. The continuous application of the criteria of party interests in judging every person and situation and the need to avoid eclecticism in doctrine and opportunism and compromise in practice.	3. The establishment of sharp boundaries between the group of which one is a member and all other groups.
4. The stress on the class characteristics of individuals and the interpretation of their actions in the light of their class position exclusively.	4. The tendency to categorize persons with respect to certain particular qualities and make "all or none" judgments.
5. The belief that all history is the history of class conflict.	5. A vision of the world as a realm of conflict.

[55] *Ibid.*, p. 28.
[56] *Ibid.*, pp. 33–34.

6. The denial of the existence of pure truth and attack on those who espouse pure science or "art for art's sake."

6. Disdain for purely theoretical or contemplative activities.

7. The belief that the expression of sentiment is an expression of weakness and that it interferes with the correct interpretation of reality and the choice of the right course of action.

7. A repugnance for the expression of sentiments, particularly sentiments of affection.

8. The belief in the ubiquitousness of the influence of "Wall Street," the "City," the "Big Banks," "Heavy Industry," "200 families," etc., and their masked control over even the most remote spheres of life and the counterbelief in the necessity to penetrate organizations and achieve complete control over them.

8. Belief that oneself and one's group are the objects of manipulative designs and that oneself and one's groups can survive only by the manipulation of others.

9. The ideal of the classless society, without private property in the instruments of production and hence without conflict, the "realm of freedom" where man will cease his alienation and become truly human.

9. The ideal of a conflictless wholly harmonious society in contrast with an environing or antecedent conflictful chaos. There are other properties as well but these will serve for illustrative purposes.

tarianly" or "democratically." This seems to be related to the two different kinds of "liberalism-conservatism" described above and delineated by Lipset. "Intellectual liberalism" may be linked *either* to "democratic" liberalism *or* "democratic" conservatism of the politico-economic kind; and "intellectual conservatism" may be linked *either* to "authoritarian" liberalism *or* "authoritarian" conservatism of the politico-economic type.

Shils's insight has been more fully developed in recent research by Milton Rokeach.[57] Rokeach has developed a measure of "Dogmatism" and measures of "Left Opinionation" and "Right Opinionation." With these measuring instruments, as well as some ingenously designed laboratory experiments, he has shown statistically what Shils had suggested theoretically and qualitatively: there are dogmatic ("closed-minded")

[57] Milton Rokeach, *The Open and Closed Mind* (New York: Basic Books, Inc., 1960).

and tolerant ways of being "liberal" as well as dogmatic and tolerant ways of being "conservative." In the terms we have been using, we may say that there are not two, but four, major ideological positions:

1. Economically liberal—intellectually liberal
2. Economically liberal—intellectually conservative
3. Economically conservative—intellectually liberal
4. Economically conservative—intellectually conservative[58]

The distinctions among them may be delineated briefly but suggestively in terms of the contrasting meanings attached to the concept of "individualism" in each of the four ideological perspectives.

ECONOMIC LIBERALISM—INTELLECTUAL LIBERALISM

In the language of this ideology, "individualism" means the furthering of individual diversity, even "nonconformity," partly through legal and social protection of minority rights, freedom of speech, and so on; and partly through collective social responsibility for the "mechanics of living": housing, health, occupational security, access to education, minimum incomes, and so on. It is an ideology represented, for example, by the ADA (Americans for Democratic Action) and what is often referred to as the "Northern Liberal Wing" of the Democratic party. From this ideological point of view, social structures are instrumental tools to be manipulated for the end of individuals' intellectual development and freedom. The "individuals," from this perspective, include all individuals, without regard to racial, ethnic, religious, or national identification. Government power, according to this ideology, is something to be used to produce equality, to prevent discrimination, to help industrialize backward nations, to promote education, and so on.

ECONOMIC LIBERALISM—INTELLECTUAL CONSERVATISM

In the language of this ideology, "individualism" tends to take on a negative connotation. In some cases, as in Communism, an extreme form of this position, it would be more correct to say that "individualism" be-

---

[58] S. M. Lipset distinguishes six major ideological positions. He does this by distinguishing three basic "positions"—Left, Center, and Right—and within each an "extremist" and a moderate or "democratic" variant. His "extremist" and "democratic" variants correspond to our "intellectual conservatism" and "intellectual liberalism," respectively; and his "Left, Center, Right" distinctions represent a finer and more complex treatment of our "economic liberalism and conservatism." See Lipset, *op. cit.*, Chap. 5, " 'Fascism'—Left, Right, and Center."

comes a dirty word. The "welfare state" is espoused, in the sense of collective social responsibility for the "mechanics of living"; but conformity is widely demanded and diversity is viewed suspiciously as a threat. This ideological position has been called by Edward Shils "Left Authoritarianism";[59] and by Milton Rokeach, "Left Dogmatism" or "Closed-minded Leftism."[60]

ECONOMIC CONSERVATISM—INTELLECTUAL LIBERALISM

In this language, "individualism" has a positive connotation, just as it does from the perspective of the first ideology discussed above, but the meaning is very different. "Individualism" here means self-reliance, competitiveness, and self-oriented (but "fair") bargaining. "Collective social responsibility" or the "welfare state" is, from this point of view, the surest way of destroying individualism—they are, in Hayek's phrase, "the road to serfdom." In this sense, the economically conservative—intellectually liberal ideology is the direct opposite of the "liberal-liberal" view of the world. But they are alike in what Rokeach would call their "open-mindedness,"[61] or what T. W. Adorno and his associates in California[62] would call their "democratic" or "antiauthoritarian" orientation. Although it tends to be secondary in the present ideology, nonconformity is not viewed with the suspicious fear that is felt toward it by the "liberal dogmatist" or by the "conservative dogmatist." This ideology tends to be supported by well-educated, big business men.

ECONOMIC CONSERVATISM—INTELLECTUAL CONSERVATISM

In this ideology (called "Right Authoritarianism" by Rokeach and Shils), "individualism" is again a dirty word when it refers to nonconformity; but it is a sacred word when it means the opposite of "collectivism" or "welfare state." At the extreme, this is the ideology that becomes fascism or Nazism. This ideology has been represented most clearly in the United States in recent years by McCarthyism, and appeals typically to small business men who tend to feel themselves threatened on all sides by labor unions, big business, and the increasing role of gov-

[59] Shils, *op. cit.*, pp. 24–29.

[60] Rokeach, *op. cit.*

[61] *Ibid.* Technically, Rokeach would not speak of an "open-minded" ideology, but rather of an open- or closed-minded *adherent* to an ideology. What we are in effect suggesting here is that "closed-mindedness" and "open-mindedness" may be conceptualized for certain purposes as ideological positions, as well as character traits.

[62] Adorno *et al.*, *op. cit.*

ernment;[63] and to some third- and fourth-generation descendants of immigrant groups who feel compelled to assert their "100 percent American-
ism" in extreme form.[64]

SOCIAL FUNCTIONS OF IDEOLOGY

In much the same way that religion and magic may be functional for
tension management, ideology may offer to individuals a psychological
release from the anxieties of fear and uncertainty. This psychological
function, in turn, has a social impact insofar as it contributes to pattern-
maintenance. In addition, like other belief-systems, ideology also *may* be
functional for the integration of a society or subgroups within it. Some
shared cognitive definition of the social order is necessary for a division
of labor. Ideology may provide a common cognitive orientation toward
goals and means for their attainment, and a rationale for the division of
labor and the position of individuals and groups within it. At the same
time, ideology provides a common universe of ultimate values that enhances solidarity by overriding and, hence, subduing social conflicts
among individuals and subgroups in a system. Paralleling the function of
sacred objects, the abstract doctrine of ideology is symbolized in objects
and signs that serve as rallying points and collective representations for
those who endorse the ideology. Solidarity is periodically vitalized by
common ritual practices, and ideological founders and leaders are memo-
ralized and venerated. Flags, such as the "stars and stripes" or the "star
and crescent"; emblems, such as the eagle or the iron cross; signs, like the
swastika or the hammer and sickle; memorial dates, such as May Day or
the Fourth of July; or veneration of such "founding fathers" as George
Washington or Karl Marx—all perform integrative and pattern-maintenance functions for the ideology they represent.

Despite the frequent claim to legitimacy of an ideology on the grounds
of empiricism and rationality, there is often as strong an element of non-
rationality and mystique in ideology as in religion. Indeed, some ideologies, such as Nazism, are grounded in mystique and extol intuition and
revelation.[65] These tendencies emerge partly as a consequence of the
integrative and pattern-maintaining nature of ideology, which may lead

[63] See Martin A. Trow, "Small Business Men, Political Tolerance, and Support for
McCarthy," *American Journal of Sociology*, 64:270–282 (1958).

[64] See Daniel Bell (ed.), *The New American Right* (New York: Criterion Books,
Inc., 1955).

[65] For a brief discussion, see Alex Inkeles, "The Totalitarian Mystique: Some Impressions of the Dynamics of Totalitarian Society," in C. J. Friedrich, *Totalitarianism*
(Cambridge, Mass.: Harvard University Press, 1954).

to ideological distortion and oversimplification. In this sense, ideology may be disfunctional for the very purposes it may be alleged to serve.

In order to appeal to a wide and diversified source of support and to communicate rapidly and effectively, there is a strong demand to express an ideology in sloganizing oversimplification. Because an ideology frequently is conceived as the "true faith," there is a tendency to reductionism, in which all of the social order is interpreted in terms of the main root thesis of the ideology. Conflicting facts and harsh realities may be submerged or glossed over in favor of the ideological definitions of reality.[66] To protect the ideology against its vulnerabilities and strengthen its values in group solidarity, scapegoats may be created. In our own society, for example, one political official believes that a wave of prison riots sweeping the country must somehow be Communist-inspired, and another asserts that organized crime would be appreciably reduced by the deportation of aliens. The failure of an ideology to cope with human dilemmas or the tendency to produce unanticipated results inconsistent with doctrine may be rationalized by a resort to scapegoating that assures there is nothing wrong with the ideology, it is only this group or that category of people that holds back the millennium. Wall Street, the Jews, the capitalists, aliens, radicals, eggheads, and the like become a focus for the projection of hostilities and a source of solidarity as the ranks are closed against the common enemy.

IDEOLOGICAL GROUPINGS: COUNTERIDEOLOGY,
SOCIAL MOVEMENTS, PARTIES, AND NATION-STATES

There has not been much systematic work in the development of a typology embracing the variety of social groupings that express ideological orientations. However, there appear to be some ideological groupings that are in some ways the structural counterparts of the various religious groupings discussed earlier.

In contemporary life the nation-state probably represents the most em-

---

[66] The writings of Marx present a particularly interesting example of some of these tendencies, since he combined the dual roles of an ideological propagandist and a penetrating analyst of society. For a searching examination of some of the fundamental doctrines in capitalistic ideology consult Thurman W. Arnold, *The Folklore of Capitalism* (New Haven, Conn.: Yale University Press, 1937) or F. X. Sutton, S. E. Harris, C. Kaycen, and J. Tobin, *The American Business Creed* (Cambridge, Mass.: Harvard University Press, 1956). For a statement of the business ideology as voiced by one set of business leaders see National Association of Manufacturers, Economic Principles Commission, *The American Industrial Free Enterprise System, Its Nature and Growth* (2 vols.; New York: McGraw-Hill Book Company, Inc., 1946).

bracing ideological grouping. People are born into the state, ideological orientations are largely shaped by it, and individual loyalties are confined to it. Totalitarian states probably represent the most closed form of ideological organization at the national level. Attempts are made to structure all subgroups in terms of national ideology, and deviations or pluralistic tendencies are suppressed. The state determines the ideological basis of activities in the arts, the economy, the family, voluntary associations, and the like; and where religion is not suppressed, its secular implications are geared to state ideology. Within the nation, a variety of subgroups may arise that express differences concerning the national ideology or that transcend it.

The term "counterideology" has been used to suggest the nature of the ideological orientation of one such grouping.[67] This ideology expresses conflict with the larger society and justifies a pattern of deviant adaptation without attempting to alter the societal ideology. It is characteristic of deviant groups that covertly adapt without seeking to change institutionalized norms, in contrast to those who attempt to get their pattern of deviant adaptation institutionalized. This distinction was pointed out in Chapter 5 in the discussion of forms of deviance. J. Milton Yinger has elaborated, with some variation, the concept of counterideology, using the term "contraculture" and focusing specifically on the sociopsychological source of the belief-system.[68] According to Yinger, a contraculture expresses, as a primary element, conflict with the larger society, directly manifests the frustration and tension of people exposed to strain as a consequence of their position in the society, and arises as a consequence of interaction of the subgroup with the larger society. These elements of conflict, personality variables, and relationship to the larger culture are involved to some degree in all subcultures, but it is only when these are central to and necessary for the understanding of the normative system of the subgroup that we speak of a "contraculture." Such ideological orientations probably are most clearly represented by some types of delinquent gangs and criminal groups, and to some extent the pattern is found among groups of drug addicts and "beatniks."[69]

The "social movement" represents another kind of ideological orienta-

---

[67] Parsons, *The Social System*, p. 355. See also Harold D. Lasswell, who speaks of "countermores" in *World Politics and Personal Insecurity* (New York: McGraw-Hill Book Company, Inc., 1935), p. 64. No special term has been suggested to identify the groups that express a counterideology.

[68] J. Milton Yinger, "Contraculture and Subculture," *American Sociological Review*, 25:625–635 (1960).

[69] For a detailed analysis of the psychogenic origins of some delinquent groups, see Albert K. Cohen, *Delinquent Boys* (New York: The Free Press of Glencoe, Inc., 1955).

tion. In a social movement, there is an ideological break with the larger society, but the members of the movement seek to legitimize their value orientation. A social movement tends to operate within the broad outlines of the ideology of the larger society, but has its special interpretation of these values or of means for their realization. A further distinction sometimes is made between a reform and a revolutionary movement. In the former, change is attempted largely within the framework of existing ideology by appeal to those strategically and preferentially placed in the authority structure. In the latter, attempts are made to alter important elements of the existing ideology, conflict with authority may be sharp, and appeal is directed toward the exploited or the deprived that the ideology purports to serve.

Most social movements in the United States have been reform movements. These include such varied ideological orientations as those found in the Prohibition movement, which culminated in the Eighteenth Amendment, the Townsend movement for pensions for the aged, the diffuse and loosely organized "progressive" movement during the two or three decades prior to World War I, and a variety of farmer and labor movements.[70] Although Communism represents the prototype of contemporary revolutionary movements, it has never been successful as a social movement in the United States. There have been some forerunners of revolutionary or quasi-revolutionary movements among workers and to a lessor extent among farmers, however. The International Workingmen's Association or, as it was commonly known, the "First International," had a brief existence in the 1860's and 1870's, and a revolutionary orientation was revived somewhat in the 1900's in the Industrial Workers of the World. Among farmers, such movements as the Farmers' Alliance and the Populists, although relatively militant in their demands, were largely reform rather than revolutionary in orientation.

Because of the tenuous relation to the larger society of a group involved in a social movement, there is an intense need for the members to convince themselves and others, in terms of the larger value system, of the legitimacy of their ideological protests and the illegitimacy of what they attack. In order successfully to recruit members to the movement, this

---

[70] Alfred McClung Lee, "Techniques of Social Reform: An Analysis of the New Prohibition Drive," reprinted in Logan Wilson and William L. Kolb (eds.), *Sociological Analysis* (New York: Harcourt, Brace & World, Inc., 1949), discusses prohibition movements past and present. Hadley Cantril discusses the Townsend movement, as well as others, in *The Psychology of Social Movements* (New York: John Wiley & Sons, Inc., 1941). The history of some major agrarian and labor movements is related in Thomas H. Greer, *American Social Reform Movements* (Englewood Cliffs, N.J.: Prentice-Hall, Inc., 1949). For a general discussion, see Rudolf Heberle, *Social Movements* (New York: Appleton-Century-Crofts, Inc., 1951).

kind of ideology must maintain a delicate balance between its opposition to the *status quo* and its appeal to certain values of the larger society. Success, in turn, implies some fairly widespread dissatisfaction and deprivation on the part of the population involving both the disparate values of individuals and the collective values of society.[71]

Frequently, perhaps necessarily, the reform or revolutionary ideology is propounded by a "charismatic" leader. "Charisma" refers to qualities of a leader that set him apart from ordinary men in the eyes of followers so that he is treated as possessing superhuman or supernatural powers or as being endowed with specific and special powers or qualities.[72] Charisma is the quality of a leader that validates the ideology of the movement and the authority of leadership, develops a sense of duty on the part of the devotees, and lends a sense of mission to the movement. Hitler is perhaps the best example of charismatic leadership in the contemporary history of social movements.

Because of these very characteristics of social movements, particularly revolutionary movements, there is a tendency for the structure and ideology of the movement to alter as it gains ascendancy.[73] Utopian emphasis, necessary to *gain* power, tends to yield to the practical necessities of concession and compromise once power is achieved; and action tends to be based more on expediency and less on principle. Propaganda and recruitment become less urgent than consolidation and organization of authority and power. A stance of protest and rebellion gives way to one of protection of orthodoxy and suppression of protest in the form of counterrevolutionary or neorevolutionary movements. The Stalin period in the instrumentation of Communist ideology in the Soviet Union represents the kind of ruthless suppression that may follow a successful social movement. Once a group has ascended to power or authority, the possibility of realizing previously suppressed needs may give rise to a dilution of idealism, schisms over the "division of the spoils," and devotion to the realization of immediate and private needs, rather than to ideological

[71] For an analysis of a successful social movement, based on six hundred life stories of members of the National Socialist party, see Theodore Abel, *Why Hitler Came to Power* (Englewood Cliffs, N.J.: Prentice-Hall, Inc., 1939).

[72] See Max Weber's discussion of charisma in *Max Weber: The Theory of Social and Economic Organization* (trans. A. M. Henderson and Talcott Parsons; New York: Oxford University Press, 1947), pp. 358–386.

[73] See Weber, *op. cit.*, for a discussion of "the routinization of charisma." For discussion of "the adaptive transformation of revolutionary movements," with reference to Communism in the Soviet Union, see Parsons, *The Social System*, pp. 525–535. Seymour Lipset, *Agrarian Socialism* (Berkeley: University of California Press, 1950) describes the adaptation of the Canadian Commonwealth Federation after it took power in Saskatchewan, Canada.

ends. The transformation of charisma into a permanent bureaucratic structure, with the creation and appropriation on the part of individuals of differentiated positions and correspondingly differentiated advantages, may dissipate the solidarity and equalitarianism that was instrumental in bringing the movement to power. The downgrading of Stalin on the part of Khrushchev appears to reflect, at least in part, an attempt to substitute bureaucratic organization for the cult of the personal leader. In sum, when the "outs" become the "ins" they are faced with many of the problems of those they deposed. This is not to say, of course, that successful revolutionary movements do not change or alter the previous structure. However, they are somewhat in the same positions as sects that have become "respectable" in denominationalism or have developed into a church.

In addition to social movements and groups based on counter-ideologies, "parties" may serve as an ideological grouping of peoples of diverse interest and need within a society. Parties are ideological groupings that develop within a legal state with a representative government.[74] Although important ideological differences may exist among parties, their primary function is the realization of differentiated interest among members of the society through influence or control of its governing structure. Party affiliation is voluntary and membership is made up, roughly, of a central group of leaders and their staff who formulate policy and direct party affairs, active party members who form the core support of the party leadership, and the mass of the inactive electorate whose support is solicited primarily through their vote. Party leadership is likely to be less ideologically oriented than leadership of a social movement, and frequently their primary motivation centers around maintenance of power in office and the satisfaction of individual interests rather than the realization of a collective ideology. Ideological support of the electorate may be sought only insofar as it is necessary to ensure election.[75] In turn, ideological commitment to a party on the part of the electorate is likely to be considerably less than commitment to a counterideology or to a social movement.

Without unduly pressing the case, we may say that ideological groupings are in some ways analogous to religious groupings. Indeed, where the secular and religious orientations overlap, they may converge. In their emergence, recruitment, and transformation, cults have their parallel in

[74] Max Weber uses the term "parties" to include a variety of types, reserving the term "legal parties" for what we here have in mind. See Weber, *op. cit.*, pp. 407–412, for a brief discussion.

[75] For the classic statement of oligarchic tendencies in parties, see Robert Michels, *Political Parties* (New York: The Free Press of Glencoe, Inc., 1958).

groups based on counterideologies; sects, in social movements, particularly conversionist sects and revolutionary movements; parties, in denominations; and churches, in states, particularly totalitarian states.

SUMMARY

Religion may fruitfully be understood
as a mixture of theology, magic, fatalism, morality, activism, and passivity, the emphasis on those elements varying from religion to religion.
Theology is a set of cognitive beliefs based, in part, on supernaturalism,
which attempts to explain the "how" and "why" of the empirical and
superempirical worlds. Although religious explanations vary from culture
to culture, injustice, suffering, death, and the meaning of life seem to provide the bases for universal themes in all religions. Once institutionalized,
answers to such questions may be functional for pattern-maintenance and
integration. Different theological answers to those questions have different consequences for the society in which they are institutionalized. One
significant consequence is the development of either an activist or a
fatalistic orientation. Theology usually, although not always, provides the
basis for religious ethics or morality. With an increase in the division of
labor and the consequent differentiation and specialization, a problem
arises of integrating religious and secular norms; and the kinds of religious beliefs that are satisfying to different subgroups may become
differentiated.

Religious belief-systems emerge, achieve their identity, and are expressed and maintained in social groups. Church, sect, denomination, and
cult are four such groupings generally recognized by sociologists. Sects
seem to emerge in response to diffuse discontent with the social order and
as a consequence of strain experienced differentially within a society.
Over time, conversionist sects, particularly, are likely to develop into
denominations. The diversity, mobility, rapid change, and loose controls
of urban areas appear to be conducive to the development of cults, which
may evolve into more stable sects or denominations.

Ideologies are secular efforts to explain injustice, suffering, death, and
the meaning of life. Ideologies vary in their conception of the relation
between man and his social structure. "Liberal" ideologies tend to be
critical of the prevailing social structure and to justify changing it or
some aspect of it. "Conservative" ideologies tend to offer justifications for

the prevailing structure and to demand man's conformity to it. Recent investigations have pointed to the necessity of distinguishing between "political-economic" and "intellectual" dimensions. This distinction further differentiates the "liberal-conservative" dichotomy. Thus, four, rather than two, major ideological positions emerge. Economic and intellectual liberalism favors diversity and regards social structures as tools to be manipulated for collective ends. Economic liberalism plus intellectual conservatism favors collective responsibility but demands conformity and is intolerant of diversity. Economic conservatism plus intellectual liberalism favors self-reliance but supports diversity. Economic and intellectual conservatism espouses self-reliance while at the same time demanding conformity.

Like religion, ideology may be functional for pattern-maintenance and integration. Similarly, it may be disfunctional by distorting reality, tending toward reductionism, and creating scapegoats. Like religion, ideologies tend to be expressed in organized groups. Counterideological groups, social movements, parties, and nation-states are typical of the organized expression of ideologies.

II

SOCIAL STRATIFICATION

"**S**tratification" is a very general term referring to a hierarchy of inequality. Traditionally the term has been applied mostly to societal rather than to other types of social systems. Most theoretical analysis and empirical research have focused upon the historical development and consequences of stratification in various *societies*, past and present. This focus should not obscure the fact that stratification may be an aspect of the basic structure of subsystems as well. Very generally speaking, it appears that any group of some size and complexity involves some degree of stratification.

Although there is disagreement among analysts as to the precise basis of inequality in the stratification sense, there is general agreement that it involves "economic," prestige, and power differences or some combination of them.[1] Disagreement centers around such questions as to which one of these dimensions is central and which derivative, what the precise relationship is among them, and to what extent, if at all, stratification is to be conceived as either unidimensional or multidimensional.[2]

---

[1] Max Weber is generally credited with the articulation of this multidimensional approach. A variety of theoretical approaches to stratification analysis have been conveniently abstracted in Chap. 1 of Reinhard Bendix and Seymour Lipset (eds.), *Class, Status, and Power* (New York: The Free Press of Glencoe, Inc., 1953). For Weber's brief discussion, see pp. 63–75 of that chapter.

[2] A detailed discussion of the distinction among "economic," prestige, and power differences with reference to stratification research in American sociology may be found in Milton M. Gordon, *Social Class in American Sociology* (Durham, N.C.: Duke University Press, 1958).

DIMENSIONS OF STRATIFICATION

As we shall use the term, the "economic" dimension of stratification refers to the unequal distribution of the material products and productive labor services of a social system. Any human group is faced with the necessity of developing some structure for the production of goods and services necessary to sustain it. Regardless of how this is accomplished, there is the further problem of distributing among its members the goods and services produced. Whenever they are distributed unequally, one basis for stratification is established.

Economic inequality tends to foster significant differences among categories of people differentially positioned in an economic hierarchy. Life chances and opportunities to experience and participate in the social and cultural life of the group are directly affected. Differences in types and amounts of goods and services used may give rise to differences in attitudes and values. Rates of death, birth, and illness may be differentiated insofar as they are affected by economic factors. Conflicting interests may emerge, particularly where similar needs are differentially met as a consequence of economic inequalities. Opportunities to develop individual capacities and skills, to pursue personal interests, and to enjoy leisure may vary widely, depending on available economic resources. As these examples remind the reader—who probably needs no reminding—economic stratification may result in significant differences among categories of people in a society.

The "prestige" dimension of stratification refers to the differential *evaluation* of statuses ranked in a hierarchy. "Prestige" should be distinguished from "esteem." Prestige refers to the relative value ascribed to a status irrespective of who occupies it; esteem refers to the evaluation of performance in a status, irrespective of the status. For example, in our society, professional statuses have relatively high prestige, although our esteem for different professional people may vary considerably. Conversely, unskilled labor has little prestige, but a particular laborer may be held in high esteem because of the way in which he does his job.

People who share similar position in a prestige hierarchy tend to share a common "style of life," and both ascribed and voluntary associations are restricted largely to those of the same prestige category. Rank differences frequently are expressed in dress, manners, speech, consumption patterns, use of leisure, and the like. Family lineage, place of residence, association with the "right" people, membership in the "correct" club, and special attitudes of deference and "honor" are associated with position in the prestige hierarchy. The degree to which these differences are explicitly and formally structured may vary from society to society—from the relatively clear demarcations of rank associated with traditional European societies to the more loosely and informally structured patterns in our own.

The "power" dimension of stratification refers to the unequal distribution of the capacity to carry out, by whatever means, a desired course of action, despite the resistance of others and without having to take into account their needs. As should now be clear from previous chapters, this ability to procure something from someone else or to get someone else to accept something may take many forms. It may take the form of illegitimate coercion, of bargaining, of authority (that is, calling on the duty of "someone else"), or of loyalty (that is, calling on the love or cathexis of "someone else"). As we also have seen, only the last three are consistent with a stable social system. The first, illegitimate coercion, represents the absence of the shared culture that is the essence of integrated social action.

To some degree, power always is distributed unequally, for different statuses provide different means and opportunities for its exercise, whether legitimate or not. Furthermore, the necessity of resolving or preventing conflicts among group members and coordinating their activities can be carried out by only a few statuses even when these rights are institutionalized in authority. However, to the degree that power is institutionalized as authority, the power wielder is as bound by his authority as other people are bound by his decisions. For example, judges and congressmen are as bound by the definitions, restrictions, and pressures of their statuses as the litigants or taxpayers who must abide by their decisions.

It should be clear from these considerations that what must be meant by "inequalities of power" has something to do with the area of discretion open to different individuals.[3] The more constricted the decision-making power of an individual, the less is the power differential between him and those bound by his decision. The hierarchy of the power dimension of stratification, then, is a hierarchy of relative freedom from external controls, whether the external controls be legal-bureaucratic rules, restricted alternatives, abundant competitors, binding loyalties, or physical coercion.

Clearly, different positions in a hierarchy of power have different consequences for people just as does position in an economic or prestige hierarchy. The probabilities of carrying out a course of action, of achiev-

---

[3] Throughout this discussion the distinction between "degree" and "scope" of power should be kept in mind. "Degree of power" refers to the extent to which it may be expected that a given decision will be carried out and not vetoed, countermanded, or overridden. "Scope of power" refers to the extent to which enforceable decision making embraces a wide or a narrow range of activities.

ing a given goal, of being relatively immune to negative sanctions, and the like, are importantly conditioned by access to or control of the sources of power in the system. Furthermore, it is clear that whenever such a hierarchy exists, those at the top *can* use their power to secure for themselves top positions on the economic dimension of stratification; that is, they may secure vastly disproportionate shares in the total supply of goods and services. In precapitalistic or noncapitalistic societies governmental power positions may be, and frequently have been, used for this purpose. With the transfer, in capitalistic economies, of certain kinds of power or discretion from governmental officials to private individuals, the use of power (or at least the *legitimate* use of power) to augment one's own wealth and income has shifted to those who have decision-making autonomy with respect to private capital equipment or with respect to their own skills and capacities.

Ownership or control of scarce productive capital, without customary legal or particularistic restrictions on their use, gives people great bargaining power that they can use to command a large share of the national income. In the same way, ownership or control of scarce skills, talents, or capacities, without customary legal or particularistic restrictions on their use, gives people great bargaining power, usable in the same way. One important issue in stratification analysis, which we shall take up below, is whether it is possible, or the degree to which it is possible, to impose such restrictions on the control of scarce instruments and talents in such a way as to prevent their transformation into unequal shares in goods and services.

IS STRATIFICATION NECESSARY?

Men have long debated whether or not the inequalities of a stratification structure are necessary.[4] In functional terms, the question is essentially to what extent, if at all, inequality is "functionally essential" for the maintenance of a social system, particularly of the size of a whole society. Starting with the question as to what the function of stratification is, Kingsley Davis and Wilbert E. Moore conclude that inequalities in the form of unequal rewards have evolved as a mechanism to accomplish the universal necessity of filling efficiently the positions in the societal division

---

[4] The brief summaries of different positions reviewed here cannot hope to convey the analyses in all their detail and complexity, and the student is hopefully urged to pursue the analyses in detail in their original form. However, the broad outlines of the positions are given in the belief that a general orientation to the field of stratification should touch on the variety of theoretical approaches now available.

of labor and motivating effective role-playing.[5] Available rewards consist of economic incentives (those contributing to sustenance and comfort), prestige incentives (those contributing to psychological gratification), and esthetic incentives (those contributing to humor and diversion). The question then is raised concerning the determinants of unequal distribution of these rewards. This is answered in terms of functional importance and scarcity of personnel. Those statuses in the division of labor that are most essential for the maintenance of the system must receive sufficient reward so that less essential positions will not compete successfully for personnel. At the same time, people who are most qualified, by virtue of training and ability, must be motivated to fill the more essential statuses and to perform adequately in them. Hence the functionality of a differential reward system that embraces two dimensions of stratification we have mentioned—economic and prestige.

Bernard Barber and Talcott Parsons have developed a somewhat similar analysis of stratification.[6] Barber's central focus is upon the necessity of differential evaluation of positions in a division of labor. He points out that there is a universal necessity for social differentiation and evaluation. Any division of labor involves some differentiation of activities, and these differentiated activities must be differentially evaluated to assure that those necessary for group existence will be performed. It is such "functionally necessary" activities that are the basis for evaluation in the stratification system. Such statuses are evaluated in a rank hierarchy according to the amount of generalized and systematic knowledge necessary to fill them and the amount of "responsibility" (the number of people whose activities are controlled by the status) attached to the status.

In a more elaborate and complex analysis, Parsons also starts with the evaluative aspect of social stratification. He points out that the units of a system, both activities (statuses) and the way in which they are carried out (performances), simply are, and inevitably will always be, evaluated differentially by the members of a system. This evaluation is in accordance with the common values of the system. The bases or standards of evaluation are fourfold. First, activities and performances are evaluated in terms of their *effectiveness* in the attainment of goals. Second, they are evaluated in terms of the importance attached to the goal to which the

---

[5] This seminal and controversial article first appeared in the *American Sociological Review*, 10:242–249 (1945), and is reproduced in Logan Wilson and William L. Kolb (eds.), *Sociological Analysis* (New York: Harcourt, Brace & World, Inc., 1949), pp. 434–443. Also see Kingsley Davis, *Human Society* (New York: The Macmillan Company, 1949), Chap. 14.

[6] Bernard Barber, *Social Stratification* (New York: Harcourt, Brace & World, Inc., 1957), and Talcott Parsons, "A Revised Analytical Approach to the Theory of Social Stratification," in Bendix and Lipset, *op. cit.*, pp. 92–129.

activity or performance is directed. Third, they are evaluated in terms of their contribution to the solidarity and integration of other units in the system. Fourth, they are evaluated in terms of their contribution to pattern-maintenance. These standards seem to correspond to what Davis and Moore as well as Barber imply by functionally "important" or "essential" activities.[7]

Parsons further contends that there will tend to be a correspondence between the allocation of *facilities* (objects that are instrumental in the attainment of desired ends or goals) and *rewards* (objects of direct gratification) and the differential contribution that activities and performances make to the "system-functions" discussed above. In other words, status and role-performances that contribute most to the attainment of goals, that are oriented toward the most valued goals, that aid most in integrating the system and maintaining its pattern will not only be most highly evaluated; they will tend to have the greater control of facilities and receive the greater rewards. Put in broad terms, in a perfectly integrated system, there would be a perfect correspondence between the prestige accorded to a person, the facilities he controls, the rewards he gets, and the power he exercises *and* his qualifications to perform in a status, his actual performance in it, and his conformity to the institutionalized expectations (both in the use of facilities and in the exercise of power) of the status. However, perfection being not of this world, a person may "cash in" on some quality he possesses without a parallel performance, he may achieve a highly evaluated status illegitimately, or he may use facilities and rewards to secure prestige.

These three theories of stratification all focus on the function of inequality in a system of stratification.[8] Although they focus in the main on what we have called the prestige dimension of stratification, the back door and side windows are wide open for the power and economic dimensions to enter in. Parsons explicitly deals with power in his analysis, and the concepts "facilities" and "rewards" encompass the economic, broadly conceived. Barber seems to include power implicitly when he deals with

[7] The standards also correspond to Parsons' functional prerequisites of all social systems: adaptation, goal attainment, integration, and pattern-maintenance, respectively. See Talcott Parsons, Edward Shils, and Robert F. Bales, *Working Papers in the Theory of Action* (New York: The Free Press of Glencoe, Inc., 1953).

[8] Whether or not these inequalities are *necessary* is another question. Davis specifically states his interest in attempting to explain the existence of stratification as actually found in "all societies," leaving open, apparently, the question as to whether or not stratification is essential to social life. Clearly, the fact that a structure is found in all societies and is analyzed as being functional for some essential end does not necessarily imply that the structure is necessary. Barber and Parsons seem to be somewhat less explicit on this matter, although both assert the necessity of differential social evaluation.

the notion that rank is partially based on amount of "responsibility," and he explicitly deals with it as a stratified "influence" (power) structure distinct from but related to the structure of "social" (prestige) stratification. The economic he handles in much the same way as do the other two analysts, but with less emphasis upon it than Davis and Moore place. They imply the power dimension in their conception of "functionally important" activities, suggesting that one criterion of importance is "the degree to which other positions are dependent upon the one in question."[9]

This type of analytical approach to stratification represents a somewhat dominant focus in contemporary stratification theory in American sociology, but it is not without its critics. One problem arises around the concept of functional importance or essentiality. Functionally essential activities appear to refer specifically to economic, political, technological, religious, military, and other activities that are or may be essential for meeting the internal (integrative) and external (adaptive) problems of social existence. Granting that such activities or their functional equivalents somehow must be accomplished and, therefore, valued, and recognizing the fact that the exercise of authority must be differentially distributed in some degree, we must raise two fundamental questions.

First, within the wide variety of activities embraced by the notion of functional essentiality, is one more essential or important than another? Is the medical doctor more essential than the garbage collector, or the captain more essential than a member of his crew? In terms of functions (consequences), the answer would seem to be no. Their activities are equally essential. Why, then, is one more highly evaluated than another? This seems to be answered in terms of scarcity of personnel and the necessity of motivating scarce but needed talents into activities requiring specialized training and capacity. This, then, raises the second question.

In order to motivate scarce but needed talent, must economic and prestige rewards be distributed differentially? In other words, is it true that people always use the bargaining power their scarce skills (or equipment or qualities, for that matter) give them in order to augment their shares in the national income?[10] To consider these questions, let us distinguish between two issues. One concerns the nature of incentives necessary to motivate people to carry out adequately and conscientiously the obligations of a status once they are in it. The other concerns the incentives necessary to motivate them to *enter* a status, or to move from one

---

[9] Wilson and Kolb, *op. cit.*, n. 3, p. 436.

[10] A persistent critic of a positive answer to this question has been Melvin M. Tumin; see his "Some Principles of Stratification: A Critical Analysis," *American Sociological Review*, 18:387–394 (1953). See Kingsley Davis' reply in same issue, pp. 394–397.

status to another. We have discussed both issues in systematic detail in the chapters on socialization; here we shall only summarize the views that have been expressed by writers in the field of stratification.

So far as the first issue is concerned, it is clear that economic and prestige rewards by no means exhaust incentives for adequate role-playing, and a desire for esteem or a sense of duty based on internalized standards of status-rights and -obligations may motivate performance without the necessity of hierarchical distribution of rewards. Indeed, it could hardly be otherwise. If people's conscientiousness in carrying out the obligations of their statuses depended entirely—or even at all—on their hierarchical positions, it would necessarily follow that the lower the status, the less conscientious the performance. And, given the importance of low-ranking statuses, a social system could hardly survive if that were so. Moreover, as Tumin has pointed out, one needs only to look at an average stable family to see that duty, love, and esteem are quite sufficient motives to guarantee adequate role-performance. Again, studies of the collective farms (*kibbutzim*) of Israel give evidence of such structuring.[11] The *kibbutzim* represent a contemporary attempt to distribute economic rewards on the basis of the credo "from each according to his abilities, to each according to his need" and to minimize prestige ranking by such measures as job rotation, socialization, mechanization of farm labor, and the like. Students of the *kibbutzim* have found that they apparently have eliminated the economic dimension of stratification but have succeeded in only reducing the prestige dimension.[12] Both the family and the *kibbutzim* are of limited relevance, however, since they are integrated into and dependent on the larger society, which has a much greater differentiation of statuses and a more differentiated reward-system. Furthermore, to what extent the strong affectional ties and loyalties within the family, which seem to be an intrinsic possibility in primary groups generally, can be extended out into secondary groups the size of a whole society is a moot question. In a highly specialized division of labor, rotation of statuses seems impractical, as it appears to have been even in the less specialized, agriculturally based *kibbutzim*. The "leveling" of statuses by mechanization offers possibilities of reducing the distance between the

---

[11] Melvin Tumin, "Rewards and Task-Orientations," *American Sociological Review*, 20:419–423 (1955) and "Obstacles to Creativity," *ETC: A Review of General Semantics*, 11:261–271 (1954).

[12] See Richard D. Schwartz, "Functional Alternatives to Inequality," *American Sociological Review*, 20:424–430 (1955); Eva Rosenfeld, "Social Stratification in a 'Classless' Society," *American Sociological Review*, 16:766–774 (1951); and Melford E. Spiro, *Kibbutz: Venture in Utopia* (Cambridge, Mass.: Harvard University Press, 1956).

extremes of prestige difference and equalizing the knowledge and skill necessary to play various roles, but it has not yet eliminated such differences.[13]

These considerations strongly suggest that inequalities may be appreciably reduced, if not eliminated, as reward-systems for status-performance in societies as we now know them. There is, however, another consideration. Providing incentives for performance in a status is one thing; providing incentives for movement from one status to another is something else. If all positions are equally rewarding, how can people with scarce capacities be motivated to use them and to undergo the extended training necessary to fill positions requiring special talent and skills? If garbage collectors and physicians were paid the same amount, who would undergo the rigorous training and accept the burdensome hours required of the physician? One possible answer to this question is that people might be motivated to accept positions by incentives similar to those just discussed. For example, the credo that each person should strive to reach his maximum potential might be elevated to an ultimate value and viewed as an end in itself. On this basis, presumably anyone who was "doing his best" would receive his full measure of esteem and have a favorable self-conception regardless of his position, as long as his activities at least were not manifestly disfunctional for the system. Standards governing both activities and their performances would be set, but as long as anyone measured up to them in terms of his potential, he would be "rewarded," but no more or no less than anyone else who also met the standards. Thus, the individual with the capacity to be a physician would find that his rewards—material as well as psychic—were dependent on his doing so: being a garbage collector would cost him self-respect, esteem, *and* income, although an individual with the capacity to be a garbage collector would not experience those costs.

Whatever the incentives may be to get people to use their talents so that all "functionally essential" positions are filled in at least an adequate enough manner, one essential would be that positions requiring capacity and training are indeed available to those who have the capacity and are motivated to undergo the training. This is precisely what many present and past systems of stratification do not do. Any structure that distributes the ownership or control of economic facilities and economic and prestige rewards differentially creates the condition and certainly the incentive for a partial or total monopoly of the means for acquiring skills and knowledge. Thus, alleged "scarcity" in these respects may be a *conse-*

---

[13] For an intriguing discussion of this possibility, see Nelson N. Foote, "The Professionalization of Labor in Detroit," *American Journal of Sociology*, 58:371–379 (1953).

quence of the structure of stratification, rather than a "cause" of it. Although ultimately a biological matter, scarcity of talent and capacity is always relative to structures that permit their development and expression. When opportunities are distributed differentially, scarcity is induced, not inherent.[14] When opportunities are linked to family transmission (socialization, inheritance, and succession), the possibility that stratification can perform the function of placing the most-qualified persons where they are most needed becomes a dim prospect indeed. Measures developed to counter this situation—such as publicly sponsored education, inheritance taxation, graduated income tax, unions, the popular vote, respect for "honest labor," and the like—all operate in the direction of *equalizing* the economic, prestige, and power dimensions of stratification.

What, then, can we say of the "necessity" of stratification? About all that can be said concerning nonstratified mechanisms of incentive is that few, if any, societies past and present have relied upon them exclusively. One must be careful in drawing inferences from this fact. On the one hand, it does not mean that what was and is must be, else why attempt to develop structural alternatives to warfare or seek to eliminate poverty? On the other hand, the weight of historical and anthropological evidence should temper our conclusion that what is conceivable is probable or even possible.

Whatever the mechanisms of placement and motivation, current analyses of stratification agree that they must meet at least the following essential conditions. First, differential prestige must be awarded to those who conform to norms and those who deviate from them in ways judged to be disfunctional. Bank robbers can hardly be given the same prestige as doctors or garbage collectors, at least "in the long run." Second, some balance must be maintained between the more and the less functionally essential activities. Although a society may be able to sustain a limited number of full-time tiddlywink players, such activity must not compete successfully with other, more productive, activities. Third, at some level within the society and in some degree, talents and capacities must be allocated effectively enough for essential activities to be accomplished. This implies some matching of capacities, knowledge, and training to specialized activities. It does not imply that everyone in a society need be an eligible candidate for any activity, only that there be sufficient

---

[14] A case may be made for the proposition that any society always has more potential capacity than it can use, since, presumably, ability is distributed in the form of a bell-shaped normal probability curve that provides more than can be absorbed by the pyramidal structure of prestige and authority. For an incisive discussion of this dilemma, see Kurt H. Wolff (trans. and ed.), *The Sociology of George Simmel* (New York: The Free Press of Glencoe, Inc., 1950), pp. 300–303.

capacity within a category of people to provide adequate performance of status-obligations, even if that category of people should have a monopoly of those statuses. In other words, castelike inheritance of statuses need not be disfunctional; it is so only if the inheriting caste does not contain people with the appropriate capacities.

The degree of urgency of these structural imperatives is dependent on conditions both internal and external to the society or subsystem in question. For example, a small-scale society living at a subsistence level cannot very well sustain a large "leisure class," and a large society cannot have a very few families maintain a monopoly of recruitment to highly specialized statuses requiring special abilities. In the latter case, the odds against the few families' producing the appropriate skills are too great. In the same way, societies experiencing severe conflict or competition from other societies cannot very well afford the luxury of "idle hands" or the inefficiencies of differential opportunity. Furthermore, as internal and external changes take place, the "functional emphasis" of a society may be altered. During periods of extended warfare, warriors may be relatively more "essential" than merchant chiefs, or with a shift from an agricultural to an industrial economy, the skills and power base of the landowner may be displaced by the skills of the merchant and his power base. Older institutionalized arrangements for allocation to statuses in the division of labor become obsolete. New fields are open to those who by design or circumstance are strategically placed or who by special capacities of guile, strength, talent, or previous training are able to move into the new positions.

Thus, in an ultimate sense, the "prize must go to the strong"; that is, if a system is to survive, personnel must be allocated and motivated so as to meet the system's adaptive and integrative problems. Just what the "prize" *must* be is debatable, although so far man has relied principally on differential reward. And once the prize has been won, there has been a strong inclination to hold onto it and transmit it through the family or to the chosen few—until the next crisis of competition or technological innovation forces a change in the rules, and the prizes are once again thrown up for grabs.

THE INTERRELATIONSHIP OF THE DIMENSIONS OF STRATIFICATION

The economic, prestige, and power dimensions of stratification are analytically distinct but empirically interrelated. For example, maintenance of a style of life characteristic of a position of high prestige usually demands high income and wealth. Although wealth is not a prerequisite for high prestige, it is unlikely that prestige can be maintained, in the long run, without it. In the United States, for example, being a member of an old and distinguished family may confer prestige without great wealth, particularly at the local community level. It is doubtful, however, that this carries much weight in the larger society, and over several generations the "halo effect" of family prestige is likely to wear thin without the support of wealth and power that frequently accompany it. Conversely, the possession of wealth and high income, per se, is no guarantee of high rank. Privileged prestige groups tend to react against the claim to prestige solely on the basis of property, particularly "new" wealth, and to maintain their exclusiveness and separateness. Cash in hand does not ensure membership in the "400"; one is likely to remain just one of the zeros, at least for some time, in the absence of the "proper" source or age of wealth, the education, family lineage, and general life style that may be prerequisites for cashing in on prestige. At the same time, because high rank tends to confer a monopoly of the means for the acquisition of property, prestige groups are able to maintain their position somewhat immune to the threat of those lower in the rank system.

What has been said of the relationship of wealth and prestige applies equally to the relationship of power to both. For example, a political "boss" has considerable power in our society, but his rank is not likely to match his power. Prestige groups may "do business" with him, but exclude him from their circle of interactions when it comes to anything other than purely instrumental action. Where wealth and prestige are in conflict, both may compete for political power. Wealth may be restricted by political control; but, equally, the possession or control of scarce but valued goods and services has implications for the control of political power. At the same time, high position in the power structure, particularly formal office, may confer high prestige and frequently is accompanied by relative wealth.

STATUS CONSISTENCY

The terms status "consistency," "equilibrium," or "crystallization" have been used to identify those situations in which the dimensions of stratification coalesce, so that high position on one is reinforced by high position on the others.[15] The degree to which wealth, prestige, and power are

---

[15] See Émile Benoit-Smullyan, "Status, Status Types and Status Interrelationships," *American Sociological Review*, 9:151–161 (1944), and Pitirim A. Sorokin, *Society, Culture, and Personality* (New York: Harper & Brothers, 1947), pp. 289–294, for a theoretical and conceptual discussion.

in precarious balance may vary from system to system. Within any particular system, individuals, groups, or categories may rank high on one dimension of stratification and low on another. This presents an inconsistency in their status-sets that may have significant social and psychological consequences. The marginality produced by such structured inconsistency may lead to strain and resort to deviant adaptation. This complexity of the relationship among the dimensions of stratification may be further complicated by the presence of ethnic categories, based on race, nationality, religion, or a combination of them. Such social categories may be ranked on a prestige continuum and geared to corresponding positions on economic or power hierarchies. The Negro physician, the poorly educated but successful businessman, the immigrant who "makes his mark in the world," the "old line" family member who has lost his wealth, or the poor but "honored" intellectual may experience similar strain as a consequence of a lack of status-consistency. Thus, the extent of status-consistency or -inconsistency in a system is an important aspect of stratification analysis, quite apart from the consideration of the dimensions of stratification themselves.[16]

THE DIVISIONS IN THE STRATIFICATION STRUCTURE

The terms "stratum" and "class" have both been used to indicate divisions within the stratification structure. A good deal of confusion has arisen from the use of these terms, because they have meant one thing to one analyst and something else to another. The problem centers around the analyst's conception of stratification. On the one hand, the structure of stratification may be conceived as organized along a *continuum* of gradual differences, in terms of wealth, prestige, or power. From this point of view, the divisions in the stratification structure are arbitrarily drawn by the analyst, depending on his purposes and the dictates of the available data. For example, the annual income of the family heads of a community might be determined and drawn up on a continuum ranging from the lowest to the highest. Divisions of this stratified continuum could then be made by arbitrarily drawing lines through it. How many divisions are made would depend on how fine the analyst wishes to make his distinctions. He might use three, five, seven, or presumably any other num-

---

[16] For a sampling of studies directed to the consequences of status-inconsistency see Gerhard Lenski, "Status Crystallization: A Non-Vertical Dimension of Social Status," *American Sociological Review*, 19:405–413 (1954); Jack P. Gibbs and Walter T. Martin, "A Theory of Status Integration and Its Relationship to Suicide," *American Sociological Review*, 23:140–147 (1958); and B. B. Ringer and D. L. Sills, "Political Extremists in Iran," *Public Opinion Quarterly*, 16:689–701 (1952–53).

ber. Frequently this also is determined by how many people fall into a division. He might find that so few have an income of say, twenty to one hundred thousand dollars, that he would include all of them with those receiving "twenty thousand dollars or more." The same would be true of a prestige continuum based on the ranking of occupations, with boot-blacks at the bottom and Supreme Court justices at the top. The analysts then might choose to call such divisions "strata" or "classes," simply im-plying that a "division" represents a category of people who hold a rela-tively similar position on the continuum. (It should be noted, however, that this way of classifying people has the inevitable result that the bot-tom person in one division is really more like the top person in the next lower division than he is like the top person in "his own" division. Some members of a division, in other words, always have more in common with members of another division than with one another.) The analyst, pre-sumably, would be interested in classifying people into such divisions in order to determine what difference the difference makes, raising such questions as the relationship of position on the continuum to use of leisure time, consumption habits, political choice, religious orientation, educa-tional or occupational aspirations, and the like. However, he would hardly be doing more than this, and this brings us to "the other hand."

On the other hand, the structure of stratification may be conceived as a *hierarchy* of *discrete* categories rather than a continuum. (For con-venience we shall refer to this structure as a "discrete hierarchy.") This implies that the divisions in the stratification structure are not the sta-tistical constructs of the analyst, but, rather, emerge as a consequence of positional awareness, consciousness, or identification on the part of the population being studied. For example, it may be found that people in a community or society tend to identify with others similarly placed in the stratification structure, share a sense of cohesiveness or solidarity with them, are conscious of their position in the structure, and define their interests in different ways from that of others in different positions.

The prototype of this conception may be found in the classic writings of Karl Marx and Friedrich Engels, who focused on the economic dimen-sion of stratification (specifically, the relationship of people to the instru-ments of production) and viewed the historical process in terms of "class struggle."[17] Briefly put, they contended that history may be roughly di-vided into several historical periods, each of which had its characteristic mode of production that formed the basis of a class structure composed

[17] As always, for the serious student, the point of departure for the study of any theory is the author's own writings. The writings of Marx on the subject of "class" are fragmentary and scattered, but a good starting point is Karl Marx and Friedrich Engels, *Manifesto of the Communist Party* (New York: International Publishers Co., Inc., 1932). Bendix and Lipset present a convenient summary, *op. cit.*, pp. 26–35.

of the rulers and the oppressed. This division within society, based on a conflict of economic interest (and a wide range of contingent activities) between those who own or control the productive instruments and those who do not, provides the dynamics of class consciousness and ultimately class organization that leads to revolutionary overthrow of the ruling class. European social philosophers and scientists, although not necessarily embracing the Marxian formulation, traditionally have focused on the stratification of society in terms of a discrete hierarchy. They have used the term "class" to indicate the nature of this expression of stratification.[18]

Because the term "class" traditionally has been used to indicate a discrete hierarchy of stratification, it seems reasonable to reserve the term for this concept. The term "stratum" may then be applied to any one of the divisions made of a *continuum* of stratified differences involving economic, prestige, or power considerations. Whether class stratification does or does not exist in a society must be determined, not assumed. Similarly, the existence of a continuum of stratification in a society does not necessarily imply a class structure.

THE UNIT WITHIN A DIVISION OF STRATIFICATION

The family rather than the individual is treated as the unit of analysis within a division in the stratification structure of a society. As we noted in Chapter 7, placement is one of the transmission functions of the family. In all societies the wife is ascribed the position of her husband, and the children are ascribed the position of their parents. Why this should be so is not fully understood. However, the organization and functions of family systems as we know them would seem to demand it. The economic solidarity of the family system, the close, intimate associations of its members, the socialization of children, and the mutual identifications entailed in family relationships would seem to require the kind of solidarity that would be incompatible with gross stratification differences among family members.[19] The position of family members, then, is determined by the

[18] There is some variation in the use of this term even in the denotation of a discrete hierarchy. Marx contended that a class exists only when its members have organized collectively to pursue their common interests. Others have applied the term exclusively to modern Western industrial societies and have used the term "caste" to indicate the fixed and rigid stratification division in a society such as India, and the term "estate" to indicate the form of stratification of medieval Europe. Still others, Max Weber, for example, reserve the term "class" to indicate the kind of stratification that allegedly results from a market economy.

[19] This is not to say, of course, that differences in authority, control of the family economy, and prestige do not exist *within* the family. We are speaking of the relationship of family members to the stratification of the society.

adult head of the household. Movement from this position may be possible when children assume adult statuses; but even in this case, family membership strongly influences what happens. Familial organization perpetuates inequalities and, as we shall see, has an impact on mobility in the stratification system.

VARIATIONS IN STRATIFICATION STRUCTURES

Although apparently all societies have some degree of stratification, there are a number of differences among them. Precisely what occasions the differences is not well understood. One thing we can be sure of is that the structure of stratification is closely interlinked with other societal considerations, such as the organization of the economy, the stage of technological development, religious and ideological belief-systems, and the like. We shall only touch upon some of the major differences and briefly indicate some probable reasons for them where pertinent.

SHAPE OF THE STRATIFICATION STRUCTURE[20]

Shape refers to the proportion of the population in the various strata or classes of a society. Polar types might range from a shape approximating a triangle, with a small elite at the top and the vast mass of the population at the bottom, to a shape approximating a diamond, with the majority of the population in the middle and few at either the top or the bottom. Any structures that tended toward leveling of the economic, prestige, or power dimensions of stratification would favor the diamond shape—the extreme result of such leveling tendencies being to flatten the diamond into a narrow horizontal band. We might picture the major possibilities of stratifications shapes, then, as follows:

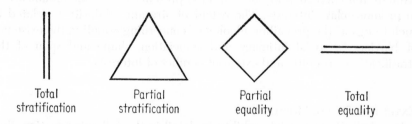

| Total stratification | Partial stratification | Partial equality | Total equality |

---

[20] Barber, *op. cit.*, pp. 87–93, has introduced the concepts of "shape" and "span" of stratification systems. Davis and Moore, *op. cit.*, contains a brief but cogent discussion of variations in stratification.

SPAN OF THE STRATIFICATION STRUCTURE

Span refers to the degree of difference in property and income, prestige, or power from the top to the bottom of the stratification structure. The span may remain constant while the shape changes. For example, there may continue to be a gap of several million dollars between the income of the top family and that of the bottom, but the proportion of total families receiving those extreme incomes may decrease, and the proportion of those in the middle increase. Thus, span and shape are different aspects of the structure of stratification.

FUNCTIONAL EMPHASIS

Functional emphasis should be distinguished from functional necessity. As we have seen, the latter refers to activities that are presumed to be essential for the existence of any society. In stratification analysis, functional emphasis refers to the relative value or significance attached to some functionally necessary activity by the members of a society. Depending on the prevailing belief-systems and the exigencies of external and internal problems of adaptation, such various activities as warfare, government, religion, production of goods, reproduction, and so forth, may be emphasized by the society in question. Thus, although both the production of goods and the justification of ultimate values may always be necessary, one society may overwhelmingly value the businessman over the priest, whereas another may reverse the emphasis.

DEGREE OF STRATUM SOLIDARITY

Societies may differ in the degree to which strata inequalities give rise to a class structure. Variation may be all the way from a simple awareness of difference that has no particular implications for a class system, to strongly felt class consciousness and the presence of specific organizations to promote class interests. The extent of stratum solidarity is related to such things as the prevailing ideologies concerning equality, the existence of barriers to social intimacy and association, shape and span of the stratification structure, and extent of conflict of interests.

EXTENT OF SOCIAL MOBILITY

We shall discuss social mobility in detail in the following section. Suffice it to say here that societies may vary in the degree of opportunity to move from one position to another in the structure of stratification.

SOCIAL MOBILITY

The analysis of social mobility among stratified statuses is a special application of the general problem of status-placement in social systems. As we have pointed out in Chapter 2, division of labor in a human social system is determined largely by culture rather than by biology. This results in the necessity of some mechanism for allocating people to statuses. Two central issues are raised in the consideration of mechanisms of status-allocation. First, if a system is to survive, its members must be allocated effectively enough so that its procurement and disposal needs are met. This means that statuses must be filled, in some degree, by the people comparatively best fitted to fill them by virtue of their talents and training. Second, the ratio of statuses to one another must be such that the system as a whole is able to meet its integrative and adaptive problems. This means that all system members cannot be Indian chiefs, nor can they all be technicians, religious functionaries, unskilled laborers, and so forth.

As a matter of fact, we find that societies vary widely in their mechanisms of placement in the stratification structure. The extent to which societies are structured so as to permit social mobility is one important way in which they vary. In stratification analysis, the term "social mobility" refers to the movement of individuals and categories of people from one to another position in the stratification structure. Pitirim A. Sorokin has made a useful distinction between vertical and horizontal mobility.[21] Vertical mobility refers to movement from one to another division in a discrete hierarchy of stratification. Horizontal mobility refers to movement *within* a division. The utility of this distinction lies in the fact that people may improve their stratum position without appreciably affecting their class position. For example, from the Marxian point of view, it would follow that any change in the income or occupations of workers would not affect their class position, since it would not alter their relationship to the instruments of production, and hence would have little effect on their class identity and consciousness. Whether or not this is true, of course, would have to be demonstrated in the empirical situation. However, it can readily be seen that in our own society a modest increase in income may not affect one's prestige position or a similar change in occupation may have little consequences for a person's style of life, life chances, or power position.

Any society may have a relatively open or closed system of stratifica-

[21] Pitirim A. Sorokin, *Social Mobility* (New York: Harper & Brothers, 1927), p. 133.

tion, but no society is completely open or closed. At one end of a continuum of social mobility stands a society such as India, where a caste system of stratification prevails that minimizes the possibility of movement. Caste membership is hereditary and fixed for life. Castes are strictly isolated socially, and traditionally caste is linked to occupational position and reinforced by religious belief. However, even here there is mobility among the several thousand castes and subcastes, although the movement is gradual and by a caste as a whole rather than on the part of individuals. At the other end of the continuum stands a society such as the United States. It is a relatively open society with considerably less status-consistency with respect to stratification dimensions than a society such as India. Yet the differential distribution of wealth, prestige, and power, coupled with the family structure and ethnic considerations, results in very significant differences in access to and use of the opportunity structure, even in the United States.

The fact that all societies have some mobility but none is completely open appears to be related to considerations we already have discussed. Differential rates of reproduction, change in functional emphasis occasioned by internal and external changes, possession of scarce but needed talents, noninstitutionalized use of power, and failure to eliminate completely economic competition may all operate in the direction of mobility, even in the most rigid caste system. The structure of the family, differential distribution of wealth, prestige, and power, the necessity of some stability and continuity in the structure of stratification, and the impossibility of accommodating all possible candidates for top positions work in the direction of inhibiting pure vertical mobility.

Familiarity with the open system in our own society should not obscure the fact that there may be certain advantages in a more closed system. The functionality of either type partly depends upon other structural features of the society and its historical position. A relatively closed system gives some assurance that all positions will be filled in their accustomed ratios, relieves people of the anxieties of competitive striving, and permits early socialization and training to position in the stratification structure. A relatively open system is more adaptable to social change, a broader base for recruitment is available, and a powerful incentive to excel may be institutionalized.

With these considerations in mind, we can turn to an examination of some of the determinants of mobility in any society. Two sets of factors should be distinguished: those that are variable for the individual or for categories of people, and those variable for the system as a whole. Those that may vary from person to person or among categories of people, irrespective of the degree of mobility in a society, include mobility resources, mobility skills, and mobility orientation. Mobility resources refer to variables conducive to mobility that are ascribed to or inherent in the individual, such as family wealth and "connections" or biologically determined abilities. Mobility skills include acquired capacities functional for upward mobility, such as manners, modes of speech, appropriate attitudes and values, learned skills, and the like. Finally, mobility orientation refers to levels of aspiration within the stratification structure that serve as points of motivation in competition for positions. These three variants would help to account for differences in upward or downward mobility among people within a stratum or class as well as differences among strata or classes.

Factors that vary from society to society and hence help to account for differences in extent of mobility among them include: the value placed on mobility by the society's general culture, differences in birth rates among the various divisions of the stratification structure, and shifts in the status-structure. Although high value placed on mobility probably does not operate independently of other considerations, it is an important, analytically distinct consideration. The importance of upward mobility in our society is a constant goad to increase equality of opportunity, whereas in India, traditionally, there has been little value basis for such change. Differential birth rates among the different divisions, of course, would have important implications for replacement. Any understaffed division would have to dip below or pull from above for new recruits. Shifts in the status-structure at the societal level would open up new statuses and close off others. Geographical exploration and colonization, a shift from an agricultural to an industrial society, an expanding economy that opens up new positions, or geographical changes that make old positions obsolete may all affect the positions that make up the structure of stratification.

Stratification in American Society

Stratification in modern Western societies differs in important respects from preceding stratification systems. Earlier systems were characterized by a much more clearly articulated, discrete hierarchy in the stratification system. Divisions in the system were more rigidly demarcated by differing standards of behavior, by dress, by education, and by general life styles that lent clear recognition to a person's place in the social hierarchy. Marked differences in prestige, in rights and obligations, and in power accompanied these tangible boundaries. Social distance was officially recognized among the divisions and reinforced by religious and ideological belief-systems. Interpersonal associations and intermarriage were more sharply limited to the individual's own division within the stratification structure.

By contrast, in Western society today the boundaries separating people in the stratification system are far less clear and sharp. The dimensions of wealth, prestige, and power are less tightly interwoven, and there is no legal and little ideological support of social classes. Equalitarian values officially deny the existence of a class structure, and, in principle, the highest positions are available to anyone who seeks them. Access to prestige symbols and life styles is based on bargaining power and vertical mobility is free of legal restriction.

Despite these very significant differences, there remains a clearly discernible system of stratification that is expressed in differences in wealth, prestige, and power. These differences, furthermore, are not merely individual in nature, but embrace categories of people and are perpetuated through the generations over time. They affect life chances, foster different life styles, and form the basis of prestige and power groupings.

Until rather recently, American sociologists had not given much attention to stratification in the United States. Beyond the writings of early American sociologists, the field lay relatively dormant until the early thirties.[22] With the appearance of the Lynds' studies of *Middletown*, a series of monographs on urban ecology emanating from The University of Chicago, and W. Lloyd Warner's beginning research on a frankly stratification-oriented study of a New England community, interest was rekindled.[23] The decade of the forties saw an acceleration of research, and by the mid-fifties the field of social stratification was firmly established in American sociology. This trend in development represents an interesting focus for the sociology of knowledge, for it seems likely that the depression of the thirties sparked the renewed interest that was so latent earlier—very probably as a consequence of strong equalitarian

[22] Charles H. Page discusses the writings of early American sociologists on class in *Class and American Sociology: From Ward to Ross* (New York: The Dial Press, Inc., 1940). The economist Thorstein Veblen presents a classic cultural and psychological treatment of class behavior in *The Theory of the Leisure Class* (New York: Modern Library, Inc., 1934).

[23] Robert S. Lynd and Helen Merrill Lynd, *Middletown* (New York: Harcourt, Brace & World, Inc., 1929) and *Middletown in Transition* (New York: Harcourt, Brace & World, Inc., 1937). Clifford R. Shaw, *Delinquency Areas* (Chicago: The University of Chicago Press, 1929), Ernest R. Mowrer, *Family Disorganization* (Chicago: The University of Chicago Press, 1927), and E. Franklin Frazier, *The Negro Family in Chicago* (Chicago: The University of Chicago Press, 1932) are representative of ecological studies. The research of Warner and associates did not appear in print until the early forties. Sorokin's previously cited analysis of social mobility should also be mentioned.

ideology, belief in unlimited social mobility, and rapidly rising standards of living.

Because of the characteristics of modern systems of stratification and the complexities and rapid social change of modern industrial society, American sociologists have been faced with many conceptual and research difficulties in the analysis of social stratification in their own society. As a consequence, analysts have approached the study of stratification from quite different points of view, have used terminology in a variety of different ways, and frequently have conducted research without adequate conceptual or theoretical formulation. In spite of these difficulties, a growing body of knowledge is developing concerning the nature and consequences of stratification in the United States.

THE ECONOMIC DIMENSION

Ours is a market economy that distributes economic goods and services on the bargaining principle. Most property can be transformed into money and is represented by money income and capital wealth. However, occupation rather than property ownership is the main source of income for the vast majority of the population. Ownership of productive property in the form of a small business, the tools of a craftsman, or a small farm increasingly has been displaced by employee status. About three quarters of the total national product takes the form of wages; the remainder flows from rents of lands and other resources, interest on capital assets, and profits. Hence, wages and salaries are a major differentiating index along the economic dimension of stratification in our society.

Private wealth figures in income primarily at the extreme upper end of the income continuum. Generally speaking, as the income continuum is ascended, the proportion of income from property ownership increases. According to a recent calculation, 1 percent of the population twenty years of age and over owned 26 percent of the tangible wealth in 1958.[24] The great bulk of this privately owned property takes the form of corporate wealth. Landownership, as such, plays a much less central role in economic stratification than it did in pre-industrial societies. Except for the brief period in the pre–Civil War South, it has not been the basis for the organization of a landed aristocracy. The outstanding characteristic of corporate wealth is its extreme concentration and the separation of

[24] Robert Lampman, "Changes in the Share of Wealth Held by Top Wealth Holders," *Occasional Paper No. 71* (New York: National Bureau of Economic Research, Inc., 1960), p. 21.

ownership of this wealth from its control. This has important implications for the distribution of power in the society, as we shall see later. As far as the distribution of income is concerned, this is one reason why most of the income of those at the top of the scale comes from corporate control or holdings. Some indication of actual ownership of corporate wealth is indicated by the fact that 1 percent of adults owned nearly 76 percent of the value of corporate stocks in 1953, despite the fact that the base of stockownership has broadened in recent years.[25]

For census purposes, income data are tabulated on the basis of families and unrelated individuals. In 1959, the median income of families and individuals was $5,300. This means that half of such groups and persons falls above and half below that figure on an income continuum. The average (arithmetic mean) income was $6,500. It is important to realize that the average is considerably higher than the median because there is a skewed distribution of income; a very few families receive extremely high incomes. According to the Bureau of Labor Statistics' "City Worker's Family Budget," a rough average of about $6,000 annual income would be necessary to "maintain a level of adequate living according to standards prevailing in large cities in the U.S. in recent years."[26] Making allowances for rural-urban and regional cost differences and the fact that individual as well as family incomes are included in the median just given, a considerable proportion of the population is unable to meet the modest standard set for the city worker.

Table 11–1 below summarizes recent statistics on income distribution in the United States. A glance at this table will indicate the skewed nature of income distribution and the considerable proportion of the population that receive relatively low incomes. For example, over a third of the families and individuals receive an income of $4,000 or less; and while 14 percent receive only 2 percent of the total income, 5 percent receive 21 percent.

Long-term trends in income distribution have been in the direction of a vast increase in real income for almost everyone, accompanied by a shorter workweek and a reduction of inequalities in the distribution of income.[27] In the first half of this century, real income has approximately doubled. At the same time, those at the very highest level of the income continuum decreased their share of the total income; those at the middle

---

[25] *Ibid.*, p. 26.

[26] Helen H. Lamale and Margaret S. Stotz, "The Interim City Worker's Family Budget," *Monthly Labor Review*, 83:785–808 (1960).

[27] It should be noted that the net gain in a shorter workweek has been appreciably offset by the increased entrance of married women into the labor force, so that the total work output of a family may not be appreciably reduced by a shorter workweek. The decrease in child labor, however, works in the direction of reduction of family work output.

TABLE 11–1

Distribution of Incomes of American Families and Individuals, 1959

INCOME CLASS	PERCENTAGE OF ALL FAMILIES AND INDIVIDUALS IN THIS CLASS	PERCENTAGE OF TOTAL INCOME RECEIVED BY FAMILIES AND INDIVIDUALS IN THIS CLASS	PERCENTAGE OF FAMILIES AND INDIVIDUALS IN THIS CLASS AND LOWER ONES	PERCENTAGE OF INCOME RECEIVED BY THIS CLASS AND LOWER ONES
Under $2,000	14	2	14	2
$ 2,000–$ 4,000	21	10	35	12
4,000– 6,000	23	18	58	30
6,000– 8,000	18	19	76	49
8,000– 10,000	10	14	86	63
10,000– 15,000	9	16	95	79
Over $15,000	5	21	100	100

SOURCE: Paul A. Samuelson, *Economics* (5th ed.; New York: McGraw-Hill Book Company, 1961), p. 113. Reprinted by permission of the publishers. Source of data from United States Department of Commerce.

increased, but those at the bottom made the major gain.[28] Graduated income and inheritance taxes somewhat reduce gross income differentials and the perpetuation of family wealth, although probably not as much as may be assumed. There are a number of ingenious ways of avoiding large tax payments, and a considerable amount of goods and services enjoyed by high-income persons may be written off as tax-deductible business expenses. On the other hand, social welfare and insurance programs have been instituted that partially protect the aged and the short-time unemployed against the extremes of economic deprivation.

Low-income categories are composed of people who occupy a number of somewhat interrelated statuses, including race, occupation, education, age, and sex. In addition, there are important regional differences. Farm labor as well as unskilled labor bulk large as sources of low income. Amount of income rises progressively from unskilled labor through semi-skilled and skilled labor and on up into the clerical, proprietary, managerial, and professional occupations. As a whole, Negroes earn much less than whites, and although this is largely due to their low occupational status, differentials remain within similar occupations and amounts of education because of discrimination. Rural income is lower than urban, is especially low in the South, and is lowest of all for rural Negroes. Inci-

---

[28] The following studies present a fairly consistent picture of this pattern: The Editors of *Fortune*, *The Changing American Market* (Garden City, N.Y.: Hanover House, 1955); Elizabeth Hoyt *et al.*, *American Income and Its Use* (New York: Harper & Brothers, 1954); and Herman P. Miller, *Income of the American People* (New York: John Wiley & Sons, Inc., 1955).

dentally, farm income is distributed even more unequally than nonfarm income. Women receive less income in wages and salary than men, and this strikes especially hard at households headed by women and at elderly widows.

There are significant differences among occupations in anticipated income during people's work history. Among manual occupations, particularly unskilled and semiskilled work, a relatively low plateau is reached early and continues at that level or decreases throughout the job history until retirement. In addition, such workers are more subject to periods of unemployment. Among white-collar occupations, particularly managerial and professional career lines, income rises progressively through successful business enterprise, consolidation of the professional career, or advancement up the bureaucratic hierarchy. The considerable differences in income spread out over a lifetime of work between the blue-collar and white-collar worker are perpetuated in retirement. As a consequence and despite social security legislation, a considerable proportion of aged people have insufficient resources to maintain adequate living standards.

THE PRESTIGE DIMENSION

Because equalitarian values are an important part of American culture and because our society is not built on a feudal base, the more obvious distinctions of title, dress, manners, and language that mark prestige lines in some other societies are not so clearly evident in our own. In addition, an abundant economy has made is possible for a wide sharing of many symbols of prestige that traditionally have divided prestige categories. On top of this, rapid social change, urbanization, and relatively active social mobility appear to have inhibited the formation of stable prestige groups or, as they are frequently called, "status groups"—groups of people holding relatively similar prestige positions in one another's view and interacting in an intimate and relatively closed social association.[29] Nevertheless, prestige differences do exist in our society and are accompanied by somewhat different life styles. Furthermore, particularly at the level of the small community, they appear to form the basis of some significant prestige group associations.

The most elaborate and extensive studies of prestige in the small community life of American society have been conducted by Professor W. Lloyd Warner and his associates. It should be emphasized that these studies were conducted in relatively small and homogeneous commu-

[29] Just as an economic continuum should be distinguished from a class hierarchy, a continuum of prestige should be distinguished from prestige groups. Prestige refers to a rank order based on a shared and differential evaluation of the activities of system members. Prestige groups of the order just mentioned may or many not develop as a consequence of prestige differences.

nities, with an established tradition and a social organization that had developed over a long period of time. For this reason, they cannot be said to reflect the urban metropolitan area. This, of course, is one of the shortcomings of these studies for the purpose of understanding the prestige hierarchy of the society as a whole. However, insofar as they reflect rank in older, small communities, they give us a picture of the prestige hierarchy of a segment of American society.[30]

An attempt was made in these studies to obtain the community prestige hierarchy from the people themselves—prestige, after all, is a shared, subjective evaluation lodged in the minds of community members. To discover the prestige hierarchy, analysts went into the community and by means of informants, who were interviewed at length, obtained information concerning the prestige structure of the community and the position of various families in that structure. To the extent that there was a high level of agreement among informants concerning the nature of the prestige categories and representative members of them, the "social class configurations" of the community were established. Once the basic prestige structure of the community was established in this way, analysts ultimately placed nearly all community members on the basis of a variety of prestige indicators that informants mentioned.[31]

As a result of his research, Warner contends that each of the communities he studied exhibited a discrete hierarchy of prestige groups, which he called "classes." These are viewed as discrete groups that reflect the

[30] Three different communities have been studied. One, known as "Yankee City," is located in New England and has been reported in the following volumes published by the Yale University Press, New Haven, Conn.: Vol. I, by W. Lloyd Warner and Paul S. Lunt, *The Social Life of a Modern Community* (1941); Vol. II, by the same authors, *The Status System of a Modern Community* (1942); Vol. III, by W. Lloyd Warner and Leo Srole, *The Social Systems of American Ethnic Groups* (1945); and Vol. IV, by W. Lloyd Warner and J. O. Low, *The Social System of the Modern Factory* (1947). The second study was of a southern community known as "Old City" and described in Allison Davis, Burleigh B. Gardner, and Mary R. Gardner, *Deep South: A Social-Anthropological Study of Caste and Class* (Chicago: The University of Chicago Press, 1941). The third was a study of a midwestern community called "Jonesville," reported in W. Lloyd Warner et al., *Democracy in Jonesville* (New York: Harper & Brothers, 1949). A study of the adolescents in this community was published separately in August B. Hollingshead, *Elmtown's Youth* (New York: John Wiley & Sons, Inc., 1949).

[31] This method of stratifying a population is known as Evaluated Participation and is described in W. Lloyd Warner et al., *Social Class in America: A Manual of Procedure for the Measurement of Social Status* (Chicago: Science Research Associates, 1949). See Ruth Rosner Kornhauser, "The Warner Approach to Social Stratification," in Bendix and Lipset, *op. cit.*, pp. 224–255, for a summary of Warner's work and the responses of his critics to his findings and methodology. A variation on this method, which makes use of a panel of community judges who rank families in accordance with prestige categories established by prior interviews, is described in Hollingshead, *Elmtown's Youth.*

way in which people think and feel about themselves and others in the community and, therefore, are not the statistical constructs of the researchers. Six "classes" were found to exist in two of the older communities and five in the third and more recently established community. These "classes" are called the upper-upper, lower-upper, upper-middle, lower-middle, upper-low, and lower-lower. The distinction between the upper-upper and lower-upper was not found in the third community; hence it exhibited only five levels. Each of these levels is distinguished by two major differences. Each has a relatively distinct style of life reflected in different tastes, attitudes and values, consumption habits, leisure-time activities, and the like. At the same time, social participation and intimate social interaction is limited largely to members of one's own prestige level. Thus, each "class" is conceived as a relatively closed clique, and an individual or family is viewed as a member of that "class" in which most of his intimate associations take place.

There is some question as to the extent to which these prestige groups actually represent the discrete, hierarchical characteristic ascribed to them. This arises from the fact that people positioned differently on the hierarchy perceive the prestige structure differently, and what the analysts end up with is a composite of these different views. Nevertheless, these studies do show significant differences in life styles and social participation at different levels in these communities. Another difficulty arises from the fact that the method of deriving the prestige levels is applicable only to small communities. This has been overcome partially by the construction of an objective index, known as the Index of Status Characteristics, that eliminates the necessity of relying directly on informants or community judges. Occupation, source of income, house type, and dwelling area are given different weights and each is ranked on a seven-point scale. People are then placed at prestige levels in accordance with the total score assigned them by this index.[32]

The problem of establishing an index of prestige for the society as a whole has been attacked primarily through the study of occupations. Alba Edwards of the Bureau of the Census has constructed a rough index consisting of a classification of occupations reported by the census. This index is based on the conception that each occupational category represents "a somewhat distinct standard of life, economically, and to a considerable extent, intellectually and socially."[33] These are the occupational

---

[32] The major difficulty with this index of prestige is that it combines in one score different things, so that no distinction can be made between the economic, prestige, and power dimensions of stratification nor can the interrelationships among them be studied.

[33] Alba E. Edwards, *Comparative Occupational Statistics for the United States,* 16th Census, 1940 (Washington, D.C.: Government Printing Office, 1943).

categories: professional persons; proprietors, managers and officials (in-cluding farm owners and tenants); clerks and kindred workers; skilled workers and foremen; semiskilled workers; and unskilled workers (includ-ing farm laborers). Edwards presents data that show a rough correlation between these "socioeconomic classes" and amount of income and educa-tion. Although Edwards simply assumed that these occupational cate-gories represent distinct standards of economic, intellectual, and social life and no direct index of prestige is given, subsequent research has indicated that occupations are ranked in a fashion approximating this hierarchy.

Probably the most methodologically refined and nationally representa-tive study of occupational rank was made in 1946 by the National Opinion Research Center (NORC). A representative sample of the American public was asked to rank ninety selected occupations on the basis of the "general standing" the job had in their "own personal opinion." The re-sults of this study were analyzed by C. C. North and P. K. Hatt, who found that there seemed to exist a prestige scale in the public mind, and that there was considerable consensus on the relative position of the various occupations on this scale.[34] Other studies have confirmed the general outlines of this prestige ranking, and there appears to be consid-erable stability in ranking of occupations over time.[35] In addition, there appears to be significant similarities in occupational ranking among indus-trial societies. Alex Inkeles and Peter H. Rossi compared the NORC find-ings with other studies made in Great Britain, New Zealand, Germany, Japan, and the Soviet Union. Although the samples and occupations were not precisely comparable, they found remarkable agreement among these foreign studies and between them and the American study.[36]

It is not surprising that occupation is a central consideration in prestige ranking in industrial societies. Family background and lineage, esthetic tastes, source of income, interpersonal associations, and the like are not so readily visible in the mass, urbanized society. At the same time, indus-trialization thrust occupational status to the forefront of life activities, differentiating and broadening the division of labor and consuming the energies and activities of man. In the process, very likely, prestige neces-sarily becomes geared to occupational status in any industrial society. The basis of this prestige seems to arise from two sources. First, occupation importantly determines shares in the national income, shares that de-

[34] National Opinion Research Center, "Jobs and Occupations: A Popular Evalua-tion," *Opinion News,* 9:3–13 (1947), and reprinted in Bendix and Lipset, *op. cit.*

[35] A review of some of these studies is contained in A. F. Davies, "Prestige of Occupations," *British Journal of Sociology,* 3:134–147 (1952).

[36] Alex Inkeles and Peter H. Rossi, "National Comparisons of Occupational Pres-tige," *American Journal of Sociology,* 61:329–339 (1956).

termine consumption possibilities and influence life styles. Occupation, then, is a rough rule-of-thumb index of a range of behavior that is used by people to rank one another. Second, occupation is a centrally valued activity, and people ascribe prestige directly to it on the basis of the functional significance and the skill, training, and knowledge they *believe* to be associated with it. Some empirical indication in support of this supposition is given when people are asked the basis of their occupational ranking. For example, the NORC study found the following responses in answer to the reason why an occupation was given high standing:

REASON	PERCENTAGE
The jobs pay so well	18
The service to humanity; they are essential jobs	16
Preparation requires much education, hard work, money	14
The jobs carry great social prestige	14
They require high moral standards, honesty, responsibility	9
The jobs require intelligence, ability	9
All other answers	20
	100

One important point to be understood is that although these prestige rankings we have reviewed are linked to income differences, they reflect more than simply differences in economic resources. In the occupational rankings there are significant differences in income within prestige categories, and the community studies show that source of income, family background, associates, and the like are given weight in prestige evaluation. This kind of independence of prestige from income (and occupation, as well) is nowhere better illustrated than in the role that race and nationality background play in prestige. Old Americans, primarily Northwestern Europeans, tend to downgrade newer immigrants from Southeastern Europe; and whites are likely to regard Negroes as their social inferiors, irrespective of their economic position. Endogamous patterns of interpersonal association and intermarriage tend to follow these prestige lines; and, in the case of race relations, are strongly supported by custom and even by law. Low economic position has accompanied low prestige among late immigrants and the American Negroes. However, prestige recognition has lagged behind economic success on the part of many nationality categories and particularly among the nonwhite races. A notable exception is found in the case of Orientals in the state of Hawaii.[37]

[37] The following references are particularly appropriate: Davis, Gardner, and Gardner, *op. cit.*, Warner and Srole, *op. cit.*, Elin L. Anderson, *We Americans* (Cambridge, Mass.: Harvard University Press, 1937); John Dollard, *Caste and Class in a Southern Town* (New York: Harper & Brothers, 1937), and Warner *et al.*, *Democracy in Jonesville.*

THE POWER DIMENSION

The structure of power in American society probably is the least understood and adequately researched dimension of stratification. This is a result both of the difficulty of obtaining the kind of data that would indicate the nature of the power structure and of the difficulties associated with unraveling the intricate interrelationships that make up our large complex society. The usual approach to the study of power is through analysis of economic and political structures. The former focuses on the ownership or control of natural resources and productive instruments; the latter, on control of the authority structure of government—power institutionalized in specialized statuses, bureaucratically organized, and possessed of a monopoly of physical coercion.

Our society grants the right of private ownership of material resources and productive instruments. The differences in income and prestige we have discussed partly reflect and partly support great differences in the distribution of such rights. As we have pointed out, vast proportions of property rights in our society take the form of corporate wealth. Just before World War II, corporations constituted about a half million of the 2 million business firms in the United States, but accounted for 90 percent of the manufacturing and distribution business.[38] Further concentration within corporations is demonstrated by the fact that, in 1947, 139 corporations held 47 percent of the manufacturing assets.[39] In 1957, ownership of publicly owned corporations was spread out over some 8.5 million shareholders.[40] However, really large holdings are owned by a relatively small number of persons, and most shareholders are concentrated in the upper reaches of the occupational and income hierarchies.

Clearly, the distribution of corporate ownership rights is such as to result in a separation of ownership from effective control. Who, then, controls the corporations? The answer is managers and large shareholders, including both private persons and large financial institutions. About the

[38] The pioneering study of corporation concentration is the work of Adolf A. Berle and Gardiner C. Means, reported in *The Modern Corporation and Private Property* (New York: The Macmillan Company, 1934). Later studies were made by the Temporary National Economic Committee and summarized by David Lynch, *The Concentration of Economic Power* (New York: Columbia University Press, 1946), Chaps. 5 and 6, from which the calculation above is abstracted.

[39] M. A. Adelman, "The Measurement of Industrial Concentration," *Review of Economics and Statistics*, 33:269–296 (1951).

[40] In addition there are an estimated 3 million owners of privately held stock, but they do not constitute a net addition to total stockholders, since many also hold public stock. See Victor Perlo, "'People's Capitalism' and Stock-Ownership," *American Economic Review*, 48:333–347 (1958).

best estimate we have of how many persons exercise this effective control is that 1,000 men held over half of the more than 3,000 positions on boards of directors of the 200 largest nonfinancial and 50 largest financial corporations in the United States in 1935.[41]

As far as control of the authority of government is concerned, access to statuses in the governmental structure, to informal means of control that may permit manipulation of the structure, and to the channels of communication and opinion making that may influence it is a major consideration. As far as the organization of power at the national level is concerned, the key question is to what extent those who control concentrated economic power constitute a homogeneous and tightly knit association and to what degree they can translate their economic power into political action.

So far no one has come up with an unequivocal answer to this question. Two models of national power have been evoked. One views power as relatively monolithic and in the hands of a few top decision makers, who by virtue of their strategic position in the economic and political structure have the power to make crucial decisions and see to it that they are enforced. The writings of the sociologist C. Wright Mills, with modification, approximate this model of the organization of power in our society.[42] He sees power as located in the vast and highly centralized domains of economic, political, and military organization. Decisions in each bear directly on decisions in the others, and this triangle of power is viewed as controlled by interlocking personnel who form a "power elite." This elite is composed of the top executors of corporate wealth, the "political directorate" located principally in the executive, and the "soldier-statesmen" in the upper echelons and the joint Chiefs of Staff of the military. Such unity as they have comes from the ease with which they move from pinnacle to pinnacle of power and their similarities of origin, experience, and life styles. Immediately below this elite are the middle levels of power in the Congress, in pressure groups, and in the upper economic classes within local communities. Although the top power elite is not viewed as fully united, nor its members as consciously aware of what they do, or joined in a conspiracy, they are taken to be the locus of decision making at the national level. Apparently Mills is not so directly concerned with the sheer concentration of power as with what he feels to be the irresponsibility of its use, the lack of rank-and-file participation in national decisions, and what he calls the "higher immorality" of the members of the elite group who wield the power.

[41] See the National Resources Committee report on "The Structure of Controls," in Bendix and Lipset, *op. cit.*, pp. 129–154.

[42] C. Wright Mills, *The Power Elite* (New York: Oxford University Press, 1956).

Opposing the extreme model of a monolithic power structure is that of a pluralistic structure. Power is seen as scattered among a wide variety of organizations embracing varied and often conflicting interests and possessing sufficient power to realize these interests only to the extent that the interests of other organizations are not impeded or denied. This model is approximated in the writings of the sociologist David Riesman.[43] According to Riesman, there is an amorphous distribution of power in America today. Whereas in the late 1800's, national power was held firmly in the hands of business leaders, today there exists "veto groups" in the form of organized associations of farm, professional, business, labor, religious, and minority persons that are capable of stopping aggressive moves on the part of anyone but can implement their own interest only within a narrow range constricted by the others. There are many "pyramids of power," each acting as a check on the other. In addition, he contends there is surprising restraint in the use of power by upper echelon members of these power units, apparently occasioned partly by the "other directed" character structure of segments of the American people.

Any conclusion concerning the hierarchy of power operations at the national level can only be an approximation, and it must be left to the reader to reach his own conclusions until more definitive studies are made. Granting that power is unequally distributed, there is no conclusive evidence as to the extent to which it is or is not controlled by an elite at the national level. The structure of power at the local community level is hardly better understood, although most of the studies made conclude that there is a power elite at the community level that makes the major decisions, formulates policy, and largely controls local politics.[44] The elite is composed of major business and industrial leaders who mobilize the support of lesser business and political figures and influence and ally themselves with local newspapers, lawyers, and officeholders. This power seems to be exercised rather informally and behind the scenes, is somewhat unplanned and uncoordinated, and is exercised primarily when the elite interests are threatened or demand strengthening. The conclusions seem to be, however, that this elite does win out in the contest where its interests are concerned. At the community as well as at the national level individual power frequently is consolidated through formal organizations, such as business and professional associations. More recently, the rise of labor unions and trade associations has added a new dimension, and at

[43] David Riesman, *The Lonely Crowd* (New Haven, Conn.: Yale University Press, 1950), pp. 242–255.

[44] Lynd and Lynd, *Middletown in Transition;* Floyd Hunter, *Community Power Structure* (Chapel Hill: University of North Carolina Press, 1953); and Hollingshead, *Elmtown's Youth.*

least one study has shown how these organizations may become a factor in altering traditional patterns of power in small communities.[45]

At least three basic questions remain unanswered in the study of the power hierarchy. First, to what extent do the interests of those who do hold areas of power coalesce so as to present a united power group?[46] Second, to what extent is it desirable and compatible with American values to bring under public control the range of decisions now left in the hands of strategically placed persons who are not institutionally responsible to the larger society? Third, to what extent do these decisions actually reflect the community's and the society's interests or simply the interests of the privileged decision makers, whether they are institutionally controlled or not? These are questions that, in part, involve more than purely sociological competence and are also the concerns of many other disciplines.

THE DIFFERENCE IT MAKES

As we have seen, the economic, prestige, and power dimensions of stratification at some points interweave and at others stand apart. It is this mixed characteristic of stratification that makes it difficult to take up the strand of the consequences of stratification and link them to the dimensions separately. In the discussion to follow, we shall comment briefly on some of the significant differences in our society that flow from stratification, indicating where we can the relative effects upon the life chances, life styles, and privileges that follow from the economic, prestige, and power differences.

Before a discussion of such evidence as we have on these associations, a word of caution is warranted. Aside from the fact that a correlation need not indicate a causal relationship, it should be noted that variables other than stratification frequently are involved in associated data. Mass data, especially, often are not corrected for these other variables, so that it is difficult to determine to what extent, if at all, stratification is the crucial variable in the relationship. This comment should be kept in mind in most of the relationships to be discussed below.

[45] James B. McKee, "Status and Power in the Industrial Community: A Comment on Drucker's Thesis," *American Journal of Sociology*, 58:364–370 (1953).

[46] See Raymond E. Wolfinger, "Reputation and Reality in the Study of 'Community Power,'" *American Sociological Review*, 25:636–644 (1960), for a searching critique of one type of research on power and many assumptions underlying research in this area.

PHYSICAL AND MENTAL HEALTH

One basic life chance, the opportunity to enjoy good health and long life, is associated with economic stratification. Studies made in the 1920's and 1930's suggest a pattern in which incidence of illness varies inversely and use of medical facilities varies directly with position in an income and occupational hierarchy.[47] Similarly, death rates appear to decrease and life expectancy at birth appears to increase as the income and occupation continuum is ascended.[48] These differentials very probably have decreased over time, however, with rapid advances in the medical field and improvements in the distribution of medical facilities.[49]

The relationships of economic position to physical health is repeated in mental health. Both amount and type of mental illness as well as extent and type of psychiatric treatment are differentiated by position in the stratification structure.[50] Generally speaking, neurosis seems to be higher in the upper reaches of the continuum, and the more severe psychoses higher in the lower reaches. Psychiatric treatment in private practice and private hospitals is greatest among the uppers. Psychotherapeutic treat-

[47] For example, see the National Health Survey of 1935–1936 based on a survey of over 2 million persons in eighty-one cities, reported in National Institute of Health, *National Health Survey, 1935–36* (Preliminary Reports, Sickness and Medical Care Series, Bulletin 2; Washington, D.C.: 1938). Also, Federal Security Agency, *Medical Care and Costs in Relation to Family Income* (2d ed.; Washington, D.C.: Government Printing Office, 1947). This study reports that families and individuals in 1941 with incomes between $5,000 and $10,000 received twice as many services from physicians and seven times as much service from hospitals as did those with incomes of less than $500.

[48] Jessamine Whitney, *Death Rates by Occupation, Based on Data of the U.S. Bureau of the Census, 1930* (New York: National Tuberculosis Association, 1934), p. 30. Albert J. Mayer and Philip Hauser, "Class Differentials in Expectation of Life at Birth," reprinted in Bendix and Lipset, *op. cit.*, pp. 281–284.

[49] For a recent study, see Richard F. Tomasson, "Patterns of Negro-White Differential Mortality, 1930–1957," *Milbank Memorial Fund Quarterly*, 38:362–386 (1960). Also see Mayer and Hauser, *op. cit.* For two recent local studies that show little relationship between illness and economic position, see Katherine B. Laughton *et al.*, "Socio-Economic Status and Illness," *Milbank Memorial Fund Quarterly*, 36:46–57 (1958) and S. Graham, "Socio-Economic Status, Illness, and the Use of Medical Services," *Milbank Memorial Fund Quarterly*, 35:58–66 (1947).

[50] The pioneer work of R. E. L. Faris and H. W. Dunham, reported in their *Mental Disorders in Urban Areas* (Chicago: The University of Chicago Press, 1938), gives an indication of the ecological and, inferentially, the economic distribution of mental illness in urban centers. For occupational distributions see, for example, Robert E. Clark, "Psychoses, Income, and Occupational Prestige," *American Journal of Sociology*, 54:433–440 (1949).

ment methods are most frequent among the uppers; organic treatment increases among the lowers; and straight custodial care is highest among the lowest placed persons.[51]

These patterns may be interpreted in either biological-genetic or sociocultural terms or both. The straight biological-genetic interpretation would hypothesize that the biologically less fit, as manifested in physical and mental health, tend to "drift" toward the lower end of the stratification continuum and there perpetuate themselves. However, this cannot be the only consideration (perhaps not even a major one), since, at the very least, social and cultural factors appear to play a role in upgrading health and longevity over time among those possessing few economic resources.

In addition, differences in disease rates seem to be accounted for largely by acute infectious diseases and by injuries, which are known to be importantly affected by dangerous occupations that lead to injury or poisoning, differences in sanitary facilities and usages, diet, and the like. Furthermore, availability of medical care and early diagnosis and treatment, both associated with economic resources, are instrumental in maintaining health and extending longevity.

Both life chances and life styles play a role in these considerations, the former in providing resources for fostering health and obtaining medical care; the latter, in structuring attitudes and values that induce concern over illness, influence knowledge about medical care, and affect dietary habits and general health practices.

As far as mental health is concerned, stratification differences in socialization and the kind and amount of strain experienced may be significant. Using the terms "upper" and "lower" very generally, we find some evidence suggesting that the "uppers" are more likely to be socialized to a pattern resulting in repressive tendencies and rigid conformity that, under conditions of frustration, are turned inward in feelings of self-guilt, shame, and anxiety. On the other hand, the "lowers" seem to be more socialized to a pattern of overt expression of frustration in rebelliousness or withdrawal. At the same time, the "uppers" may be more exposed culturally to strains centering around status-anxiety, mobility striving, and conformity, whereas the lowers may be more exposed to situations of severe crisis and deprivation as well as social isolation, or to the difficul-

---

[51] For a recent and carefully carried out research that supports and extends earlier studies see A. B. Hollingshead and F. G. Redlich, *Social Class and Mental Illness* (New York: John Wiley & Sons, Inc., 1958). Also see T. Rennie, L. Srole, M. Opler, and T. Langner, "Urban Life and Mental Health," *American Journal of Psychiatry*, 113:831–836 (1956–57). The former reports a study in New Haven, Conn.; the latter, in New York City.

ties of finding a meaningful and purposeful existence.[52] In addition, occupational hazards, life styles, or dietary habits may expose them to injury, poisoning, or disease that damage the brain and are more likely to be expressed in psychoses than in neuroses. Finally, differences in amount and kind of treatment may affect early diagnosis and effective therapy, so that neurotic symptoms are "nipped in the bud" among the uppers before these symptoms develop into the more severe psychoses.

MARRIAGE AND FAMILY

In Chapter 7 we indicated some of the stratification patterns as they are expressed in marriage, family, and kinship. Briefly put, we found that marriage tends to be endogamous by income, occupational, and educational categories; rates of divorce seem to be inversely correlated with these categories; fertility rates are also inversely correlated; and to some extent the authority structure of the family is differentiated by stratification position. There remains one crucial area for more extended discussion, and that is concerned with socialization.

A number of studies based on a variety of stratification indexes suggest a pattern of differential child-rearing practices among strata.[53] These practices center around such considerations as amount of permissiveness, extent of supervision of activities, regularity and consistency of training, control and expression of aggression, goal orientations, and sources of social and psychological gratification. In general, differences in strata are such that it might be expected that those in the middle range, in contrast with those in the lower reaches, are more likely to develop a personality and character structure involving status-anxiety, socially acceptable expression of aggression, strong mobility orientation, deferred gratification patterns, conformity, persistence, strong superego, and the like. However,

[52] A report on an intensive study of fifty cases selected from Class III and Class V of the New Haven research previously cited indicates this sort of pattern. See Jerome K. Myers and Bertram H. Roberts, *Family and Class Dynamics in Mental Health* (New York: John Wiley & Sons, Inc., 1959) and consult footnotes 9 and 39 of Chap. 1 for related studies too extensive to indicate here. The interpretation of data on suicide and homicide set forth by Andrew F. Henry and James F. Short, Jr., in *Suicide and Homicide* (New York: The Free Press of Glencoe, Inc., 1954) is also germane. Relatively high rates of suicide and low rates of homicide for the "uppers" and the reverse for the "lowers" is viewed as a tendency for the former to turn aggression inwardly and the latter to turn it outwardly.

[53] These studies have focused primarily on middle and lower strata. See, for example, Allison Davis and Robert J. Havighurst, *Father of the Man* (Boston: Houghton Mifflin Company, 1947) for a general discussion.

it is one thing to demonstrate the existence of differences in child-rearing practices; it is another to demonstrate that these differences result in the personality and character traits ascribed to them. Most studies only infer the difference from a study of the practices.

As a matter of fact, a number of studies have found differences of the order mentioned above.[54] These studies have focused on attitudes, values, and behavior patterns, rather than on the socialization processes themselves. The problem here is to determine to what extent, if at all, these attitudes and behavioral patterns are manifestations of personality variables or simply a response to the differentiated statuses involved in the stratification structure.[55] Different personalities may conform to the same statuses and, conversely, similar personalities may conform adequately to different statuses. Perhaps the most that can be said at present is that some significant differences of attitude, value, and behavior have been indicated, and that these differences have important implications for a range of social activities and relationships.

RELIGION

In our discussion of religious belief systems in Chapter 10 we described major types of religious groupings and indicated some clues as to their membership. As far as the church type is concerned, the Roman Catholic Church in American society draws a greater proportion of its membership from the lower end of the stratification continuum than do the Protestant denominations, with the single exception of the Baptists. This appears to be largely a consequence of the late immigration of peoples from Catholic countries. To what extent Weber's thesis concerning the interplay of Protestantism and capitalism, as discussed in the chapters on industrialism and science, may have played a role is difficult to determine. It seems unlikely that it is an important consideration at this time in our society.

[54] See, for example, Herbert Hyman, "The Value Systems of Different Classes: A Social Psychological Contribution to the Analysis of Stratification," in Bendix and Lipset, *op. cit.*, pp. 426–442; Genevieve Knupfer's summary of a number of studies in "Portrait of the Underdog," in *Public Opinion Quarterly*, 11:103–114 (1947); Louis Schnieder and Sverre Lysgard, "The Deferred Gratification Pattern: A Preliminary Study," *American Sociological Review*, 18:142–149 (1953); and W. Lloyd Warner and James C. Abegglen, *Big Business Leaders in America* (New York: Harper & Brothers, 1955), Chaps. 4 and 5.

[55] For two studies that derive personality differences from psychological tests rather than from inference, see Bernard C. Rosen, "The Achievement Syndrome: A Psychocultural Dimension of Social Stratification," *American Sociological Review*, 21:203–211 (1956) and the British study by B. M. Spinley, *The Deprived and the Privileged* (London: Routledge and Kegan Paul, Ltd., 1953).

Among Protestant denominations, the Episcopal, Congregational, and Presbyterian have the highest proportions from the upper strata. Sects and cults have a heavy representation among the poorer economic strata. The heavy representation in the Baptist denomination seems to be accountable in terms of the southern Negro wing of the Baptist Church.[56] Such differentiation as exists among Jews seems to be that the uppers are more likely to belong to the Reformed or Conservative denominations and the lowers to the Orthodox synagogues.

It should be stressed that these various religious groupings draw members from the total range of the stratification continuum. The differences are differences in tendencies and trends and probably indicate a combination of differences in life chances (different economic demands made by religious denominations), life styles (differences in education, communication, and expression), and exposure to strain (differences in isolation, deprivation, and marginality). In addition, religious membership may serve as a symbol of prestige position for some people, or a way of belonging to social groups of high prestige. In such instances, social mobility may be accompanied by change in denominational affiliation.

SOCIAL PARTICIPATION

In our discussion of prestige we gave some indication of the extent to which interpersonal relationships correlate with stratification position, and certainly the geographical distributions of people according to ability to secure housing would tend to reinforce endogamous patterns as a matter of sheer propinquity. Beyond this, however, there is indication that membership in voluntary and other types of formal associations are differentiated by strata. In the public schools, recognition of strata-based differences seems to start relatively early, and cliques develop from them that extend on through high school. Differences have been found in the kinds of recreation and leisure-time activity engaged in, the amount of participation in extracurricular activities, school office holding, formal organization membership such as Scouting and the "Y," and the like.[57] This

---

[56] These generalizations are taken from both national and local studies. See Liston Pope, "Religion and the Class Structure," *Annals of the American Academy of Political and Social Science*, 256:84–91 (1948) and Herbert W. Schneider, *Religion in 20th Century America* (Cambridge, Mass.: Harvard University Press, 1952) for national sample data. For a local study in Los Angeles, see Thomas F. Hoult, "Economic Class Consciousness in American Protestantism," *American Sociological Review*, 15:97–100 (1950); see also Louis Bultena, "Church Membership and Church Attendance in Madison, Wisconsin," *American Sociological Review*, 14:384–389 (1949).

[57] Celia Burns Stendler, *Children of Brasstown* (Urbana: University of Illinois Press, 1949) discusses these patterns among grammar school children. Hollingshead, *Elmtown's Youth*, describes the pattern in high school.

pattern is repeated in adult life. Middle- and upper-strata adults participate in and hold office in more voluntary associations, belong to a greater
variety of such associations, and show a higher degree of participation
and involvement in the community than do the lower-strata adults.[58]

Again, such differences as these appear to express differences in economic resources and life styles. Organizational membership also has prestige value in symbolically validating one's position. In addition, a wide
variety of voluntary associations have implications for the consolidation
of power and for the cementing of interpersonal relationships that may be
used instrumentally. Strategically placed community organizations that
are relatively closed to the nonprivileged compound and perpetuate the
latters' disadvantage. This is particularly true where racial, religious, or
ethnic lines also are drawn.

LIFE SATISFACTION

On the basis of much of what has been said thus far concerning stratification in our society, it might be expected that differences in life satisfaction would be expressed by the various strata. Although such a subjective and diffuse feeling is difficult to quantify and measure precisely, a
number of studies have shown that those in the lower strata express less
satisfaction than those in the upper. In fact, a wide range of these studies
show that job satisfaction increases up the occupational continuum.[59]
This is not simply, or even most importantly, a matter of differences in
income. It involves the nature of the work itself and the extent to which
the job is routinized, as well as the extent to which it permits involvement
in decision making, offers opportunities to "get ahead," permits a sense of
accomplishment and personal involvement, offers security of employment,
and so on. This suggests that, although higher wages may offer compensa-

---

[58] See, for example, Mirra Komarovsky, "The Voluntary Associations of Urban
Dwellers," *American Sociological Review*, 11:686–698 (1946) and Leonard Reissman,
"Class, Leisure, and Social Participation," *American Sociological Review*, 19:76–84
(1954).

[59] See, for example, Donald E. Super, "Occupational Level and Job Satisfaction,"
Journal of Applied Psychology, 23:547–563 (1939) and Daniel Katz's general discus-
sion, "Satisfactions and Deprivations in Industrial Life," in Arthur Kornhauser *et al.*
(eds.), *Industrial Conflict* (New York: McGraw-Hill Book Company, Inc., 1954),
pp. 86–106. For an excellent study of blue-collar workers, see Lloyd G. Reynolds and
Joseph Shister, *Job Horizons: A Study of Job Satisfaction and Labor Mobility* (New
York: Harper & Brothers, 1949). For an analysis of the white-color workers, see
Nancy C. Morse, *Satisfactions in the White-Collar Job* (Ann Arbor: Survey Research
Center, Institute for Social Research, University of Michigan, 1953).

tory sources of satisfaction, alienation of manual workers may not be entirely eliminated by increasing their share in the national income. More general sources of differentials in life satisfaction involve the extent to which people feel they are getting out of life what they should and that they and their children have the opportunities they should. Such research as we have in this area indicates that the lowers are considerably more dissatisfied in these respects than the uppers.[60]

To the extent that these expressed opinions are deeply felt and are a central consideration, it might be expected that they would have significant implications for understanding a wide range of contingent attitudes and behavioral responses. Their implications for various types of deviant adaptation should be clear from previous discussions. Two areas of attitude in which they might be expressed are discussed directly below.

ECONOMIC AND POLITICAL ATTITUDES

It might be expected that the more relatively satisfied would be more content with the *status quo* than the less satisfied. As conformity to the *status quo* is expressed in attitudes toward the prevailing economy, this seems to be the case. The lowers seem to favor more government intervention in the economy, more equal distribution of wealth and income, more government ownership of business and industry, strong labor unions, and the like.[61] Generally speaking, the most extreme attitudes are expressed at the terminal ends of a stratification continuum, but the attitudes seem to be more firmly held and more consistently shared by those at the upper end. More of the respondents among the lowers in these studies say they "don't know" or are uncertain about economic issues, and they are less likely to present a solid front. However, there is some indication that organized worker movements, such as unions and trade associations, more nearly approximate the uppers in their solidarity and more extreme position. Those in the middle range take an intermediate position.

These differences concern economic ideology, largely. Beyond the

[60] For an early local study of Chicago, see Arthur W. Kornhauser, "Analysis of 'Class Structure' of Contemporary American Society—Psychological Basis of Class Divisions," in G. W. Hartmann and T. M. Newcomb (eds.), *Industrial Conflict* (New York: Holt, Rinehart and Winston, Inc., 1939). For a later study of a national sample, see Richard Centers, *The Psychology of Social Classes* (Princeton, N.J.: Princeton University Press, 1949).

[61] The research of Kornhauser and Centers cited in the previous footnote gives evidence of this pattern. Also see attitudes toward corporate property in the study by A. W. Jones, *Life, Liberty, and Property* (Philadelphia: J. B. Lippincott Company, 1941).

matter of the role of government in controlling the economy, political questions are not so sharply differentiated. As we pointed out in the chapter on political ideology, the terms "conservative" and "liberal" embrace a rather wide range of attitudes, and not all are caught up in studies of attitudes concerning the economy. Furthermore, political action is concerned with external adaptation as well as internal integration. Attitudes concerning foreign policy, international relationships, and the like may not be differentiated by position on the continuum. Recent studies seem to indicate that the lowers tend to be more authoritarian and less "liberal" in their attitudes toward civil rights and minority groups. Caution is warranted in interpretation of these data, however. "Working class" movements in Europe and America have shown little notable tendency in this direction, possibly because leadership, guidance, and direction have been influenced by intellectuals who have played an ideological role in such movements.

In the United States, the two-party system has been and is the major mechanism for the expression of ideology in the political arena. Studies of voting behavior indicate two trends that are strata-linked. First, people in the lower strata participate less in political action and vote less than those in the middle and upper. Apparently this is due to a number of factors related to their structural position, such as exposure to political processes, visibility of governmental action, contact with political office and organizations, social pressure to vote, and so forth.[62] Second, a greater proportion of the lowers tend to vote for the Democratic party; and a greater proportion of the uppers, for the Republican party.[63] Paralleling economic attitudes, the uppers seem to express more uniform party preference than the lowers. This pattern, of course, varies over time and is differentiated by ethnicity and by rural-urban, regional, and sex differences.

In addition, status-inconsistency appears to result in alternative patterns that cut across the main pattern. Some studies have shown that inconsistencies in status-set, as indicated by education, income, ethnicity, and occupation, motivate toward a more liberal economic attitude and

[62] For a detailed analysis of factors affecting voting see, Seymour Lipset *et al.*, "The Psychology of Voting: An Analysis of Political Behavior," in Gardner Lindzey (ed.), *Handbook of Social Psychology* (Reading, Mass.: Addison-Wesley Publishing Company, 1954), Vol. II, Chap. 30.

[63] A wide variety of studies conducted over the past thirty years or so indicate this pattern. See P. E. Davidson and H. D. Anderson, *Ballots and the Democratic Class Struggle* (Stanford, Calif.: Stanford University Press, 1943); B. R. Bereleson *et al.*, *Voting: A Study of Opinion Formation in a Presidential Campaign* (Chicago: The University of Chicago Press, 1955); and Paul F. Lazarsfeld *et al.*, *The People's Choice* (2d ed.; New York: Columbia University Press, 1949).

registers in support for the Democratic party. More speculative analysis has suggested, also, that status-inconsistency may be registered in a reactionary or a "pseudoconservative" ideology. The former response seems to be in the direction of opening up opportunity and leveling ethnic prestige differences by governmental intervention; the latter, in the direction of consolidating and reinforcing a prestige position by attacking authority figures and downgrading members of out-groups.[64]

SOCIAL MOBILITY

In our earlier theoretical discussion of social mobility we pointed out that the extent of mobility in any society is determined by the ideology governing its desirability, the availability of statuses at any given time, and shifts in the status-structure over time. All three of these factors operate in our society in favor of a relatively open system of stratification. Credoes in support of freedom, equality, self-reliance, and competition tend to support a structure within which mobility is valued and fostered. Strata-differentiated birth rates demand recruitment from below to some extent. Industrialization has altered the occupational structure in the direction of increasing the number of positions in the upper end of the stratification continuum and decreasing those in the lower end. One additional factor should be mentioned. In our society, there has been a steady influx of immigrants, most of whom entered at the bottom of the stratification continuum. This probably accelerated the upward movement of the native-born since it offered a "fresh" supply of workers at the lower levels and gave the native-born workers an opportunity to move up in a rapidly expanding economy. In total impact, the desirability and the possibility of social mobility are both supported by the societal system.[65]

Given these conditions, to what extent and in what ways does the position of individuals and categories of people in the stratification system affect their mobility chances? Most studies of mobility have used occupation, grouped in broad categories, to indicate position in a stratified continuum. Movement usually is measured in one of several ways. Recruitment to all occupational positions is indicated by comparing the present occupations of a representative sample of workers with their fathers' oc-

[64] For a series of essays on the latter, see Daniel Bell, *The New American Right* (New York: Criterion Books, Inc., 1955).

[65] These conditions, in varying degree, seem to have accompanied industrialized societies in general. For a comparative analysis of mobility in industrial societies, see Seymour Lipset and Reinhard Bendix, *Social Mobility in Industrial Society* (Berkeley: University of California Press, 1959).

cupations to see how many have moved up or down from their fathers' occupational strata or have remained at the same level. Recruitment to only the highest positions in an occupational continuum may be studied by tracing back to their point of origin (usually indicated by the fathers' occupations) a sample of people who occupy these top positions. This would indicate the extent to which recruitment is selective by strata or simply random. Sometimes certain specialized workers, such as political officers, scientists, or civil service people, are studied in this way. The same is true of certain elite categories.

Although varying in technique and population studied, a number of mobility studies have all indicated a fairly consistent pattern of social mobility in American society. Research that focuses upon recruitment to the total occupation structure by means of intergenerational comparisons suggests the following generalizations.[66] There is a very high degree of occupational mobility, and the net balance of this mobility is upward. However, a considerable proportion of this mobility is horizontal rather than vertical. Somewhere around 40 percent of sons remain in the occupational stratum of their fathers; although few follow the same occupation as their fathers, a considerable number thus remain in the same occupational category. Those who do move, do not move far. Most of the movement is one step up or one step down from the fathers' occupational stratum. Roughly two thirds of the mobility appears to be of this sort. At the same time, however, the sons of fathers in any one occupational stratum can be found in all of the other strata. Movement from top to bottom or bottom to top is rare. In sum, although the amount of mobility is great, the extent of movement is limited.

Studies of occupational elites show a highly selective rather than random pattern of recruitment, in contrast to some interpretations of the "rag to riches" ideology.[67] The top business and industrial leaders are largely recruited from middle and upper strata. It might be said, in general, that the chief barrier to mobility lies between the white-collar and the blue-collar occupations, although this barrier is by no means insurmountable. A similar pattern exists among the very wealthy, the major

[66] For an early local study see Percy E. Davidson and H. Dewey Anderson, *Occupational Mobility in an American Community* (Stanford, Calif.: Stanford University Press, 1937). For a more recent study based on a national sample see Centers, *op. cit.*, also see National Opinion Research Center, *op. cit.*, and Natalie Rogoff, *Recent Trends in Occupational Mobility* (New York: The Free Press of Glencoe, Inc., 1953). For a general summary consult Lipset and Bendix, cited in preceding footnote.

[67] For an early study of the business elite, see F. W. Taussig and C. S. Joslyn, *American Business Leaders* (New York: The Macmillan Company, 1932). For a later comparative study, see W. Lloyd Warner and James C. Abegglen, *Big Business Leaders in America* (New York: Harper & Brothers, 1955).

professions, in political office, and among various social and intellectual elites.[68]

These patterns of mobility appear to have remained relatively stable over time.[69] On the one hand, there does not seem to have been a "Golden Age" of opportunity in the past in which immigrants, poor farm boys, the uneducated and urban slum dwellers were on an equal footing with the more privileged members of the society.[70] On the other hand, mobility opportunity does not seem to be closing off in response to the vanishing frontier and the concentration of industry in the way that some analysts have suposed.[71] However, as indicated in our discussion of income distribution, the span and shape of the economic continuum have changed. In addition, shifts in the occupational structure also have altered span and shape. There has been a major decrease in unskilled labor, particularly farm labor, and a substantial increase in professional and clerical positions. This has been accompanied by smaller decreases in skilled labor and increases in semiskilled work and among proprietors and officials.

To what extent is this general pattern of mobility based on inequalities of opportunity and privilege rather than on ability and capacity? As we have pointed out, the mobility of individuals and categories of people is determined by their ascribed resources, acquired skills, and mobility orientations. Ascribed resources include genetically determined abilities and access to material goods and services, both of which are transmitted through the family. This intertwining of biological and cultural inheritance in the family makes separate analysis extremely difficult. Studies measuring "intelligence" differentials by strata do show higher scores for the uppers than for the lowers. However, there is considerable over-

[68] The following is a representative selection among a number of studies in these areas: Ferdinand Lundberg, *America's Sixty Families* (New York: Vanguard Press, Inc., 1937); Stuart Adams, "Trends in Occupational Origin of Physicians," *American Sociological Review*, 18:404–409 (1953); Donald R. Mathews, *The Social Background of Political Decision-Makers* (New York: Doubleday & Company, Inc., 1954); R. H. Knapp and H. B. Goodrich, *Origins of American Scientists* (Chicago: The University of Chicago Press, 1952); Beverly Davis, "Eminence and Level of Social Origin," *American Journal of Sociology*, 59:11–19; E. Digley Baltzell, " 'Who's Who in America' and 'The Social Register': Elite and Upper Class Indexes in Metropolitan America," in Bendix and Lipset, *Class, Status, and Power*, pp. 172–185.

[69] For a convenient summary of a variety of studies in time analysis of mobility, see Ely Chinoy, "Social Mobility Trends in the U.S.," *American Sociological Review*, 20:180–186 (1955).

[70] William Miller (ed.), *Men in Business: Essays in the History of Entrepreneurship* (Cambridge, Mass.: Harvard University Press, 1952) for data on the social background of the business elite in the 1870's and in the first decade of the twentieth century.

[71] See the findings of Rogoff, *op. cit.*, and Warner and Abegglen, *op. cit.*

lapping among strata: the highest scores among the lowest stratum are about as high as the lowest scores of the highest stratum.[72] In addition, the influence of cultural factors in conditioning scores has not been eliminated from such tests. Certainly there is considerably more capacity, as measured by intelligence tests, throughout the stratification continuum than is being used (or can be used, for that matter) in the upper reaches of the continuum.[73]

This raises the consideration of the development and training of this capacity. Despite the very considerable extension of education in our society it remains selective on bases other than innate capacity, and this is particularly true of higher education. Although amount of education is dependent on capacity, resources to pursue education and the desire to do so play an important role as well. Regional and rural-urban differences in economic resources differentiate educational resources, and differences in family income differentiate pursuit of education, even when intelligence test scores are held constant.[74] Even in higher education, college attended and curriculum selected is associated with stratum position.[75] Since education is a significant prerequisite for the higher income and occupation positions, unequal access to this avenue of mobility inhibits life chances. The same is true, of course, for family economic resources that are instrumental in financing a profession or a business and in the direct inheritance of the economic, prestige, and power position of the family.

As far as mobility orientation is concerned, it appears to be a consequence of both a recognition of the realities of life chances and differences in life styles. Studies of mobility orientation, as indexed by verbally expressed occupational, income, and educational aspirations, indicate that the uppers set higher goals than the lowers. However, it is difficult to know whether these goals express relatively realistic perceptions of life

[72] For a review and analysis of such studies see, for example, Otto Klineberg, *Social Psychology* (New York: Holt, Rinehart and Winston, Inc., 1940). For a critique of intelligence tests and an attempt to indicate their stratum-based bias, see Kenneth Eels *et al., Intelligence and Cultural Differences* (Chicago: The University of Chicago Press, 1951). Then see John G. Darley's review of this study in *Journal of Applied Psychology,* 36:141–143 (1952).

[73] See Walter V. Bingham, "Inequalities in Adult Capacity—from Military Data," *Science,* 104:147–152 (1946) for analysis of World War II Classification Tests of some 10 million men. This shows, among other things, that 1 million of the 3 million men in the upper two brackets of the intelligence test had not completed high school.

[74] See the convenient summary of a range of studies by Raymond A. Mulligan in "Socio-Economic Background and College Enrollment," *American Sociological Review,* 16:188–196 (1951).

[75] See Ernest Havemann and Patricia S. West, *They Went to College* (New York: Harcourt, Brace & World, Inc., 1952), especially Chap. 15.

chances on the part of respondents or, as is so frequently alleged, are self-imposed barriers on the part of the lowers representing a particular life style.[76]

CLASS, CLASS CONSCIOUSNESS, AND CLASS CONFLICT

In our theoretical discussion of stratification we pointed out that the term "class" is used in different ways by different analysts. We have chosen to use the term to apply to a discrete hierarchy that involves elements of class consciousness and identification that may be expressed in conflict of interests. The discussion above would seem to indicate an awareness of differences in income, prestige, and power on the part of the American people. The crucial questions are to what extent do people feel the differences are justified, to what do they ascribe the differences, and how salient is the conflict. Our discussion of differences in life satisfaction, in attitudes toward certain economic and political questions, and in voting behavior appears to indicate some awareness of interests that are divisive along an economic continuum. However, it can hardly be said that these interests override other divisive interests or other unifying interests. Cleavages along class lines are often cut across and submerged by cleavages along racial, religious, regional, and rural-urban lines. In addition, status-inconsistencies and mixed ideologies (the pattern of "economic" and "intellectual" liberalism and conservatism) further blur sharp class division. On the other hand, commonly shared national loyalties, equalitarian values, materialistic orientations, belief in mobility and opportunity, and the like, tend to unite rather than divide; and economic differences are likely to be perceived as a result of individual, rather than class, differences. The net upward pattern of mobility in our society, the horizontal mobility that may mean some real gain, projection of aspirations on children, the extension of education and expansion of income, and an expanding pattern of social legislation all operate in the direction of blurring class interests and dissipating feelings of class solidarity and identification.

Studies calculated to measure class identification reflect this rather vague and ill-defined image of "class" among Americans. Studies that ask people to name the "class" they think they belong to (so called open-

[76] For one study of the interrelationship of aspiration and realism in occupational orientation, see Richard M. Stephenson, "Mobility Orientation and Stratification of 1,000 Ninth Graders," *American Sociological Review*, 22:204–212 (1957). For a comparison with British studies see the same author's "Stratification, Education, and Occupational Orientation: A Parallel Study and Review," *British Journal of Sociology*, 9:44–52 (1958).

ended questions) give a very wide variety of responses without any clear pattern of class identification.[77] Many people say they do not know and some deny the existence of class altogether. On forced choice questions (where respondents are asked to place themselves in one of several listed "classes") responses vary depending on the divisions and the terminology used. If only "upper," "middle," and "lower" class terms are used, the overwhelming response falls in the "middle class" category.[78] This appears to express equalitarian ideology and a negative connotation of the term "lower class." Where a fourfold distinction is made, in terms of "upper class," "middle class," "working class," and "lower class," most respondents place themselves in either the "middle" or the "working class." When these subjective attitudes are correlated with occupation there is some correspondence with objective position, but there also is considerable overlapping.[79] When all three of these techniques are used on the same sample, the following pattern emerges.[80] There are some business, professional, and lower white-collar people who call themselves "middle class" no matter how the question is asked. The same is true for some manual laborers who call themselves members of the "working class." There is a category composed of some manual workers and white-collar people who sometimes call themselves "middle class"; sometimes, "working class." There is another category that tend to say that there is no class system, but if a forced-choice is presented, they tend to call themselves members of the "working class." In sum, there appears to be a relatively low degree of class identification in American society, insofar as it is measured by such questions.

There is even less evidence for the existence of strong class conflict and class organization. Probably the clearest patterns in these directions are found toward the ends of the stratification structure. Wealthy and powerful business people seem to be aware of their economic interests and organize in association to foster them. Labor unions among manual workers appear to reflect the same tendency, although short-range goals frequently dominate, and the interests of organized business and organized workers sometimes converge in conflict with the interests of unorganized workers or other businesses. People in the middle range seem to have the least clear and sharp image of where their interests lies and have little formal organization to express whatever may be their interests.[81]

[77] "The People of the U.S.A.—A Self-Portrait," *Fortune,* 21:14 (February, 1940).
[78] G. H. Gallup and S. F. Rae, *The Pulse of Democracy* (New York: Simon and Schuster, Inc., 1940).
[79] Centers, *op. cit.*
[80] Joseph A. Kahl and James A. Davis, "A Comparison of Indexes of Socio-Economic Status," *American Sociological Review,* 20:317–325 (1955).
[81] See C. Wright Mills, *White Collar* (New York: Oxford University Press, 1951), for an extended discussion and evaluation.

Is America a class-stratified society? The answer to this question depends on the definition of "class." According to Max Weber's definition, for example, we are class-stratified, because he defines classes as categories of families and individuals who have similar life chances, represented by economic goods and opportunities for income, and determined by a market situation. If, however, class is defined in terms of class consciousness, identity of interests, and class organization—or any one of these—there does not seem to be much evidence for clearly articulated class stratification in American society. The overview of "class" that we have briefly described may vary over time and in response to economic depression and prosperity. The indications of latent consciousness and conflict mentioned may become more manifest with shifts in the occupational structure, in the recruitment pattern, or in the availability of upper positions as the variables that give rise to them change. At the present time, however, it seems fair to conclude that the United States cannot be characterized as a class-stratified society in the sense that "class" involves a hierarchy of discrete categories who are conscious of a separate identity and conflicting interests.

SUMMARY

Social stratification refers to the unequal distribution of economic goods and services, prestige, and power, which are analytically distinct but empirically interrelated. The structure of stratification may take the form of a continuum of inequality or a hierarchy of discrete categories of inequality. The divisions of the former may be called "strata"; the latter, "classes." In stratification analysis, the family rather than the individual is treated as a unit of analysis within a stratum or a class.

The extent to which economic and prestige rewards must be distributed unequally is debatable, although no known society has succeeded in institutionalizing equality in their distribution so far. With respect to provision of incentives for placement and performance, differential prestige as between conformity and deviance, balance between the more and the less essential activities, and effective allocation of talent and ability would seem to be essential for the persistence of a social system. The degree of urgency of these imperatives and, therefore, the structure of stratification, may vary, depending on conditions internal and external to the system.

Stratification structures vary in shape and span, functional emphasis, degree of stratum solidarity, and extent of mobility.

Social mobility refers to movement of individuals and categories of people from one to another position in the stratification structure. Societies vary in the extent of mobility, depending on the ideological support for mobility, the availability of statuses, and shifts in the status structure over time. Within a given society, movement of individuals and categories is differentiated by their mobility resources, skills, and orientations.

In American society all three of the dimensions of stratification are distributed unequally, giving rise to differential life chances and differences in life styles and power. These are accompanied by significant differences in a wide range of contingent attitudes and behavior. Despite such differences, and because of other salient characteristics of the society, class consciousness, identity of interests, and class organization have not developed to any notable extent.

12

POLITICS

As we have noted several times, a basic dilemma of human group life is the fact that, on the one hand, each person is dependent on other people for certain goods and services; but, on the other hand, there are no instincts compelling B to give A what the latter needs—or, at least, claims. Only A's ability to make it worth B's while, or B's love or care for A, or B's obligation can result in B's giving A what he asks for. It is this last mechanism that is one of the roots of "politics."

When B has an obligation to meet A's claims, A has a *right* to the goods or services being claimed. It is important to get clear what is meant by the term "right." A right is a claim on some goods or service that someone else has an *enforceable obligation* to grant. You may make a claim to anything—a job, a date, housing, food, education, and so on; but you have a *right* to it only if someone (an employer, for example) has an enforceable obligation to give it to you.

The heart of the matter lies in the term "enforceable." In everyday speech we sometimes use the term "right" when we mean that someone else has a "moral obligation" to honor the claim, meaning that he should "feel guilty" if he does not, or perhaps that God will enforce the obligation either later on in this world or in the next. It is not in this sense that we shall use the term.

By "enforcement" we shall mean the use, or the threat of use, of physical compulsion as a last resort. In our usage, then, A has a right to something from B, when, and only when, as a last resort, B can be physically compelled to honor A's claim. We do not, of course, mean physically compelled by A, necessarily, or by just anyone. If your "rights" were contingent on your ability physically to coerce other people, the entire difference between human groups and jungle systems would evaporate, as civilization degenerated into Hobbes's war of each against all.

367

In stable human groups, the ever-present possibility of physical coercion is monopolized in certain statuses. Those are political statuses. Political statuses, in fact, are defined as those with a monopoly of the use of physical compulsion.[1] "Rights," then, are claims on good or services that other people will be physically compelled, by political status-occupants, to honor.

From these simple but fundamental considerations, the basic issues of politics stem: (1) *Which* of the innumerable claims and counterclaims that can run riot in human affairs should be "rights," and which should be left to the arena of bargaining or to the structure of in-group loyalties? (And for those claims that are recognized as rights, who should bear the corresponding obligations?) (2) How should the statuses with the power to decide such questions, and with the monopoly of physical compulsion to enforce the decisions, be defined? and how should they be filled?

In the rest of this chapter we shall discuss the nature of these two issues, and some of the mechanisms for dealing with them.

Sources of Potential Conflict

The necessity for political decision making stems, we have said, from the fact that, unlike the members of termite groups, human individuals may differ sharply in their definitions of how goods and services should be allocated. Without some mechanism of making decisions that are binding on *all* the members of a group, the group is likely to be torn by conflict. Appreciation of the need for, and problems of, political structures can be increased by understanding the sources of potential conflict and cleavage.

One of the major sources of potential conflict among the members of a group is differences in notions of "ultimate truth" and "morality." As we noted earlier, religious or ideological explanations of the "meaning" or "purpose" of life and of "virtue" and "wickedness" are beyond the reach of objective scientific discussion. If you and I disagree about the relative importance of saving souls versus enjoying "this" life, or if we disagree about *how* to save souls, or about the "goodness" or "badness" of various sexual practices; and if both of us refuse to change our minds, there are really only three things left for us to do. We can either agree that you

---

[1] Cf. Gabriel Almond's excellent analysis in Gabriel Almond and James S. Coleman (eds.), *The Politics of the Developing Areas* (Princeton, N.J.: Princeton University Press, 1960), Introduction.

will go your way and I will go mine while we continue to cooperate in other areas of life; or we can refuse to be contaminated by associating with one another; or we can fight. The first amounts to redefining the situation so that the scarcity problem simply disappears—there ceases to be a question of how to allocate resources, since nothing you want interferes with anything I want. In the kinds of cases we are considering, however, it is usually difficult to prevent that solution from collapsing into one of the other two. Should I pay taxes, for example, to help you disseminate your ideas? Do I have to risk exposing my children to your propaganda in magazines, movies, schools, or on radio or television? Do I have to observe your immoral behavior when you wear "indecent" attire on the beach or neck too ardently in the movie I'm attending?

Over such questions as these we are likely to come to blows, or to part company altogether—in either of which case, we disintegrate the group of which we are members. The same kind of issue arises in many different areas of life. Should the resources of South Africa (or the sovereign state of Mississippi) be used to protect "white supremacy," or to produce "equality"? Is the "mission" of the United States to spread the gospel of free enterprise, or is it to help industrialize other countries by whatever means? And so on, virtually ad infinitum. Over such issues there is no such thing as a "reasoned" solution. In the absence of *political* solutions—solutions made and enforced by acceptable monopolists of force—there remain only disintegration and civil war.

A second though closely related source of potential conflict stems from the intrinsic tension between "rights" and "obligations," or between "freedom" and "restriction." To have a *right* to do something means that someone else must have some obligation to facilitate your doing it. To have a right to education, for example, means that someone has an obligation to build schools and to teach. To say that someone has a right but that no one has a corresponding obligation is simply a contradiction in terms.

What this means is that rights are inherently scarce. The more rights you have, the more obligations someone else has. Similarly, the more freedom you have, the less freedom someone else has to interfere with you. (If you are free to speak your mind, I cannot be free to stop you; and if you have a right to censor my publications, I have less freedom to write.) Whenever someone is granted a right or a privilege or a freedom, then, someone else is handed a duty or has his privileges or freedom restricted. Since this is so, there is always a potential conflict between those who are asking for rights or freedoms and those who would have to assume the corresponding duties or restrictions. And here, too, science and reason are not likely to solve the problem; if there are solutions, they are *political* solutions.

A third source of potential conflict is the fact that in a division of labor that is at all complex, some individuals and subgroups are significant to other individuals and subgroups only as means. File clerks in an insurance office or dairy farmers, for example, are likely to be, for you and me, only necessary cogs in a machine. If someone invents better cogs—electronic sorting devices or automatic milkers—you and I are likely to be in favor of replacing the old human cogs with the more efficient mechanical ones. The "old human cogs," however, are equally likely to have a rather different view of the matter; and if you and I were they, we might consider smashing the machinery. The general point is that, as we have noted in earlier chapters, the cost of social change is likely to fall unevenly on people differently situated in the social structure.

A fourth source of conflict is also related to the division of labor. Major organizations and subsystems are specialized to produce services or goods for other people or groups. The recipients of these services and goods may, at any time, be divided—or may see themselves as divided—into two categories, the haves and the have nots. For example, the recipients of the wealth produced by industrial activities are always divisible into those who receive more and those who receive less. This, of course, was the phenomenon that Karl Marx focused his attention on, and which led him to the prediction that the gap beween the two would finally become so great that civil war would result. As Talcott Parsons has pointed out,[2] the same analysis might be made of the potential cleavage of the recipients of *any* service produced in the division of labor. Educators, for example, produce education; and the population might be divided into those who go to college and those who do not. Religious role-players produce assurances about "meaning" and "salvation"; scientists produce empirical knowledge; and so on. The recipients of all those services might be divided into those who get their questions answered satisfactorily and those who do not, and the resulting cleavage is a *potential* source of conflict.

A fifth endemic source of potential conflict is the conflict between the present population and posterity. More accurately, this is a potential conflict between those members of the present population who think in terms of the future of the group after all its present members are long dead, and those who do not, or who do so less. The potential conflict stems from the fact that the distribution of resources that might maximize the welfare of future generations is likely to be different from that which is "best" for the present generation. For example, it might have been better for us if our ancestors had not despoiled our woodlands and soil as they did, and it would have been better for them (and worse for us) if they had not driven so furiously toward industrialization. In the same way,

[2] Talcott Parsons, "Sociological Theory" in R. K. Merton and Leonard Broom (eds.), *Sociology Today* (New York: Basic Books, Inc., 1960).

present-day Chinese might be better off if they worked less arduously and at such vast sacrifice to industrialize China, but their grandchildren may be better off for their having done so. In the same way, the present-day stockholders of a corporation might be better off if they distributed all the profits as dividends, investing none of them in modernization or research; but that would mean the end of the corporation within a generation or two.

Finally, a sixth source of potential conflict stems again from the division of labor. It results from the fact that the perspective in which most specialists see the entire social structure is almost bound to be distorted by their special positions within it. Sheer ignorance produced by necessarily narrow vision might lead subgroups to misperceive their own interests. Two motorists in a traffic jam, for example, may delay themselves interminably by bickering with one another, whereas both would agree if they had the over-all perspective of the policeman circling overhead in a helicopter.

The Structure of Decision Making

DECISION-MAKING MINORITIES

The disagreements stemming from the six bases of cleavage discussed above have to be resolved in some way if the Hobbesian war is to be avoided.[3]

Some statuses must exist with the responsibility and power to make decisions that settle disputes one way or another and that are binding on all the disputants. These are political statuses, whether they appear in nations, states, cities, families, hospitals, or universities.

The decision-making statuses are always fewer in number than those whose occupants are being coordinated and controlled by the decisions. One reason for this has been stated in a leading text on public administration as follows:

> When an organization has a large number of members . . . they must be divided into groups sufficiently small that each can be coordinated by a single supervisor. Again, one of the principal devices used to co-

---

[3] The empirical evidence for such an assertion, by the way, is readily available. One has only to look at what happens when such mechanisms are not present—that is, at the relations among nations. War continues to be the way of settling disputes on that level, and will continue to be so long as the mechanisms we shall consider below are not institutionalized.

ordinate the activities of these separate groups is to designate a second-level supervisor to supervise a number of them. And if there are more first-level supervisors than can be coordinated by one man, there must be several second-level supervisors, to be coordinated in turn by the establishment of a third supervisory level.[4]

Robert Michels has expressed the necessity for minority leadership in still other terms:

> Though it will grumble occasionally, the majority is really delighted to find persons who will take the trouble to look after its own affairs. In the mass, and even in the organized mass of the labor parties, there is an immense need for direction and guidance.[5]

Michels has also noted that "the most striking proof of the organic weakness of the mass is furnished by the way in which, when deprived of their leaders in time of action they abandon the field of battle in disordered flight."[6]

STRUCTURAL VARIATIONS

The decision-making statuses of different groups may vary in certain familiar ways. They may vary, first of all, in terms of how they are filled. The major points of variation here concern the questions of *what people are to decide* who will occupy them, and *by what criteria* they decide. The essential difference between a democratic political system and a non-democratic one is that in the former the people to be governed by the decisions are the ones who decide who will make them.[7] More frequently, those who do the allocating to decision-making statuses are persons other than those to be governed by the decisions. Children, for example, who are governed by parental decisions do not select their decision makers; litigants in courts of law do not select the judge or (except partially) the jury; students do not allocate personnel to professorial or administrative

---

[4] H. A. Simon, D. W. Smithburg, and V. A. Thompson, *Public Administration* (New York: Alfred A. Knopf, Inc., 1950), p. 132.

[5] Robert Michels, *Political Parties* (trans. E. Paul and C. Paul; New York: The Free Press of Glencoe, Inc., 1949), p. 53.

[6] *Ibid.*, p. 56. Compare Chap. 1 of Chester I. Barnard, *The Functions of the Executive* (Cambridge, Mass.: Harvard University Press, 1938), p. 170: "The practical difficulties in the operation of an organization seldom lie in the excessive desire of individuals to assume responsibility for the . . . action of themselves or others, but rather lie in the reluctance to take responsibility . . . ."

[7] More accurately, *some* of the people decide. The suffrage is always restricted by age and often (in the United States until 1920) by sex. It is also often restricted by wealth, income, or property holdings. More or less institutionally, it may also be restricted by race and nativity.

statuses; neither workers nor consumers select the managers of corporations; Hungarians do not choose their Communist rulers; privates in the army do not vote for officers; subjects do not choose kings; and Catholic laymen do not elect the pope.

The significance of the difference between these two basic types of structure is that the decision makers in each structure look in different directions, so to speak, to validate and justify their decisions, or to validate and justify their right to make the decisions. In both cases, the decision makers must attempt to satisfy the persons on whom they depend for office. In the first case, when followers choose their leaders, the leaders must attempt to satisfy the followers—or, more precisely, the most important or the most influential or the most numerous of their followers. In the second case, when *non*followers choose the decision makers, decision makers use different standards for making their decisions.

Several different illustrations of this nondemocratic kind of structure were mentioned above: business organizations, the army, the Catholic Church, kingdoms, universities, families, the judiciary—and national dictatorships. Merely to list those few cases, however, is to suggest that within this category of "nondemocratic" political structures there may be several different subtypes. Exactly what are the differences?

We suggest that there are four major ways in which nondemocratic systems may differ from one another.[8] First, there are differences in the *degree* to which the decision makers are independent of the wishes of those they govern. No leaders are ever totally immune to the needs and aspirations of all their followers: they must always temper their orders, to some extent, to the convictions, attitudes, and beliefs of those whom they command. *How* dependent they are on their subjects depends basically on how easy it is for the subjects to leave the group and join another group. Thus the fact that it is ordinarily easier for workers to leave a business firm than it is for soldiers to leave the army is a major reason why business organizations are somewhat more democratic than the army. (But it is important to bear in mind that the harder it is for workers to change their employment, the less sharp the distinction becomes.) Second, there are differences in the *scope* of the subjects' lives that are within the jurisdiction of the decision makers—that is, differences in the range of followers' status-sets that are subject to control. Much of the controversy over the "undemocraticness" of the Catholic Church centers precisely around the issue of how *much* of Catholic laymen's lives is

[8] Thus, if we were to dichotomize each of those four dimensions of variation for purposes of simplification, we could distinguish sixteen logically possible different types of nondemocratic political systems. We shall not undertake such a detailed analysis in this introductory text (but we invite the reader to do so for his own edification).

under the jurisdiction of the clergy. Third, there are differences in the
subjects' sense of legitimacy of the nondemocratic structure. Children,
for example, are probably at least as rigidly controlled by their parents
as the average Chinese citizen is by the Communist party, but most of us
perceive a vast difference between the two situations, the difference being
that in the one case we think the decision making is legitimate and in the
other we think (and we think that Chinese citizens think) it is not.
Fourth, there are differences in the degree to which decision makers are
independent of *anyone* else, including those who allocated them to their
decision making statuses. For example, although Supreme Court justices
and college professors are relatively immune to the sanctions of litigants
and students, they are still accountable to the legal and teaching *professions*—to their peers—and this distinguishes them sharply from, say, a
classical monarch. No judge can say with Louis XIV, "Le loi—c'est moi."

Turning to the other major kind of decision-making structure—in which
the persons (or some of the persons) to be bound by decisions choose
the people to make them—we must notice first of all that they also may
differ from one another in the same four ways. First, there are differences
here, too, in the degree to which decision makers, even though elected
by their constituents, are responsive to them. For one thing, by definition
of the six sources of cleavage discussed above, democratic decision
makers cannot be responsive to *all* the members of a group: if everyone
were equally pleased by every decision, there could be no disputes to
resolve, or prevent in the first place. For another thing, even democratic
decision makers are often in a position to manipulate their followers'
perceptions and control the information available to them; hence, although followers *nominally* choose their leaders, the leaders in fact may
tell them how to choose.

Second, there are differences among democratic groups as well as
among undemocratic ones with respect to the *range* of subjects' lives that
are controlled by political decisions. A majority of voters can be just as
totalitarian, in the sense of totally controlling people's lives, as any undemocratic decision maker. The democratically controlled Puritan communities of early New England, for example, were more tyrannous, by
anyone's standards, than the Supreme Court of the United States, the
members of which are completely unresponsive, in a political sense, to
all those whom their decisions control.

Third, there are differences among democratic groups in the subjects'
sense of legitimacy of the *democratic* structure. Many people feel, for
example, that no judges should be elected—they should all be appointed
for life, precisely in order to free them from the pressures of those they
"serve." And the completely democratic family is criticized almost as often

these days as the completely "authoritarian" family was a generation ago.

Fourth, there are also differences among democratic groups in the degree to which the elected decision makers are (or are even supposed to be) independent of influence from people *other* than their constituents. It is often the case—perhaps more often than not—that a democratic decision maker's constituents have no opinion on the issue in question. The decision maker may then be dependent on other sources for clues as to the "best" decision.

However decision makers are chosen, their function is to allocate, by the exercise of authority, goods and services and rights and obligations among the members of the group. Political decision making, in other words, is competitive with the two other ways of allocating goods and services that we mentioned earlier—through bargaining and through primary group attachments. Indeed, as we noted at the outset, one of the central political issues of modern societies is that of determining the boundaries and relationships among these three allocative principles. Whether education should be allocated on the basis of ability to pay or through political decision making was once a burning issue in the United States; how housing and medical care should be allocated is an issue today. Similarly, to what extent people's needs should be met through such primary-group mechanisms as Community Chests and United Funds, rather than by governmental decisions, is a source of considerable disagreement.

Even in these issues, however, it must be clearly understood that the decision on which mode of allocation is to be utilized is still a *political* one. That is to say, when we discuss political decision making, we are discussing not only the problem of how to allocate tax receipts, for example, but also the problem of *whether or not* to allow automobiles, say, to be allocated by "the market"; and if so, under what rules. The decision on the part of a legislature or a board of directors or the father in a family *not* to settle a dispute is still a political decision. It might just as well have gone the other way.

The Effectiveness of Decision Making

Since this is so, it should be clear that both the integration and the adaptation of a group depend finally on the quality of the decisions made by the group's leaders—and by the degree to which they are accepted by the group members. Whether a member or a subgroup of a group gets its needs met or not, and whether the group as a whole gets its needs met from its environment, both depend on what decisions the groups' leaders make or do not make, and on the followers' response.

LEADERSHIP AND ADAPTATION

The making of decisions that are functional for adaptation requires that knowledge about the environment be gathered and communicated to decision makers, ideas about how to cope with it be developed and communicated, and decision makers be motivated and able to put those ideas and knowledge to work—which requires that they have a clear conception of what the "ideal" relationship of the system and its environment is. None of these conditions may be taken for granted. If they are to exist, special structures are needed, and these structures may not be present in any given concrete case.

Science and technology, as we noted in Chapters 8 and 9, are the specialized social structures that have evolved to gather information about, and to develop ideas for coping with, the physical and biological environments. Diplomacy, espionage, and military engineering are their counterparts in the context of social environments.

As we also noted in our earlier discussion of science and technology, the major requirement of science is *permission* and *encouragement* to speculate and experiment. As this implies, political decisions are likely to be functional for science to the degree that they provide freedom of speculation and to the degree that they provide rewards for exercising such freedom. They are likely to be disfunctional to the degree that they taboo certain inquiries or create risks of punishment for certain lines of thought. In addition, but perhaps not at first so obvious, political decisions are likely to be functional to the degree that the new ideas and novel speculations have free and open channels of communication. This is true for at least two reasons.

In the first place, they cannot be criticized or subjected to test if they are not publicly exposed; and in the second place, new ideas are generated in large part by the exposure of people to new ideas. That is to say, science, like technology, grows as a result of individuals' putting together in a new way symbolic definitions that had formerly existed separately. If anyone is to develop a new way of looking at things, he must be exposed to ways of looking at things that are new to him, however old they may have been to others. The exercise of power to diminish the dissemination of ideas, then, is likely to be a political decision disfunctional for science.

These same considerations are equally relevant when the environment to be adapted to is a social environment. The essential consideration is that accurate knowledge about anything—social, physical, or biological phenomena—can be secured only by objectively accepting the thing as it is, encouraging cognitive speculation about it, and exposing those cognitive speculations to the widest possible testing—by criticism and, ideally, by experimentation.[9]

Definitions of reality that blur the distinction between cathexes or evaluations on the one hand and cognitions on the other reduce the posibility of accepting reality as it is—at least as a prerequisite to turning it into something else, more pleasant or more "worthy." So long, for example, as it is impious to consider the possibility that the earth is not the center of the universe, so long is it impossible to discover what the solar system is really like. In the same way, so long as it is treason to consider that one's own system is not the final word in civilization, so long is it impossible to discover what other social systems are really like.

Free, encouraged, and widely communicated speculation about environing social systems, then, together with experimental or at least critical testing, is as indispensable to the gathering of knowledge in this area of adaptation as in the area of biology or physics. The use of political power to increase the risks or decrease the rewards for such speculation is always likely to be disfunctional in the long run.

But it is not enough—difficult as it may be—to improve the chances of gathering knowledge. It is also necessary that the knowledge be *communicated* to decision makers, and this requires that scientists and intellectuals of all kinds have access to decision makers' attention. Furthermore, if the decision makers are to make adaptively functional decisions on the basis of the knowledge made available to them, *they must have clear criteria defining a desirable relationship between the system and its environment.* This last point, obvious as it is, points to a condition that is sometimes missing from the decision-making process. On the level of societies as social systems, it is precisely a conception of the *purpose* of the system that is often missing. The result tends to be for decisions to be based on considerations of what will preserve the adaptive mechanisms, rather than on considerations of what the adaptive mechanisms are supposed to be *for*. As a political scientist, Henry A. Kissinger has described the problem in a stimulating essay on American policy making:

[9] Cf. John Dewey and James Tufts, *Ethics* (New York: Holt, Rinehart and Winston, Inc., 1932, 1959), pp. 364–366.

> The smooth functioning of the administrative apparatus absorbs more energies than the definition of criteria on which decision is to be based. . . .[10]
>
> Few if any of the recent crises of U.S. policy have been caused by the unavailability of data. Our policymakers do not lack advice. . . . *They do lack criteria on which to base judgment.* In the absence of commonly understood and meaningful standards, all advice tends to become equivalent. . . . The dilemma of our policy is not so much that it cannot act on what it has defined as useful . . . but that the standards of utility are in need of redefinition.[11]

The need of decision makers for clear criteria of the group's "ideal" relation to its environment is more readily met on the level of groups smaller than nations. In the case of corporations, the army, universities, hospitals, families, and so on, the goal of the group is likely to be less ambiguous.

Even if decision makers have accurate knowledge about the group's environment, have effective ideas about how to cope with it, have clear images of *what* to do, and are motivated to act—even under these ideal conditions, the group's adaptation is by no means assured. There remains the problem of getting the resulting decisions accepted and carried out by the members of the group. This is a "problem" simply because of the endemic sources of conflict in a complex group that we discussed above. Because of the different meaning and consequence of events to people differently situated in a social structure, it is more likely than not that the allocation of resources, statuses, and rights and obligations that would be best for the group's long-run adaptation is *not* the allocation that would be best for some unit's short-run adaptation. What is best for the United States in the long run may very well not be best for General Motors in the short run, just as what is best for a marriage in the long run may be far from best for one of the partners in the short run. The pursuit by each unit of its immediate interests can never be relied on to maximize the welfare of the group, and hence can never be relied on to maximize the long-run welfare of the units. Indeed, this is simply another way of stating the basic necessity for political decision making: as we noted earlier, if human groups had the same built-in identity between the units' conception of their welfare and the group's welfare as termite groups, there would be as little need for politics in the former as in the latter (and as little humanness).

As we noted in Chapter 2, the tension between the group's adaptation and that of its units is a special case of the problem of the group's inte-

[10] Henry A. Kissinger, "The Policymaker and the Intellectual," A Reporter Essay, *The Reporter* 20:30 (March 5, 1959).
[11] *Ibid.*, p. 34.

gration—that is, the mutual adaptation of units to one another. Before we consider the mechanisms by which leaders secure acceptance of their adaptive decisions, we must consider the political dimensions of the integrative problem.

LEADERSHIP AND INTEGRATION

If the decisions made by the leaders are to further integration, the first requirement obviously is that there be mechanisms by which information concerning integrative difficulties is communicated to them. When a subgroup or category of the population is having difficulty in procuring or disposing there must be some way in which that fact is cognized as a fact, interpreted as a difficulty, communicated to decision makers, and understood by them. (Then, just as in the case of adaptation, they must be motivated to correct the difficulty, they must have or be given some ideas about *how* to correct it, and they must get their decisions accepted.)

Both the way in which integrative difficulties are communicated to decision makers and the kinds of action the decision makers then take depend on which mechanisms of integration are institutionalized. If bureaucratic mechanisms are institutionalized, there are likely to be specialized statuses with the responsibility for gathering information about the state of the group's integration and interpreting it, as well as formalized machinery for communicating that information to the final decision makers. The cost-accounting procedures of modern business corporations are an example of such arrangements. Other examples include systematic surveys of morale, time-and-motion studies, the requirement of periodic reports from section chiefs to bureau chiefs to division chiefs, and so on. Police surveillance, health inspections, surveys of unemployment by the Department of Labor, congressional investigations—these also function, in part, to gather and report data on the degree of malintegration prevailing.

Insofar as primary group mechanisms are institutionalized, awareness of some unit's problems depends on the sensitivity and empathic ability of others. In families, for example, the recognition of a child's or a spouse's frustration rests on that intangible and elusive but nonetheless real intuition that is difficult to describe but that every reader has probably experienced. And every reader has also, no doubt, experienced its breakdown—has experienced the failure of a parent or a friend to "understand" his needs and the pain of his frustration, as well as the bafflement of being unable to understand why someone else is obviously feeling hurt or deprived. Outside such small groups, wherever the needs of individuals are dependent on "charity" of some kind, the gathering of information

about malintegration requires that some people be "humanitarianly" sensitive to the difficulties of others. Annual Community Chest or United
Fund appeals, for example, represent efforts to persuade people to empathize with the adaptive difficulties of others.

Insofar as bargaining is institutionalized, action on the part of decision
makers to correct malintegration is complicated by the fact that whatever
state of procurement and disposal on the part of units exists is, in one
sense, the right one. That is to say, under bargaining mechanisms, if
unit A has difficulty in procuring from unit B, unit A is simply not making
it worth B's while. For example, if the only housing that some people can
afford is slum housing, then, under the bargaining institution, slum housing is precisely what they should have. The existence of slums, poverty,
unemployment, unmet health needs, and so on, never represents the
failure of bargaining institutions; it simply represents the operation of the
bargaining mechanism. Feelings that slums and poverty and the like are
wrong stem from the "intrusion" into the picture of sentiments stemming
from one of the other two mechanisms of integration: either the sentiment stemming from legal-bureaucratic modes of thought that people
ought to have some "right" to "decent housing"; or the sentiment stemming from primary-group feelings of empathic dismay at another person's
squalor. In addition, decision makers may feel—or other people may
attempt to persuade them to feel—that a given state of integration determined by the market is bad for the *adaptation* of the group or some
subgroup to *its* environment. For example, even though the bargaining
mechanism results in slum housing or unhealthful living conditions, it
may be felt that the consequent waste of human resources puts the nation
at a competitive disadvantage vis-à-vis other nations or that the bad condition of the "underprivileged" constitutes a health, fire, or safety hazard
for the "privileged."

When some bargaining-determined allocation of satisfaction is felt, for
one of the above reasons, to be "wrong," another dilemma confronts
decision makers. The remedy for malintegration produced by bargaining
modes of allocation is either to abandon the bargaining mechanism by
substituting for it bureaucratic-legal mechanisms (as in the case of public
education or public housing) or primary-group mechanisms (as in the
case of Community Chest activities) or else to change the distribution of
bargaining power. But changing the distribution of bargaining power
means giving "have nots" more alternatives or fewer competitors, which
again can be done only bureaucratically-legally or through the development of primary-group bonds of loyalty. Both methods are to be observed, for example, in the improvement of workers' bargaining power
through the reduction of competition among themselves by bargaining
collectively rather than individually.

In short, since the "wrong" degrees of integration that exist were produced by the "right" mechanism (bargaining), political action means either accepting the "wrong" state of affairs for the sake of preserving the mechanism, or interfering with the mechanism for the sake of correcting the conditions. Either choice tends to alienate some members of the group, which raises the question, How do decision makers secure compliance with decisions that go counter to the convictions of followers?

Leader-Follower Relations: Political Equilibrium

If we view the leaders of a social group as one specialized set of role-players and their followers as another, it is apparent that their relationships are like those of any two sets of "specialists" that are dependent on one another for procurement and disposal.

What leaders must procure is *support for their occupancy of leadership statuses*. They must, in other words, secure the permission of status-allocators to occupy those statuses. Their disposal problem is that of getting their decisions accepted, just as the disposal problem of automobile manufacturers is to get their automobiles accepted.

Those on whom the decisions are binding, on the other hand—followers—have as *their* procurement problem the *obtaining of decisions*. More precisely, they need leadership and direction, they need the enforcement of their rights, and they need a binding determination of what their rights and obligations are. What followers have to offer in exchange for leadership, of course, is precisely what the leaders need, support. Table 12–1 illustrates these relationships.

TABLE 12–1

Relationship between Leaders and Followers

LEADERS	FOLLOWERS
Seek support	Give support
Issue decisions	Receive directions

The political process is the process by which leaders procure the support they need from followers and get followers to accept restrictions on their freedom, and it is the process by which followers procure direction and decisions and give necessary support. Those procurement and disposal problems may be solved through any of the modes of adaptation reviewed in Chapter 2.

POLITICAL EXPLOITATION: RULE BY FORCE

At the extreme of noninstitutionalization, the ability of decision makers to occupy their statuses comes from might, not right. They have not been allocated to their roles by any institutionalized means, and they secure compliance with their decisions by the use or threat of superior naked force. Delinquent and criminal gangs, for example, are sometimes ruled in this way; and it is the method of government illustrated in such times and places as the defeated American Confederacy immediately after the Civil War, the Soviet Union immediately after the October Revolution in 1917, and Hungary and East Germany today.

In this case, it is obviously not correct to speak, as we have done in Table 12–1, of followers giving support in order to receive direction. When rule is by force, followers give support in order to save their lives or to stay out of concentration camps. The exploitative method, moreover, is obviously not available to followers as a way of solving *their* adaptive problems—although it is by no means unknown for racketeers or pressure lobbies to coerce legislators, judges, police chiefs, district attorneys, and others into making the decisions desired by the special-interest group. In such cases, however, *de facto* leadership is in the hands of the coercing group, whatever the formal *de jure* allocation of authority. This is a case of deviance, to be analyzed in terms of the principles discussed in Chapter 5.

POLITICAL BARGAINING: RULE BY COMPROMISE

Requiring a giant step toward normative consensus is the trading or bargaining method of procuring support and getting decisions accepted. This is one aspect of the political mechanism institutionalized in modern political campaigns. Candidates for political office compete with one another for support by promising to make the decisions their potential supporters want. Interest groups among the electorate compete with one another and "bargain" with candidates by offering to throw their support to candidates who will make decisions favoring their special interests.

Leaders get acceptance of their decisions in this bargaining case by making other decisions desired by followers. In exchange for lower taxes, for example, the electorate may accept the decision not to build more schools; or in exchange for more schools, it may support the decision to levy a sales tax.

The success of the ruled in getting their political needs met depends on their political bargaining power. Here, as always, bargaining power depends on the ratio of alternatives to competitors for both sides. In the political case, this means most obviously that if system members are to have any control at all over their leader, the leader must have competition. There must be at least a "two-party" system if bargaining is institutionalized.

It also means that the system members who seek to bargain successfully with leaders must have control over the support needed by those leaders. In practice, this means not only that they must be able to vote, but, of at least equal importance, that they must be members of solidary collectivities that vote as a bloc and that share the interests for which protection is being sought. Under the "bargaining" structure of political order, in other words, only those interests are likely to be protected by political decisions that are (a) widespread or (b) expressed by well-organized groups.

Idiosyncratic or individualistic interests or even interests that are widespread among *unorganized* segments of the population cannot be protected when political bargaining is institutionalized. For this reason, in such political systems as that of the United States, political effort and energy must be focused in the first instance on the organization of interest groups among the population. That is to say, if you want the legislature to enact a law in your interest, your first effort had better be addressed not to the legislature at all but to the organization of other people to support you when you do appeal to the legislature.

Legislators cannot, by definition of the bargaining mechanism, vote for your interest unless you can persuade them either (a) that there is no opposition or (b) that the opposition controls fewer votes than you do. Or, of course, (c) that you control more financial campaign support than the opposition controls.

Within the organized pressure groups, the entire analysis of political structure that we have presented so far must be made all over again. That is, your ability to "control" a bloc of votes depends on your power to get the organization to vote as you wish. Such power may be based on exploitation of the organization's members, it may be based on bargaining within the organization, or it may be based on any of the other mechanisms for securing support that we shall discuss below.

In large complex systems, the masses of followers cannot rationally bargain with their leaders, however, even when, as in the United States, the mass of voters elect their leaders directly. As Talcott Parsons has put it:

> There must be mechanisms by which the average voter can come to a "responsible" decision which is meaningful to him. He must not, in too many cases, withdraw to nonvoting, nor be too susceptible to appeals which would be grossly disruptive of the stability of the system. Since

the intellectual problems involved in a rational solution are not practically soluble, my thesis is that the mechanisms are typically nonrational. They involve stabilization of political attitudes *in terms of association with other members of the principal solidary groups in which the voter is involved*. In terms of party affiliation this may be called "traditionalism." The traditionalistic operation of nonrational mechanisms is a condition of the stability of the system.[12]

POLITICAL BUREAUCRACY: RULE BY LAW

Requiring the highest degree of value consensus are the procurement of support and the disposal of decisions as a matter of institutionalized rights and obligations. In patriarchal family structures, for example, the male head of the household has an unquestioned right to the decision-making role, and it is the duty of the other family members to accept his decisions as final and binding. Similarly, on the level of national social systems, hereditary aristocracies rule as a birthright. In the United States, although trading and bargaining are institutionalized with respect to decision makers' *procurement* problems, once they are elected and once their decisions are made, it is the *duty* of all Americans to accept the decisions as binding.

When the decision makers are, say, members of the United States Supreme Court, bargaining is eliminated altogether. Neither procurement nor disposal is a matter of political horse trading.

Under a structure of "rule by law," the right to make certain kinds of decisions is part of the cultural definition of certain statuses. *Whoever* occupies the status (provided, of course, he entered it according to the institutional prescriptions) has the right to make the decisions defined as within the boundaries of the status, and everyone else has the correlative duty to comply with them. In this case, we speak of an "authority structure." Policemen, for example, "have the authority" to make arrests by definition of the status "policeman."

Support and compliance are sometimes based on authority in a slightly different but related sense. This is the case when people comply with decisions because of their belief in the decision maker's special *expertise* in a certain specified area. In such cases, as it is ordinarily put, the expert does not "have" authority; he "is" an authority. Patients obey their physicians, for example, and clients follow the instructions of their lawyers because they define those decision makers as experts.

[12] Talcott Parsons, "'Voting' and the Equilibrium of the American Political System," in Eugene Burdick and Arthur Brodbeck (eds.), *American Voting Behavior* (New York: The Free Press of Glencoe, Inc., 1959), pp. 91–92.

When decision making is based on authority, a follower's duty to comply with decisions is balanced by his *right* to have the decisions made and to have them made according to specific standards. For example, policemen are authorized to make arrests, but only under certain circumstances and in accordance with certain procedures. Moreover, given those circumstances, they *must* make the arrest. Their power is matched by your power (a) to prevent them from acting, except under specified circumstances by specified procedures, and (b) to *require* them to act in the presence of those circumstances.

Similarly, in the usual case, the officials of your local municipality have not only the authority but the obligation to provide you with water, sewage disposal, garbage collection, fire protection, health code enforcement, and so on. Again, there may be certain things that legislators, no matter what their potential gain in political support, may *not* do to you. For example, in the United States, they may not take away your life, liberty, or property "without due process of law," they may not interfere with your religious practice, they may not cause you to be arrested without a prompt hearing.

The decisions desired by system members under this institutional structure are procured not by persuading decision makers that it is worth their while to issue them but by showing them that it is their *duty* to do so. This requires, of course, that there be some institutionalized way of making final determinations of who has what duty to whom. On the national level, this is the basic function of the courts. System members who claim the freedom to act in a certain manner or who claim that other people should not have the freedom to act in a certain manner must argue their claims before the courts of law. They attempt to prove that the judges *must*, in view of established principles, the evidence, and logic, make a decision in their favor. Power, in this case, is based neither on might nor on the ability to bargain successfully, but on "principle"—that is, on "right."

POLITICAL IDENTIFICATION: RULE BY LOYALTY

As we noted above in discussing the bargaining relationship between decision makers and followers, rational calculations as to which leader can offer the most in exchange for one's support are, in a complex group, extremely difficult. Support, rather, may be given to leaders on the basis of deep loyalties of a primary-group nature. In the United States, for example, a large proportion of voters are Democrats or Republicans, not so much on the basis of rational calculations of self-interest as on the basis of traditional loyalty, reinforced, as Parsons says, by "association with other members of the principal solidary groups in which the voter is involved." Put otherwise, for many people being a Democrat or a Republican is not terribly different from being a man or a woman: it is a matter of basic identity. For many people, it would require almost as big a wrench to change their political identities as it would to change their sexual identities.

A somewhat different kind of loyalty is that involved in "charismatic" leadership—leadership in which followers give support and accept decisions because of what they perceive as the "charisma" of the leader.[13] He personally, without regard to his status and even perhaps in spite of it, seems in his followers' eyes to have a special dynamic, "magnetic," confidence-inspiring personality. Followers' support is for him personally, and tends to be diffuse rather than specific as in the case of institutionalized "authority." That is, followers are willing to accept the leader's decisions over an often-unlimited area of affairs. Religious leaders such as Moses, Jesus, or Mohammed are outstanding examples.

As in any adaptive process, the cultivation of such personal loyalty among followers may be more or less deliberate on the part of the charismatic leader. The barrage of propaganda attempting virtually to deify Stalin in the eyes of Russian masses was an example of carefully calculated cultivation; but charismatic qualities are often imputed to leaders "spontaneously," as it were. Certainly, many of Franklin Roosevelt's followers as well as many of Dwight Eisenhower's came close to conceiving their leaders as idols who could do no wrong. Again, it is not unusual for people in positions of authority based on *expertise* to acquire a diffuse charismatic aura in the eyes of others. Patients of physicians, for example, especially when they are of a lower educational or social class than the physician, often tend to see the physician as an awe-inspiring, "special," "set-apart" person, whose decisions carry weight far outside his area of competence. Not a little of the terminology, trappings, and carefully learned demeanor of such technical experts has the latent function of contributing to such definitions.[14]

Very little is really known about this phenomenon—about the attributes of the leader that make him charismatic, about the attributes of followers that make them susceptible to such hero worship, or about the conditions under which this type of leadership and followership emerges. The most plausible theory, for which there is more than a little suggestive evi-

[13] Cf. Max Weber, *The Theory of Social and Economic Organization* (trans. A. M. Henderson and Talcott Parsons; New York: Oxford University Press, 1947), Part III.

[14] The amateur sociologist Stephen Potter has stripped the veil from some of these techniques used by physicians and tells some useful elementary ploys the student might wish to brush up on before he next assumes the patient role. See *One-Upmanship* (New York: Holt, Rinehart and Winston, Inc., 1952), pp. 15–36.

dence,[15] is that people become susceptible to the charismatic influence of a leader under conditions of *anomie*. When the social structure fails to meet integrative, adaptive, or pattern-maintenance requirements, people become disorganized and fearful. They become susceptible to the simplistic reassurances of a "savior" on whom they can pin their hopes and to whom they gladly surrender their own wills.

One of the easiest formulas for offering simplistic diagnoses of malintegration, maladaptation, and the collapse of traditional culture patterns is the scapegoating formula. "The reason for your troubles is the perfidy and wicked plotting of _____"; and there may be inserted, "the Jews," "Wall Street," "the Communists," "capitalist encirclement," "eggheads," "foreigners," "Yankee labor agitation," "the yellow menace," "the black menace," "Western imperialists," and so on. The solution is alleged to be a return to old virtues (occasionally, a giant leap forward to new virtues), and the vigorous suppression of whatever scapegoat had been chosen.

Since this formula lies so ready to hand, charismatic leadership is often accompanied by exploitative techniques of getting decisions obeyed. The passionate submission of the charismatic leader's followers, in other words, tends to be accompanied by another basis of compliance on the part of the group chosen as scapegoat—that of fear. The McCarthy period of demagoguery in the United States provided the most recent American example of the joining of these two bases of compliance.[16]

POLITICAL EQUILIBRIUM AND DISEQUILIBRIUM

In equilibrium, the mechanisms reviewed above operate in such a way that

1. leaders receive all the support they want;
2. all the decisions they want to make are voluntarily accepted;
3. followers receive all the decisions they want; and
4. there are leaders whom they trust and feel able and willing to support.

Just as in similar cases we have discussed in earlier chapters, there are

[15] See Erich Fromm, *Escape from Freedom* (New York: Holt, Rinehart and Winston, Inc., 1941); T. W. Adorno *et al.*, *The Authoritarian Personality* (New York: Harper & Brothers, 1950). Also see Seymour Lipset, "Democracy and Working Class Authoritarianism," *American Sociological Review*, 24:482–501 (1959); and Daniel Bell (ed.), *The New American Right* (New York: Criterion Books, Inc., 1955).

[16] See Richard Rovere, *Senator Joe McCarthy* (New York: Harcourt, Brace & World, Inc., 1959). See also Bell, *op. cit.*

two major types of breakdown that might occur in this political equilibrium.

"Inflationary disequilibrium," it will be recalled, is in general a condition in which the disposal problems of the subsystems are met satisfactorily, but procurement problems are not. The result is a straining of resources with attendant dissatisfaction, feelings of frustration at the failure to procure enough, and, at the extreme, consequent frenzied preoccupation with efforts to procure what is wanted.

In the political case, this kind of disequilibrium is a condition in which competitors for leadership statuses strive to bid support away from one another by making stronger and stronger appeals and more and more extreme promises as well as, sometimes, making more and more extreme attacks and charges against their competitors. Analogous to the situation in periods of economic inflation when employers vie with one another for workers by offering higher wages, shorter hours, better conditions, more opportunities for advancement, and so on, in periods of political inflation competitors for decision-making statuses vie for support with claims that under their leadership the group will have greater victories, more wealth, more efficiency, less corruption, higher levels of "grandeur," and so on. Their appetites whettled and their expectations raised, followers, in turn, press more and more claims for new and expanded rights. At the extreme, expectations and demands become unrealistic, as they exceed the willingness of other groups to assume the corresponding obligations; and leaders' promises approach worthlessness as they exceed the ability of those who made them to "deliver."

In part, the leaders' inability to redeem their promises may stem from their inability to secure the compliance of various subgroups in the group. Their authority or charisma may not be widely enough recognized, and they may be unable to secure enough of a monopoly of physical compulsion to enforce the obligations they dispense. In part also, when the time of reckoning arrives, it may develop, to the shock of the followers who had so enthusiastically embraced the promises of greater "rights" (and perhaps to the surprise of the leaders as well), that the followers themselves must accept many of the restrictions and obligations corresponding to their new rights and freedoms.

David E. Apter has provided an apt description of this sort of problem in his excellent analysis of Ghana. A possible difficulty, he wrote in 1955,

> results from the fact that political office . . . has given the fruits of victory to the C.P.P. [the Convention People's party, the dominant political party in Ghana, led by the charismatic leader, Kwame Nkrumah] almost prematurely. That is to say, the responsibilities of office, while they help to indoctrinate and teach nationalists the processes of government, also by the very demands of parliamentary and bureaucratic roles require a kind of purging in the party. Some of those

who made the "revolution" are no longer appropriate to consolidate its gains. More and more, access to top positions demands a kind of training which bars many of the radical, dispossessed, partially educated young C.P.P. members from important political posts. . . . the important factor here is that one of the major appeals of the C.P.P. was its provision of new roles, new jobs, new sinecures for those barred by lineage or clan ties from positions of importance, and for those from rural areas whose ideas, expectations, and desires had gone beyond the local purview. Now a closing down of political awards, a more stringent set of demands on behavior, and the very requirements of government itself, tend to undermine the fruits of political victory.[17]

In much the same fashion that the colonial regime accelerated wants and desires beyond its ability to satisfy, the nationalist movement too must shoulder the same burden. Its main accomplishment, independence, is soon taken for granted. Revolutionary fervor can easily be dissipated in the difficult tasks of governing. Nkrumah not only faces the danger of public disenchantment as he achieves his goal, but a disenchantment all the more pressing because of the lofty heights which so many of his followers had envisioned for themselves.[18]

Either anarchy or a reign of terror and oppression may be the result. It is not surprising, then, that Nkrumah's democratically oriented regime has, in recent years, taken on many of the forms of totalitarian dictatorships, or, to cite another example, that Fidel Castro's revolutionary government in Cuba has moved in the same direction.

The other kind of equilibrium breakdown—deflation—is a condition in which people cannot find acceptance for the goods or services they want to dispose of. The result is a "slack" period, a period in which resources become idle at the same time that wants are unsatisfied. In the political case, deflation is a condition of widespread apathy. Leaders do not really lead. They make no effort to "rouse the people" to new accomplishments, they hold out no vistas of improvement, they drift and go through the motions of leadership either perfunctorily or ritualistically and routinely— or even, though not necessarily a characteristic of political deflation, with cynical preoccupation with their own graft and corruption. Either there is no competition for decision-making statuses or the nominal competition is itself perfunctory, listless, or perhaps even fraudulent—that is, nominal competitors are actually in collusion.

At the same time, followers are also apathetic. Partly—or in some cases primarily—because they are unorganized and leaderless and partly because they have become cynical or resigned, they do not press or even raise claims for rights. They may even become habituated to their "rightless" state, as many unemployed men during the depression of the 1930's adapted submissively to the lassitude of their workless state.

[17] David E. Apter, *The Gold Coast in Transition* (Princeton, N.J.: Princeton University Press, 1955), p. 309.
[18] *Ibid.*, p. 312.

The outcome of the inflationary or deflationary breakdown may be the establishment of a new equilibrium at a "higher" or a "lower" level—that is, a level at which political rights are more abundant and widespread than during the previous equilibrium, or a level at which rights are restricted and political activity is at a lower ebb. Alternatively, the outcome may be a complete disintegration of the system—anarchy or widespread secessionism, the "depression of politics"—in which *none* of the four equilibrium conditions prevails.

What causes equilibrium at whatever level, once established, to break down?

Inflationary pressures are produced by anything that increases the competition for the available supply of goods and services without increasing the supply of those goods and services.[19] Competition for goods and services might be increased in either of two major ways:

By a Decrease in the Costs of Procuring

For example, if old notions of "staying in one's place," or "accepting the decisions of authority" begin to weaken through education or propaganda, there need be less sacrifice of "respectability" or "pride" or "loyalty" in demanding more rights. Thus, the breaking up of traditional feudal relationships in Africa, as natives were invited, seduced, or coerced into leaving their villages and working in the white man's mines and factories, contributed to a weakening of the ancient restraints. As Apter writes in the case of Ghana,

> For those who moved to Westernized patterns of life, the pressure of traditional social obligations appeared as a millstone. . . . Among the general public, both in the tribe and in the urban centers, the old allegiances tended more and more to be subverted. Young men turned sourly against them. Pressures on the family were greater and the family tended to be less a source of strength than an obstacle. The old tended to view the young with fear. In the process new aspirations toward independence, status, reward, and wealth were being defined for those who composed this marginal group. In some cases the gap between aspiration and achievement was met with apathy; in most parts of the Gold Coast . . . it was met with nationalism.[20]

By an Increase in the Estimated Costs of Not Demanding More

For example, movies and other mass media of communication, as well

---

[19] Inflationary pressures may also be produced by anything that decreases the supply of goods and services, without decreasing competition for them; but for simplicity's sake we shall not analyze this source in the present text.

[20] Apter, *op. cit.*, p. 158.

as formal education and the personal examples of Westerners, have con-- tributed heavily to making Africans, Asians, and Middle Easterners aware of the "glories" of nationalism and industrialism, thus often raising sharply their awareness of what they are missing through their docile acceptance of the existing state of affairs.

Deflationary pressures, on the other hand, are produced by anything that decreases the competition for goods and services without decreasing their supply. This, similarly, may come about in two major ways:

By an Increase in the Estimated Cost of Procuring

For example, when people are deterred from asserting political demands through fear of reprisals or of public ridicule, or when they are deterred by a labyrinth of bureaucratic obstacles so that it takes considerable *expertise*, not a little money, and great quantities of time even to find the critical decision maker, submission or withdrawal may be the most profitable mode of adjustment. Again, when there are alternative ways of gaining the same or substitute satisfactions—as, for example, through personal or private business—the sacrifice of those rewards that would be entailed in political activity might provide an effective deterrent.

By a Decrease in the Costs of Not Procuring

When interest in political rights wanes, through discouragement or through preoccupation with personal or other matters, the rewards that could be achieved through the pressing of political claims may seem relatively unimportant. If so, the costs of not getting them are obviously low.

So far we have been looking at the sources of political disequilibrium from the point of view of followers and the costs and rewards of their activity or passivity. From the point of view of leaders, similar considerations apply.

Inflationary pressures are generated by anything that increases competition among leaders for support; deflationary pressures are generated by anything that decreases such competition (in both cases, of course, assuming that counterbalancing changes do not occur in the supply of support). Thus, if leaders' or would-be leaders' estimates of the costs of trying to win more support decline, they are likely to increase their competition for support. Similarly, if their estimates of the costs of *not* attempting to win more support increase, they are likely to step up their support-seeking efforts. In either case, they are led to intensify their efforts to woo potential supporters with promises, harangues, alarums, exhortations, and appeals of all kinds, as well, perhaps, as with deals, threats, blackmail, and assassination.

On the other hand, if leaders' estimates of the costs of procuring support rise, or if their estimates of the costs of *not* procuring support decline, their support-garnering activities are likely to decline. Thus, a deflationary tendency might result from leaders' convictions that the population was so seriously cleaved that any attempt to gain the support of one segment would cost the support of another. Or their estimates of follower apathy, ignorance, lack of organization, or manipulability might lead them to think that they did not need to bother with winning support. In either case, leadership is likely to be relatively lusterless and superficial. Again Apter seems to suggest that something like this was the definition held by most of the British-educated African intelligentsia in Ghana, shortly before they were thoroughly eclipsed by the more aggressive and bolder tactics of Kwame Nkrumah and his Convention People's party. According to Apter, "most of the intelligentsia viewed politics and political parties with some distaste, tending to think of a council as a deliberative body of educated gentlemen."[21]

SUMMARY

Political mechanisms are the social processes and interactions by which decisions concerning the allocations of resources and of rights and obligations are made and enforced. Special structures for such decision making are necessary because of six major sources of disagreement and cleavage endemic in complex groups: cleavages concerning "morality" and "ultimate truth"; the tension between "rights" or "freedom" and "obligations" or "restrictions"; the uneven incidence of the costs of social change; the relative shares of "haves" and "have-nots"; the present versus the future; and the partial vision of specialists.

Decision-making statuses, which are always a minority, may be filled either "democratically" or "undemocratically." In either case, political structure may vary according to the degree to which decision makers are independent of those they govern; according to the scope of the lives of the subjects governed by the decision makers; according to the sense of legitimacy felt by the subjects; and according to the degree to which decision makers are independent of anyone else.

[21] *Ibid.,* p. 178.

If decisions are to be functional for integration and adaptation, knowledge about the environment and the needs of subsystems must be gathered and communicated to decision makers, who must have clear criteria for making decisions and must be motivated to act in the interests of the group. The various ways in which these requirements are more or less met depend upon which mechanisms of adaptation are institutionalized in the group—bargaining, bureaucratic-legal, or primary-group.

Finally, decision makers must get their decisions accepted by followers, through the use or threat of force, bargaining, authority, or charismatic appeal. Political equilibrium may break down in either inflationary or deflationary directions, and at the extreme the breakdown may result in anarchy, the "depression of politics."

NOTES TO
COLLECTED READINGS

*Below is a list of the titles referred
to in the chart on the following pages.*

[a] Harry C. Bredemeier and Jackson Toby, *Social Problems in America* (New York: John Wiley & Sons, Inc., 1960).

[b] Samuel Koenig, Rex D. Hopper, and Feliks Gross, *Sociology: A Book of Readings* (Englewood Cliffs, N.J.: Prentice-Hall, Inc., 1953).

[c] Raymond L. Lee, James A. Burkhart, and Van B. Shaw, *Contemporary Social Issues* (New York: Thomas Y. Crowell Company, 1955).

[d] Seymour Martin Lipset and Neil J. Smelser, *Sociology: The Progress of A Decade* (Englewood Cliffs, N.J.: Prentice-Hall, Inc., 1961).

[e] Arthur Naftalin, Benjamin N. Nelson, Mulford Q. Sibley, Donald W. Calhoun, Andreas G. Papandreou, *An Introduction to Social Science* (Philadelphia: J. B. Lippincott Company, 1953).

[f] Eleanor E. Maccoby, Theodore M. Newcomb, and Eugene L. Hartley, *Readings in Social Psychology* (3d ed.; New York: Holt, Rinehart & Winston, Inc., 1958).

[g] Robert W. O'Brien, Clarence C. Schrag, and Walter T. Martin, *Readings in General Sociology* (2d ed.; Boston: Houghton Mifflin Company, 1957).

[h] Logan Wilson and William L. Kolb, *Sociological Analysis* (New York: Harcourt, Brace & World, Inc., 1949).

[i] Edgar A. Schuler, Thomas F. Hoult, Duane L. Gibson, Maude L. Fiero, and Wilbur B. Brookover, *Readings in Sociology* (2d ed.; New York: Thomas Y. Crowell Company, 1960).

[j] Kimball Young and Raymond W. Mack, *Principles of Sociology: A Reader in Theory and Research* (New York: American Book Company, 1960).

[k] Robert K. Merton and Robert A. Nisbet, *Contemporary Social Problems* (New York: Harcourt, Brace & World, Inc., 1961).

Collections of Readings	1 Culture	2 Groups	3 Social- ization	4 Social- ization	5 Deviance
BREDEMEIER AND TOBY [a]	3-12	104-144 224-239 250-262 321-339 483-504		86-96	15-57 145-249 288-317 347-350
KOENIG, HOPPER, AND GROSS [b]	43-62 429-435 436-444	101-105 499-501 505-510	65-96 429-435 467-474		550-575 112-130
LEE, BURKHART, AND SHAW [c]	2-45 458-473		388-414		261-371
LIPSET AND SMELSER [d]	220-255	46-63 299-311	262-268		166-193 449-457 522-591
NAFTALIN, et al. [e]	(I) 80-97		I, 64-73 212-222	I, 183-189	I, 32-38 189-199; 260- 264; 356-381; II, 126-175
MACCOBY, NEWCOMB, AND HARTLEY [f]	1-9 85-94 102-131	265-291 437-447 465-472	32-40 164-174	174-265 291-371 472-483 532-546	447-464
O'BRIEN, SCHRAG, AND MARTIN [g]	139-158 211-216	33-40 313-316	186-192 200-204	204-208 216-224 234-239 308-313	18-22 44-48 230-234 299-305
WILSON AND KOLB [h]	61-82 120-146	160-163 287-290 683-711	163-180 185-207	223-230 592-603	236-260 575-579 740-761 767-797
SCHULER, et al. [i]	32-40; 68-81; 92-102; 238- 252; 109- 117; 641- 647	22-32; 92- 102; 179-182; 203-208 225-237 680-687	56-64 131-140 175-179 182-187	140-151 158-175	40-46 187-195 812-821
YOUNG AND MACK [j]	31-40 47-62 102-111				91-101 120-126
MERTON AND NISBET [k]					3-290 697-737

6 *Social Control*	7 *Marriage Family & Kinship*	8 *Indus-trialism*	9 *Magic and Science*	10 *Religion & Ideology*	11 *Strati-fication*	12 *Politics*
	106-110 276-284 318-319	96-102 339-347 352-373		63-82 386-396 412-418 436-482	119-122 373-386	262-276 418-431
343-346 359-367 481-495	131-138 152-157	158-180 513-527 533-546	513-549 527-533 546-549	5-14 209-237 390-419 461-466	106-111 312-332	181-208 371-389 576-601
	373-388 414-451	629-701		74-145 552-628 702-757	606-613 634-638 708-716	146-260 758-846
241-248 580-591	255-262 356-377	81-89 378-421	166-193	206-220 592-603	262-292 433-438 469-522	421-433 449-457 608-623
I, 145-174 332-337 II, 190-200	I, 329-332	I, 108-113 209-212 II, 3-137 235-279		I, 97-104 121-130 381-392 II, 279-335	I, 306-319 II, 150-153 179-237 340-357 III, 200-216	III, 38-51 64-70 233-370
596-602 612-636		583-596		636-653	371-437	72-85 489-532 546-564
256-282 328-333 414-419	74-79 361-379	158-162 316-323	172-180	167-172 379-394	98-112 192-200 334-359 419-424	98-103 323-328 394-414 424-433
335-343 479-488	603-618	324-335 557-575 579-586		655-677 812-831	236-248 378-391 429-474 624-650 489-509 716-726	513-551 831-840
122-131 260-273 714-730	81-87 386-415 746-754	187-203 213-221 376-386 416-436 787-797	46-56 102-109 754-777	510-530	309-362 489-501	464-482
40-46 63-76 264-272	246-264 273-278	77-83 120-125 237-245	246-264	84-90 299-309	20-30 111-116 127-187 203-213 282-291 310-316	337-342
	262-290 390-458	291-323 459-514			324-389	553-650

NAME INDEX

Abegglen, J. C., 345n, 360n
Abel, Theodore, 314n
Adams, Stuart, 361n
Adelman, M. A., 347n
Adorno, T. W., 84n, 139n, 305n, 309, 387n
Alexander, A., 161n
Alman, David, 135n
Almond, Gabriel, 368n
Anderson, Elin L., 346n
Anderson, H. D., 358n, 360n
Apter, David E., 388, 390n
Arensberg, Conrad M., 184, 185, 196n
Argyris, Cris, 34n, 233
Arnold, Thurman W., 311n
Asch, S. E., 13, 14, 112n

Babchuk, Nicholas, 242, 243, 244, 245
Bacon, Seldon D., 160n
Bakke, E. W., 131n
Bales, Robert F., 85n, 204n, 323n
Baltzell, E. Digbey, 361n
Barber, Bernard, 265n, 268n, 322, 333n
Barnard, C. I., 33n, 372n
Barton, Allen, 23n, 24
Battis, Emery, 292n
Beach, F. A., 187n
Becker, Howard, 295n
Beecher, Henry Ward, 291, 292
Bell, Daniel, 310n, 359n, 387n
Bendix, Reinhard, 318n, 359n
Benedict, Ruth, 63, 81, 101, 113n, 114, 164n, 198n, 209n, 211–212, 252n, 253n, 257n, 258n, 259n, 261n
Benoit-Smullyan, Emile, 329n
Berelson, Bernard, 241n, 358n
Berle, Adolf A., 347
Bingham, Walter V., 362n
Blau, Peter, 142n, 149–150, 243, 244, 245, 246n
Bloomberg, Warner, Jr., 157n
Blumenthal, Albert, 168n, 200n
Bolles, Blair, 166n
Bossard, J. H. S., 142n
Bredemeier, Harry C., 122n, 130n, 132n, 238n
Brill, A. A., 158n
Bronner, Augusta F., 143n
Burgess, Ernest W., 99n, 203n, 211n
Bultena, Louis, 355n
Burma, John H., 158n

Calhoun, A. W., 200n
Campbell, A. A., 161n
Cantril, Hadley, 313n
Caplow, Theodore, 202n
Cayton, Horace R., 196n
Centers, Richard, 357n, 360n, 364n
Child, Irvin L., 66, 67n
Chinoy, Ely, 361n
Christenson, C. R., 234n
Christie, Richard, 305n
Clark, Robert E., 351n
Clemmer, Donald, 97n
Cloward, Richard A., 143n
Cohen, Albert K., 135n, 143, 150n, 312n
Cohn, Richard, 168
Coleman, James S., 368n
Conant, James B., 265n
Cook, Alistair, 166
Cooley, Charles H., 32n, 75
Cottrell, Leonard S., Jr., 110n
Cressey, Donald R., 112n
Crowell, John F., 222n
Curti, Merle, 291–292

Daniel, V., 294
Davidson, P. E., 358n, 360n
Davies, A. F., 345n
Davis, Allison, 127n, 153n, 200n, 343n, 353n
Davis, Beverly, 361n
Davis, James A., 364n
Davis, Kingsley, 41n, 79, 113n, 183, 186n, 199n, 206n, 276n, 321, 333n
Davison, W. Phillips, 302n
Deutsch, Morton, 112n
Dewey, John, 377n
Dickson, W. J., 230n
DiDonato, Pietro, 135n
Dollard, John, 135n, 346n
Dornbusch, Sanford M., 100, 109
Dubin, Robert, 123n, 134n
Dunham, H. W., 351n
Durand, J. D., 207n
Durkheim, Emile, 16n, 43, 132n, 173n, 287n

Edman, Irwin, 240
Edwards, Alba, 344
Eels, Kenneth, 362n
Ehrmann, Winston, 202n

399

SUBJECT INDEX